VISUAL QUICKSTART GUIDE

3DS MAX 4

FOR WINDOWS

Michele Matossian

 **Peachpit Press**

Visual QuickStart Guide
3ds max 4 for Windows
Michele Matossian

Peachpit Press
1249 Eighth Street
Berkeley, CA 94710
510/524-2178
800/283-9444
510/524-2221 (fax)
Find us on the World Wide Web at: http://www.peachpit.com
Peachpit Press is a division of Pearson Education

Editor: Rebecca Gulick
Production Coordinator: Lisa Brazieal
Compositor: Maureen Forys, Happenstance Type-O-Rama
Indexer: Karin Arrigoni
Cover Design: The Visual Group

Notice of rights

Notice of liability

Trademarks

ISBN 0-201-73429-X

9 8 7 6 5 4 3 2 1

Printed and bound in the United States of America

Dedication

For Chris, my wonderful husband without whose support this book would never have been written

and

In memorium to my loving grandmother, Katharine Hillix Kilbourne

and

To my beloved cat Crystal and his delightful successors Metta and McCoy

and

To Robert D'Arista, the great artist and teacher, whose memory continues to inspire us.

Acknowledgements

I would like to thank everyone who contributed to this work: my editor, Rebecca Gulick, for her sensitivity, thoughtfulness, encouragement, and support; Lisa Brazieal, for coordinating the production of the book; Maureen Forys, for skillfully compositing the text and graphics; and Karin Arrigoni, for indexing. I would also like to thank the founders of Peachpit Press for their clarity of vision, and all those who have refined that vision over the years.

A special acknowledgement is due to Steven D. Elliot, who, over the course of his 15-year association with Autodesk, designed and produced many wonderful books, manuals, guides, and tutorials on 3D Studio, 3D Studio MAX, and countless other Autodesk products. Thank you, Steven, for all you have taught me.

In addition, I thank my friends and family for all their love and support, and all my readers for their motivation and inspiration.

May all beings be peaceful, happy, and free of suffering.

Michele Matossian
May 11, 2001

CONTENTS AT A GLANCE

TABLE OF CONTENTS

TABLE OF CONTENTS

INTRODUCTION

3ds max is one of the most powerful and popular desktop 3D graphics programs available today. Formerly known as 3D Studio MAX, the program is used for a wide variety of commercial and artistic applications, including architecture, computer games, film production, Web design, forensics, medical and scientific visualization, virtual reality, and fine art.

This book was written for artists, designers, students, teachers, working professionals, and anyone who wants to build their dreams. To guide you through the process of learning, over 1,200 illustrations accompany the text. At the beginning of each chapter, the introduction gives you a sense of the possibilities. The section headings present the theory you need just in time to do the step-by-step tasks that follow. Tips give you important clues about pitfalls, advanced techniques, and related tools. By studying both the theory and the mechanics, you will be equipped to not only push the right buttons, but to create art, solve problems, and invent solutions.

Like other Visual QuickStart Guides, this book is designed to be visually clear and easy to read, and it presumes no prior experience on the part of the reader. If you are a beginner, the best thing to do is start at the beginning and work your way through the topics in order. More advanced students may want to skip around to areas of particular interest. To use this book as a how-to reference, look up your task in the table of contents, reference the shortcut commands in the appendices, or look up the topic in the index.

In order to get the most out of this book, you should be familiar with the Windows environment and have access to 3ds max 4. You should also have a good understanding of 2D graphics programs, such as Adobe Photoshop and Corel Painter.

There are as many ways to work in 3ds max as there are artists who use the program. Throughout this book, I have tried to select the easiest and most direct ways of using the program, while showing you the larger design of its workings. My aim is to explain complex ideas in simple terms and organize the information in such a way that you can find what you need when you need it.

Chapter 1 gets you up and running, from installing the program to navigating the interface and learning file commands.

Chapters 2 through 4 teach you how to create and select objects, control display, and navigate 3D space.

Chapters 5 through 7 show you how to manipulate and animate objects using transforms, modifiers, and animation controllers.

Chapters 8 through 10 explain more advanced modeling techniques, including sub-object editing and creating compound objects.

Chapters 11 and 12 describe the use of lights and cameras for illuminating scenes and taking pictures.

Chapters 13 and 14 cover materials and mapping, so you can paint your scenes with color and pattern and assign surface qualities such as shininess, reflectivity, and transparency.

Chapter 15 rounds out the book with rendering, which further develops the concepts of taking pictures and adding effects to produce high-quality still images and movies.

By the end of this book, you will have learned how to create, model, map, animate, and render objects in 3ds max 4. When you are ready to put it all together, visit the Peachpit Press companion Web site for this book at www.peachpit.com/vqs/3dsmax, or go to www.lightweaver.com to see artwork and examples from my new CD-ROM of self-paced tutorials and classroom teaching materials.

Enjoy!

GETTING STARTED

Figure 1.1 By combining 3D objects with 2D bitmaps, you can build your own paradise using 3ds max 4.

Welcome to the world of 3d studio max, where you can create alien planets, towering ruins, heroes, and villains, or build your own paradise. (**Figure 1.1**). By harnessing your imagination to 3D animation, you can make animals prowl and mountains tumble, as people run through quivering jungles. You are not bound by the rules of this sphere: pigs can fly and fleas can rumble.

But before you start creating chaos and conquest, you need to learn some basic skills. This chapter starts at the very beginning: how to install and configure the program; how to manage files; and how to get around the user interface.

Once you have mastered the skills discussed in this first chapter, the following chapters will teach you how to navigate viewports, control the display, create and select objects, and transform your creations—making your first animations! Then you will learn how to model objects in greater detail. Toward the end of the book, you will find out how to change the entire look of a scene by setting up lights and cameras, applying materials, and adding special effects.

As with other Visual QuickStart books, procedures are short and to the point; each step is designed to get you from point A to point B without needless wandering. Tips provide information about shortcuts, pitfalls and related tools. I suggest you pay attention to these closely; there's more to this book than its simple format would suggest.

Installing 3ds max 4

3ds max 4 is designed to run on an Intel-compatible processor that has Windows 98 or Windows 2000 installed. It can also run on Windows NT 4.0 or Windows Millennium Edition, but it is not supported on these platforms. See the sidebar "System Requirements" for more details.

The following steps guide you in setting up a typical installation of 3ds max 4.

To install 3ds max:

1. Close any open programs, making sure sufficient free space is available on the hard drive, and gather the serial number and CD Key located on the back of the 3ds max CD-ROM case.

2. Place the 3ds max 4 CD-ROM in the CD-ROM drive and double-click on the CD-ROM drive letter.

3. In the 3ds max 4 installation wizard, click Install 3ds max 4 (**Figure 1.2**).

4. Enter the serial number and CD Key (**Figure 1.3**). Then click Next.

5. Follow the steps as prompted by the messages in the installation routine; accept the Typical installation option.

6. If you do not have Internet Explorer 5 or QuickTime 4 installed, install these components.

7. Click Finish to finish the 3ds max installation and restart your computer.

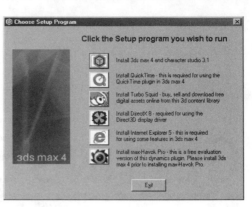

Figure 1.2 Choose Install 3ds max from the Choose Setup Program dialog box.

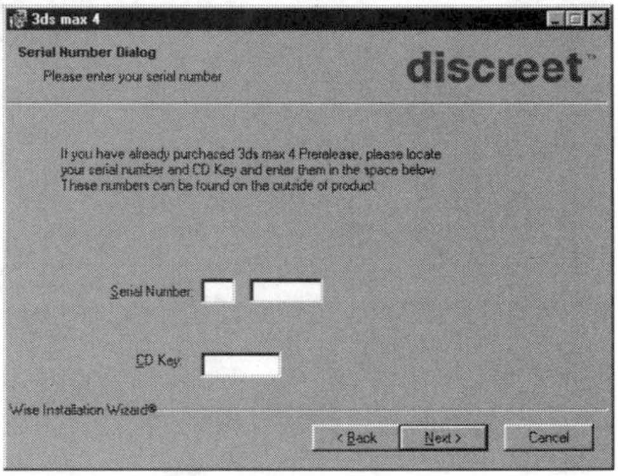

Figure 1.3 Enter the serial number and CD key from the back of the CD case.

System Requirements

Software

◆ Windows 2000

◆ Windows 98

◆ Windows Millennium Edition (not officially supported)

◆ Windows NT 4.0 (not officially supported)

Hardware

◆ An Intel-compatible processor that runs at a minimum speed of 300 MHz. (3ds max 4 provides full support of multiple-processor systems; a dual Pentium III system is recommended.)

◆ 128 MB RAM (256 MB or more is recommended)

◆ 374 MB hard drive space (for a typical installation)

◆ 300 MB swap disk space (minimum)

◆ A graphics card that supports 1024-by-768 pixels per inch (ppi) at 16-bit color (OpenGL and Direct3D hardware acceleration supported; 24-bit color, 3D graphics accelerator with Direct X8 preferred)

◆ A mouse or other pointing device (the program is optimized for a Microsoft Intellimouse)

◆ A CD-ROM drive

◆ Optional: sound card and speakers, cabling for TCP/IP compliant network, 3D graphics hardware acceleration, video input and output devices, joystick, midi instruments, three-button mouse.

✔ Tips

■ Click the Turbo Squid option to install a special client for buying or selling models, textures, and other 3D assets online. For more information see www.turbosquid.com.

■ The DirectX option installs a program that tests and diagnoses and configures DirectX components and drivers. DirectX is a set of APIs (application programming interfaces) that allow 3ds max to take full advantage of high-performance hardware, such as 3D accelerator cards. If you don't have any of this type of hardware, DirectX can improve the performance of your system by emulating hardware services with software drivers.

■ max-Havoc Pro is a plug-in for creating dynamic simulations, including rigid body, cloth, soft body, and fluid dynamics. For more information, see www.havok.com.

INSTALLING 3DS MAX 4

Setting up 3ds max 4

When you first start up 3ds max, you will be prompted to choose a display driver and authorize the program with a code that you obtain from Autodesk. If you do not authorize the program, it will run for only 30 days.

To configure the display driver:

1. Open 3ds max 4 by double-clicking the icon it installed on your desktop. You can also choose Start > Programs > discreet > 3dsmax4 > 3dsmax4.

2. In the 3ds max Driver Setup dialog box, choose a display driver.

   Unless you have a GLINT, OpenGL, or other hardware accelerator card, stick with the default Heidi driver Software Z-Buffer. You can always change it later in Customize > Preferences > Viewports.

3. Click OK.

To authorize the program:

1. Start up 3ds max 4.

2. In the Authorization Code dialog box, choose Authorize 3ds max 4.

3. Register the program by filling in all the required fields in the Register Today routine.

   When you have filled out all the information, you will be asked how you want to contact Autodesk (**Figure 1.4**).

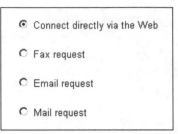

Figure 1.4 The User Reference describes the features of 3ds max.

4. If you have an online connection, choose Connect directly via the Web. You will then be prompted to connect. The registration program uploads the information you entered, plus the CD-key and serial number of the program. It then downloads your authorization code and enters it automatically.

5. If you choose one of the other options, you will be given directions and contact information for submitting your registration and obtaining your authorization code. For your convenience, the contact information for North America and Europe is reproduced at left.

6. Click Finish. The program starts.

Authorizing 3ds max from North America

Web: https//:register.autodesk.com

email: authcodes@autodesk.com

Fax: (800) 225-6490 or (415) 507-4690

Call: (800) 551-1490 or (415) 507-4690

Mail: Product Registrations
          Autodesk Inc.
          111 McInnis Parkway
          San Rafael, CA 94903

Authorizing 3ds max from Europe

Web: https//:register.autodesk.com

email: authcodes@eur.autodesk.com

Fax: +41-32-723-9169

Mail: Autodesk Development S.a.r.l.
          Puits-Godets 6
          Case Postale 35
          CH-2005 Neuchatel
          Switzerland

SETTING UP 3DS MAX 4

Accessing Technical Support

If you have any problems with your 3ds max installation or use, the following resources are available to help you:

♦ The Installation Notes in the Readme file located in the 3dsmax 4 main directory.

♦ The Authorized Dealer who sold you the product. To obtain the number of an Authorized Dealer, call (800) 879-4233.

♦ The 3ds max User Reference files, located in the Help menu (**Figure 1.5**).

♦ The Discreet Support Pages on the Web at http://support.discreet.com/. A well-referenced source of questions and answers.

♦ The Product Support HelpFile in the 3ds max Help menu under Additional Help Updated quarterly and posted on the Web.

♦ Product Support: (425) 489-7519, Monday through Friday, 6 a.m. to 5 p.m. Pacific Standard Time. Installation and configuration support is available for free for 30 consecutive business days. Have your product serial number ready when you call.

After the first 30 days telephone support costs $65 per incident. From the United States and Canada: (800) 225-6531

♦ Autodesk 24-hour FAX Support Information System at (415) 446-1919. Select option 2 and enter 100# to receive a fax of available support documents and their document numbers.

♦ The Autodesk Product Information Line at (800) 964-6432.

For display problems, make sure that you have the latest display driver and video card BIOS installed by checking the technical support pages of your video-card manufacturer's Web site. If problems persist, contact the manufacturer directly.

Figure 1.5 The Help System is an interactive system of reference accessed from the Menu Bar. You can open it from the Help menu within 3ds max.

Touring the Interface

3ds max 4 is a very powerful program that includes tens of thousand commands. To save desktop real estate, many commands are initially hidden from view. Consequently, it can take a while to learn where they are located. This section takes you on a tour of what you typically see as you work with the program.

The 3ds max 4 interface is visually organized by function. Commands are layered in menus, toolbars, tab panels, modules, and dialog boxes to maximize the screen real estate without compromising workspace. Graphical icons and right-click menus supply handy shortcuts to the most commonly used commands.

The main user interface is organized into five main regions, as shown in **Figure 1.6**.

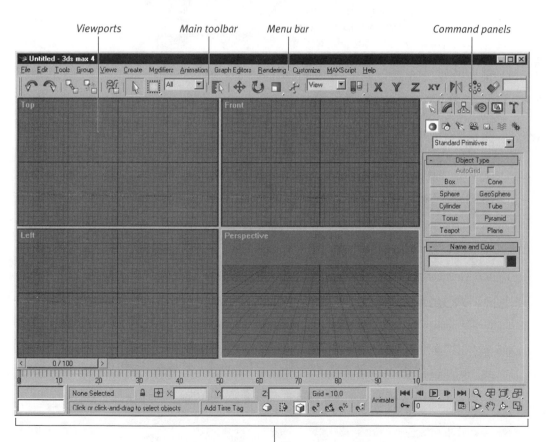

Viewports   Main toolbar   Menu bar   Command panels

TOURING THE INTERFACE

Status bar, locks and controls area

Figure 1.6 The default 3ds max user interface contains a menu bar, the Main toolbar, command panels, viewports, and an assortment of controls at the bottom of the interface.

Special Controls

The following special controls of the user interface make program easier to use.

- Tooltips (**Figure 1.7**) are pop-up labels that appear when you rest your cursor over an icon without clicking it.

- Drop-down menus (**Figure 1.8**) are indicated by an inverted black triangle just to the right of the current menu item.

- Context-sensitive menus, including the new viewport quad menus (**Figure 1.9**), are extensive hidden menus that exist throughout 3ds max 4. You access these menus either by right-clicking, by holding down the CTRL key and right-clicking, or by holding down the ALT key and right-clicking.

- Rollouts (**Figure 1.10**) contain additional commands. The titlebar of a rollout displays a plus sign (+) when the rollout is closed; clicking the titlebar opens the rollout and changes the plus sign to a minus sign (-). To scroll a long rollout so that you can see all the commands, place the cursor over an empty area so that it changes to a panning hand. Then drag up or down. As an alternative, you can drag the thin scrollbar that appears to the right of the rollout.

Figure 1.7 If you rest the cursor over an icon without clicking it, tooltips appear to tell you what the icon represents.

Figure 1.8 Downward-pointing triangles indicate the presence of a drop-down menu.

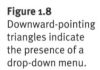

Figure 1.9 When you right-click on most elements of the program interface, a context-sensitive menu appears.

Figure 1.10 Scrolling a Parameters rollout by dragging with the panning hand. The Keyboard Entry rollout is closed.

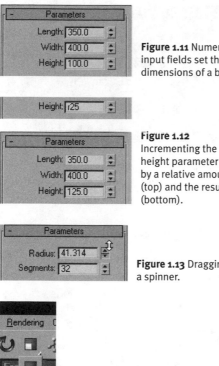

Figure 1.11 Numeric input fields set the dimensions of a box.

Figure 1.12 Incrementing the height parameter by a relative amount (top) and the result (bottom).

Figure 1.13 Dragging a spinner.

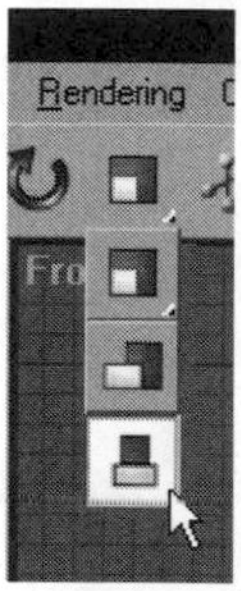

Figure 1.14 You can find flyouts on the Main Toolbar, the status bar, and in the Material Editor.

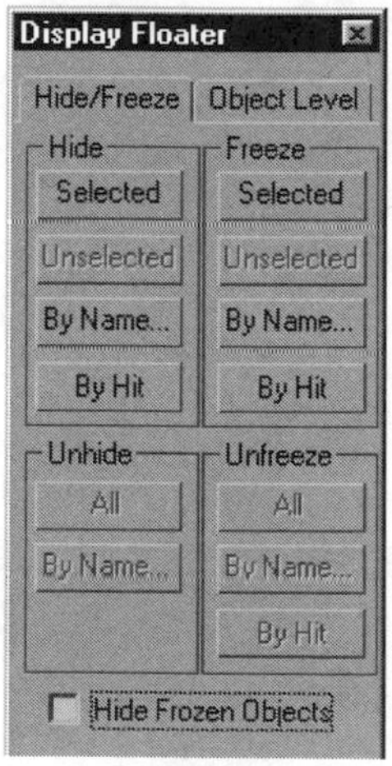

Figure 1.15 Floaters, dialog boxes of commands that stay on top of the interface, are found in the Tools menu.

◆ Numeric Input Fields (**Figure 1.11**) allow you to enter parameter values from the keyboard. To increment a parameter value by a certain amount, enter the letter "r" and the amount you want to add into the field. Then press the Enter key (**Figure 1.12**). To decrement a value, enter "r-" instead of "r," and the amount you want to subtract, and then press Enter.

◆ Spinners (**Figure 1.13**), designated by a pair of little up- and down-facing triangular arrows to the right of an input field, give you a quick way to change the value of a parameter. Click or drag the up arrow to increase a parameter. Click or drag the down arrow to decrease a parameter. Holding down the CTRL key speeds up the rate of change. Holding down the ALT key slows down the rate of change. Right-clicking a spinner zeroes out the parameter.

◆ Flyouts (**Figure 1.14**) are sets of related tool icons that appear when you click and hold any icon that displays a small black triangle in its lower-right corner. You pick a tool from the flyout by rolling the mouse over its icon and then releasing the mouse button.

◆ Floaters (**Figure 1.15**) are modeless dialog boxes that "float" in the foreground and stay available as long as you need them.

continues on next page

- Floating and docking toolbars (**Figure 1.16**) are groups of commands that float in the foreground. Drag a toolbar to detach it, move it, or dock it at the edge of the display.

- Cursors (**Figure 1.17**) in 3ds max change to indicate the selected action. They usually match the icon of whatever tool you select.

The Menu bar

Thirteen drop-down menus are available from the menu bar (**Figure 1.18** (below) and **Figure 1.19**). Commands that cannot be used with the current selection are grayed out.

- The File menu contains commands for managing files and viewing file information.

- The Edit menu contains commands for selecting and editing objects. It also contains the Undo, Redo, Hold and Fetch commands.

- The Tools menu accesses tools and tool modules. Many of these tools (but not all) are also found in the toolbar.

- The Group menu contains commands for grouping and ungrouping objects.

- The Views menu contains commands that control viewport display.

- The Create menu commands access Create panel rollouts for creating standard primitives, extended primitives, shapes, lights, and particles.

- The Modifiers menu contain commands for modifying objects and sub-object selections.

Figure 1.16 You can drag 3ds max toolbars around the interface or attach them alongside the viewports.

Figure 1.17 The cursor changes shape to indicate which tool is active.

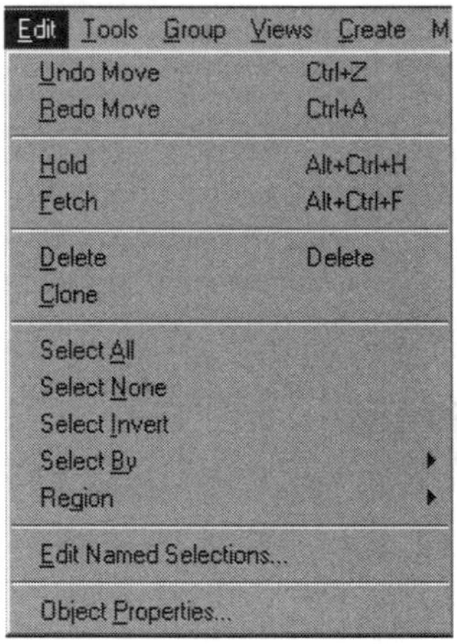

Figure 1.19 The Edit menu contains commands, keyboard shortcuts and arrows that lead to submenus.

File   Edit   Tools   Group   Views   Create   Modifiers   Animation   Graph Editors   Rendering   Customize   MAXScript   Help

Figure 1.18 The 3ds max menu bar contains 13 menus that work just like other Windows menus.

SPECIAL CONTROLS

◆ The Animation menu contains advanced commands for character animation.

◆ The Graph Editors menu commands access modules that manage hierarchies and animations.

◆ The Rendering menu commands access modules that control the rendered appearance of objects and backgrounds.

◆ The Customize menu contains commands that allow you to customize the user interface and set program preferences.

◆ The MAXScript menu contains commands for working with MAXScript, the program's built-in scripting language.

◆ The Help menu provides access to the 3ds max 4 help system.

The Main toolbar

The Main toolbar contains the most important tools (**Figure 1.20**). Most of these tools are accessed by tool icons. To see all of the tool icons at once, your display must be set to a minimum resolution of 1280-by-1024 ppi. If the resolution is set to less than this amount, some of the icons will disappear off to one side or the other. To view the hidden icons, place the cursor in an empty area of the main toolbar. When the cursor turns into a hand, drag the toolbar to the right or the left until the rest of the icons appear.

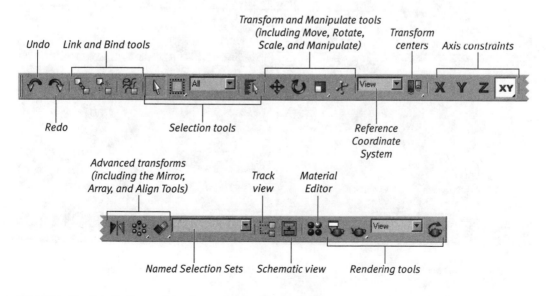

Figure 1.20 The Main Toolbar contains the most commonly used tools.

The viewports

The viewports are the four main viewing areas in the center of the interface (**Figure 1.21**). Viewports can be resized by dragging the borders between two viewports or by dragging the intersection of all four viewports. Right-click a viewport boundary and choose Reset to reset the layout.

Chapter 2, "Navigation and Display," covers in detail how to work with the viewports and viewport controls.

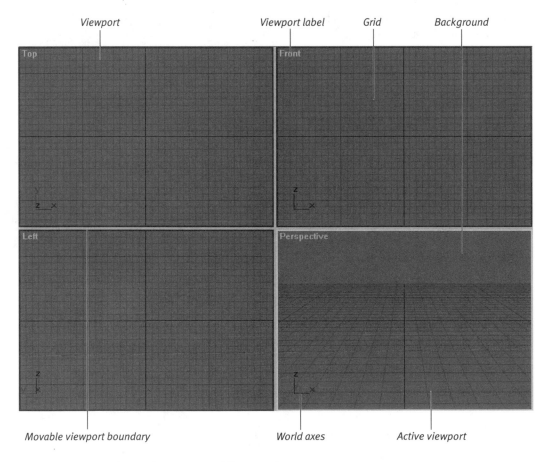

Figure 1.21 Viewports display the scene from different angles.

Figure 1.22 3ds max has six command panels of related tools. Click a tab to bring the panel that you want to the foreground.

The command panels

The command panels give you access to the majority of modeling and animation commands. They also provide display controls and an assortment of utilities. You access command panels by clicking tabs at the top of each panel (**Figure 1.22**). Long command panels can be expanded horizontally to form two or more columns by dragging their edges left or right.

Table 1.1

Command panel icons and functions		
	Create panel	Contains commands for creating objects.
	Modify panel	Contains commands for reshaping objects.
	Hierarchy panel	Contains commands for manipulating linked hierarchies.
	Motion panel	Contains commands for controlling motion.
	Display panel	Controls the display of objects.
	Utilities panel	Contains a miscellaneous assortment of tools. (A subpanel of the Create panel.)

The status bar, locks, and controls area

This area at the bottom of the interface includes command prompts, status information, grid and snap settings, snap and selection locks, animation controls, and viewport controls (**Figure 1.23**). It also includes the MAXScript Mini Listener for scripting commands and the degradation override button for locking display resolution.

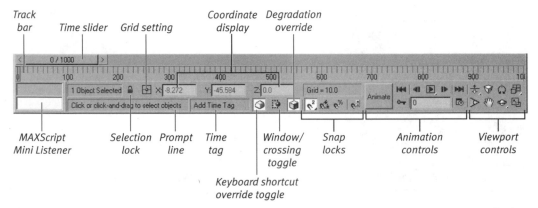

Figure 1.23 The status bar, locks and controls area includes tools for controlling cursor movement, viewport display, animation, and scripting.

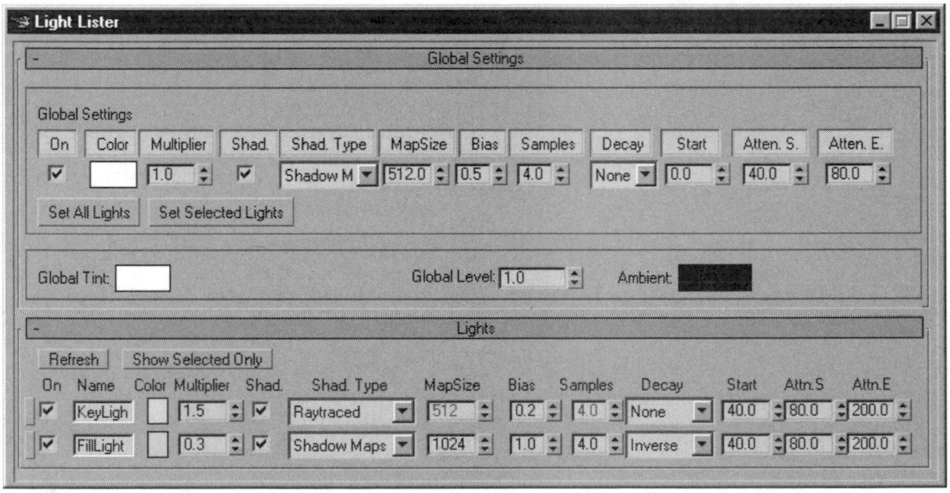

Figure 1.24 The Light Lister dialog box allows you to compare and adjust settings for all of the lights in a scene.

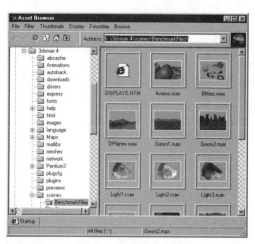

Figure 1.25 Use the Asset Manager to browse external images and scene files and to drag elements into your scene.

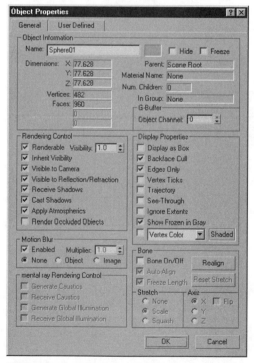

Figure 1.26 The Object Properties dialog box displays parameters of selected objects.

Additional features

3ds max has a large number of utilities, modules, and dialog boxes. Among them, these three stand out as being particularly useful:

◆ The Light Lister dialog box (**Figure 1.24**) allows you to view and adjust light settings for all of the lights in the scene—all at once. You can access the Light Lister from the Tools menu or from the Lights tab panel.

◆ The Asset Browser (**Figure 1.25**) allows you to browse your entire system for image files and scene files. Use the Asset Browser, which can be found in the Utilities command panel, to drag files directly into your scene.

◆ The Object Properties dialog box (**Figure 1.26**) allows you to access and manipulate essential object settings. Access this dialog box by right-clicking a selected object and choosing Properties from the menu.

SPECIAL CONTROLS

Managing Files

When you first initialize the program, a new untitled scene is displayed. At this point, you can either start building a new scene, or build upon an existing file.

Building a scene generally starts by setting preferences and creating some objects. This is covered in the next chapter. If you want to save your scene or work with a previously saved file, you need to know the following File commands:

- Open a scene (Ctrl + O)
- Open a new scene (Ctrl + N)
- Save a scene (Ctrl + S)
- Save selected objects in the scene
- Reset the program
- Merge objects into your scene
- Replace objects in your scene
- Hold the scene in a special Hold file (Alt + Ctrl + H)
- Fetch the scene from the Hold file (Alt + Ctrl + F)
- Import a scene from a different format
- Export a scene to a different format
- View an image file
- Configure paths
- Archive the scene
- Exit the program

The following tasks can be done any time, as you need them. They are also laid out in such a way that if you have never used 3ds max before, you can follow them in a step-by-step sequence.

The native file format for 3ds max scenes is called a max file. The name comes from the three-letter extension for scene files, which is .max.

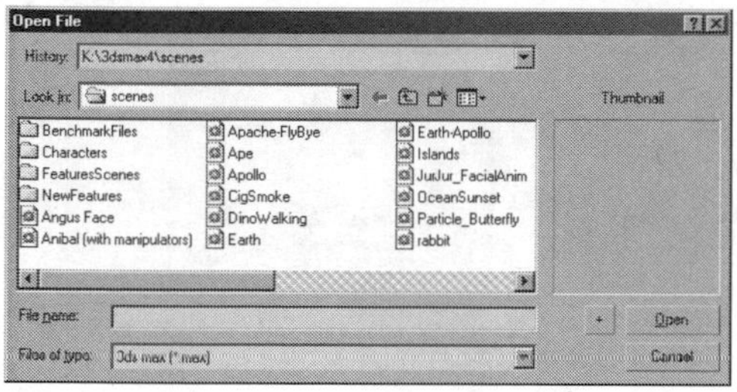

Figure 1.27 The Open File dialog box opens to the 3dsmax4\scenes directory by default

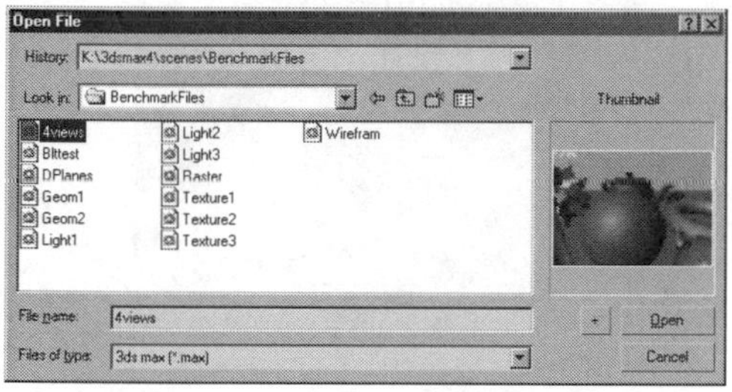

Figure 1.28 The thumbnail in the Open File dialog box displays contents of the selected scene file.

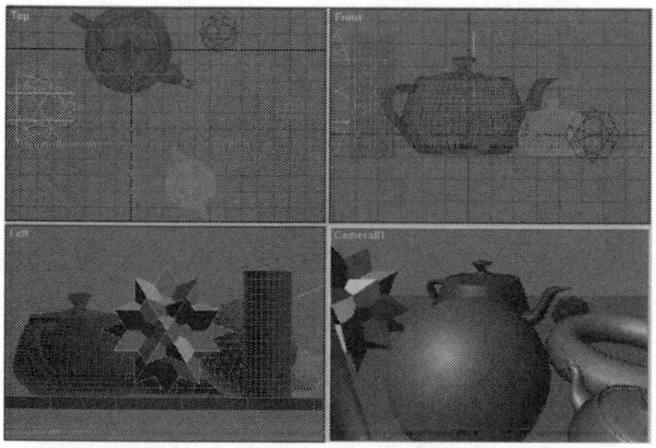

Figure 1.29 The contents of the 4views.max scene file.

Obsolete data format found -- Please resave file.

☐ Don't display this message.   [OK]

Figure 1.30 3ds max runs only one scene at a time. If you have made changes to an open scene, you are asked if you want to save them before opening a new scene.

To open a scene:

1. Choose File > Open.

The Open File dialog box appears. It opens to the 3dsmax4\scenes directory by default (**Figure 1.27**).

2. Navigate to the max scene file you want to open and click the name of the file.

A thumbnail image of the scene appears in the dialog box (**Figure 1.28**).

3. Click Open.

The file opens. The layout of the viewports changes to match the layout that was saved with the scene file. The objects in the scene are displayed in the viewports (**Figure 1.29**).

If the file you are opening was saved with an earlier version of the program, you will be prompted to resave the file (**Figure 1.30**).

✔ Tips

■ To reopen scene that was opened just recently, open the File menu and choose the name of the scene from the list of recently opened files at the bottom of the menu.

■ 3ds max opens only one scene file at a time. If you have enough RAM and you are using Windows 2000 or Windows NT, you can run multiple sessions of the program and open a different scene file in each.

MANAGING FILES

17

The New command saves settings from the previously loaded scene and places them in a new, untitled scene. You are also given the option of keeping objects and their hierarchy of links.

To open a new scene:

1. Choose File > New.

   If you have made changes to the current scene, you are asked whether you want to save your changes (**Figure 1.31**). If you have not made any changes to the current file, the New Scene dialog box appears (**Figure 1.32**) and you can skip to step 3.

2. If you have made changes to the current file, click Yes to bring up the Save File As dialog box and save your changes.

   or

   Click No to leave any changes unsaved.

   If you click No, the New Scene dialog box appears.

3. In the New Scene dialog box, choose the elements you want to preserve, if any. Then click OK.

   A new, untitled scene is displayed. Settings for viewport configuration, user interface customization, snap settings, materials, and others are preserved in the new scene.

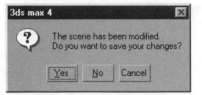

Figure 1.31 If you click yes, the Save As dialog box will appear.

Figure 1.32 The New Scene dialog box lets you incorporate objects and structures from the current scene into the new scene.

MANAGING FILES

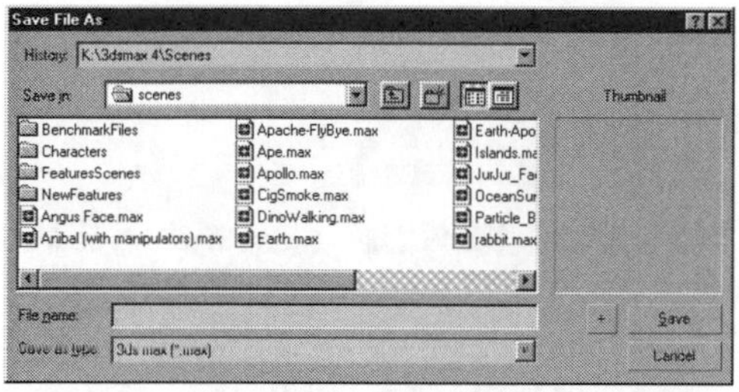

Figure 1.33 You save scene files using the Save File As dialog box.

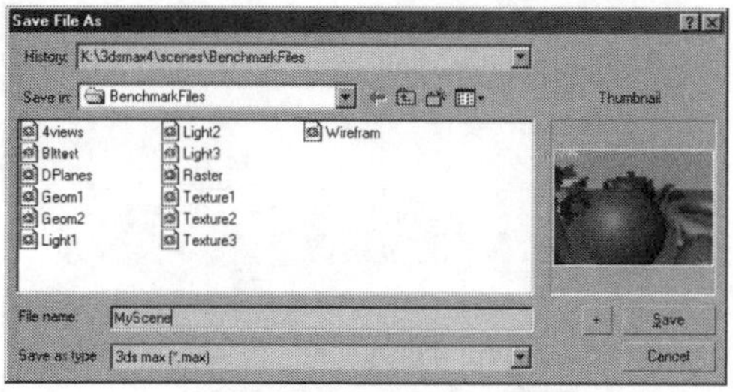

Figure 1.34 Rename scene files using the Save File As dialog box.

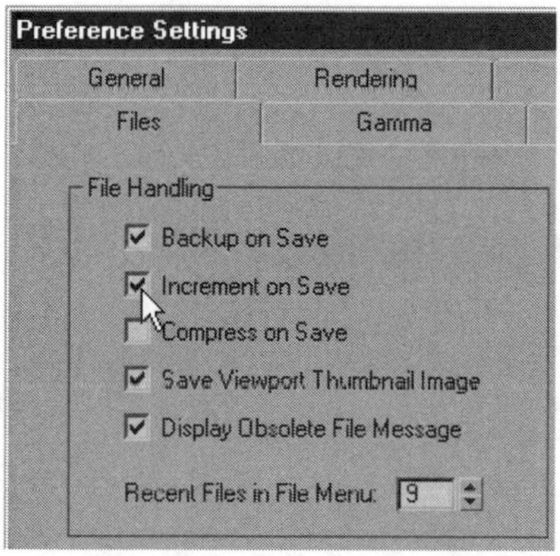

Figure 1.35 Checking Increment on Save causes the program to save to a new file each time you save.

To save a scene:

1. Choose File > Save.

If you are saving a previously saved scene, the file is saved.

If the scene has never been saved and named before, the Save File As dialog box appears (**Figure 1.33**).

2. Navigate to the directory where you want to save the file.

3. In the Save File As dialog box, type a name for your scene in the File Name field (**Figure 1.34**).

4. Click Save.

The file is saved under the new file name. A snapshot of the active viewport (the one with the yellow boundary) is saved as the thumbnail image for the new file.

If you want to save the scene under a different name, use the Save As command.

To save as:

1. Choose File > Save As.

2. Follow steps 2 through 4 above.

✔ Tips

- To increment a file name by +01, click the plus sign (+) in the Save As dialog box. For example, a scene called Apple would be saved as Apple01.

- To increment a file on save automatically, choose Customize > Preferences and click the Files tab. Then check Increment on Save (**Figure 1.35**).

- To save selected objects in your scene, choose File > Save Selected.

The Reset command returns the program to its initial state. All objects, hierarchy, animation data, and materials are eliminated. A new, untitled scene is displayed using the default viewport layout.

To reset the program:

1. Choose File > Reset.

   If you have not saved all of your changes, you will be prompted to do so. Then the Reset dialog box appears (**Figure 1.36**).

2. Click Yes in the Reset dialog box.

   The original 3ds max 4 settings are restored.

✔ Tips

- If the layout of the interface has been changed, the Reset command will not restore the original layout. Instead, choose Customize > Revert to Startup UI Layout.

- If the colors of the interface have been changed, choose Customize > Customize User Interface, and click the Colors tab (**Figure 1.37**). Then click Load, and choose DefaultUI (**Figure 1.38**). When you click Open, the default colors of the user interface are restored.

To exit the program:

1. Choose File > Exit.

2. If necessary, save changes to the current file.

   The program window closes and the program quits.

✔ Tip

- To quit the program, you can also close the program window.

Figure 1.36 This series of dialog boxes is the program's way of letting you know you are about to lose some changes unless you save.

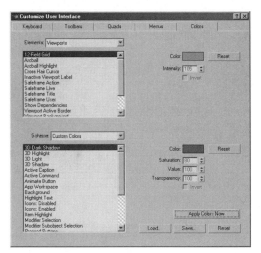
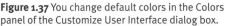

Figure 1.37 You change default colors in the Colors panel of the Customize User Interface dialog box.

Figure 1.38 Choose the DefaultUI.clr file to restore the default program colors.

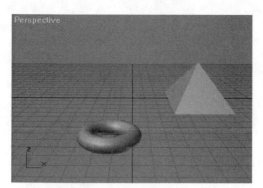

Figure 1.39 Blttest.max before merging it with another file.

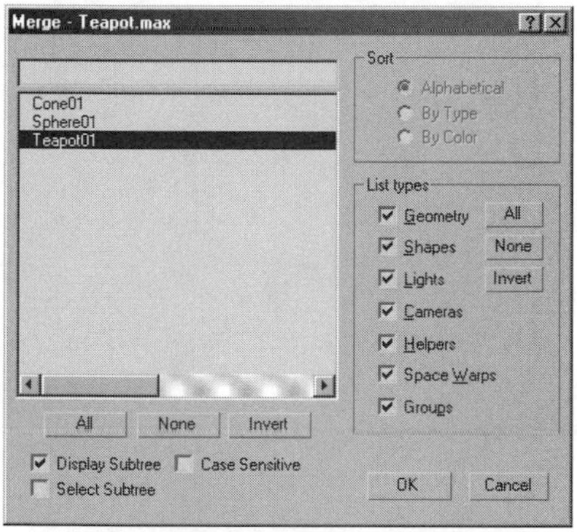

Figure 1.40 In the Merge dialog box, choose the objects that you want to add to your scene.

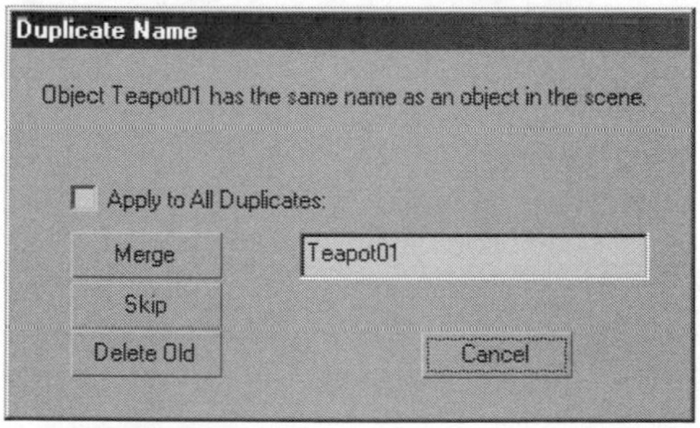

Figure 1.41 If there are any objects with duplicate filenames, you are offered the choice of merging the object and/or deleting the original.

By merging files, you can bring objects into your current scene from other scene files, along with their materials and animation data. This allows you to develop parts of your scene in different files and then combine them into a single scene.

To merge objects into a scene:

1. Choose File > Reset

   or

   Open a scene file (**Figure 1.39**).

2. Choose File > Merge.

3. Select and open the file that contains the objects you want.

   The Merge dialog box appears with a list of objects in the scene file.

4. Select the objects you want to merge (**Figure 1.40**). Then click OK.

5. If there are any objects with duplicate names, you will be prompted to merge the object, skip merging the object, or delete the old object in your current file (**Figure 1.41**).

   continues on next page

MANAGING FILES

When you are finished with your selections, the objects you chose to merge appear in the scene (**Figure 1.42**).

✔ Tip

■ Your merged objects may be selected when they arrive. Selected objects have box corners around them in shaded views, and appear white in wireframe views. To deselect them, just click in the background.

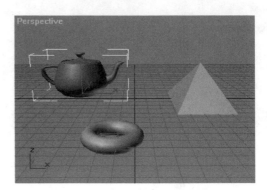

Figure 1.42 The scene after merging in the object.

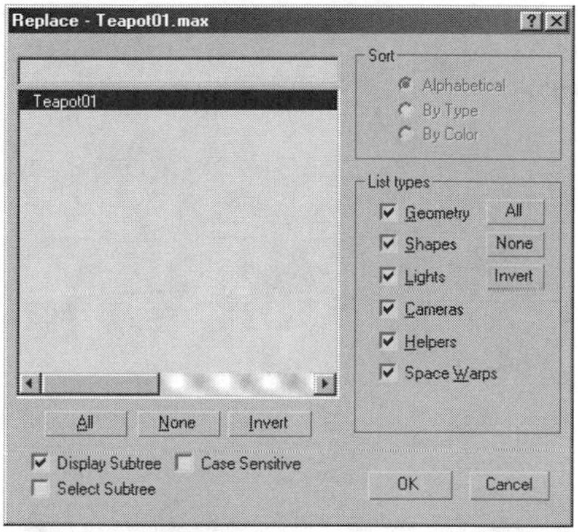

Figure 1.43 In the Replace dialog box you choose the substitute objects for your scene.

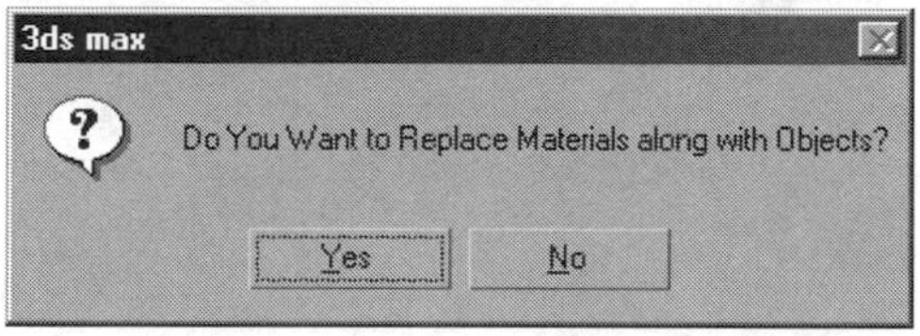

Figure 1.44 When you replace objects, you can import their materials with them, or simply substitute geometry.

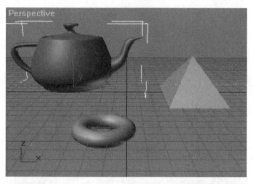

Figure 1.45 After replacing all the objects. The white corners indicate that the replacement objects are currently selected.

Using the Replace command, you can substitute an object in your scene with another object by the same name that is saved in another scene. The substitute object takes on the properties and animation data of the object it replaces. This allows you to animate your scene faster using simple objects and then substitute complex objects later when you have developed them.

To replace objects in a scene:

1. Open a scene file (Figure 1.42).

2. Choose File > Replace.

3. In the Replace dialog box, open the scene that has the object you want to substitute into your file. If the file you want to open does not have an object with the same name as an object in your current scene, you will not be able to access the file.

4. Select the objects you want to replace (**Figure 1.43**).

   The Replace Materials dialog box appears (**Figure 1.44**).

5. Click Yes to replace materials along with the objects or No to bring in objects only.

   The replacement objects appear in the scene (**Figure 1.45**). All the replacement objects are selected. To deselect them, just click in the background.

MANAGING FILES

If you want to try making some changes that you are not sure you will like, you can save your scene to a temporary file called a *hold file*. To restore the hold file, you use the fetch command.

To hold and fetch a file:

1. Open a scene file (**Figure 1.46**).

2. Choose Edit > Hold.

3. Try out some changes to your file (**Figure 1.47**).

4. Choose Edit > Fetch.

5. In the About to Fetch. OK? dialog box, click Yes to restore the hold file without saving the current state of the scene. Click No if you want to cancel (**Figure 1.48**).

   If you click Yes, the program restores the hold file and changes its name to the name of the scene it replaces (**Figure 1.49**).

✔ Tip

■ The hold file is named maxhold.mx and it is located in the Autoback directory. You can open this file with the File > Open command if you change Files of type to All files.

Figure 1.46 The file before you have made any changes.

Figure 1.47 The file after deleting the character's face.

Figure 1.48 Click yes to fetch the hold file; no to cancel.

Figure 1.49 After restoring the hold file.

MANAGING FILES

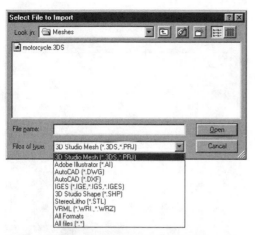

Figure 1.50 When you import a file, start by choosing a file type from the Select File to Import dialog box.

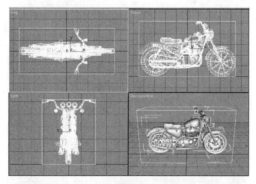

Figure 1.51 The imported files appear in the 3ds max viewports.

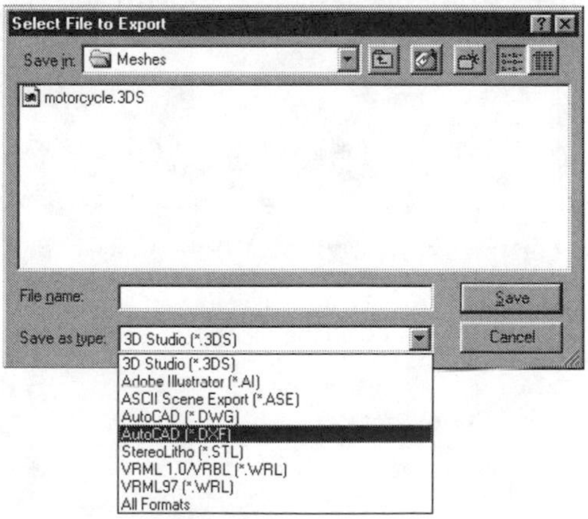

Figure 1.52 When you export a file, you select a file and an export file format.

Use the Import and Export commands to exchange geometry with other 3D modeling programs. You can also import .AI files from Adobe Illustrator.

Exporting files causes 3ds max to translate the native .max scene information into universal 3D file formats such as .3ds or .dxf. Because these universal files are usually less robust, some of the scene information may change or disappear. 3ds max usually warns you of such changes, while preserving the most important information.

To import a file:

1. Choose File > Import.

   The Select File to Import dialog box appears.

2. Select a file format from the Files of Type menu (**Figure 1.50**).

3. Double-click the name of the file you want to import.

4. In the dialog box that appears, choose Completely Replace Current Scene.

5. Click OK to accept the default settings.

   The imported file appears on the screen (**Figure 1.51**).

To export a file:

1. Choose File > Export. The Select File to Export dialog box appears.

2. Select an export file format from the Save As Type menu (**Figure 1.52**).

3. Choose a directory to hold the exported file.

4. Name the file, and click Save.

MANAGING FILES

The File menu offers a quick way to view image files, including both still images and animations.

To view an image file:

1. Choose File > View Image File.

2. Navigate to the image or animation you want to view (**Figure 1.53**).

3. Click View (if you want to view the image and keep surfing)

   or

   Click Open (if you want to open the image and close the dialog box).

   The image file appears on your screen (**Figure 1.54**). If it is an animation file, it opens in Windows Media Player or QuickTime Player (**Figure 1.55**).

✔ Tip

■ You can also view image files from other dialog boxes, including the Asset Manager, the Select Bitmap Image dialog box in the Material Editor, or the Browse Images for Output dialog box that opens when you click Save Bitmap in the Virtual Frame Buffer.

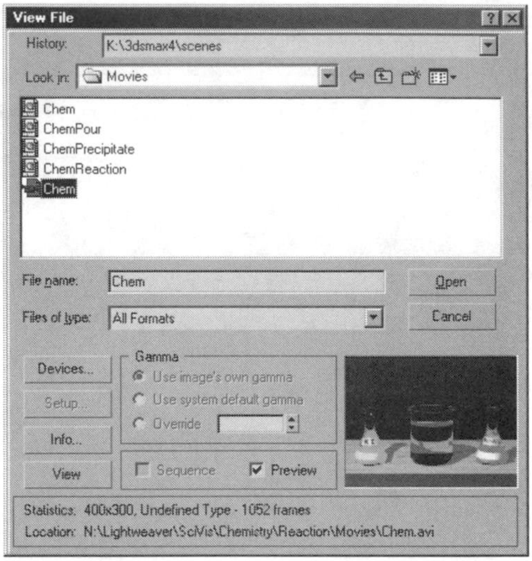

Figure 1.53 The View File dialog box displays viewable image files.

Figure 1.54 The image file that you select appears in a special window called the virtual frame buffer.

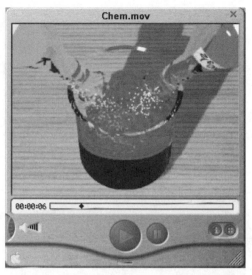

Figure 1.55 Animated image files appear in Windows Media Player or QuickTime Player, depending on the file type.

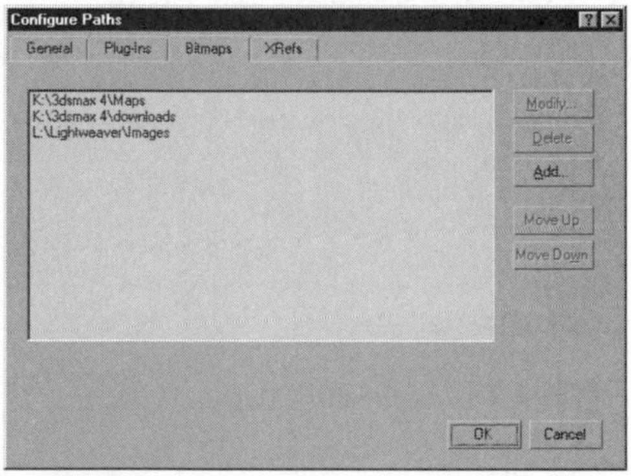

Figure 1.56 The Bitmaps panel of the Configure Paths dialog box allows you to add paths for finding bitmaps. Paths are searched from the top of the list on down.

File paths cause the program to look for certain types of files in specific directories and folders. Configuring paths can help you work more efficiently on a project when you need to organize files in different locations.

Bitmaps can have multiple paths, which 3ds max searches in this order:

1. The path of the image file last loaded.

2. The directory of the current scene.

3. The subdirectories below the current scene.

4. The paths listed in the Bitmaps panel of the Configure Path dialog box, starting at the top of the list (**Figure 1.56**).

MANAGING FILES

To configure a file path:

1. Choose Customize > Configure Paths.

   The Configure Paths dialog box appears (**Figure 1.57**).

2. Select a file type and click Modify.

3. In the Choose Directory for Scenes dialog box, navigate to a folder, or click Create New Folder and open the new folder.

4. Click Use Path.

5. Click OK.

   The program goes to the designated folder whenever you attempt to open a file of that type. If the path is a scene file path, the program will begin saving scene files to the newly designated folder, instead of to the default 3dsmax4\scenes directory.

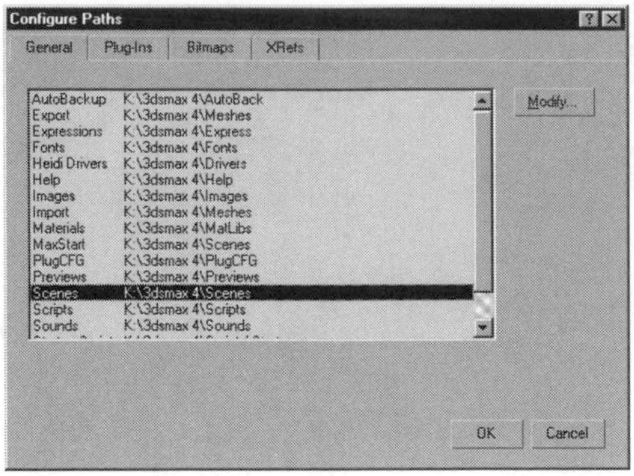

Figure 1.57 The Configure Paths dialog box tells the program where to find different types of files.

File Pathnames

File pathnames are stored in the 3dsmax.ini file, located in the main 3dsmax4 directory. You can edit this file directly with a text editor such as Notepad. If you delete the file, the program will create a new .ini file the next time it boots using default pathnames and preferences.

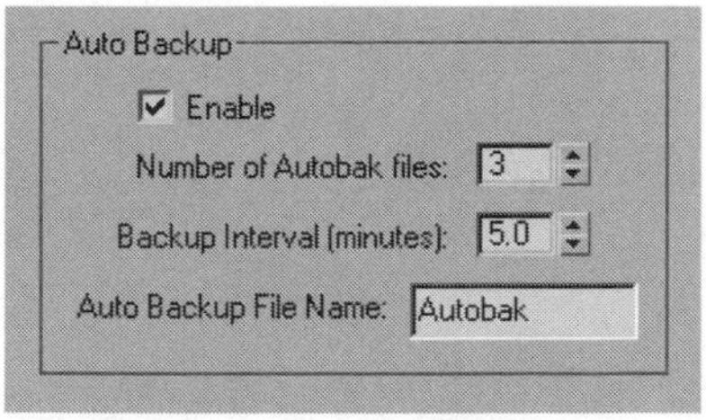

Backing Up Files

Figure 1.58 The Files panel of the Preference Settings dialog box. These settings govern saving, backing up, and archiving files.

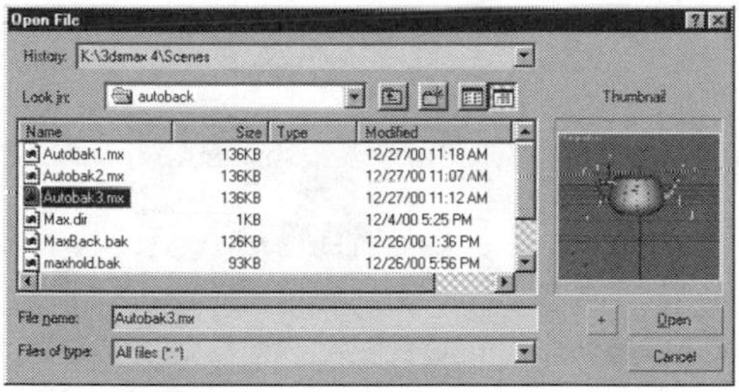

Figure 1.59 When restoring a scene file from the Autobak directory, click Details and Files of type: All files to see which file was modified the most recently.

Backing up files is crucial to the success of any project. Besides saving files manually, you can set a preference to back up files automatically.

To back up files automatically:

1. Choose Customize > Preferences.

2. In the Preferences dialog box, click the Files tab.

3. In the Auto Backup area, check Enable (**Figure 1.58**).

4. Enter the maximum number of backup files to maintain, or use the default of three files.

5. Enter the backup interval in minutes, or use the default of five minutes.

6. Click OK.

To recover a file from automatic backup:

1. Choose File > Open.

2. Navigate to the 3dsmax3\autoback directory.

3. In the File Type drop-down menu, choose All Files (*.*).

4. Click the Details icon in the upper-right corner of the dialog box.

   The modification dates of the Auto Backup files appear (**Figure 1.59**).

5. Open the most recently modified file.

6. Choose File > Save As. Navigate to the scenes directory and rename your file.

Backup File Naming

The automatic backup process saves a limited number of backup files at set intervals of time. 3ds max automatically names the files Autobak1.mx, Autobak2.mx, Autobak3.mx, AutobakN.mx, where N is the maximum number of backup files you have set the program to save. When the number of backup files exceeds the maximum, the backup process saves over the oldest file starting with Autobak1.mx.

BACKING UP FILES

Saving files is a good thing, right? Not when you save changes over work you had wanted to keep. Fortunately, you can set a preference in 3ds max that automatically backs up your previously saved file every time you save it again. This nonincrementing file is saved in the 3dsmax4\Autoback directory.

To backup on save:

1. Choose Customize > Preferences.

2. Click the Files tab.

3. Check Backup on Save (**Figure 1.60**).

   3ds max will now automatically back up your file to the Autobak directory every time you use Save.

To recover a backup file after a save:

1. Choose File > Open.

2. Navigate to the 3dsmax4\Autoback folder.

3. In the Files of Type drop-down menu, choose All Files (*.*) (**Figure 1.61**).

4. Open MaxBack.bak.

5. Choose File > Save As. Navigate to the scenes directory and rename your file.

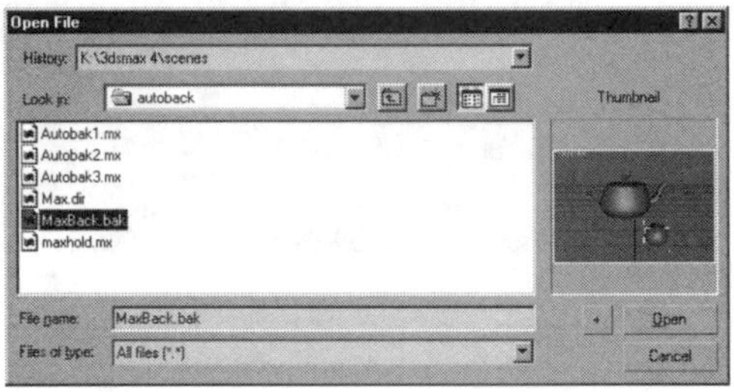

✔ Tips

■ Checking Compress on Save causes the program to compress saved scenes to as little as one fifth of the original size.

■ Checking Increment on Save causes the program to automatically increment your filename by +01 every time you use Save.

■ You can also increment on save manually by clicking the "+" button in the Save File As dialog box.

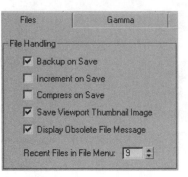

Figure 1.60 Check Backup on Save in the Files panel of the Preference Settings dialog box.

Figure 1.61 Choose All Files (*.*) in the Files of Type drop-down menu to see the MaxBack.bak file.

BACKING UP FILES

CREATING OBJECTS

Everything in nature can be represented as a combination of geometric forms. As the painter Paul Cézanne once wrote, "Treat nature in terms of the cylinder, the sphere, the cone; everything in proper perspective." He also is reported to have said, "One must first of all study geometric forms: the cone, the cube, the cylinder, the sphere."

Today, 3D artists use geometric forms called *objects* to create and animate entire worlds. Starting with a foundation of the cone, the cube, the cylinder, and the sphere (**Figure 2.1**), you can combine and manipulate basic objects to create highly complex and realistic scenes.

This chapter explains how to create mesh objects and shape splines, which are the basic building blocks of 3D scenes. You will also learn how to create helper objects to assist you in placing objects in your scene. In later chapters, you will learn how to create lights and cameras, and how to combine objects into compound objects.

Figure 2.1 The cone, the cube, the cylinder, and the sphere are basic objects in 3ds max.

About Creating Objects

When you create an object in 3ds max, it is automatically assigned certain attributes, including a name, a color, a position, an orientation, a pivot point, an axis tripod, and display properties and rendering properties. If an object is can be rendered to an image output file, a white *bounding box* appears at the dimensional extents of the object when it is selected (**Figure 2.2**).

When you place objects in a scene, the viewports display them from different angles. The Front, Left, and Top viewports always view objects from the front, left, and top, respectively. By default, objects in these views are displayed in *wireframe*. In contrast, the Perspective viewport can display an object from any angle. By default it looks at the scene from in front and a little above, and draws objects using a smooth shaded mode of display (**Figure 2.3**).

The grids that you see in the viewports are all part of the *home grid*. The home grid provides construction planes for creating objects. What this means is that objects automatically sit on top of the grid when they are created. Because the grids of the home grid are perpendicular to one another, objects created in different viewports may orient in different directions (**Figure 2.4**).

For more information on navigating viewports and viewport modes of display, see Chapter 3, Viewport Navigation and Display.

The method that you use to create an object depends on how it is defined:

Parametric objects are defined by parametric equations that determine the overall structure of the object. By entering a few parameters, you can quickly create entire objects. In 3ds max, you enter parameters from the keyboard, or by clicking and dragging in a viewport.

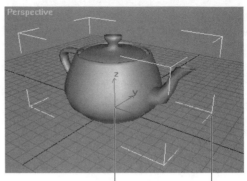

Axis tripod   Bounding box

Figure 2.2 The axis tripod and bounding box indicate that the object is selected. The origin of the axis tripod is located at the pivot point of the object; the bounding box is drawn at the object's extents.

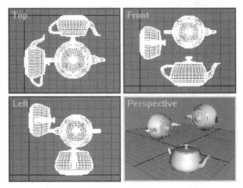

Figure 2.3 Viewing a scene from four different angles. Three of the views are displayed in wireframe; the Perspective view is shaded, and rotated to a new viewing angle.

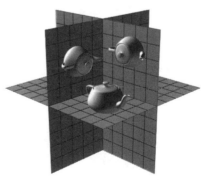

Figure 2.4 The home grid consists of three intersecting grids. Creating objects on different grids results in different orientations.

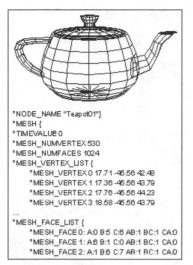

```
*NODE_NAME "TeapotO1"}
*MESH {
*TIMEVALUE 0
*MESH_NUMVERTEX 530
*MESH_NUMFACES 1024
*MESH_VERTEX_LIST {
    *MESH_VERTEX 0 17.71 -46.56 42.48
    *MESH_VERTEX 1 17.36 -46.56 43.79
    *MESH_VERTEX 2 17.76 -46.56 44.23
    *MESH_VERTEX 3 18.58 -46.56 43.79
...
*MESH_FACE_LIST {
    *MESH_FACE 0: A:0 B:5 C:6 AB:1 BC:1 CA:0
    *MESH_FACE 1: A:6 B:1 C:0 AB:1 BC:1 CA:0
    *MESH_FACE 2: A:1 B:6 C:7 AB:1 BC:1 CA:0
```

Figure 2.5 This teapot started out as a parametric object but was converted to a non-parametric object.

Figure 2.6 The Create menu has shortcuts to commonly used object-creation commands.

Figure 2.7 The Tools menu has shortcuts to just a few object-creation commands.

Non-parametric objects are defined by an explicit description of every part, and the relationship of those parts to their neighbors. Because they have no predefined structure, you create each part by clicking and dragging. You can also create non-parametric objects by converting parametric objects (**Figure 2.5**). Most non-parametric objects include built-in commands for editing their structure. Such objects are called *editable objects* in 3ds max.

All commands for creating objects from scratch are found in the Create command panel. For your convenience, 3ds max provides shortcuts to some of these commands:

◆ The Create menu in the Menu bar. Limited to Standard Primitives, Extended Primitives, shapes, lights, and particles (**Figure 2.6**).

◆ The Tools quad menu. Object choices are limited to the Rectangle, Circle, Line, Sphere, Cylinder, and Box. Access this menu by Ctrl + right-clicking in any viewport (**Figure 2.7**).

◆ The Tab panels. Includes every object type. Hidden by default; right-click on the Main toolbar and choose Tabs to access (**Figure 2.8**).

This book does not employ object-creation shortcuts because it is usually more efficient to go straight to the command panel. But if you find a shortcut to be useful, by all means, take advantage of it.

ABOUT CREATING OBJECTS

Figure 2.8 The Tab panels contain shortcuts to all of the object-creation commands.

To create an object by clicking and dragging:

1. In the Create panel, click the button for the object you want to create. In this example, I will choose the Teapot.

   The creation rollouts for the object appear below (**Figure 2.9**).

2. Choose an option from the Creation Method rollout, or simply use the default.

3. In the Perspective viewport, click and drag across the grid to create the object or its base. Release the mouse button when the object or base is the right size (**Figure 2.10**).

4. If the object is not complete, drag and click to set other dimensions as needed.

5. Adjust the creation parameters by entering new values in the Parameters rollout or by dragging the spinners next to the input fields of the rollout (**Figure 2.11**).

   The object updates in the viewport interactively (**Figure 2.12**).

6. Right-click in a viewport to exit object creation mode.

Figure 2.9 The Parameter rollouts for creating a teapot.

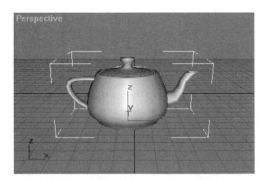

Figure 2.10 The quickest way to create a mesh object is to click and drag.

Figure 2.11 Adjusting a parameter by dragging a spinner.

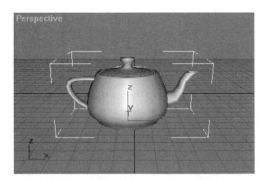

Figure 2.12 Decreasing the value of the radius parameter reduced the size of the teapot.

Figure 2.13 After entering the location and dimensions of an object, click Create.

Figure 2.14 The object appears at the location you entered.

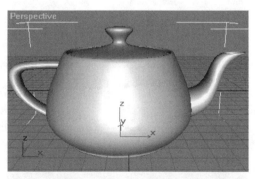

Figure 2.15 Increasing the number of segments makes the teapot object appear smoother.

Figure 2.16 You make variations on a theme by changing settings before you click Create.

To create an object using the keyboard-entry method:

1. Activate the Perspective viewport.

2. In the Create panel, click on the button for the object you want to create.

3. Open the Keyboard Entry rollout and enter the dimensions of the object.

   If you want to position the object in a place other than the origin, enter location coordinates for X, Y, and Z as well.

4. Click Create (**Figure 2.13**).

   The object you specified appears in the viewports (**Figure 2.14**).

5. Adjust the creation parameters in the Parameters rollout of the Create panel or the Modify panel (**Figure 2.15**).

✔ Tip

■ You can create as many objects as you like by clicking the Create button repeatedly. Or you can change the settings a little each time to get variations on a theme (**Figure 2.16**).

Disappearing Parameters

Creation parameters disappear as soon as you exit object-creation mode, or start creating a new object. It is this last point—creating a new object—that sometimes causes trouble because if an object-creation button is still selected, all you have to do is click in a viewport and the parameters of the first object disappear. To get them back, choose the Select Object tool in the Main Toolbar and click on the object to reselect it. Then open the Modify panel by clicking on the Modify tab. The creation parameters reappear in the Modify panel in the state that you last set them. Now you can adjust the parameters as much as you like.

ABOUT CREATING OBJECTS

3ds max automatically assigns names to objects based on the object type and the order in which it was created. For example, the first, second, and third sphere that you create will be named Sphere01, Sphere02, and Sphere03. After you create your objects, it is helpful if you assign more descriptive names so you can find them more easily when your scene gets more complex.

3ds max also assigns colors to objects as you create them. By default, color assignment is random, but you can change the color of objects after they are created, or set an option so that all objects are assigned the same color.

To assign a name and color to an object:

1. Create an object, or select an existing object by clicking on it.

2. In the Create panel, highlight the name of the object in the Name and Color rollout (**Figure 2.17**).

3. Enter a new name (**Figure 2.18**).

4. Click on the color swatch located just to the right of the name field.
   The Object Color dialog box appears (**Figure 2.19**).

5. Click on a swatch to pick color, and click OK.
   The object changes to the new shade.

✔ Tips

- To assign the same color to objects as you create them, uncheck Assign Random Colors in the Object Color dialog box.

- To assign the same color to existing objects, drag a selection region around them before picking a color (**Figure 2.20**). Note that you cannot assign a name to a multiple selection.

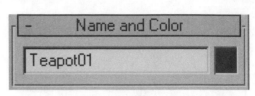

Figure 2.17 Highlight the name of the object.

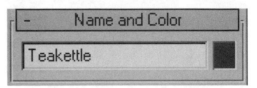

Figure 2.18 Enter a new name.

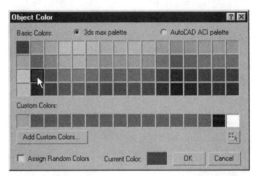

Figure 2.19 Pick a color from the Object Color dialog box.

Figure 2.20 Select a group of objects by dragging a selection window.

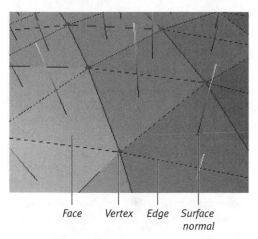

Face   Vertex   Edge   Surface
                          normal

Figure 2.21 The three components of a mesh are the vertex, edge, and face. The surface normal determines which side of the face is rendered.

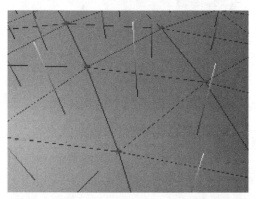

Figure 2.22 After smoothing the mesh.

Creating Mesh Objects

Mesh objects are surfaces (not solids) that are subdivided by three types of sub-object components: *vertices*, or point locations in space; *edges*, which are straight line segments that connect vertex points; and *faces*, which are triangular surfaces made up of three vertices and three edges that connect them. At the center of each face lies a perpendicular vector called a *surface normal* that indicates the side of the face to be shaded in, or *rendered* (**Figure 2.21**).

Smoothing creates gradations of value across the surface of mesh objects by averaging the intensity of light at each vertex based on surrounding normals (**Figure 2.22**). The more vertices that are present, the subtler the gradations will be, and the smoother the mesh surface will appear when rendered.

Parametric objects that define regular geometric forms are also known as *parametric primitives*, or just primitives for short. Mesh primitives come in two varieties: *Standard Primitives*, which include basic geometric forms; and *Extended Primitives*, which include more complex objects.

The easiest way to create mesh primitives is by using the click and drag method.

Creating standard primitives

There are 10 Standard Primitives in 3ds max 4: the Sphere, GeoSphere, Box, Pyramid, Plane, Cylinder, Cone, Tube, Torus, and Teapot (**Figure 2.23**).

Standard Primitives are found in the Geometry branch of the Create panel, which is "on deck" when you start the program (**Figure 2.24**). Shortcuts to theses commands are found in the Create menu and in the Objects Toolbar.

You create a sphere (or, in the same way, a GeoSphere) by dragging out its radius.

To create a sphere:

1. In the Create panel, click Sphere.

   The Sphere rollout appears (**Figure 2.25**).

2. In the Perspective viewport, drag a sphere of any size.

   The object grows outward as you drag (**Figure 2.26**).

3. Release the mouse button to set the radius.

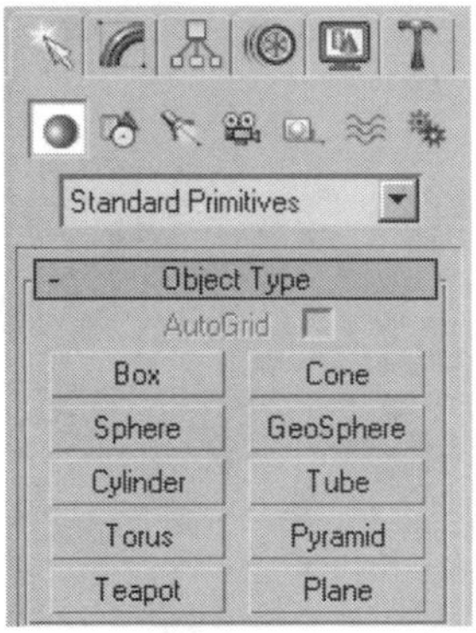

Figure 2.23 Standard Primitives are used to make basic geometric forms.

Figure 2.24 The menu of Standard Primitives is located in the Geometry branch of the Create panel.

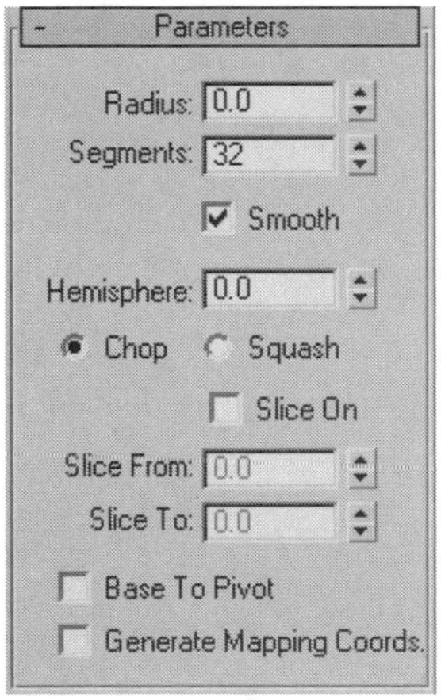

Figure 2.25 The main parameter of the Sphere rollout is the Radius.

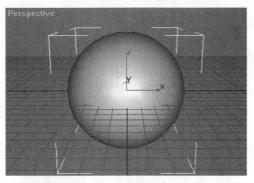

Figure 2.26 Drag to set the length of the radius.

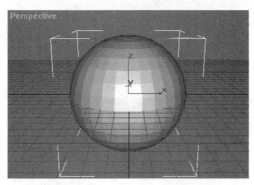

Figure 2.27 You unsmooth a sphere by unchecking the Smooth parameter.

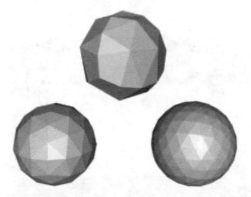

Figure 2.28 Low-poly variations on the GeoSphere.

✔ Tips

- To make a curved surface appear smoother, increase the number of surface subdivisions by increasing the Segments value.

  To unsmooth a surface, so that faces are shaded without gradation, uncheck the Smooth parameter (**Figure 2.27**).

- To make a sphere sit on top of the grid, check Base to Pivot. This moves the pivot point of the object to its base.

  If you drag the Hemisphere spinner up and down with Base to Pivot checked, the sphere will disappear into or emerge from the grid.

- To create slices, like cutting pieces from an apple, check Slice and enter the size of the slice in terms of the degrees of angle.

- With a GeoSphere, you can create low-polygon spheres such as a tetrahedra, an octahedra, and an icosahedra (**Figure 2.28**).

CREATING MESH OBJECTS

The box and the pyramid use a similar method of creation. The first click-drag sequence defines the base; the second click defines the height. Planes are even simpler; you just click and drag once to set the proportions.

To create a box:

1. In the Create panel, click Box.
   The Box rollout appears (**Figure 2.29**).

2. In the Perspective viewport, drag diagonally to form the base of the box.

3. Release the mouse button to set the length and width of the box (**Figure 2.30**).

4. Without clicking, move the cursor upward in the viewport.

5. Click to set the height (**Figure 2.31**).

✔ Tips

■ To create a box that hangs below the grid plane, drag downward in step 4.

■ To create a box or a pyramid that has a square base, hold down the Ctrl key as you drag to create the base. In this method, the first click sets the center of the base, and dragging causes the base to grow equally in all directions.

■ To create a box with equal sides, choose Cube in the Creation Method rollout.

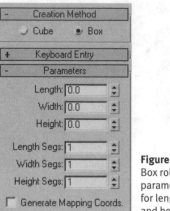

Figure 2.29 The Box rollout has parameter inputs for length, width, and height.

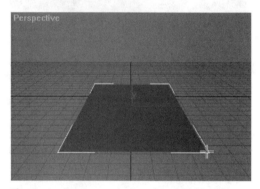

Figure 2.30 Drag to set the length and width of the box.

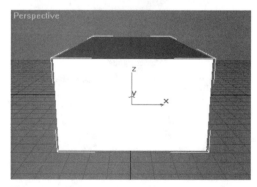

Figure 2.31 Click to set the height.

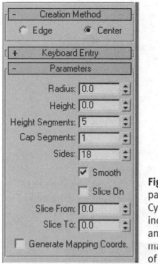

Figure 2.32 The parameters for the Cylinder primitive include dimensions and settings for making slices out of the cylinder.

Cylinders, cones, and tubes are all variations on a theme. Each one has a radius and a height. In addition, cones and tubes have a second radius.

To create a cylinder:

1. In the Create panel, click Cylinder. The Cylinder rollout appears (**Figure 2.32**).

2. In the Perspective viewport, drag the base of the cylinder.

3. Release the mouse button to set the base radius (**Figure 2.33**).

4. Without clicking, move the cursor up in the viewport.

5. Click to set the height (**Figure 2.34**).

✔ Tip

■ Check the Slice On box and then set the Slice From and Slice To parameters (in degrees) to create a pie chart (**Figure 2.35**).

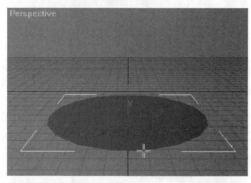

Figure 2.33 Drag to make the base of the cylinder.

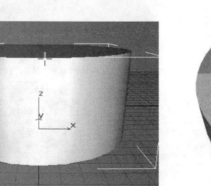

Figure 2.34 Then you set the height.

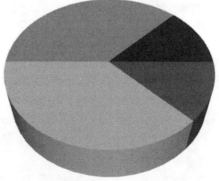

Figure 2.35 Use the Slice parameters to make separate wedges of a cylinder "pie."

To create a cone:

1. In the Create panel, click Cone.

   The Cone rollout appears (**Figure 2.36**).

2. In the Perspective viewport, drag the base of the cone.

3. Release the mouse button when the base is the right size (**Figure 2.37**).

4. Without clicking, move the cursor upward in the viewport.

5. Click to set the height (**Figure 2.38**).

6. Without clicking, move the cursor downward to establish the radius for the top.

   If you want to close up the point at the top of the cone, drag downward from the top till it closes up.

7. Click to set the radius of the top (**Figure 2.39**).

✔ Tips

■ You can make the radius of the top wider than the radius of the base by dragging upward in the viewport in step 6.

■ To slice the cone, choose Slice On from the Parameters rollout and adjust the values of the Slice From and Slice To parameters.

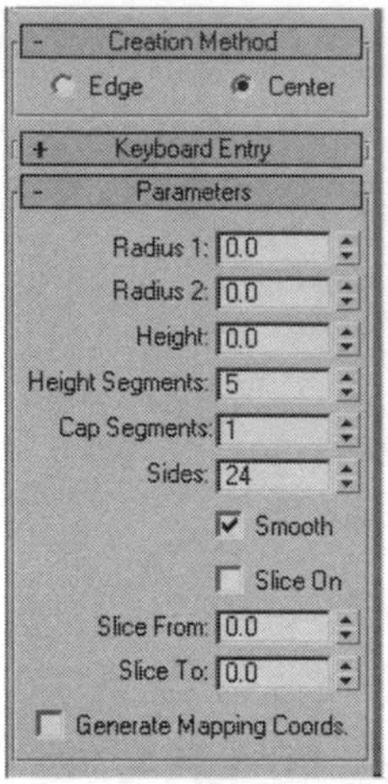

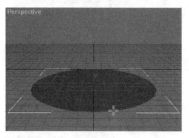

Figure 2.36 The Cone rollout has parameter inputs for height and two radii.

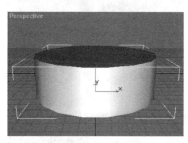

Figure 2.37 Drag to set the base radius of the cone.

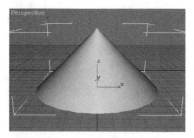

Figure 2.38 Move the cursor upward and click to set the height of the cone.

Figure 2.39 Move the cursor down and click to complete the cone.

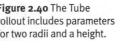

Radius 1: 0.0
Radius 2: 0.0
Height: 0.0
Height Segments: 5
Cap Segments: 1
Sides: 18
☑ Smooth
☐ Slice On
Slice From: 0.0

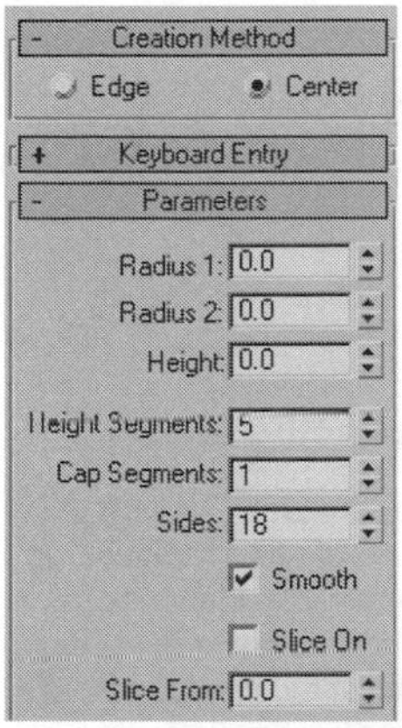

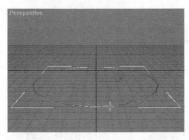

Figure 2.40 The Tube rollout includes parameters for two radii and a height.

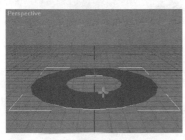

Figure 2.41 Drag to set the base of the tube.

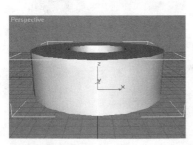

Figure 2.42 Move and click to set the second radius.

Figure 2.43 Move and click to set the height and complete the tube.

To create a tube:

1. In the Create panel, click Tube.

   The Tube rollout appears (**Figure 2.40**).

2. In the Perspective viewport, drag the base of the tube (**Figure 2.41**).

   By default you drag from the center of the base, but you can change the setting in the Creation Method rollout to drag from the edge.

3. Release the mouse button to set the first radius.

4. Move the cursor toward (or away from) the center of the tube.

5. Click to set the second radius (**Figure 2.42**).

6. Move the cursor upward in the viewport.

7. Click to set the height (**Figure 2.43**).

CREATING MESH OBJECTS

The teapot has preset parts for a body, handle, spout, and lid. All you need to do is drag the radius.

To create a teapot:

1. In the Create panel, click Teapot.

   The Teapot rollout appears (**Figure 2.44**).

2. In the Perspective viewport, drag a teapot of any size.

   The entire teapot grows outward and upward from the grid (**Figure 2.45**).

3. Release the mouse button to set the radius.

   For variations, try turning off (unchecking) the body, handle, spout, or lid in the parameters rollout (**Figure 2.46**).

✔ Tip

- You may have noticed that the inside of the teapot is invisible. By default, mesh objects are rendered only on one side. To make a mesh object render on both sides, check Force 2-sided in the Rendering dialog box, or assign it a two-sided material (Chapter 12).

Figure 2.44 The Teapot rollout has a radius parameter input and checkboxes for including the body, handle, spout, and lid.

Figure 2.45 Drag to set the radius of a teapot.

Figure 2.46 Variations on a teapot.

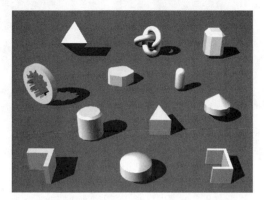

Figure 2.47 Extended Primitives are more specialized forms.

Creating extended primitives

Extended Primitives are more complex objects that include the Chamferbox, ChamferCyl, Oil Tank, Capsule, Spindle, Gengon, Prism, L-Ext, C-Ext, Hedra, Torus Knot, Ringwave, and Hose (**Figure 2.47**).

Extended Primitives are found in the drop-down menu of the Geometry category. Shortcuts to theses commands are found in the Create menu and in the Objects Toolbar.

The easiest way to create Extended Primitives is by clicking and dragging.

The Utah Teapot

People often ask me why the Teapot is included among the Standard Primitives. After all, how many forms are based on teapots? It all started in the 1970s at the University of Utah when Martin Newell created an elegant wireframe model of a teapot. His colleague, James Blinn, used the teapot to experiment with different methods of surface rendering. Soon, everyone was making reflecting teapots. Eventually, the "Utah Teapot" became so identified with 3D graphics that it became immortalized as a symbol for the field.

To create an extended primitive:

1. Open the drop-down menu of the Geometry branch of the Create panel. Then choose Extended Primitives.

   A menu of Extended Primitives appears in the Object Type rollout (**Figure 2.48**).

2. Click the name of the extended primitive you would like to create.

   The parameters for that object appear in the Create panel.

3. In the Perspective viewport, click and drag the radius or base of the object (**Figure 2.49**).

4. Keep moving and clicking the cursor to set additional parameters, such as length, width, height, radius, fillet, or cap height (**Figure 2.50**).

Figure 2.48 Extended Primitives are found in the Geometry drop-down menu.

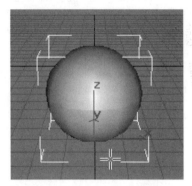

Figure 2.49 Dragging the radius of a Capsule.

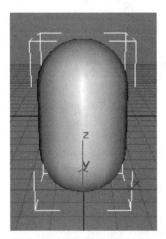

Figure 2.50 After setting the object's height.

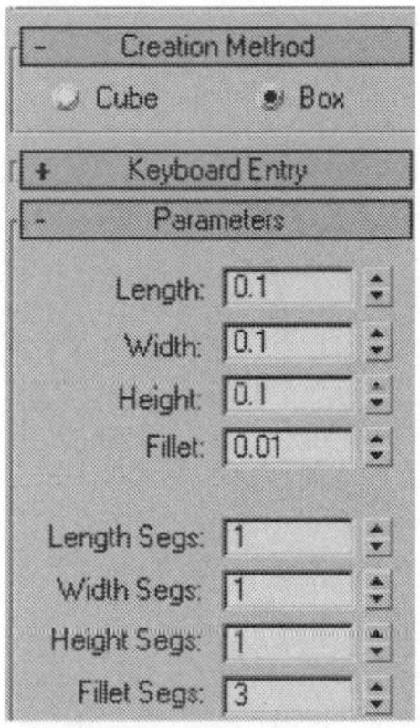

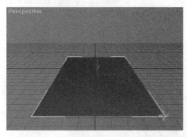

Figure 2.51 The ChamferBox rollout has length, width, and height parameters as well as fillet.

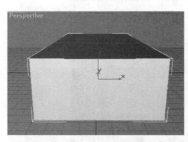

Figure 2.52 First, drag to create the base.

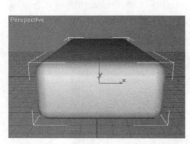

Figure 2.53 Next, click to set the height.

A ChamferBox is a box with filed edges, or fillets. It is a useful replacement for the standard box because most real-world objects have rounded edges and corners. Other objects that have fillets include the ChamferCyl, Oil Tank, Capsule, Spindle, and Gengon. These objects are variations on spheres, cones, and cylinders.

To create a ChamferBox:

1. In the Extended Primitives Object Type rollout, click ChamferBox.

   The ChamferBox rollout appears (**Figure 2.51**).

2. In the Perspective viewport, drag diagonally to make the base of the ChamferBox (**Figure 2.52**).

3. Release the mouse button to set the base length and width.

4. Move the cursor and click to set the height (**Figure 2.53**).

5. Move the cursor up again and click to set the fillet (**Figure 2.54**).

✔ Tip

■ Uncheck Smooth in the Parameters rollout to see the actual shape better.

Figure 2.54 Click again to set the fillet.

To create a ChamferCyl:

1. In the Create panel, click ChamferCyl. The ChamferCyl rollout appears (**Figure 2.55**).

2. In the Perspective viewport, drag diagonally to make the base of the ChamferCyl (**Figure 2.56**).

3. Release the mouse button to set the radius of the base.

4. Move the cursor and click to set the height (**Figure 2.57**).

5. Move the cursor up again and click to set the fillet (**Figure 2.58**).

✔ Tip

■ Uncheck Smooth in the Parameters rollout to see the actual shape better.

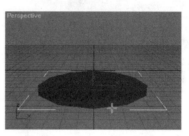

Figure 2.55 The ChamferCyl rollout has radius, height, and fillet parameters.

Figure 2.56 First, drag to create the base.

Figure 2.57 Next, click to set the height.

Figure 2.58 Click again to set the fillet.

CREATING MESH OBJECTS

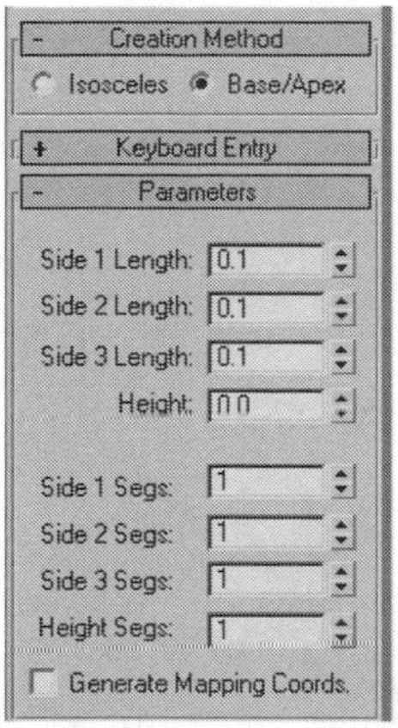

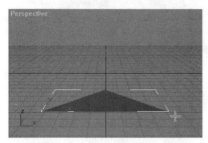

Figure 2.59 The Prism rollout has parameters for height and the length of each side.

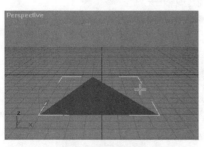

Figure 2.60 Drag to set the length of side 1.

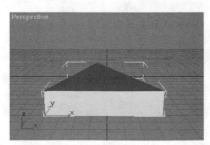

Figure 2.61 Move the cursor and click to set the apex. This sets the length of sides 2 and 3.

Figure 2.62 Move and click to set the height.

The Prism is a triangle projected into three dimensions.

To create a Prism:

1. In the Create panel, click Prism.
   The Prism rollout appears (**Figure 2.59**).

2. In the Perspective viewport, click and drag horizontally.

3. Release the mouse button to set the width of the base (side 1) (**Figure 2.60**).

4. Move the cursor up or down in the viewport. Then click to set the apex (**Figure 2.61**).

5. Move the cursor and click to set the height (**Figure 2.62**).

✔ Tip

■ Hold down the Ctrl key while dragging the base to create an equilateral triangle.

A C-Ext looks like an office cubicle. You set the thickness, or width, of the walls after you establish the length and height. After you create the C-Ext, try creating its sibling, the L-Ext.

To create a C-Ext:

1. In the Create panel, click C-Ext.

   The C-Ext rollout appears (**Figure 2.63**).

2. In the Perspective viewport, drag diagonally to create the base of the C-Ext (**Figure 2.64**).

3. Release the mouse button to set the length of the back, side, and front of the base.

   The initial width, or thickness, of the walls is assigned by default.

4. Move the cursor up and click to set the height (**Figure 2.65**).

5. Move the cursor up and click to set the width of the walls.

   The three sides all adopt the same width (**Figure 2.66**).

✔ Tip

■ To constrain the base of the C-Ext to sides of equal length, hold down the Ctrl key as you drag the base.

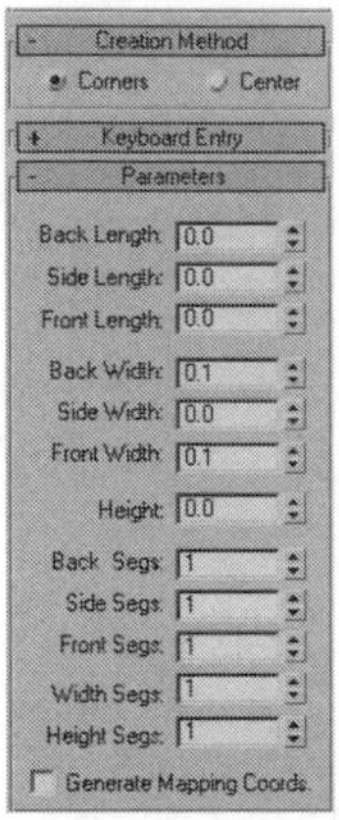

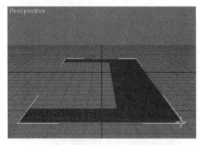

Figure 2.63 The C-Ext rollout has length and width parameters for all three sides.

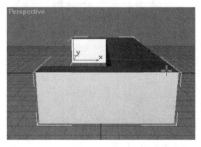

Figure 2.64 Click and drag diagonally to set the length of the front, back, and side walls. A default width is used while you drag.

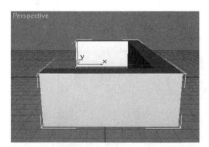

Figure 2.65 Move and click to set the height.

Figure 2.66 Move and click again to set the width of the walls.

CREATING MESH OBJECTS

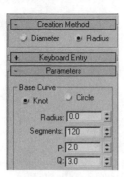

Figure 2.67 The Torus Knot rollout has inputs for the radius of the base and the radius of the cross section.

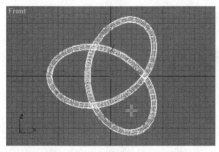

Figure 2.68 Drag to set the first radius. A three-lobed Torus appears by default.

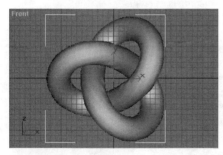

Figure 2.69 Next, set the radius of the cross section.

Figure 2.70 After changing the P and Q parameters. In this illustration, Segments = 2000, P = 6, and Q = 18.5.

Torus Knots look better if you create them in an orthogonal viewport, such as the Front viewport.

To create a Torus Knot:

1. In the Create panel, click Torus Knot. The Torus Knot rollout appears (**Figure 2.67**).

2. In the Front viewport, position the cursor where you want the center of the Torus Knot, and then drag out from the center. A three-lobed knot appears as you drag.

3. Release the mouse button to set the radius of the base (**Figure 2.68**).

4. Slowly move the cursor up or down to establish the cross-section radius.

5. Click to set the radius of the cross section. Press F3 to view the object in shaded mode (**Figure 2.69**). When you are done, press F3 to toggle the viewport back to wireframe mode.

✔ Tip

■ The P parameter of the Base Curve controls the number of times the Torus Knot winds around the center. Q controls the number of lobes it makes as it winds. In combination, the two parameters work together as a ratio, often creating surprising results (**Figure 2.70**).

CREATING MESH OBJECTS

A Hedra is so complicated that it does not have a keyboard-entry method. The real fun of using this object is playing with its parameters.

To create a Hedra:

1. In the Create panel, click Hedra.
   The Hedra rollout appears (**Figure 2.71**).

2. In the Perspective viewport, drag a Hedra (**Figure 2.72**).

3. Release the mouse button to set the radius.

4. Select a family in the Parameters rollout.
   The Hedra dramatically changes form (**Figure 2.73**).

5. Drag the P and Q spinners for family parameters up and down.
   The edges of the polyhedron change position (**Figure 2.74**).

6. Change the axis-scaling parameters to make the points more or less prominent.

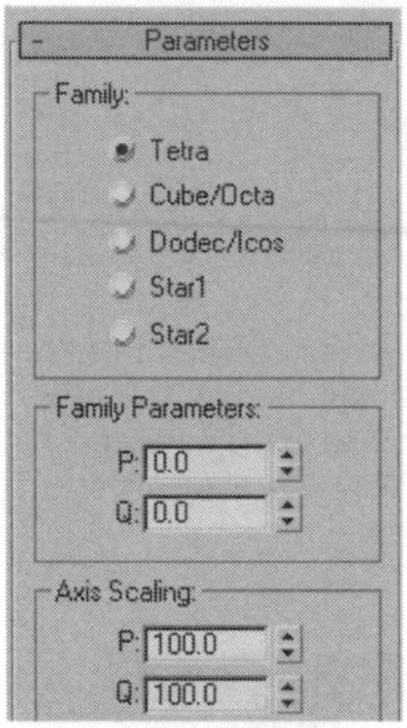

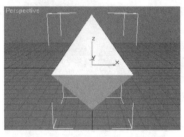

Figure 2.71 The Hedra rollout has no keyboard-entry rollout. Here you see the Hedra parameters.

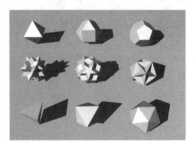

Figure 2.72 The most basic parameter of a polyhedron is its radius. Here, a Hedra is being dragged into view.

Figure 2.73 Examples of each of the families of Hedra.

Figure 2.74 A Star1 Hedra with P = .38 and Q = .62

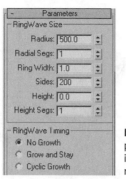

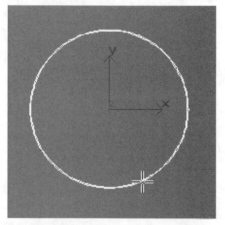

Figure 2.75 The basic parameters of a RingWave include a radius and a ring width.

Figure 2.76 Click and drag to set the radius.

Figure 2.77 Move and click to set the ring width.

The Hose and RingWave are radial objects that have built-in animation parameters. For a complete description of these parameters, please see the Online Help Files.

To create a RingWave:

1. In the Create panel, click RingWave.
   The RingWave rollout appears (**Figure 2.75**).

2. In the Front viewport, position the cursor where you want the center of the RingWave to be, and drag outward (**Figure 2.76**).

3. Release the mouse button to set the first radius.

4. Move and click to set the second radius. You can make it larger or smaller than the first (**Figure 2.77**).

5. In the Parameters rollout, adjust the number of sides and the Ring Width as needed. You can also assign a height and adjust height and radial segments.

6. Click Play Animation 🔲 in the animation controls to play back the default animation.
   The inner ring of the Ring Wave ripples in and out from the center of the object.

✔ Tip

- The RingWave timing group provides basic controls for the RingWave animation:

   No Growth means that the radius of the RingWave will stay at a constant size throughout the animation.

   Grow and Stay causes the RingWave to increase its radius from 0 to the current setting beginning at the frame number entered for the Start Time, until it reaches full size at the Grow Time frame number.

   Cyclic Growth causes the RingWave to start a new growth cycle after it reaches the end of its growth, as described above.

CREATING MESH OBJECTS

Creating Shape Splines

The term spline dates back to the 18th century, when shipbuilders and architects used a thin strip of wood or metal called a spline to create curved lines, such as the profile of a ship's hull. Today, splines are linear objects that are curved using controls that lie on or near their path.

3ds max provides two types of splines. Shapes are basic all-purpose splines that are used to create flying logos for television, low-polygon models for 3D games, geometric shapes for architecture and engineering, and motion paths for animation. NURBS are non-uniform rational B-splines that have advanced curvature controls suitable for modeling complex organic forms. The topic of NURBS is beyond the scope of this book.

Shapes are made up of three sub-object components: *vertices*, which are point locations in space; *segments*, which are straight or curved lines; and *splines*, which are made from a sequence of vertices that are connected by segments (**Figure 2.78**). Controls located at each vertex determine the curvature of the two adjacent. In between vertices, *steps* subdivide segments to make their curves appear smoother.

Shapes are non-rendering by default. This means that when you render an image to an output file, spline shapes do not appear in the scene unless you set them to be renderable.

3ds max 4 provides 11 shape primitives: the Circle, Rectangle, Ellipse, NGon, Donut, Star, Line, Arc, Text, Helix, and Section (**Figure 2.79**). The Shapes menu is found in the Shapes branch of the Geometry category (**Figure 2.80**). Shortcuts to the Shape commands are found in the Create menu and in the Shapes Toolbar.

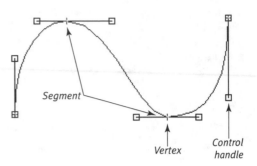

Figure 2.78 Shapes are made up of vertices, segments, and splines. Curvature controls determine the curvature of each segment.

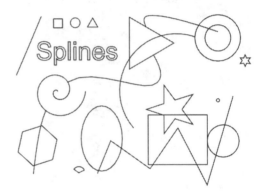

Figure 2.79 Shape splines are composed of open and closed shapes.

Figure 2.80 The Shapes menu contains 11 different object types.

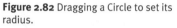

Figure 2.81 The Circle rollout has only one parameter.

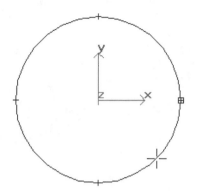

Figure 2.82 Dragging a Circle to set its radius.

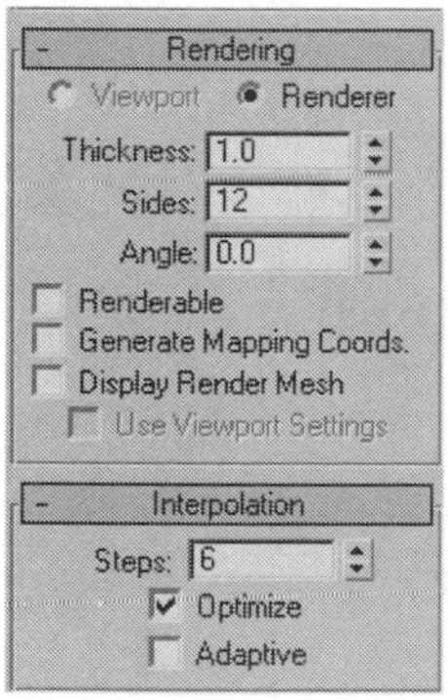

Figure 2.83 The Rendering and Interpolation rollouts allow you to make shapes renderable and control their smoothness.

As with mesh objects, shapes can be created either by dragging or from the keyboard. Unlike mesh objects, you can create compound shapes at the time of object creation, instead of combining them later with a series of commands. Because most shapes initially lie flat on the grid, it is usually easier to create them in the Top viewport where you look straight down at them.

To create a shape:

1. Open the Shapes branch of the Create panel and choose the shape you want to make. In this example, I will create a Circle.

   The shape rollout appears (**Figure 2.81**).

2. In the Creation Method rollout, choose a creation option, or use the default.

   For a circle, the default is Center.

3. In the Top viewport, position the cursor where you want to start the object. Then drag out the first parameter of the object.

   For a circle, you simply define its radius (**Figure 2.82**).

4. Move and click the mouse to set additional parameters as needed.

5. Adjust the parameters in the Create panel or the Modify panel.

✔ Tips

- To make a spline object visible during rendering, open the Rendering rollout and check Renderable. Then enter settings for the thickness of the rendered spline, and the number and angle of its sides (**Figure 2.83**).

- To make a spline shape curve more smoothly, open the Interpolation rollout and increase the number of steps in its segments. You can also check Adaptive to make the program do this automatically.

To create a compound shape:

1. Create a shape.

2. Uncheck Start New Shape at the top of the Shape menu (**Figure 2.84**).

3. Create any additional shapes that you want to include in the compound objects.

   As you complete each shape, its extents are added to the extents of the compound shape.

The rectangle is created by dragging its length and width in a single click-and-drag sequence. Ellipses are made in a similar fashion; the only difference is the edges are round.

To create a rectangle:

1. In the Create panel, click Rectangle. The Rectangle rollout appears (**Figure 2.85**).

2. Choose the edge creation method in the rollout.

3. In the Top viewport, position the cursor where you want to start the rectangle and drag diagonally from the upper left-hand corner to the lower right-hand corner (**Figure 2.86**).

4. Release the mouse button when the rectangle is the right size.

✔ Tip

■ To round the corners of a rectangle, increase the Corner Radius parameter (**Figure 2.87**).

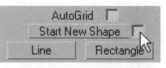

Figure 2.84 Uncheck Start New Shape to begin creating a compound shape.

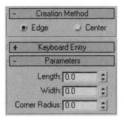

Figure 2.85 The Rectangle rollout has parameters for length and width.

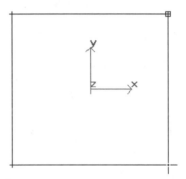

Figure 2.86 Drag a rectangle to set its length and width.

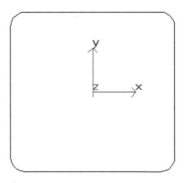

Figure 2.87 You make a rectangle with rounded corners by increasing the Corner Radius parameter.

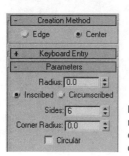

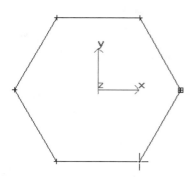

Figure 2.88 The NGon rollout allows you to create a regular polygon of up to 100 sides.

Figure 2.89 Dragging an NGon in the Top viewport. The default number of sides is six.

NGons are regular polygons of up to 100 sides. You adjust the number of sides after you create the basic shape.

To create an NGon:

1. In the Create panel, click NGon.
   The NGon rollout appears (**Figure 2.88**).

2. In the Top viewport, position the cursor where you want the center of the NGon and drag outward to make the NGon.
   A regular hexagon appears in the viewport (**Figure 2.89**).

3. Release the mouse button to set the radius.

4. In the Parameters rollout, adjust the sides to the number that you want.
   By default, the number of sides is six.

✔ Tips

■ An NGon is a good way to make an equilateral triangle. Just set the Sides parameter to 3.

■ You can create a snowflake by setting the radius and Corner Radius parameters to extremely high values (**Figure 2.90**).

Figure 2.90 An NGon with Radius = 60, Sides = 12, and Corner Radius = 1152.

CREATING SHAPE SPLINES

Stars have two radii that define a perimeter of anywhere from three to 100 points. The first click defines the outer radius; the second click defines the inner radius.

If you can make a Star, you can easily make a Donut, which is simply two concentric circles.

To create a Star:

1. In the Create panel, click Star.

   The Star rollout appears (**Figure 2.91**).

2. In the Top viewport, position the cursor where you want the center of the Star to be, and drag outward (**Figure 2.92**).

3. Release the mouse button to set the first radius.

4. Move and click to set the second radius. You can make it larger or smaller than the first (**Figure 2.93**).

5. In the Parameters rollout, adjust the number of points as needed.

✔ Tips

■ You can fillet the points of a star to round them off or distort them to make them twist (**Figure 2.94**).

■ There are no creation method options for the Star other than dragging from the center.

Figure 2.91 The most important parameters of the Star rollout are the two radii and the number of points.

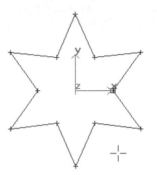

Figure 2.92 Dragging a Star.

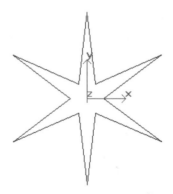

Figure 2.93 Setting the second radius alters the shape considerably.

Figure 2.94 After filleting, distorting, and changing the number of points.

CREATING SHAPE SPLINES

Figure 2.95 The Line rollout has parametric inputs for the type of vertex points used to create the line.

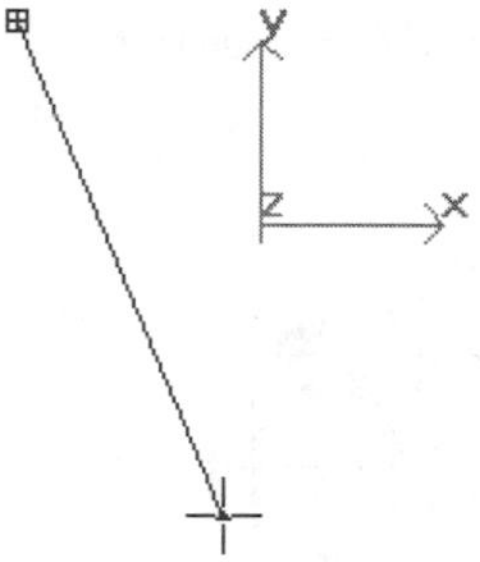

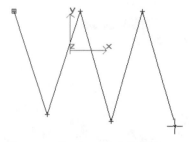

Figure 2.96 Click to set the second vertex point.

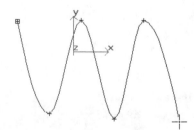

Figure 2.97 Create a zigzag line by moving and clicking in a zigzag pattern.

Lines are non-parametric objects. You create them by defining the location of their vertices.

To create a line:

1. In the Create panel, click Line.
   The Line rollout appears (**Figure 2.95**).

2. Set the first vertex point by clicking in the Top viewport.

3. Move the cursor to a new position and click to set the next vertex (**Figure 2.96**).

4. Continue creating vertex points until the line is complete (**Figure 2.97**).

5. Right-click to end the line.

✔ Tips

- To create a closed shape from line segments, set the last point on top of the first point. When prompted, click Yes to close the spline.

- To create a curved line, select Drag Type Smooth or Bézier in the Creation Method rollout. Then click and drag to create smooth or Bézier vertex points (**Figure 2.98**).

  Note that Bézier points are particularly hard to control during the line creation process. For better control, start with all Corner points, and then convert and adjust them, as shown on the next two pages.

Figure 2.98 Create a wavy line after setting Initial Type and Drag Type to Smooth.

To smooth a line, you convert its vertex points. Creating an angular line and then smoothing it makes the curves easier to control.

To convert vertex points:

1. Select the line.

2. Open the Modify panel.

3. Click on the point you want to convert. To convert multiple points at once, drag a selection region around them (**Figure 2.99**).

4. Right-click on a selected point.

5. In the Quad Tools1 menu, choose Bézier Corner, Bézier, or Smooth (**Figure 2.100**).

   The vertex points convert to the new type. The corners of the line become curved (**Figure 2.101**).

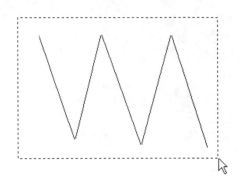

Figure 2.99 Drag a selection region around the points you want to convert.

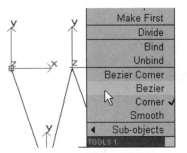

Figure 2.100 Choosing a Bézier vertex type.

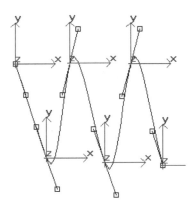

Figure 2.101 The result is a curved Bézier line.

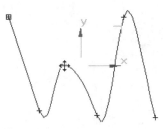

Figure 2.102 Using the Move tool to adjust a vertex point.

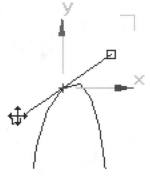

Figure 2.103 Using the Move tool to drag a Bézier handle.

Because lines are non-parametric objects, you adjust each vertex individually.

To adjust a line:

1. Select the line.

2. Open the Modify panel.

3. In the Selection rollout, click the Vertex button.

4. Choose the Select and Move tool ⊹ from the Main toolbar.

5. Adjust vertex points by dragging them (**Figure 2.102**).

6. To adjust the curvature of a Bézier point, drag its handles (**Figure 2.103**).

You create arcs by defining their endpoints and defining the shape of the curve between them.

To create an arc:

1. In the Create panel, click Arc.

   The Arc rollout appears (**Figure 2.104**).

2. Make sure that End-End-Middle is selected in the Creation Method rollout.

3. In the Top viewport, position the cursor where you want the arc to begin.

4. Drag from the beginning point to the end point.

   The click sets the beginning point; releasing the mouse button sets the end point. It still looks like a straight line (**Figure 2.105**).

5. Without clicking, slowly move the cursor along the line toward the middle of the arc.

6. Move the cursor to either side of the line.

   The arc appears to stick to the cursor (**Figure 2.106**).

7. Click to set the curvature of the arc.

✔ Tips

■ To create a closed form called a pie slice, check the Pie Slice parameter (**Figure 2.107**).

■ The Center-End-End creation method allows you to establish a center point and radius before drawing the arc around the center.

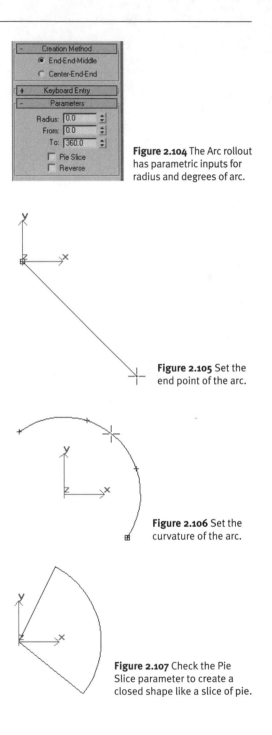

Figure 2.104 The Arc rollout has parametric inputs for radius and degrees of arc.

Figure 2.105 Set the end point of the arc.

Figure 2.106 Set the curvature of the arc.

Figure 2.107 Check the Pie Slice parameter to create a closed shape like a slice of pie.

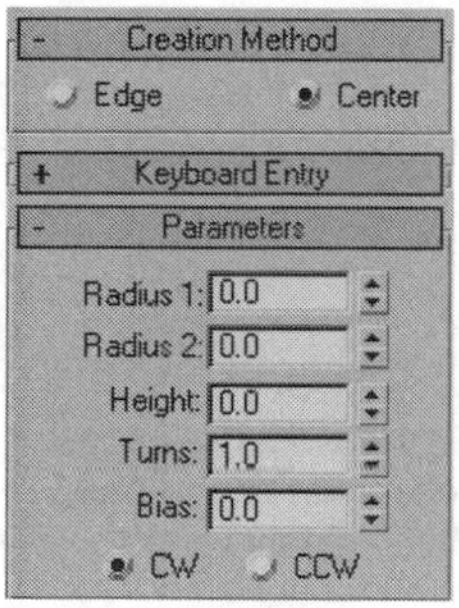

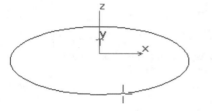

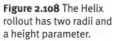

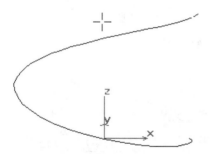

Figure 2.108 The Helix rollout has two radii and a height parameter.

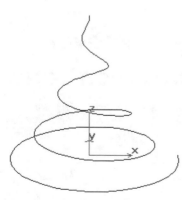

Figure 2.109 Set the first radius of a helix.

Figure 2.110 Set the height of a helix.

Figure 2.111 After setting the second height, turns, and bias.

The Helix is the only spline that has three-dimensional creation parameters. It is usually easier create helices in Perspective viewports.

To create a helix:

1. In the Create panel, click Helix.
   The Helix rollout appears (**Figure 2.108**).

2. In the Perspective viewport, drag the base of the helix. Release the mouse button to set the first radius (**Figure 2.109**).

3. Move the cursor upward and then click to set the height (**Figure 2.110**).

4. Move the cursor up or down in the viewport and click to set the second radius.

5. Enter the number of turns and the bias amount to give your helix its final shape (**Figure 2.111**).

CREATING SHAPE SPLINES

To create text:

1. In the Create panel, click Text.

   The Text rollout appears (**Figure 2.112**).

2. Click in the center of the Front viewport.

   The words MAX Text fill the viewport (**Figure 2.113**). This is the default text, which you will replace.

3. In the Text input field, highlight the default text. Then type in the text you want.

   This text replaces the default text in the scene (**Figure 2.114**).

4. Adjust the Size parameter.

   The text shrinks or grows, based on a percentage of the original size.

5. Choose a font from the font drop-down list.

   The text changes to the new font (**Figure 2.115**).

6. Use the alignment buttons to align, center, and justify multiple lines of text.

7. If you want to italicize or underline the text, click I for italics or U for underline.

8. Spread out the text with more space between letters by increasing the kerning amount.

   If you need more room, click the Zoom Extents button in the lower right-hand corner of the interface.

9. To spread out multiple lines of text vertically, increase the Leading parameter.

✔ Tip

- Apply an Extrude modifier to fill in the text or make it appear three-dimensional (**Figure 2.116**). (See Chapter 6, Modifying Objects.)

Parameters
Arial
I
U
Size: 100.0
Kerning: 0.0
Leading: 0.0
Text:
MAX Text

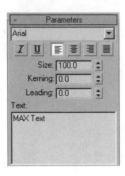

Figure 2.112 The Text rollout has settings for different fonts and styles of text.

MAX Text

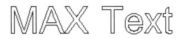

Figure 2.113 The default text appears in the view.

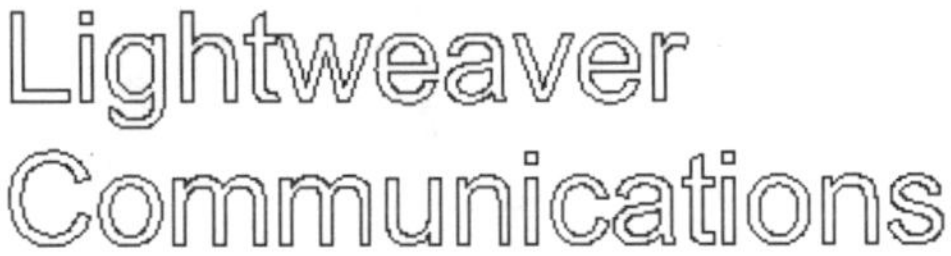

Lightweaver
Communications

Figure 2.114 Changing the default text gives immediate results.

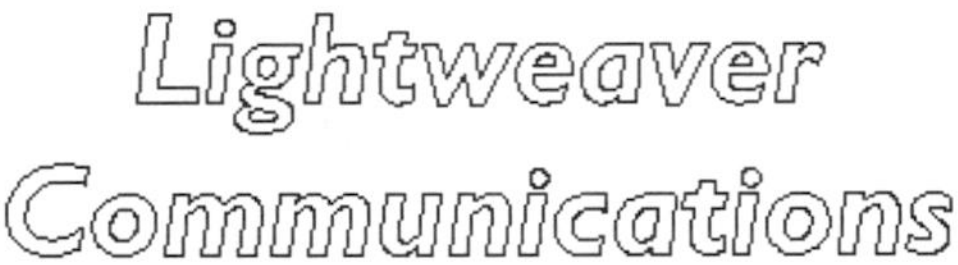

Lightweaver
Communications

Figure 2.115 After changing the font.

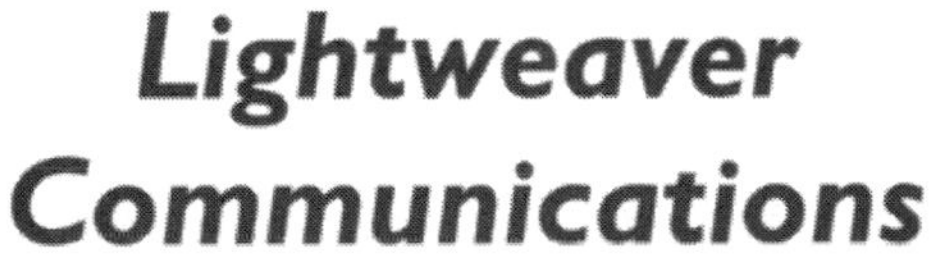

Lightweaver
Communications

Figure 2.116 Applying an Extrude modifier fills in the text.

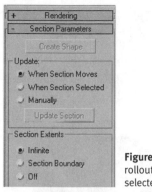

Figure 2.117 The Section rollout with Infinite selected in Section Extents.

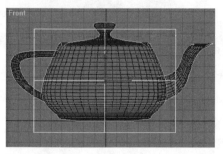

Figure 2.118 Dragging a section causes a yellow line to appear at the "waterline" of the teapot.

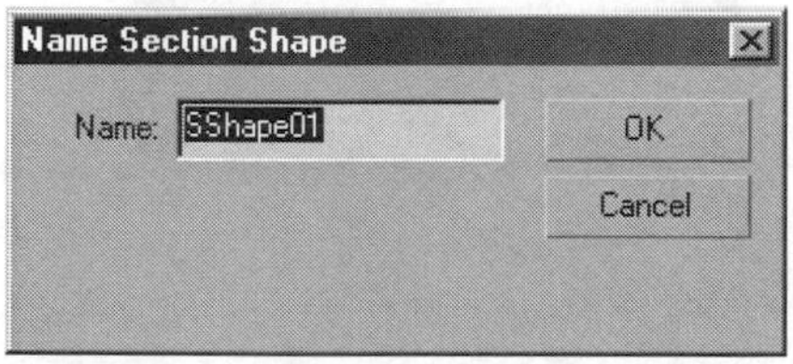

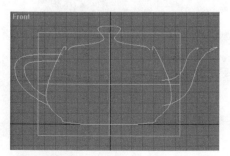

Figure 2.119 Clicking Create Shape brings up the Name Section Shape dialog box.

Figure 2.120 The resulting cross-section shape.

A section is a plane that slices the objects it intersects into cross-section shapes.

To create a section:

1. In the Perspective viewport, create a mesh object using keyboard entry.

   Leave x, y, and z at zero.

2. In the Create panel, click the Shapes button. Then click Section.

   The Section rollout appears (**Figure 2.117**).

3. In the Front viewport, drag a section of any size.

   A yellow line appears where the section bisects the object (**Figure 2.118**).

4. In the Section Parameters rollout, click Create Shape.

   The Name Section Shape dialog box appears (**Figure 2.119**).

5. Click OK to accept the default name or type a new name.

   A cross section of the object is created.

✔ Tip

■ To get a better look at the teapot cross-section shape, select and delete the teapot (**Figure 2.120**).

CREATING SHAPE SPLINES

Precision Aids

When you want to create objects to precise specifications, you can customize your units of measurement, grid spacing, and cursor snaps. You can also create custom grids to use as alternative construction planes.

If you want to create objects that align to the surfaces of other objects, you use an AutoGrid. This feature allows you to place a temporary construction grid on the surface of an object, aligned to the surface normal under your cursor.

To create objects on an AutoGrid:

1. In the Create panel, select an object type.

2. Turn on the AutoGrid feature in the Object Type rollout (**Figure 2.121**).

3. Move the cursor over the surface of a mesh object. Then click and hold to check the orientation of the grid (**Figure 2.122**).

4. When the grid is aligned properly, drag to create the object.

   The object is created on top of the AutoGrid (**Figure 2.123**).

   If no object is present under the cursor, the object will align itself to the home grid.

When you want to create objects on a different construction plane, you use a helper grid.

To create objects on a helper grid:

1. In the Create panel, open the Helpers subpanel by clicking the Helpers icon .

2. In the Helpers subpanel, click Grid.

   The Grid creation rollout appears (**Figure 2.124**).

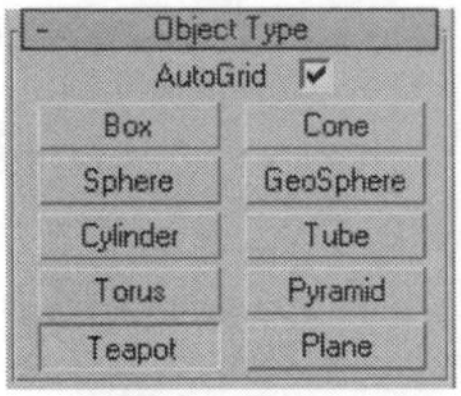

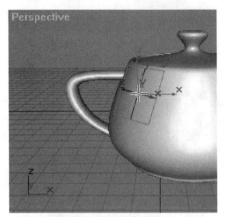

Figure 2.121
The Section rollout with Infinite selected in Section Extents.

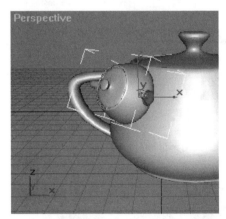

Figure 2.122 Click and hold to see the orientation of the AutoGrid.

Figure 2.123 Drag to create the object on top of the AutoGrid.

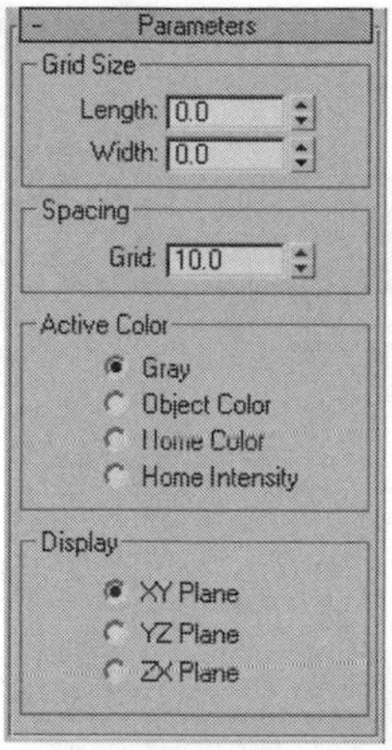

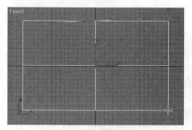

Figure 2.124 The Grid creation Display rollout allows you to choose the active plane.

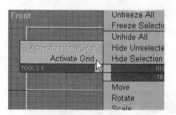

Figure 2.125 The XY plane of the grid aligns to the home grid of the viewport in which you are working.

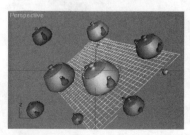

Figure 2.126 Activate the grid using the right-click Quad menus.

3. In any viewport, drag diagonally to create a grid of any size (**Figure 2.125**).

4. Choose the Select and Rotate tool 🔄 from the Main toolbar.

5. In the Status Bar, Locks and Controls area, orient the grid by dragging the X, Y, and/or Z spinners.

6. Right-click the grid object and choose Activate Grid (**Figure 2.126**).

The grid object becomes active, and grid line subdivisions appear. The home grid becomes inactive, and grid line subdivisions disappear.

7. Create some objects.

The objects appear on the construction plane that is defined by the grid (**Figure 2.127**).

8. When you are done, click the grid to select it and then right-click. Then choose Activate Home Grid from the Quad menu.

The helper grid becomes inactive and the home grid becomes active.

✔ Tips

■ To make user grids activate automatically upon creation, choose Customize > Grid and Snap Settings and click the User Grid panel. Then check Activate grids when created.

■ Another way to create a grid object is by holding down the Alt key when creating an AutoGrid. Use this method when you want to create a grid that is aligned to an object

Figure 2.127 Objects on the construction plane defined by the grid.

By default, 3ds max measures space in generic units of measurement equivalent to inches. But if you want to build a house or a highway, you may want to use an exact system of measurement, such as feet and inches or kilometers.

To set units of measure:

1. Choose Customize > Units Setup.

   The Units Setup dialog box appears.

2. Choose a unit of measurement: Metric, U.S. Standard, Custom, or Generic (**Figure 2.128**).

3. Click OK.

   Once you set the units of measurement, you will want to set the spacing of the grid to match.

To set grid spacing:

1. Choose Customize > Grid and Snap Settings, and click on the Home Grid tab (**Figure 2.129**).

2. Enter a Grid Spacing amount that matches your unit of measure.

   The grid spacing changes to the unit of measure (**Figure 2.130**).

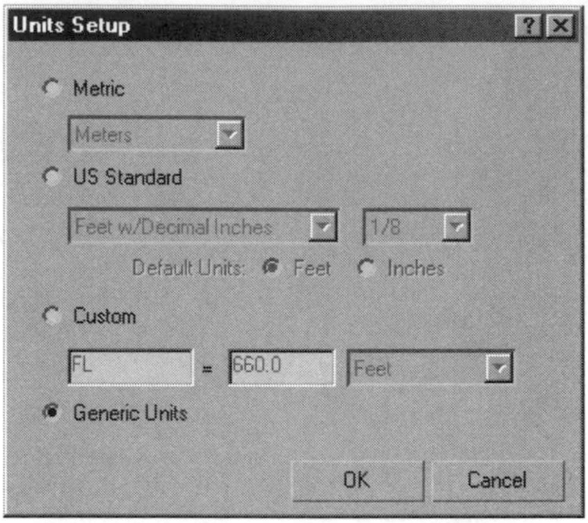

Figure 2.128 Setting the units to centimeters.

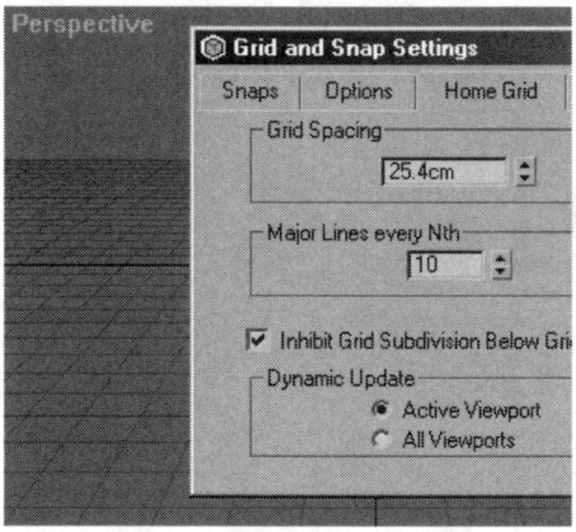

Figure 2.129 The default 1" grid spacing is now measured in centimeters.

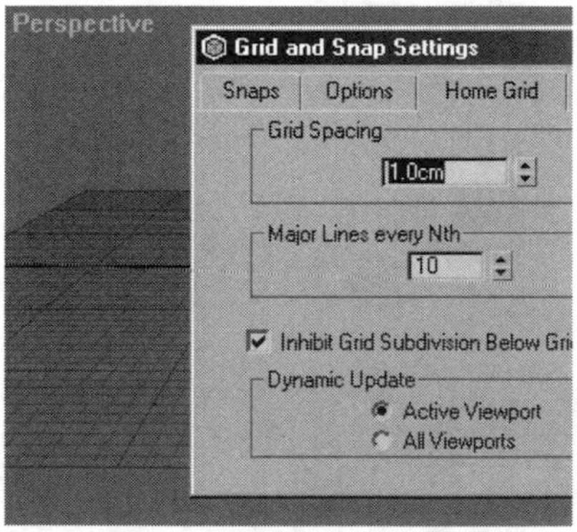

Figure 2.130 Change the grid spacing to match the units of measure.

PRECISION AIDS

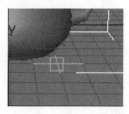

Figure 2.131 Snapping the corner of an object to a grid point during object creation.

Use 3D snap when you want to create objects to exact dimensions using the drag method.

To use 3D snap:

1. Click the 3D Snap tool ![icon] in the Status Bar, Locks and Controls area.

2. Create an object by dragging.

   As you drag the base of the object, the cursor jumps to points of grid intersection, and a blue square appears at the tip of the cursor (**Figure 2.131**).

   In setting the height of an object, the cursor snaps to an interval equivalent to the space between grid lines.

3. When you are done, turn off 3D snap by clicking the 3D Snap button. You can also toggle the snap tool by pressing the S key.

You can snap to other targets besides grid points. This feature comes in handy when you need to create exact arrangements of objects.

VIEWPORT NAVIGATION AND DISPLAY

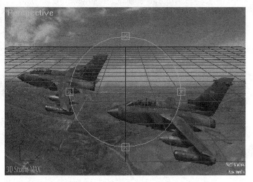

Figure 3.1 Navigating 3D space is a lot like flying.

Navigating 3D space is a lot like flying. You can wheel around, fly in fast and low, or fly up high for a bird's eye view. If you have ever played 3D games, you know how exhilarating it is to fly.

To be the master of this 3D universe, you need to get your bearings and learn how to operate the controls. Once you learn how the universe is laid out, you will teleport from place to place to see how things look from different perspectives. You will also learn how to customize the cockpit and change the display resolution of the captain's window.

Then you get to go to flight school (**Figure 3.1**).

Getting Your Bearings

In this section, we take a page out of your old planar geometry textbook and expand it to the third dimension.

In 2D space, any two lines that intersect define the surface of a plane. To locate any position in space, all you need to know is how far along each line you must travel from their intersection.

To define 3D space, all you need to do is introduce a third line that does not lie on the plane of the first two. To locate a position in 3D space, you need to measure distance along three lines instead of two.

In planar geometry, the lines that define space are called the *X* and *Y axes*. The point where they intersect is called the *origin*. The coordinates of the origin are (0,0) (**Figure 3.2**).

In 3D geometry, the third line is called the *Z axis*, and it intersects the other two axes at the origin.

The coordinates of the origin in 3D space are (0,0,0) (**Figure 3.3**).

When the X, Y, and Z axes are assigned to a fixed position and orientation in space, they define an absolute frame of reference called the *world coordinate system*. This system keeps track of all objects in space relative to the world axes (**Figure 3.4**).

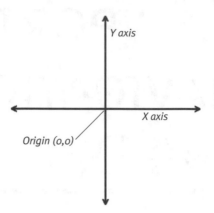

Figure 3.2 Rectangular coordinates measure space using perpendicular axes that meet at the origin.

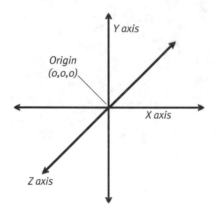

Figure 3.3 Adding the Z axis to rectangular coordinates makes it possible to measure depth.

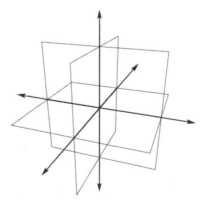

Figure 3.4 The world coordinate system uses a fixed system of reference to define world space.

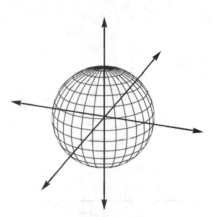

Figure 3.5 The local coordinate system uses a relative system of reference to define object space.

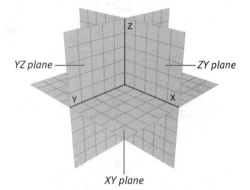

Figure 3.6 The home grid is made of three intersecting grids that are aligned to the XY, YZ, and ZX planes of the world coordinate system.

Figure 3.7 The orthogonal views face the origin from six fixed directions to help you keep track of your orientation in space.

When axes are tied to an object instead of fixed in space, they define a *local coordinate system*. This relative frame of reference keeps track of individual objects as they change position, orientation, and scale relative to their local axes (**Figure 3.5**).

Putting it in Perspective

The axes of the world coordinate system define three planes: the XY, YZ, and ZX planes. When you divide these planes at regular intervals, they form three perpendicular grids that intersect at the origin. Together, these three grids make up the home grid. In 3ds max, only one part of the home grid is shown in each viewport: the grid that defines the construction plane for creating objects in that viewport (**Figure 3.6**).

For the purposes of viewing and navigating space, 3ds max defines six views that squarely face the origin from six directions: Front, Back, Left, Right, Top, and Bottom. These directions are called *orthogonal views* because they face the planes of the world coordinate system and the home grid perpendicularly (**Figure 3.7**). They are also a type of *axonometric view* because they use parallel projection to draw the scene.

If you rotate an orthogonal view, it turns into a User view. A User view is a user-defined axonometric view that looks at a scene from any direction, rather than from one of the six fixed directions assigned to orthogonal views.

Because parallel projection systems draw objects without any foreshortening, objects in orthogonal and User views always appear true to size, no matter how far away they are from the viewer. In addition, parallel lines always appear to be parallel no matter how far they project into space (**Figure 3.8**).

In contrast, perspective views such as Perspective, Camera, and Light views use *perspective projection* to draw the scene. Objects in perspective views appear to get smaller as they recede in the distance, and parallel lines appear to converge as they move further into space (**Figure 3.9**).

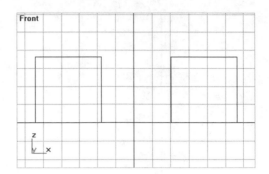

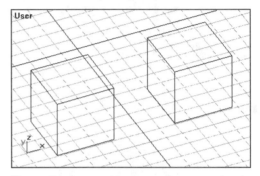

Figure 3.8 In axonometric views, cubes appear true to size. Parallel lines remain parallel no matter how far the project in space.

Perspective

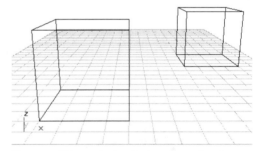

Figure 3.9 The same cubes in the perspective views appear to get smaller as they recede. Parallel lines converge as they get farther away

Figure 3.10 The viewports can show up to four views at once

Viewport label   Viewport background   Viewport boundary

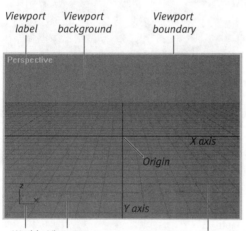

World axis   Viewport grid   Bounding box

Figure 3.11 Viewport elements may be customized.

Customizing Viewports

You need to view a scene from three directions in order to understand where you are in space. In 3ds max, you can view a scene from up to four directions at once by assigning different views to each of the viewports (**Figure 3.10**). To look at the details of a scene, you can maximize a viewport to fill the display. You can also change the layout and proportions of the viewports.

Elements that are common to all viewports include a grid for navigation, a label for identification, a world axis for orientation, a boundary to delimit the view, and a background that goes behind the scene (**Figure 3.11**). You can change these elements by turning them on and off, or by changing their colors.

In order to change a viewport in any way, you must first select it, or *activate* it. Activating a viewport not only tells the program which viewport to change, but it also establishes a spatial orientation for creating, manipulating and rendering objects. For these reasons and perhaps others, only one viewport can be active at a time.

To activate a viewport:

◆ Right-click in a viewport that has a black boundary and is not active (**Figure 3.12**). The viewport activates, and the boundary of the viewport turns yellow (**Figure 3.13**).

✔ Tip

■ Left-clicking also activates viewports, but it can cause you to lose a selection. For this reason, it is better to develop a habit of right-clicking in a viewport to activate it.

To change a view:

1. Right-click on the viewport label. The viewport right-click menu appears.

2. Choose Views > [view name]. The viewport display changes to display the view you selected.

✔ Tips

■ Press Shift + Z to undo a view change. Press Shift + A to redo a view change.

■ For convenience, most of the view-change commands have keyboard short-cuts, as summarized in **Table 3.1**.

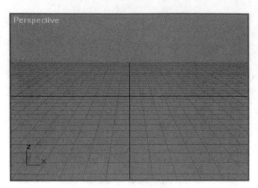

Figure 3.12 An inactive viewport has a black boundary around it.

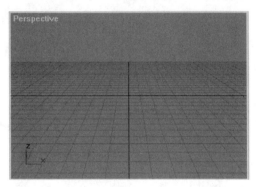

Figure 3.13 The viewport boundary turns yellow when the viewport is active.

Table 3.1

Keyboard Shortcuts for Changing Views	
KEY	**VIEW**
F	Front view
K	Back view
R	Right view
L	Left view
T	Top view
B	Bottom view
P	Perspective view
U	User view
C	Camera view
$	Light view
G	Display Grid
W	Minimize/Maximize view
D	Disable/Enable view
Shift + Z	Undo view change
Shift + A	Redo view change

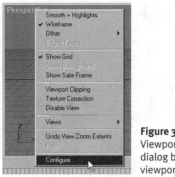

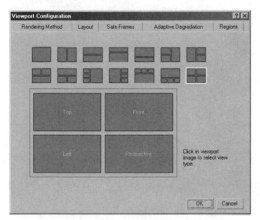

To change the layout of the viewports:

1. Right-click on any viewport label, and choose Configure (**Figure 3.14**).

2. In the Viewport Configuration dialog box, click on the Layout tab.
   The Layout panel appears (**Figure 3.15**).

3. Click in a layout at the top of the panel.
   A diagram that previews the new layout appears in the lower part of the panel.

4. Click in the diagram to assign views to each viewport (**Figure 3.16**).

5. Click OK.
   The new layout appears (**Figure 3.17**).

Figure 3.14 Access the Viewport Configuration dialog box from the viewport menu.

Figure 3.15 The Layout panel of the Viewport Configuration dialog box contains 14 layout options for configuring the viewport display area.

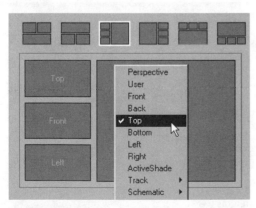

Figure 3.16 Click the preview diagram to open a pop-up menu where you select a view for each viewport.

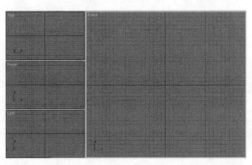

Figure 3.17 The new layout appears in the viewport.

To change the proportions of the viewports:

1. 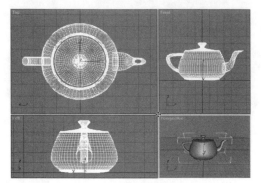 Move the cursor over the center of the viewports where the four corners meet, or in between two viewports.

2. Click and drag the viewport boundaries to the new proportion.

   The viewports redraw with the new proportions (**Figure 3.18**).

The Min/Max Toggle button toggles the display between the current viewport layout and a single viewport that expands to fill the entire display area. Use this feature whenever you want to view your scene on a grand scale.

To maximize a viewport:

◆ Click on the Min/Max Toggle button . The active viewport enlarges to fill the display area (**Figure 3.19**).

   If a viewport is maximized, clicking the Min/Max Toggle button returns the display to the original layout.

To minimize a viewport:

◆ Click on the Min/Max Toggle button . The viewports are redrawn using the current layout (**Figure 3.20**).

✔ Tip

■ The keyboard shortcut for the Min/Max button is W.

Figure 3.18 Dragging the boundaries between viewports gives your layout new proportions.

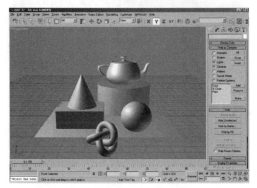

Figure 3.19 Clicking the Min/Max tool enlarges the viewport to fit the entire display area.

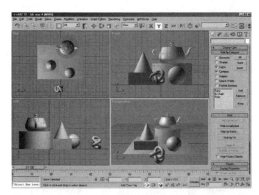

Figure 3.20 Clicking the Min/Max tool a second time returns the viewports to the previous layout.

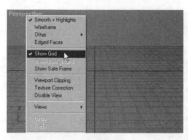

Figure 3.21 Turning off the grid display.

Figure 3.22 The viewport with the grid display turned off.

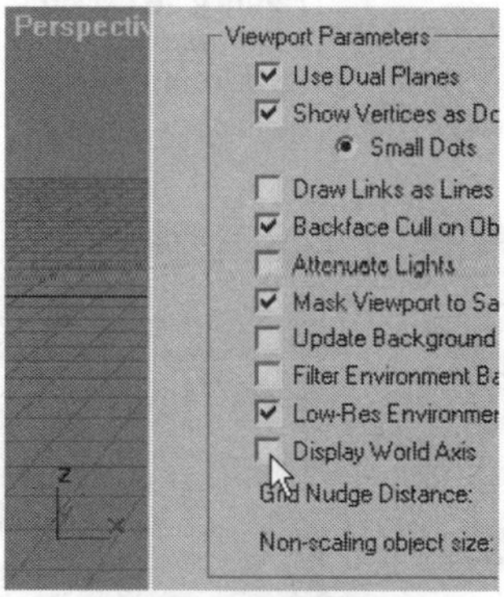

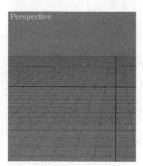

Figure 3.23 Uncheck Display World Axis in the Viewport Preferences to turn off the World Axis display.

To turn the grid display off and on:

1. Right-click on the viewport label, and choose Show Grid (**Figure 3.21**).
   The grid display turns off (**Figure 3.22**).

2. To turn the grid display back on, repeat step 1.

✔ Tips

- Press G to toggle the grid display from the keyboard.

- If pressing G does not toggle the grid display, make sure that the keyboard shortcuts are set to DefaultUI.kbd. To do so, choose Customize > Customize User Interface, and click the Keyboard tab. Then click Load and select DefautUI.kbd from the list of shortcut files.

To turn the world axis off and on:

1. Choose Customize > Preferences.

2. In the Preferences dialog box, click the Viewports tab.

3. In the Viewport Parameters group, uncheck Display World Axis (**Figure 3.23**).

4. Close the Preferences dialog box.
   The world axis disappears (**Figure 3.24**).

✔ Tip

- To turn the world axis back on, reopen the Preferences dialog box and check Display World Axis.

Figure 3.24 The World Axis no longer appears in this or any other viewport.

CUSTOMIZING VIEWPORTS

To customize viewport colors:

1. Choose Customize > Customize User Interface.

   The Customize User Interface dialog box appears.

2. Click the Colors tab.

3. In the Elements drop-down menu, choose Viewports.

4. In the scrolling window, choose the viewport element you would like to change (**Figure 3.25**).

5. Click the color swatch at right (**Figure 3.26**).

   The Color Selector dialog box appears (**Figure 3.27**).

6. Click on the color palette to select a Hue. Then drag the Whiteness slider to choose a value. You can also use the RGB or HSV settings if you prefer.

7. In the scrolling window, choose the next element that you would like to change. You do not need to close the Color Selector.

8. Click Apply Colors Now to see the effect. If you do not like a color, click the Reset button and reapply the color (**Figure 3.28**).

9. Repeat steps 6, 7, and 8 until you have changed all the colors you want to change.

10. Close the Color Selector and the Customize User Interface dialog boxes.

✔ Tip

■ To change viewport grid color or intensity, choose Grids from the Elements drop-down menu, and follow the steps above.

Figure 3.25 To change the color of the viewport background, choose Viewport Background from the Viewport Elements menu.

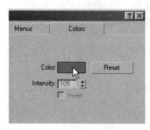

Figure 3.26 Click the color swatch to bring up the Color Selector dialog box.

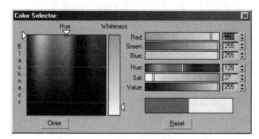

Figure 3.27 Use the Hue and Whiteness sliders to pick a color from the palette.

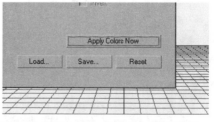

Figure 3.28 When you click Apply Colors Now, the colors update.

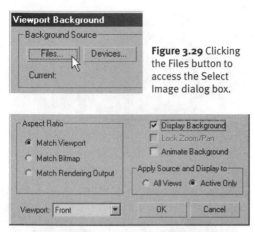

Figure 3.29 Clicking the Files button to access the Select Image dialog box.

Figure 3.30 These options will display the image so it fits the dimensions of the background.

Figure 3.31 The image appears in the background. Note that the grid display has been turned off.

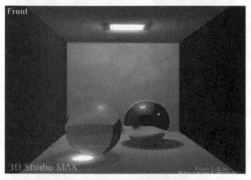

Figure 3.32 Toggle the background image display using the viewport menu.

To place an image in a background:

1. Activate the viewport that you want to place a background image in.

2. Choose Views > Viewport Background.
   or
   Press Alt + B.

3. In the Viewport Background dialog box, click the Files button (**Figure 3.29**).

4. In the Select Background Image dialog box, navigate to the image you want to place in the background.

5. Select the image, and click Open.

6. In the Viewport Background dialog box, check Display Background.

7. In the Aspect Ratio group, decide if you want to match the image to the dimensions of the viewport or the output size specified in the Render dialog box, or keep the proportions of the bitmap true to size (**Figure 3.30**).

8. Click OK.
   The image appears in the background of the viewport (**Figure 3.31**).

✔ Tips

■ To toggle a background image on or off, right-click in the viewport in which it is displayed and choose Show Background (**Figure 3.32**).

■ Viewport background images do not render to output files unless they are also used in the Environment background. For more information, see Chapter 15, Rendering.

CUSTOMIZING VIEWPORTS

Changing Viewport Display

Objects may be displayed in different modes to suit the needs of the work at hand. Higher resolution display modes are good for applying materials because they provide more information about surface color and lighting. Lower resolution display modes are good for modeling and animation because they show structure and update faster on playback.

In 3ds max, you control the display of an object individually or for an entire viewport. In this section, we will find out how to change object display for entire viewports. For information on how to change the display of individual objects, see Chapter 4, Object Selection and Display.

◆ ActiveShade is a display mode that uses the highest level of resolution. It updates interactively to show the effect of changing light. It can also display colors and textures on the surfaces of objects (**Figure 3.33**).

◆ Smooth display modes use the next-highest level of resolution. They can display surface texture and object shading but do not usually show cast shadows (**Figure 3.34**).

◆ Facets display modes use a moderate level of resolution. They show light falling across the faces of a mesh as if each one were the facet of a gem (**Figure 3.35**).

◆ Wireframe display modes use a low level of resolution that delineates faces by tracing just their edges (**Figure 3.36**).

◆ Bounding-box display modes use the lowest level of resolution. Bounding boxes display objects as the edges of a box that is just big enough to enclose the object (**Figure 3.37**).

Figure 3.33 An object displayed with ActiveShade turned on.

Figure 3.34 An object displayed in smooth mode.

Figure 3.35 An object displayed in facets mode.

Figure 3.36 An object displayed in wireframe mode.

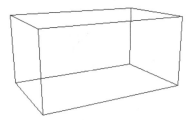

Figure 3.37 An object displayed in bounding-box mode.

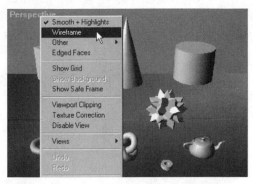

Figure 3.38 Choosing Wireframe display from the viewport menu.

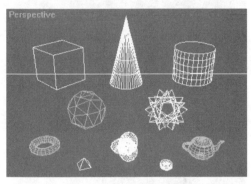

Figure 3.39 The viewport display changes to wireframe.

To change a display mode for a viewport:

1. Right-click on the viewport label.

2. Choose a display mode from the menu (**Figure 3.38**).

   Objects in the viewport change to the new mode of display (**Figure 3.39**).

✔ Tips

- You can set keyboard shortcuts to toggle display modes in Customize > Customize User Interface > Keyboard. Look for the Shade Selected and Wireframe toggles.

- Press the number 1 on your keyboard when you need the program to redraw the interface.

- By default, 3ds max degrades display resolution when the playback speed exceeds the speed at which your system can redraw. If you prefer to maintain a high resolution display, no matter how much it slows down playback, set the Degradation Override 🗗 in the Status Bar, Locks and Controls area at the bottom of the interface so that is looks like this 🗗.

ActiveShade is found on the Views menu, but it is really a high-resolution mode of display. As such, it takes a little bit longer to render than a simple screen redraw.

To change views to ActiveShade:

1. Right-click on the viewport label, and choose Views.

   The Views menu pops out.

2. Select ActiveShade (**Figure 3.40**).

   The viewport display changes to ActiveShade (**Figure 3.41**).

To toggle the ActiveShade toolbar:

1. Right-click in the ActiveShade viewport.

2. Choose Toggle Toolbar from the Tools quad menu (**Figure 3.42**).

   The ActiveShade toolbar appears in the viewport (**Figure 3.43**).

3. Repeat steps 1 and 2 to turn off the toolbar display.

To close the ActiveShade view:

1. Right-click in the viewport.

2. Choose Close from the Tools quad menu.

✔ Tip

■ Viewport window controls do not work with ActiveShade views. Instead, use the following keyboard shortcuts:

   Ctrl + left click to zoom in

   Ctrl + right click to zoom out

   Ctrl + wheel to zoom in and out

   Alt + right click to sample colors

Figure 3.40 Choose ActiveShade from the Views pop-out menu.

Figure 3.41 The viewport after changing to ActiveShade display.

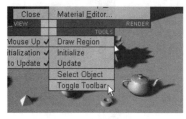

Figure 3.42 Choose Toggle Toolbar from the Tools quad menu.

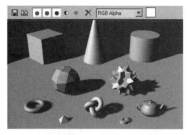

Figure 3.43 The ActiveShade toolbar has buttons for saving and cloning the viewport image, as well as viewing different color channels.

Figure 3.44
Viewport Window Controls for navigating axonometric views.

Figure 3.45
Viewport Window Controls for navigating Perspective views.

Figure 3.46 Camera Viewport Controls allow you to manipulate cameras and navigate camera views.

Figure 3.47 Light Viewport Controls allow you to manipulate spotlights and directional lights and navigate their views.

Navigating Viewports

Viewport navigation buttons allow you to look around a scene by manipulating the viewports. Each of the three sets of viewport navigation buttons appears automatically to match the view in the active viewport:

◆ Viewport Navigation Controls allow you to navigate axonometric views, including Front, Back, Left, Right, Top, Bottom, and User views (**Figure 3.44**). In Perspective views, the controls are the same except for the Region Zoom button, which changes to Field-of-View control (**Figure 3.45**).

◆ Camera Viewport Controls manipulate Cameras and Camera views. They are similar to the controls for Perspective views (**Figure 3.46**).

◆ Light Viewport Controls are used for manipulating spotlights and directional lights as well as the views seen from those lights. They are similar to the controls for Camera views (**Figure 3.47**).

Table 3.2 outlines the function of each viewport control button. (See Chapter 12, Cameras, and Chapter 11, Lights, for more information about the controls for Camera and Light viewports.)

Table 3.2

Viewport Controls and Shortcuts

BUTTON	KEYBOARD SORTCUT	NAME	DESCRIPTION
	Z	Zoom	Zooms in or out of a viewport
	assignable	Zoom All	Zooms in or out of all viewports
	Alt + Ctrl + Z	Zoom Extents	Centers all objects in the viewport
	E	Zoom Extents Selected	Centers selected objects in the viewport
	Shift + Ctrl + Z	Zoom Extents All	Centers selected objects in the viewport
	assignable	Zoom Extents All Selected	Centers selected objects in all viewports
	Ctrl + W	Region Zoom	Enlarges selected area to fill the viewport
	assignable	Field-of-View	Changes the angle of the Perspective view
	Ctrl + P	Pan	Moves the view parallel to the view plane
	V, Ctrl + R	Arc Rotate	Rotates the view around its current center
		Arc Rotate Selected	Rotates the view around selected objects
		Arc Rotate SubObject	Rotates the view around selected sub-objects
	W	Min/Max Toggle	Toggles between the viewport layout and a full-screen display of the active viewport
	[		Zoom in around cursor
	]		Zoom out around cursor
	Shift + "+" on numeric keypad		Zoom in 2x
	Shift + "-" on numeric keypad		Zoom out 2x

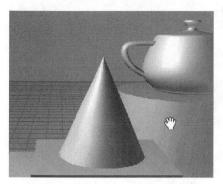

Figure 3.48 Dragging the hand-shaped Pan tool moves the viewport across a scene.

Panning viewports

Panning allows you to see beyond the edges of the current view by moving viewports across the scene parallel to the view plane (the plane of the screen).

To pan a viewport:

1. Click on the Pan tool 🖑 .

2. Drag the pan cursor across a viewport. The viewport moves across the scene (**Figure 3.48**).

✔ Tips

- Holding down the Ctrl key speeds up panning. Pressing Alt slows it down.

- The IntelliMouse wheel zooms the viewport when you are in Pan mode.

- Holding down the Alt key in Pan mode temporarily changes to Arc Rotate mode.

- The keyboard shortcut to enable the Pan tool is Ctrl + P.

NAVIGATING VIEWPORTS

Zooming viewports

Zooming moves viewports closer or farther away from a scene so you can examine details or see the big picture.

By default, orthographic viewports, such as the Front viewport, zoom around the cursor. Perspective viewports zoom around the center of the view.

To zoom a viewport:

1. Click on the Zoom tool 🔍.
   The cursor changes to the Zoom cursor.

2. Slowly drag up or down in a viewport.
   The viewport zooms in as you drag up (**Figure 3.49**) and out as you drag down (**Figure 3.50**).

✔ Tips

- To undo a zoom, choose Views > Undo View Change, or press Shift + Z. To redo a view change, choose Views > Redo View Change, or press Shift + A.

- Holding down the Ctrl key speeds up zooming. Pressing Alt slows it down.

- The keyboard shortcut for Zoom is Z.

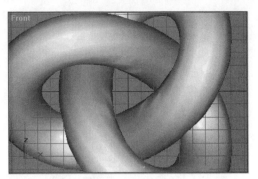

Figure 3.49 Dragging the Zoom tool up increases the viewport magnification.

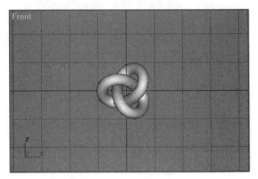

Figure 3.50 Dragging the Zoom tool down decreases the viewport magnification.

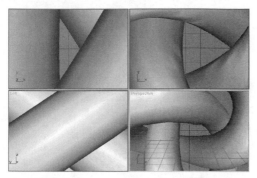

Figure 3.51 Zoom All magnifies all four viewports at once.

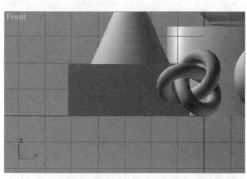

Figure 3.52 Here, objects in a scene do not fit neatly in the viewports.

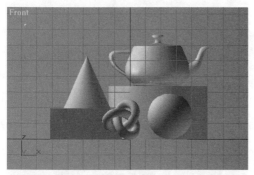

Figure 3.53 Zoom Extents makes the scene fit in the active viewport.

The Zoom All command zooms the scene in all viewports as you drag.

To zoom all viewports:

1. Click on the Zoom All tool ⊞.
   The cursor changes to the Zoom All cursor.

2. Drag up or down in any viewport.
   All the viewports zoom at once (**Figure 3.51**).

✔ Tips

- To zoom in and out around the cursor using the keyboard, press the bracket keys, [and], respectively. If you have a mouse with a wheel, such as an Intellimouse, you can use the wheel to zoom.

- To make an orthographic viewport zoom around the center of the view, choose Customize > Preference Settings > Viewports > Mouse Controls, and uncheck Zoom About Mouse Point (Orthographic).

Zoom Extents centers the scene in the active viewport. Use it when you want to get the big picture on how your scene is developing.

To zoom extents:

1. Activate a viewport in which the objects have been panned away from the center (**Figure 3.52**).

2. 🔲 Click Zoom Extents.
   The object becomes centered in the viewport (**Figure 3.53**).

✔ Tips

- The keyboard shortcut for Zoom Extents is Alt + Ctrl + Z.

- To make Zoom Extents ignore selected objects, such as a distant lights, check Ignore Extents in the Display command panel.

NAVIGATING VIEWPORTS

Zoom Extents Selected centers the current selection in the active viewport. Use it to focus in on your work.

To zoom extents selected:

1. Select one or more objects by clicking them with the Select Object tool ![icon] (**Figure 3.54**).

2. Choose Zoom Extents Selected ![icon] from the Zoom Extents flyout.

   The active viewport changes its view to frame the object in the viewport (**Figure 3.55**).

✔ Tip

■ The keyboard shortcut for Zoom Extents Selected is E.

The Zoom Extents All command centers the scene in all viewports at the same time. Use it whenever you need to reorganize your views.

To zoom all extents:

◆ Choose Zoom Extents All ![icon] from the Zoom Extents flyout.

   The objects become centered in all the viewports (**Figure 3.56**).

✔ Tips

■ To center a viewport around the cursor, press I.

■ The keyboard shortcut for Zoom Extents All is Shift + Ctrl + Z.

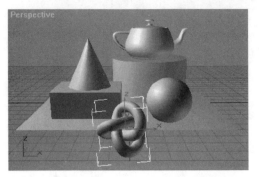

Figure 3.54 Select the object you want to zoom in on.

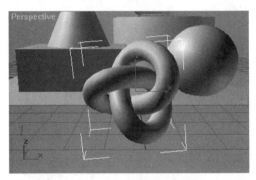

Figure 3.55 After you select one or more objects in the scene, click Zoom Extents Selected to zoom in on your selection.

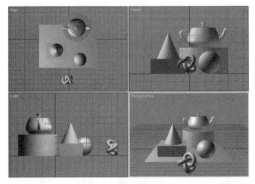

Figure 3.56 Zoom Extents All instantly centers objects in all of the viewports at once.

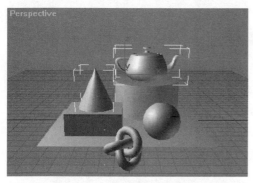

Figure 3.57 Select the objects you want to zoom in on.

Figure 3.58 After clicking Zoom Extents All, the selected objects become centered in all viewports.

Zoom Extents All Selected centers the current selection in all viewports at the same time. Use it to see your work from all sides.

To zoom all selected extents:

1. Select one or more objects (**Figure 3.57**).

2. Choose Zoom Extents All Selected from the flyout Zoom Extents All flyout.

   All viewports zoom up to the objects that you have selected (**Figure 3.58**).

✔ Tips

- To zoom to the extents of multiple objects in all viewports, select all the objects, and then click on Zoom Extents All Selected.

- You can assign a keyboard shortcut for Zoom Extents All Selected in the Customize > Customize User Interface > Keyboards tab panel.

The Isolate Tool zooms to the extent of the current selection and hides all other objects. Use it when you want to work without distraction.

To isolate an object:

1. Select an object.

2. Ctrl + right-click. In the Display quad menu, choose Isolate Tool (**Figure 3.59**).

   or

   Choose Tools > Isolate.

   The object becomes centered in the viewport, and all other objects are hidden from view (**Figure 3.60**). The Isolated floater appears.

3. When you have finished with operations that require the object to be isolated, click Exit Isolation.

✔ Tip

■ You can assign a keyboard shortcut to the Isolate Tool in the Customize > Customize User Interface > Keyboards tab panel.

Region Zoom enlarges an area to fill a viewport. Use it for working on the details of your models.

To zoom a region:

1. Activate an orthogonal viewport.

2. Click on the Region Zoom tool 🔍.

3. Drag a region in the viewport (**Figure 3.61**). When you release the mouse button, the viewport zooms in on the selected region (**Figure 3.62**).

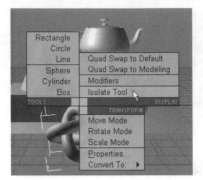

Figure 3.59 You find the Isolate Tool command by opening an object's menu; hold down the Ctrl key while you right-click the object.

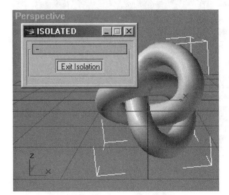

Figure 3.60 When you isolate an object, the Isolated floater appears; use it to exit isolation mode.

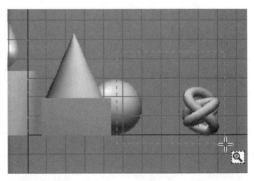

Figure 3.61 Drag to select a region for zooming in an axonometric view.

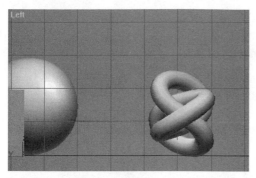

Figure 3.62 The result of zooming the region.

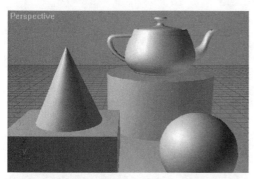

Figure 3.63 The Perspective viewport before using the Field-of-View tool.

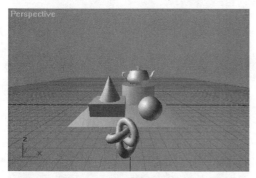

Figure 3.64 After using the Field-of-View tool, the viewport display changes magnification and perspective.

✔ Tips

- The Region Zoom tool does not appear in the Perspective viewport controls.

  To use Region Zoom in a Perspective view, change the Perspective view to a user view by pressing U. After you are finished, press P to restore the Perspective view.

- The keyboard shortcut to enable the Region Zoom tool is Ctrl + W.

The Field-of-View tool zooms and changes perspective at the same time. This tool is only available in Perspective viewports and Camera viewports.

To change the field of view:

1. Activate a Perspective viewport or a Camera viewport (**Figure 3.63**).

2. Click on the Field-of-View tool ▷.

3. Drag the Field-of-View cursor up or down in the Perspective viewport.

   The viewport changes magnification and perspective (**Figure 3.64**).

✔ Tips

- To undo a Field-of-View change, choose Views > Undo View Change, or press Shift + Z. To redo a viewport change, choose Views > Redo View Change, or press Shift + A.

- You can assign a keyboard shortcut to Field-of-View in the Customize > Customize User Interface > Keyboards tab panel.

NAVIGATING VIEWPORTS

Rotating viewports

The Arc Rotate command orbits a viewport around its center so you can see your objects from different sides.

To rotate around a scene:

1. Click on the Arc Rotate tool 🔄.

   A yellow circle appears in the active viewport. Four square handles are positioned around the circle (**Figure 3.65**).

2. Drag across the inside of the circle.

   The viewport orbits around the center of the view in a motion similar to a track ball (**Figure 3.66**).

3. Drag around the outside of the circle.

   The viewport rotates around the center of the view and parallel to the screen, or *viewplane*, like a disk spinning upon a platter (**Figure 3.67**).

✔ Tips

- Drag the handles of the Arc Rotate circle to rotate the view vertically or horizontally.

- Rotating an orthogonal view changes that view to a user view.

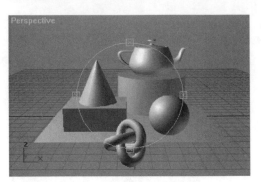

Figure 3.65 The Arc Rotate tool places a green navigation circle in the viewport.

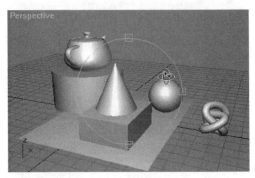

Figure 3.66 Rotate the viewport by dragging in the circle.

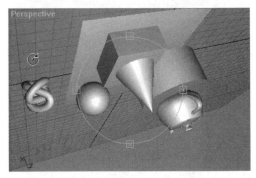

Figure 3.67 Rotating the viewport by dragging around the outside of the circle causes the viewport to spin parallel to the viewplane.

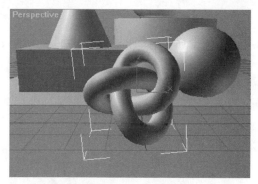

Figure 3.68 Usually you will want to zoom in on your selection first.

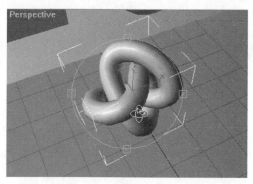

Figure 3.69 Rotating around the selection. Note that the object stays centered in the viewport

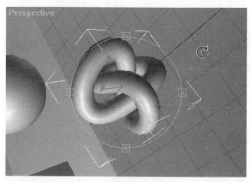

Figure 3.70 Dragging around the outside of the circle causes the viewport to spin around the selection parallel to the viewplane.

Arc Rotate Selected rotates a viewport around a selection so you can freely review your work from all sides.

To rotate a viewport around a selection:

1. Select one or more objects.

2. Optional: Click on Zoom Extents Selected 🔲 from the Zoom Extents flyout.

   The viewport zooms in on the selection (**Figure 3.68**).

3. Choose Arc Rotate Selected 🔄 from the Arc Rotate flyout.

2. Drag across the inside of the circle.

   The viewport rotates around the object (**Figure 3.69**).

3. Drag around the outside of the circle.

   The viewport rotates around the object and parallel to the screen (**Figure 3.70**).

✔ Tips

- Holding down the Alt key during a pan action temporarily switches to Arc Rotate.

- The keyboard shortcuts to enable the Arc Rotate tool are V and Ctrl + R.

- Arc Rotate Sub-Object works the same way, except it rotates the view around a sub-object selection.

OBJECT SELECTION AND DISPLAY

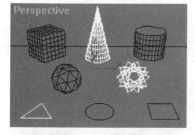

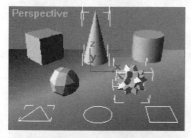

Figure 4.1 Selection allows you to apply commands to objects. Top: In wireframe views, objects turn white when they are selected. Middle: In shaded views, the corners of the bounding boxes appear. Bottom: Selection does not affect rendered images.

In order to apply commands to an object, you must first select it (**Figure 4.1**). Selection tells the program which sorts of commands may be applied, based on the object type. Only those commands that can be applied to the object in its current state are enabled. Commands that cannot be applied are grayed out.

In Chapter 2, you learned how to select an object by clicking it with the Select Object tool . You also found out how to select multiple objects by dragging a selection region around them. In this chapter, you will learn more about selecting multiple objects, and how to save selections in sets and groups.

At the end of the chapter, you will learn how to control most aspects of object display, including how to hide and freeze objects so that they cannot be accidentally selected.

Selecting Objects

The most basic way to select objects is by clicking them. When you select an object by clicking, other objects become deselected, unless you hold down the Ctrl key at the same time.

To select an object by clicking:

1. Choose Select Object from the Main Toolbar, if it is not already in use.

2. Move the cursor over an object.

3. Click an object.

   The object is selected, replacing the previous selection (**Figure 4.2**).

To add an object to a selection:

1. Choose the Select Object tool.

2. Hold down the Ctrl key, and click on an object.

   The object is added to the current selection (**Figure 4.3**).

3. Repeat step 2 until you have selected all the objects you want.

To subtract an object from a selection:

1. Choose the Select Object tool.

2. Hold down the Alt key, and click on an object.

   The object is subtracted from the current selection (**Figure 4.4**).

3. Repeat step 2 until you have deselected all the objects you want to subtract from the selection.

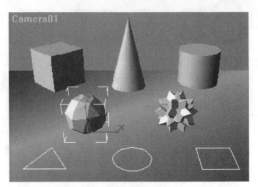

Figure 4.2 The corners of the bounding box indicate that the GeoSphere is selected.

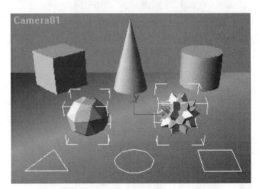

Figure 4.3 After adding the star to the selection.

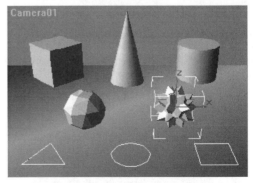

Figure 4.4 After subtracting the GeoSphere from the selection.

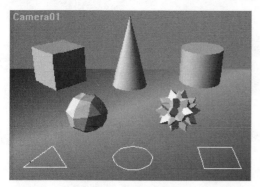

Figure 4.5 Click in the background to deselect objects.

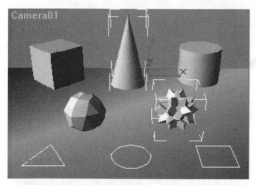

Figure 4.6 Select the objects that you want to exclude from the selection.

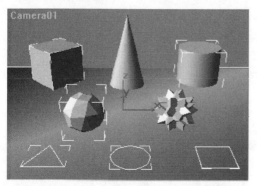

Figure 4.7 After inverting the selection.

Deselecting objects is easy. All you have to do is click in the background.

To deselect all objects:

1. Choose the Select Object tool.

2. Click the background of one of the viewports (**Figure 4.5**).

   All of the objects become deselected.

   Locking a selection prevents objects from being deselected accidentally.

To lock a selection:

1. Make a selection.

2. Click the Selection Lock Toggle 🔒 in the Status Bar, Locks and Controls area.

   or

   Press the spacebar.

   The objects stay selected, no matter where else you click in the viewports.

To unlock a selection:

◆ Click the Selection Lock Toggle 🔒 in the Status Bar Locks and Controls area.

   or

   Press the spacebar.

   Now the objects can be deselected.

Inverting deselects the current selection of objects, and selects everything else in the scene.

To invert a selection:

1. Make a selection (**Figure 4.6**).

2. Choose Edit > Select Invert.

   The selection is inverted so that everything except the objects you selected in step 1 are now selected (**Figure 4.7**).

Region Selection

Region selection is the fastest way to select multiple objects. You accomplish this by dragging a window around the objects you want to select. Every object inside the window is selected, no matter how far away it is in space.

There are two basic methods of region selection: selection by window and selection by crossing. When you select by window, you must surround objects completely in order to select them. When you select by crossing, you need only to cross the edge of an object in order to select it.

To select a region of objects by window:

1. Choose the Select Object tool.

2. Set the Window/Crossing button ⊞ to enable Window Selection.

3. Drag a selection region completely around the objects you want to select (**Figure 4.8**).

4. Release the mouse.

   The objects that are entirely enclosed by the selection window are selected (**Figure 4.9**).

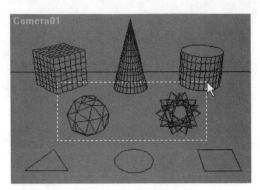

Figure 4.8 Dragging a window selection region around some objects.

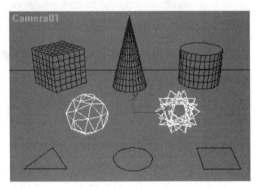

Figure 4.9 The resulting selection includes only the two objects that were fully enclosed by the selection region.

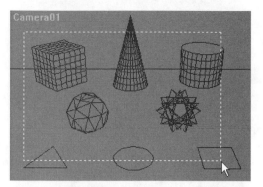

Figure 4.10 Dragging a selection region around and across some objects.

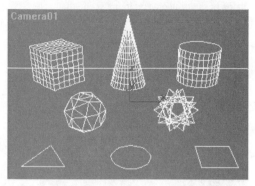

Figure 4.11 The resulting selection includes everything that was enclosed or touched by the selection region.

To select a region of objects by crossing:

1. Choose the Select Object tool.

2. Set the Window/Crossing toggle to enable the Crossing Selection.

3. Drag a region around or across the objects you want to select (**Figure 4.10**).

   The objects that are crossed by the selection region are selected (**Figure 4.11**).

✔ Tips

- To add objects to a selection, hold down the Alt key, and drag a region around the objects you want to add.

- To subtract objects from a selection, hold down the Alt key, and drag a region around the objects you want to subtract.

Selecting by Name

One reason we give objects meaningful names is to make it easy to select them from a list. This is especially useful when scenes contain a large number of objects.

You can select one or more objects by name, or select a named set of objects.

To select objects by name:

1. Click the Select by Name button 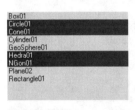.

   or

   Press the H key.

   The Select Objects dialog box appears with a list of all selectable objects in the scene (**Figure 4.12**).

2. Click to highlight the names of the objects you want to select (**Figure 4.13**).

3. Click OK.

   The objects are selected (**Figure 4.14**).

✔ Tips

- You can double-click an object in the list of names in order to both select it and close the Select Objects dialog box.

- If you have a lot of objects to choose from, you may want to switch to a different sorting order or filter the list of names (**Figure 4.15**).

- To bring up a selection list floater that stays open while you work, choose Tools > Selection Floater.

Figure 4.12 By default, the Select Objects dialog box lists all objects in the scene that are not hidden. Here the scene contains 10 unhidden objects.

Figure 4.13 Choose the names of the objects you want to select.

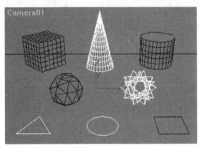

Figure 4.14 The resulting selection.

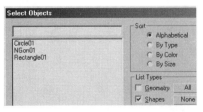

Figure 4.15 When you uncheck an object type, the objects of that type disappear from the list. Here, the mesh objects disappear when you uncheck Geometry, leaving only three spline objects on the list.

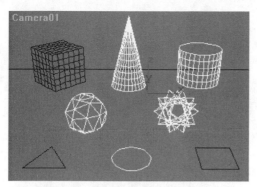

Figure 4.16 Select objects for the set.

Figure 4.17 Type a name in the Named Selection Sets input field.

Figure 4.18 Choose the selection set from the Named Selection Set drop-down list.

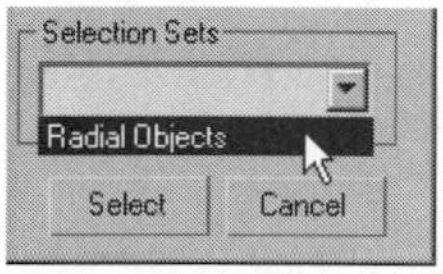

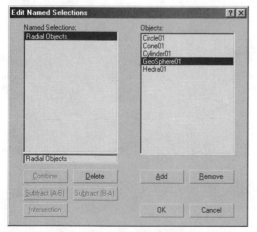

Figure 4.19 You can choose a selection set from the drop-down list in the Select Object dialog box.

Figure 4.20 In the Edit Named Selection Sets dialog box you can combine sets, add objects to sets, or remove objects from sets.

If you want to be able to select the same set of objects over and over again, consider assigning them to a named selection set.

To create a named selection set:

1. Select the objects you want to assign to the set (**Figure 4.16**).

2. In the Main Toolbar, enter a name for the set in the Named Selection Sets field (**Figure 4.17**).

3. Press Enter to save the set.

Before you do the next exercise, click in the background to deselect the set.

To select a named selection set:

◆ Choose a selection set from the Named Selection Set drop-down menu (**Figure 4.18**).

The objects in the set are selected.

✔ Tips

■ Another place you can select named selection sets is from the Selections Sets drop-down menu in the Select Objects dialog box (**Figure 4.19**).

■ To add or subtract objects from a named selection set, choose Edit > Edit Named Selections (**Figure 4.20**).

Grouping Objects

Grouping combines objects into a single unit called a group. You can select, transform, modify, and animate groups as if they were a single object. Objects in the group cannot be selected individually unless you open the group or ungroup the objects.

If you want to work with the objects together only part of the time and expect to select individual objects the rest of the time, create a named selection set, as described on the previous page, instead of making a group.

To define a group:

1. Select some objects (**Figure 4.21**).

2. Choose Group > Group.
   The Group dialog box appears (**Figure 4.22**).

3. Name the group, or accept the default name, Group01.

4. Click OK.
   The name of the group appears in the command panel in boldface. In the Select Objects dialog box, the name of the group appears in brackets (**Figure 4.23**).

✔ Tips

■ To add an object to a group, select the object and choose Group > Attach. Then click on the group to which you want to attach the object.

■ To nest groups within groups, select the groups you want to nest and choose Group > Group.

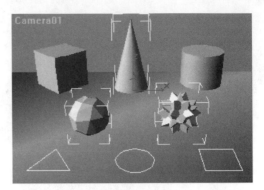

Figure 4.21 Select some objects to group.

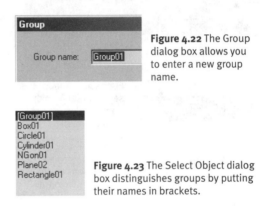

Figure 4.22 The Group dialog box allows you to enter a new group name.

Figure 4.23 The Select Object dialog box distinguishes groups by putting their names in brackets.

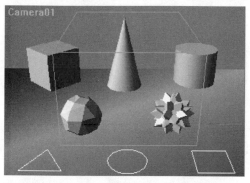

Figure 4.24 A pink bounding box appears when a group is open. Objects in an open group can be selected individually.

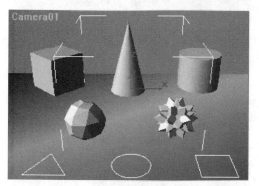

Figure 4.25 The bounding box disappears when the group closes. The objects are selected as a whole group.

To open a group:

1. Select a group.

2. Choose Group > Open.

   A pink bounding box appears around the group, indicating that the group is open (**Figure 4.24**).

To close a group:

1. Select an open group.

2. Choose Group > Close.

   The pink bounding box disappears, and the group closes (**Figure 4.25**).

GROUPING OBJECTS

105

To detach an object from a group:

1. Open the group.

2. Select the object you want to detach (**Figure 4.26**).

3. Choose Group > Detach.

   The object frees itself from the group (**Figure 4.27**).

To ungroup objects:

1. Select a group (**Figure 4.28**).

2. Choose Group > Ungroup.

   The objects are ungrouped (**Figure 4.29**).

✔ Tip

■ To ungroup nested groups all at once, choose Group > Explode.

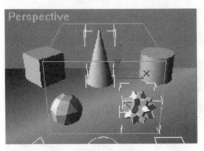

Figure 4.26 Select the objects you want to remove from the group.

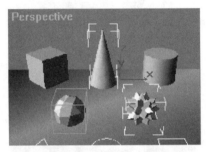

Figure 4.27 The group is reduced to a single object. The detached objects can now be selected individually.

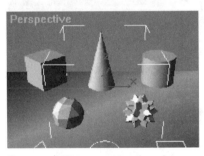

Figure 4.28 Click on any member of a group to select the entire group.

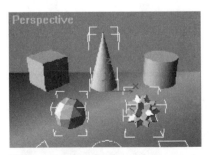

Figure 4.29 When the group is ungrouped, objects become selected individually.

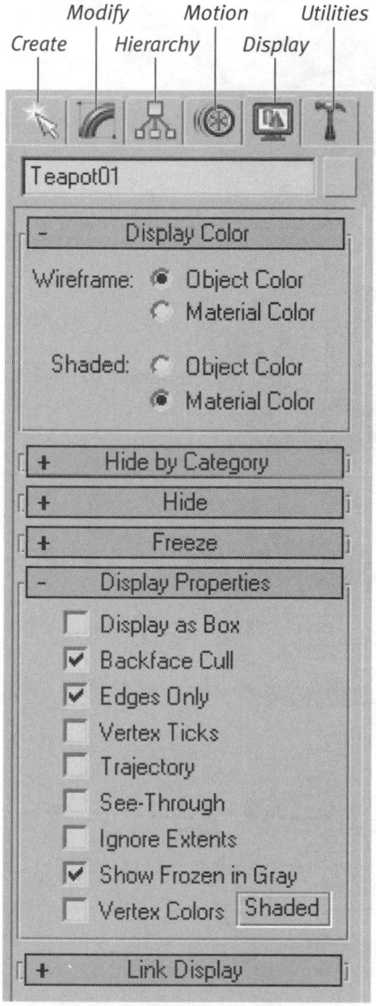

Create *Modify* *Motion* *Utilities*
Hierarchy *Display*

Teapot01

Display Color

Wireframe: ⦿ Object Color
○ Material Color

Shaded: ○ Object Color
⦿ Material Color

+ Hide by Category
+ Hide
+ Freeze
− Display Properties

☐ Display as Box
☑ Backface Cull
☑ Edges Only
☐ Vertex Ticks
☐ Trajectory
☐ See-Through
☐ Ignore Extents
☑ Show Frozen in Gray
☐ Vertex Colors [Shaded]

+ Link Display

Figure 4.30 You control object display with the Display command panel.

Display Properties
☐ Display as Box
☑ Backface Cull
☑ Edges Only
☐ Vertex Ticks
☐ Trajectory
☐ See-Through
☐ Ignore Extents
☑ Show Frozen in Gray
☐ Vertex Color ▾ [Shaded]

Figure 4.31 The Display Properties group of the Object Properties dialog box is nearly identical to the Display Properties rollout in the Display panel.

Changing Object Display

In 3ds max, you control the display of an object individually or for an entire viewport. In this section, we will find out how to change the object display by manipulating the properties of the individual object. For information on how to change the viewport display, see Chapter 3, Viewport Navigation and Display.

The commands in the Display panel affect the name, color, and visibility of objects and their components (**Figure 4.30**). In addition, the hide and freeze commands control the ability to select objects.

Any changes that you make to objects in the Display panel are reflected in the Object Properties dialog box, and vice versa (**Figure 4.31**). The Object Properties dialog box contains all the same display commands except hiding and freezing by category. To access the Object Properties dialog box, choose Edit > Object Properties, or right-click on a selection and choose Properties from the Transform menu. To call up a floating dialog box of display commands, choose Tools > Display Floater.

The color commands of the Display panel let you switch between the colors that you assign to objects in the Name and Color rollout and the colors of materials you assign to them. This provides an additional way of distinguishing between objects in a complicated scene.

Object display property commands affect the way in which viewports display objects in smooth modes, wireframe modes, or both. Display properties that affect only smooth shaded modes include:

◆ **See-Through**—Causes an object to appear translucent. Affects viewport but not rendered output.

Display properties that affect only wireframe modes include:

◆ **Backface Cull**—Hides the wireframe display of the inside of an object. Uncheck this box when you want to see the entire structure.

◆ **Edges Only**—Hides the common edge between pairs of *coplanar* faces, which are adjacent faces that can be selected as a polygon. Uncheck this box to see the true number of faces that make up a mesh surface.

◆ **Vertex Ticks**—Displays vertices as small or large dots, depending upon the preference you set in the Viewports panel of the Preference Settings dialog box.

Display properties that affect both smooth and wireframe modes include:

◆ **Display as Box**—Displays an object in box mode, even when the viewport display is set to a higher level of resolution.

◆ **Trajectory**—Displays the animation path of an object.

◆ **Ignore Extents**—Causes the Zoom Extents command to disregard the object.

◆ **Show Frozen in Gray**—Causes objects to turn gray when they are frozen.

◆ **Vertex Colors**—Displays vertex colors that have been assigned during sub-object editing (see Chapter 8). May be displayed with or without light-to-dark surface shading.

Examples of display modes are shown in **Figure 4.32**.

See-Through—on

Backface Cull—off

Edges Only—off

Vertex Ticks—on

Figure 4.32 A teapot displayed on a white background using different options.

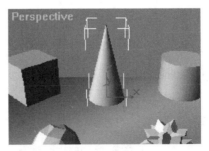

Figure 4.33 Select an object to hide.

Figure 4.34 The Hide rollout contains commands for hiding and unhiding objects.

Figure 4.35 After hiding the selected object.

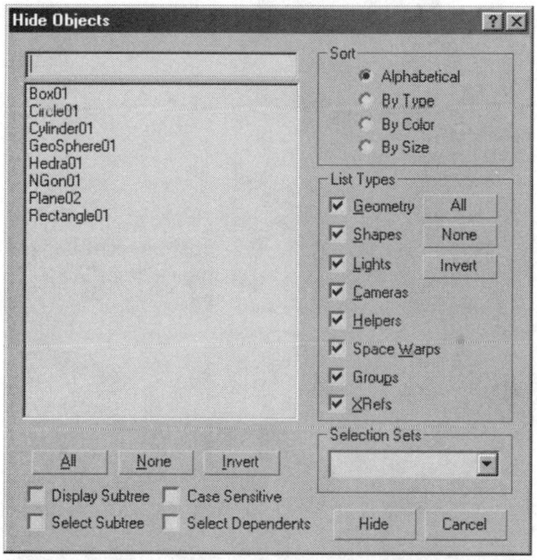

Hiding objects helps you to manage complex scenes by simplifying the viewport display and speeding up redraw time. Hidden objects disappear from view and cannot be selected until they are unhidden.

To hide an object:

1. Select an object that you want to hide (**Figure 4.33**).

2. Open the Hide rollout of the Display command panel ▣ (**Figure 4.34**).

3. In the Hide rollout, click Hide Selected. The object disappears from view (**Figure 4.35**).

✔ Tips

- Hide Unselected hides unselected objects.

- Hide by Name allows you to select objects from a list (**Figure 4.36**).

- Hide by Hit allows you to hide objects by clicking on them.

- Frozen objects cannot be hidden unless you enable Hide Frozen Objects.

Figure 4.36 You can select objects to hide in the Hide by Name dialog box. Note the similarity to the Select Objects dialog box.

To unhide an object:

1. Click Unhide by Name.

   or

   Press 5 on your keyboard.

   A list of all the hidden objects appears (**Figure 4.37**).

2. Select the object that you want to unhide.

3. Click OK.

   The object reappears (**Figure 4.38**).

To unhide all objects:

◆ In the Hide rollout, click Unhide All.

   All the hidden objects reappear.

The Hide by Category rollout allows you to hide objects according to type. I often hide lights and cameras when I am not working on them so I can zoom to the extents of a scene more closely. Another good use for this set of commands is for hiding helper objects and for hiding objects that have been used in building compound objects.

To hide an object by category:

1. In the Display panel, open the Hide by Category rollout (**Figure 4.39**).

2. Place a check in the boxes next to the types of objects you would like to hide.

   The objects disappear.

✔ Tip

■ To unhide objects by category, uncheck the object types you want to make visible.

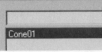

Figure 4.37 Select an object to unhide in the Unhide by Name dialog box.

Figure 4.38 After unhiding the object.

Figure 4.39 You hide objects according to type in the Hide by Category.

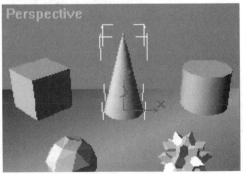

Figure 4.40 Select an object to freeze.

Figure 4.41
The Freeze rollout contains commands that make objects unselectable.

Figure 4.42 The frozen object turns dark gray.

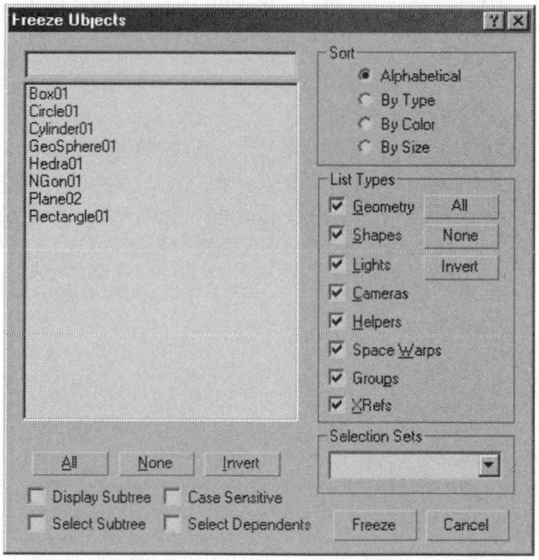

Freezing prevents objects from being manipulated without hiding them from view. When objects are frozen, they turn dark gray and cannot be selected until they are unfrozen.

To freeze an object:

1. Select an object (**Figure 4.40**).

2. Open the Display command panel.

3. Open the Freeze rollout.
   The Freeze rollout appears (**Figure 4.41**).

4. In the Freeze rollout, click Freeze Selected.
   or
   Press 6 on your keyboard.
   The object freezes (**Figure 4.42**).

✔ Tips

- Freeze Unselected freezes all visible objects that are unselected and unfrozen.

- Freeze by Name brings up a list of unhidden and unfrozen objects to freeze (**Figure 4.43**).

- Freeze by Hit allows you to freeze objects by clicking on them.

- If you do not want an object to turn gray when it freezes, uncheck Show Frozen in Gray in the Display Properties rollout.

Figure 4.43 You can select objects to freeze in the Freeze by Name dialog box.

CHANGING OBJECT DISPLAY

To unfreeze objects:

1. Click Unfreeze by Name.

   or

   Press 5 on your keyboard.

   A list of all the frozen objects appears (**Figure 4.44**).

2. Select the objects that you want to unfreeze.

3. Click OK.

   The objects become unfrozen (**Figure 4.45**).

To unfreeze all objects:

◆ In the Freeze rollout, click Unfreeze All

   or

   Press 7 on your keyboard.

   All the frozen objects become unfrozen.

✔ Tips

■ Unfreeze by Hit allows you to unfreeze objects by clicking on them.

■ The right-click Display quad menu contains most of the Hide and Freeze commands (**Figure 4.46**).

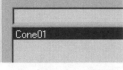

Figure 4.44 Select an object to unfreeze in the Unfreeze by Name dialog box.

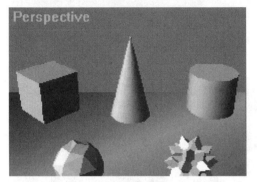

Figure 4.45 The unfrozen object returns to its original color and can now be selected.

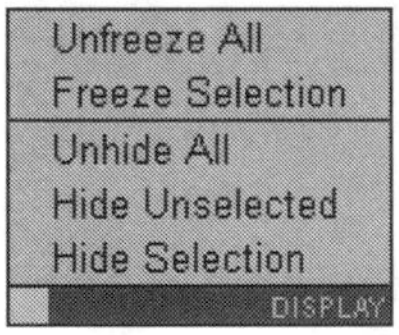

Figure 4.46 The Display quad menu contains shortcuts to the hide and freeze commands.

CHANGING OBJECT DISPLAY

TRANSFORMS

Transforms are the most basic commands for animating objects. With transforms, you make objects bounce, squash, spin, and fly. At the sub-object level, you use transforms to edit models. This chapter covers basic transforms as well as advanced transforms that create arrays of cloned objects.

Transforms are a set of mathematical functions called *affine transformations* that change the coordinates of geometry objects. With affine transformations, parallel sides of the objects they act on must remain parallel.

Basic transformation functions include:

- **Translation**—Moving along a straight line
- **Rotation**—Revolving around a point
- **Scaling**—Enlarging or reducing
- **Reflection**—Mirroring

Figure 5.1 illustrates each of these transformations.

Translation, rotation, and scaling are known as transforms in 3D graphics. In 3ds max, these are called the *move*, *rotate*, and *scale transforms*.

In this chapter, to show the before-and-after view of transforms, two views of an object appear in some figures. The transparent image represents the object before transformation; the opaque image represents the results of the transform.

Figure 5.1 From top to bottom: translation along a diagonal line, rotation around the tip of the spout, scaling from large to small, reflection from side to side.

Object Data Flow

To master transforms and other commands, it helps to see how they fit in the big picture.

3ds max is written in C++, an *object-oriented* programming language. This means that the definition of an object and its current status determine which commands may next be applied.

As commands are applied to an object, the object's data is passed from one command subroutine to another. The program's *object data flow* determines the order in which the commands are evaluated (**Figure 5.2**).

The object data flow for 3ds max starts with the master object. The master object is the basic definition of an object. When you start creating an object, the master object is assigned a position, orientation, scale, and parameters.

Modifier commands are applied next. Typically, modifiers deform the structure of objects.

Transforms are always applied after modifiers. They change the position, orientation, and scale of objects.

Space warps are applied after modifiers and transforms. They cause objects to deform as though they were passing through a force field.

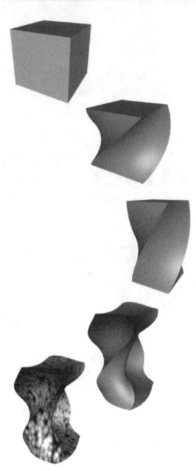

Figure 5.2 Object data flow. From top to bottom: Defining a master object by creating a cube, then applying a Twist modifier, a scale transform, an FFD space warp, and a material property.

Figure 5.3 The order of evaluation can affect the outcome. Top: Evaluating a squash before a Bend. Bottom: Evaluating a Bend before a squash.

Object properties are applied last. They include the name, color, material assignments, display properties, and rendering properties, including the ability to cast and receive shadows.

It is important to note that the order in which commands are evaluated can differ from the order of their application. For example, if you scale an object and then apply a Bend modifier, the scale transform will be evaluated after the modifier. This may produce a different result than if the scale were to be evaluated first, especially an uneven scale, such as a non-uniform scale or a squash (**Figure 5.3**). To get around this problem, experienced animators scale objects with an XForm modifier (which places the scale transform in the modifier stack), or change the original size parameters instead. (See Chapter 7 for more information on XForms.)

OBJECT DATA FLOW

Systems of Reference

Systems of reference track the position, orientation, and scale of objects as they are transformed. In Chapter 3, you reviewed two systems of reference: local coordinate systems, which use moveable axes to define object space (**Figure 5.4**), and the world coordinate system, which uses a fixed axis to define world space (**Figure 5.5**).

A third system of reference is implicit in viewing scenes: the plane of the monitor screen. Because this system is based on the viewer, it is very easy to understand: up and down along the Y axis is always up and down the screen; left and right along the X axis is always on your left and right (**Figure 5.6**).

3ds max uses a combination of local, world, and screen coordinates to provide you with a reference system for every occasion. The default system is View. View coordinates use screen coordinates in "flat" orthogonal views, and world coordinates in "3D" views that use parallel or converging perspective. In all views, the X and Y axes are marked by the darkest horizontal and vertical grid lines, while the Z axis sticks up at a perpendicular angle, invisible to the viewer.

Coordinate systems, transform centers, and axis constraints determine how transforms are executed. Each choice "sticks" to the transform it has been chosen for until you make a new assignment.

Coordinate systems define the point of origin and the direction of the current transform. To find out how each coordinate system aligns to the scene, see **Table 5.1**, "How They Line Up."

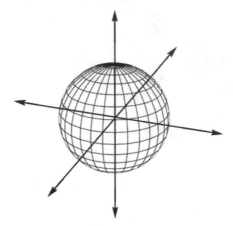

Figure 5.4 The local coordinate system is based on object space

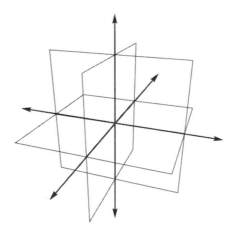

Figure 5.5 The world coordinate system is based on world space

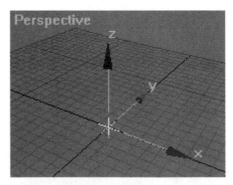

Figure 5.6 No matter which system of reference you are using, the X and Y axes lie on the grid.

Figure 5.7 The Reference Coordinate System drop-down list allows you to choose a system of reference for each transform.

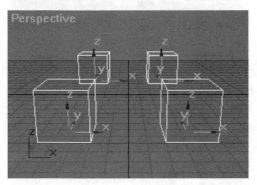

Figure 5.8 The axes of the selected objects align to the current system of reference.

Table 5.1

How They Line Up	
Screen	X and Y are parallel to the display screen; Z is perpendicular to the screen.
World	X, Y, and Z align to the world coordinate system.
View	Combination of Screen and World. X and Y lie on the visible grid plane of the active view; Z is perpendicular to the grid.
Parent	X, Y, and Z align to the local coordinates of an object's parent. If the object is not linked to a parent, it is a child of the world and uses world coordinates.
Local	X, Y, and Z align to the local coordinates of an object.
Grid	X, Y, and Z align to the coordinate system of the active grid.
Pick	X, Y, and Z align to the local coordinate system of any object in the scene that you pick.

To select a coordinate system:

1. In the main toolbar, open the Reference Coordinate System drop-down list (**Figure 5.7**).

2. Choose a system from the list.

   The coordinate system is assigned to the current move, rotate, or scale transform. The *axis tripods*—the three-pronged icons indicating the orientation of the axes—of all the current selections align to the new coordinate system (**Figure 5.8**).

Transform centers provide alternative points of origination for rotate and scale transforms. They do not affect move transforms. Choices include:

◆ Use Pivot Point Center

   This is the pivot point of the selected object. The default for selections of a single object.

◆ Use Selection Center

   This is collective center of a selection. The default for multiple selections of objects.

◆ Use Transform Center

   This is the origin of the current coordinate system that has been selected from the reference coordinate system drop-down list.

SYSTEMS OF REFERENCE

To select a transform center:

◆ From the Transform Center flyout in the main toolbar, choose a transform center (**Figure 5.9**).

The transform center is assigned to the current transform. Axis tripods and *transform gizmos*—the markers and handles that indicate the transform's direction—update to show the position and orientation of the transform center you have selected.

Axis constraints restrict the direction of transforms to certain axes.

To constrain a transform:

1. In the Main Toolbar, click button of the transform you would like to constrain .

2. In the Main Toolbar, click one of the Restrict Axis buttons ᶻˣ (**Figure 5.10**).

The transform is limited to the positive or negative direction of the axis you have chosen. If you chose a dual axis constraint (XY, YZ, ZX), the transform is limited to the plane that is defined by those axes.

✔ Tips

■ Axis restrictions stay with each transform until a new constraint is assigned.

■ The keyboard shortcuts for axis restrictions are:

F5—Restrict to X

F6—Restrict to Y

F7—Restrict to Z

F8—cycles thru Restrict to XY, YZ, and ZX

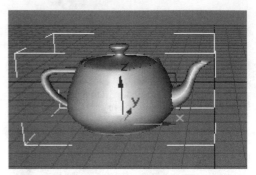

Figure 5.9 The Transform Center flyout allows you to choose the center of rotation and scaling.

Figure 5.10 The Restrict Axis buttons limit the direction of a transform to a line or a plane.

Tracking Transforms

3ds max uses a matrix to keep track of transforms with respect to local and world coordinate systems. Because this matrix is constantly updated, only the net effect of transforms is preserved. Compare this to modifiers, which are tracked in an ordered list that you can edit anytime.

SYSTEMS OF REFERENCE

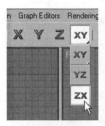

Figure 5.11 The transform gizmo with the X axis selected.

Figure 5.12 Moving a teapot to the right in the positive X direction.

Figure 5.13 Dragging the corner of the gizmo to move an object in the XZ plane.

The move transform changes the position of an object by translating it along the axes of the current system of reference.

To move an object:

1. From the Main Toolbar, choose the Select and Move tool ⊕.

2. Choose an axis constraint from the Main Toolbar ⊞.

   The current axes turn yellow, indicating the directions that the object can move (**Figure 5.11**).

3. Click and drag the object in the direction of the current transform axis.

   The object moves, following the gizmo (**Figure 5.12**).

4. To change the axis restriction on the fly, drag the axes of the transform gizmo. For dual axis constraints, drag the corners of the gizmo (**Figure 5.13**)

✔ Tips

- If you have any difficulty dragging an object, try locking your selection before you choose a constraint. Then drag anywhere in the viewport. The object will follow.

- The keyboard shortcut for locking and unlocking a selection is the space bar.

- You can select transforms from the Tools quad menu by right-clicking in a viewport.

The rotate transform changes the orientation of an object by spinning it around a center point.

By default, an object's center of rotation is its pivot point, located at the origin of its local axes. You can also assign the center of rotation to the origin of the current coordinate system. For multiple selections, the default center of rotation is the average center of the selection.

To rotate an object:

1. From the Main Toolbar, choose the Select and Rotate tool 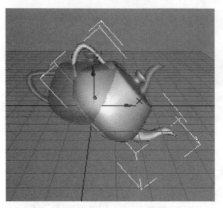.

2. Choose a transform axis from the Main Toolbar, or use the default Z axis.

3. From the Transform Center flyout, choose a transform center 🞂 to be the center of rotation, or use the default.

4. Click on object and drag up or down.

   The cursor changes to a rotate cursor, and the object spins around the current transform center (**Figure 5.14**).

✔ Tips

- By choosing different transform centers, you can rotate a multiple selection of objects around:
  🞂 Their individual pivot points
  (**Figure 5.15**)
  🞂 The center of the selection
  (**Figure 5.16**)
  🞂 The origin of the current system of reference

- To change the position or orientation of an object's pivot point, use the Adjust Pivot rollout in the Hierarchy panel 🞂.

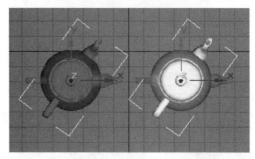

Figure 5.14 Rotating a teapot in Y using the object's pivot point as the center of rotation.

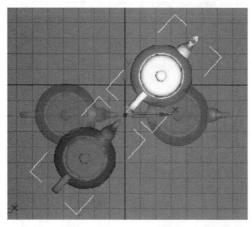

Figure 5.15 Rotating teapots around their individual pivot points.

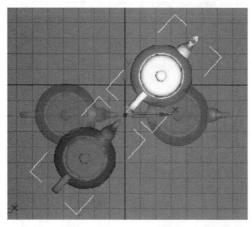

Figure 5.16 Rotating teapots around the center of the selection. This is the default setting.

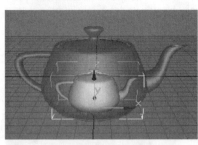

Figure 5.17 The three scale tools are located in the scale flyout.

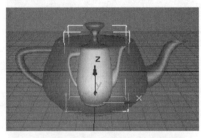

Figure 5.18 A uniform scale—Scaling an object down in all three axes.

Figure 5.19 A non-uniform scale—Scaling an object down in the X and Y axes.

Figure 5.20 A squash—Scaling and object down in X and Y is compensated by a gain in Z.

Scale transforms expand or shrink objects along their axes, using the current transform center as the origin of transformation. Located in the scale flyout of the main toolbar (**Figure 5.17**), scale tools include:

◆ **Select and Uniform Scale**—Selects and scales objects equally in all three axes, regardless of the current axis constraints (**Figure 5.18**).

◆ **Select and Non-Uniform Scale**— Selects and scales an object in up to two axes, resulting in a change in its proportions (**Figure 5.19**).

◆ **Select and Squash**—Selects and scales objects up in one or two axes and inversely scales objects in the remaining axes, resulting in a deformation of proportions in which the volume remains constant (**Figure 5.20**).

SYSTEMS OF REFERENCE

To scale an object:

1. From the Main Toolbar, choose a scale tool from the scale flyout ▣ ▣ ▣.

   If you choose Non-Uniform Scale or Squash, a warning may appear (**Figure 5.21**). Click Yes to ignore it for now.

2. ▣ Choose an axis constraint from the Main Toolbar. If you chose Uniform Scale in step 1, all three axes activate automatically.

3. Click on an object and drag up or down. The object scales in the direction of the current transform axes (**Figure 5.22**).

4. To change the scaling axis on the fly, click and drag the axes or corners of the transform gizmo.

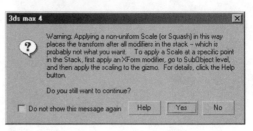

Figure 5.21 The Non-Uniform Scale Warning tells you that modeling objects with scale transforms may not turn out the way you expect if you apply modifiers to it afterwards.

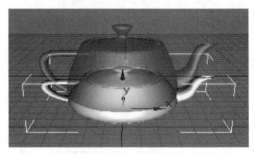

Figure 5.22 Squashing an object in Z causes it to expand proportionally in X and Y.

SYSTEMS OF REFERENCE

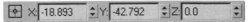

Figure 5.23 The coordinate display allows you to type in transforms when a transform tool is selected.

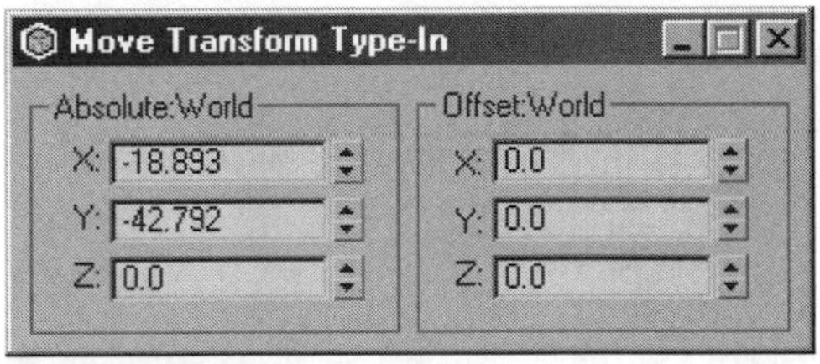

Figure 5.24 The Transform Type-In dialog box varies according to the transform that is selected.

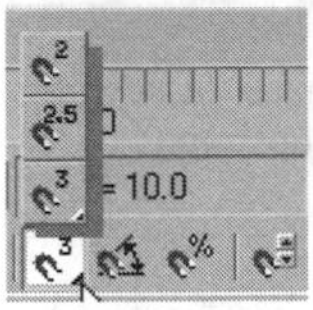

Figure 5.25 Snap locks constrain transforms to preset intervals or targets.

Precision Transforms

When you need to transform objects with precision, you use transform type-ins and snaps.

Transform type-ins transform objects by dragging spinners or using input from the keyboard. You can enter transform type-ins from coordinate display in the status bar, locks and controls area (**Figure 5.23**) or in one of the transform type-in dialog boxes (**Figure 5.24**).

Snaps constrain transforms to preset intervals or targets. Snap locks, the buttons that turn snaps on and off, are found in the status bar, locks and controls area (**Figure 5.25**).

3D, 2.5D and 2D Snaps constrain transforms to targets on a grid, to object components, or to relative distances.

Angle Snap constrains rotations to increments of degrees.

Percent Snap constrains scale transforms to a percentage of the size of an object.

Spinner Snap constrains spinners to increment or decrement by set intervals when you click on them.

Transform type-ins offer two ways to transform objects: by offsetting them a relative amount, or by transforming them to absolute settings.

To type-in a transform from the status bar, locks and controls area:

1. Choose a transform tool ⊕ ↻ ☐.

2. Select an object.

3. In the status bar, locks and controls area, choose a transform type-in mode. Choose Absolute Mode ⊞ for transforming objects to exact locations in world space. Choose Offset Mode ⬍ for transforming objects by preset increments.

4. In the coordinate display area just to the right, enter absolute coordinates or offset amounts by typing in the input fields or dragging the spinners next to them (**Figure 5.26**)

   The object is transformed (**Figure 5.27**).

✔ Tip

■ Transform type-ins override snap locks and axis constraints.

To type-in a transform using the transform type-in dialog box:

1. Choose a transform tool.

2. Select an object.

3. Choose Tools > Transform Type-In.
   or
   Right-click on the transform tool.
   The Transform Type-In dialog box for the current transform appears.

4. In the Transform Type-In dialog box, enter absolute coordinates or offset amounts by typing in the input fields or dragging the spinners next to them (**Figure 5.28**).
   The selection is transformed (**Figure 5.29**).

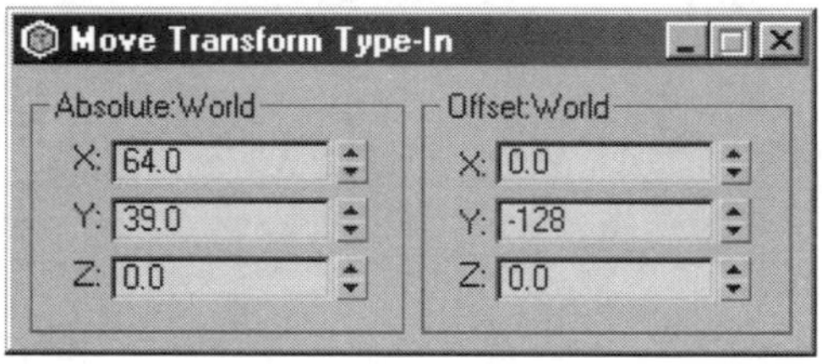

✔ Tip

■ The keyboard shortcut for opening the Transform Type-In dialog box is F12.

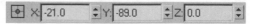

Figure 5.26 Typing an absolute move transform in the coordinate display.

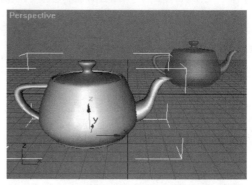

Figure 5.27 The object moves to the exact coordinates that you entered, regardless of axis constraints.

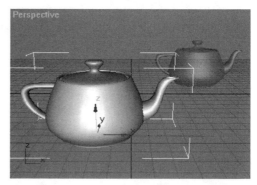

Figure 5.28 Entering an offset value for Y.

Figure 5.29 After offsetting the position of the teapot in X and Y.

PRECISION TRANSFORMS

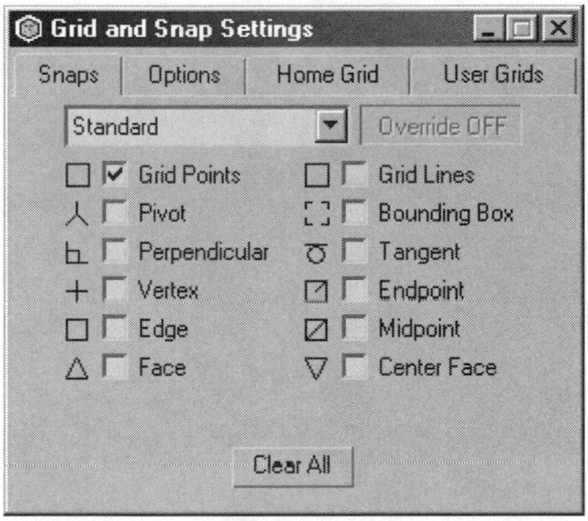

Figure 5.30 You set options for grids and snaps in the Grid and Snap Settings dialog box.

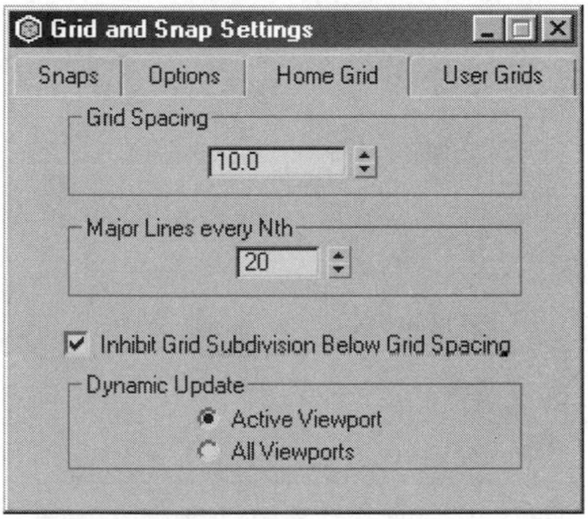

Figure 5.31 You enter grid spacing settings in the Home Grid panel.

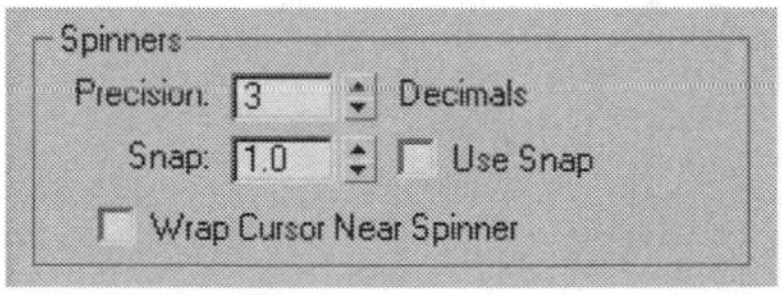

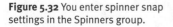

Figure 5.32 You enter spinner snap settings in the Spinners group.

You configure most snap settings in the Grid and Snap Settings dialog box. The exception is the Spinner Snap tool, which you configure in the Preference Settings dialog box.

To configure snap settings for 2D, 2.5D, 3D, Angle, and Percent Snaps:

1. Choose Customize > Grid and Snap Settings.

   or

   Right-click on any snap lock except Spinner Snap.

   The Grid and Snap Settings dialog box appears (**Figure 5.30**).

2. Open the panel you want to access.

3. Set the options you want by checking boxes or entering values (**Figure 5.31**).

4. Close the dialog box.

✔ Tip

■ The Shift + right-click menu allows you to configure snap targets and certain snap options on the fly.

To configure snap settings for spinners:

1. Choose Customize > Preferences

   or

   Right-click on the Spinner Snap lock.

   The Preference Settings dialog box appears.

2. In the General panel, set the spinner precision and snap amounts. You can also set the cursor to wrap near the spinner (**Figure 5.32**).

3. Click OK or close the dialog box.

2D and 3D snaps constrain move transforms to preset targets. Snap targets include grid points, grid lines, bounding boxes, perpendiculars, tangents, and intervals of sub-object components. The default target is grid intersections.

To snap a move:

1. Choose the Select and Move tool from the Main Toolbar.

2. Click the 3D Snap button in the Status Bar Controls.

3. Move an object.

   The object snaps from one target to another as you move it (**Figure 5.33**).

To set snap targets:

1. Choose Customize > Grid and Snap Settings.

   or

   Right-click on any snap tool.

   The Grid and Snap Settings dialog box appears.

2. Open the Snaps panel (**Figure 5.34**).

3. Click Clear All to clear all the check boxes.

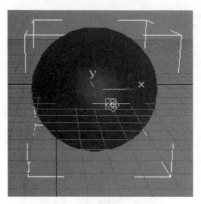

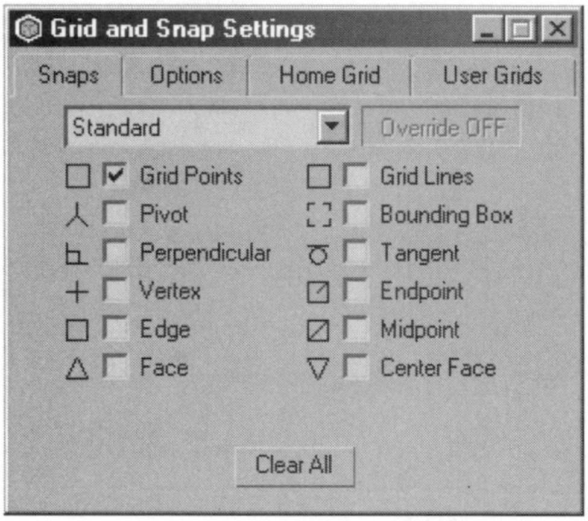

Figure 5.33 Snapping a move to grid intersections. Notice that the cursor changes to a snap icon.

Figure 5.34 You set snap targets in the Snaps panel. The snap icons are located just to the left of the snap targets.

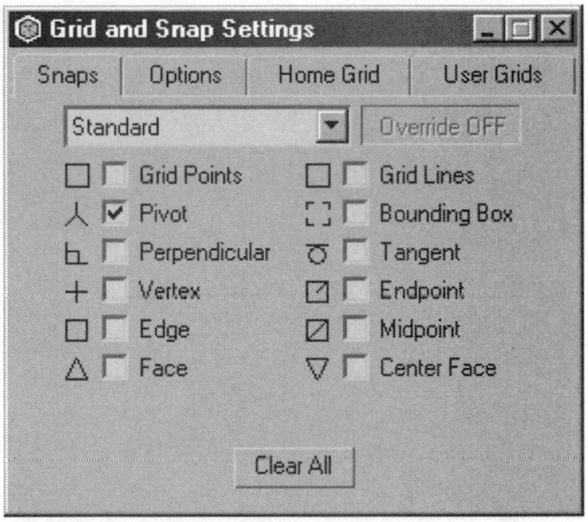

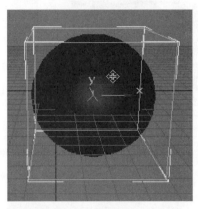

Figure 5.35 Setting the snap target to Pivot will snap the cursor to object pivot points.

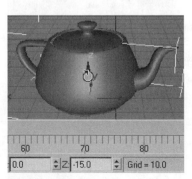

Figure 5.36 Snapping a cursor to a target changes the cursor to the target's snap icon.

Figure 5.37 Snapping a Z axis rotation in 5° increments.

4. Check the snap targets you want to use (**Figure 5.35**).

5. Close the dialog box.

The next time you snap a cursor to a target, the cursor will change to the snap icon that matches that target (**Figure 5.36**).

✔ Tips

- You increase the strength of a snap—the distance a cursor jumps to its target—in the Options panel of the Grid and Snap Settings.

- Press S to turn 2D, 2.5D, and 3D Snaps on and off.

Angle snaps constrain rotations to degree increments. The default increment is 5°.

To snap a rotation:

1. Choose the Select and Rotate tool from the Main Toolbar.

2. Turn on Angle Snap by clicking Angle Snap in the status bar, locks and controls.

3. Rotate an object.

The object snaps to degree increments as it rotates (**Figure 5.37**).

PRECISION TRANSFORMS

To set angle snap increments:

1. Open the Options panel of the Grid and Snap Settings dialog box.

2. Set the Angle value in degrees (**Figure 5.38**).

3. Close the dialog box.

✔ Tips

■ To rotate an object around a 3D snap target, such as a vertex or edge, turn on 3D Snap and set the snap targets in the Snaps panel of the Grid and Snap Settings dialog box.

■ Press A to turn angle snaps on and off.

Percent snaps constrain scales to percentage increments. The default increment is 10%.

To snap a scale:

1. Choose the Select and Uniform Scale tool from the Main Toolbar.

2. Turn on Percent Snap by clicking on the Percent Snap button in the Status Bar Controls.

3. Scale an object.

    The object snaps to percentage increments as it scales (**Figure 5.39**).

To set percent snap increments:

1. Open the Options panel of the Grid and Snap Settings dialog box.

2. Enter a new percentage in the Percent field (**Figure 5.40**).

3. Close the dialog box.

✔ Tip

■ Press Shift + Ctrl + P to turn percent snaps on and off.

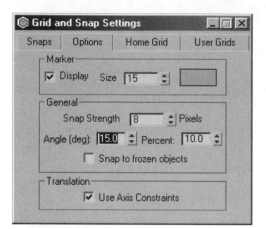

Figure 5.38 Changing the angle snap increment to 15°.

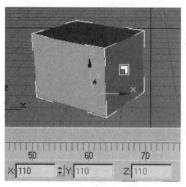

Figure 5.39 Snapping a uniform scale by 10%.

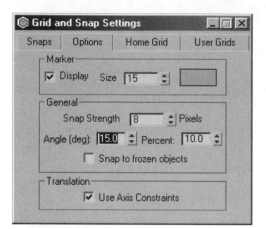

Figure 5.40 Setting the percent snap to 20%.

Cloning

Cloning creates duplicate objects (and sub-objects) that look exactly like the original. Clones can be created singly or in multiples, and they can be placed in different spatial configurations.

When combined with transforms, cloning is an incredibly powerful tool. You can create arrays of duplicate objects that have been moved, rotated, or scaled incrementally. By cloning animated objects, you can make arrays of objects that inherit the animation of the original. Think flocks of birds or schools of fish: where the leader goes, all the others follow instantly.

There are three basic clone types:

◆ A *copy* is a duplicate object that you can modify without affecting the original object. Use copies for objects that will be animated independently.

◆ An *instance* is a duplicate object that shares all its creation parameters and modifiers with the original. Any modification that you make to one affects the original and all other instances. They are great for creating flocks of birds, swarms of bees, schools of fish, etc.

◆ A *reference* is a duplicate object that shares its creation parameters but only some of its modifiers with the original and its instances. Use them to create variations on a theme: birds that veer from a flock, bees that split into smaller swarms, or fish that pause to look at the camera.

Modifiers are covered in Chapter 6. Generally speaking, they are parametric commands that are stored in a stack so you can access them afterwards. Transforms can also be placed in the modifier stack using an XForm modifier as a container. This gives you more control over the animation process and allows you to transform instances in unison.

The simplest way to make a clone is to use the Edit > Clone command. This method creates a clone in the same place as the original object.

To clone an object:

1. Select an object (**Figure 5.41**).

2. Choose Edit > Clone.

   The Clone Options dialog box appears (**Figure 5.42**).

3. Choose a clone type.

4. Enter a name or accept the default, which is the name of the original object with numbered suffix.

5. Click OK.

   The clone is created. It occupies the same spot as the original. To see the clone, move it away from the original (**Figure 5.43**).

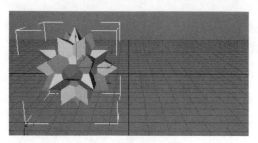

Figure 5.41 Select the object you want to clone.

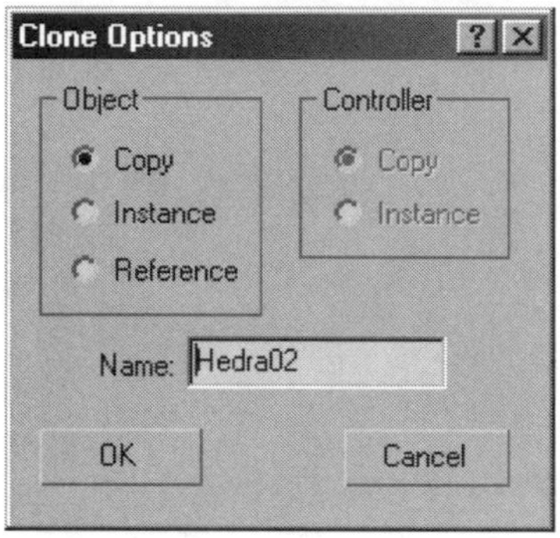

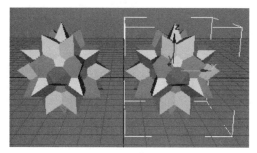

Figure 5.42 The Clone Options dialog box allows you to choose a clone type and name the clone.

Figure 5.43 After moving the clone, you see it is an exact duplicate of the original.

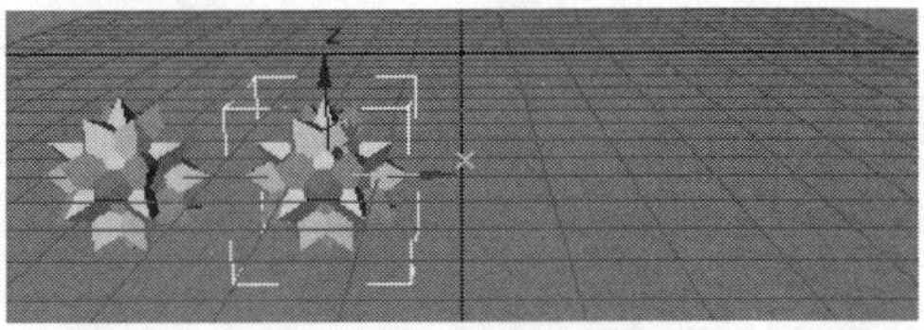

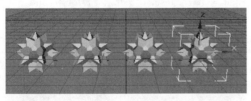

Figure 5.44 Shift-cloning an object using the Move tool.

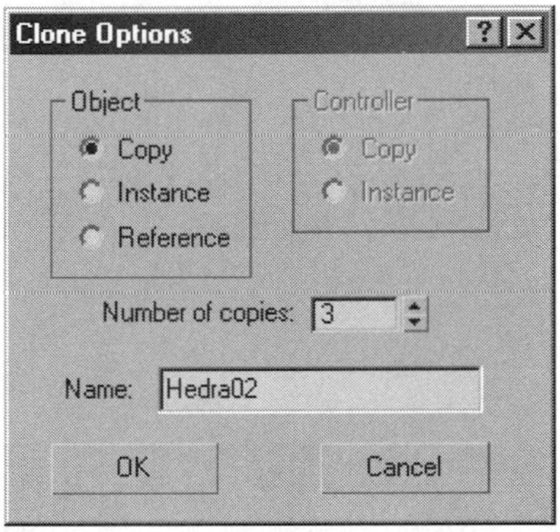

Figure 5.45 In the Clone Options dialog box, you enter the number of clones you want to create.

Figure 5.46 The resulting clones of a move transform are always spaced an even distance apart.

You can create multiple clones if you hold down the Shift key before transforming an object.

To shift-clone an object:

1. Choose a transform tool from the Main Toolbar ⊕ ↻ ◻.

2. Hold down the Shift key.

3. Transform an object by dragging it.

   A second object is dragged out of the first one (**Figure 5.44**), and the Clone Options dialog box appears. This time there is place to enter the number of copies (**Figure 5.45**).

4. Enter a value for Number of copies.

5. Click OK.

   The clones appear. Each one is transformed incrementally from the original object (**Figure 5.46**).

✔ Tip

■ To Shift-clone an object in place so that the clones completely overlap the original, click the object instead of dragging it.

CLONING

Advanced Transforms

The Mirror, Array, and Align commands apply a combination of move, rotate, and scale transforms to objects and their clones.

The Mirror tool reflects an object along one or two of its axes.

To mirror an object:

1. Select an object.

2. From the main toolbar, choose the Mirror tool .

   The Mirror dialog box appears (**Figure 5.47**).

3. Choose a mirror axis, or use the default.

4. Enter an Offset value to specify how far away the mirrored object will be.

5. Choose a clone type, or choose No Clone to mirror the original object.

   A mirrored object is created, offset in the direction of the mirror axis (**Figure 5.48**).

✔ Tip

■ To create a symmetrical pattern, create an object and mirror it. Then select the object and its clone and mirror them together (**Figure 5.49**).

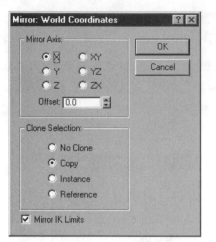

Figure 5.47 In the Mirror dialog box, you choose the axes of reflection and the clone type.

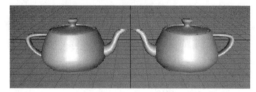

Figure 5.48 The result of mirroring an object and offsetting its clone in X.

Figure 5.49 By selecting and mirroring objects repeatedly, you can create repeating patterns.

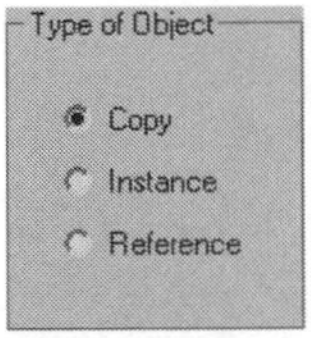

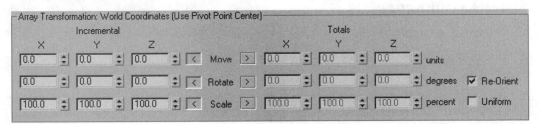

Figure 5.50 You choose a clone type in the Type of Object group.

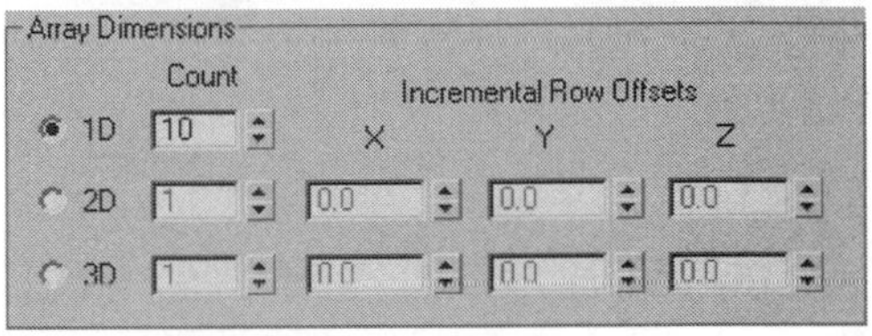

Figure 5.51 In the Array Dimension group, you set the number of dimensions you want in the array and the number of objects in each dimension.

Figure 5.52 The Total in Array value is the number of objects that will appear in the final array.

The Array tool creates an array of clones by transforming them in up to three dimensions.

The Array dialog box includes:

◆ **The Type of Object group**—Allows you to choose a clone type of copy, instance, or reference (**Figure 5.50**).

◆ **The Array Dimensions group**—Allows you to choose the number of dimensions you want in your array and the number of objects you want in each dimension of the array. The Incremental Row Offsets set the amount of space you will have between each row (**Figure 5.51**).

◆ **The Total in Array indicator**— Indicates the total number of objects in the final array. Calculated by multiplying together the number of objects in each dimension (**Figure 5.52**).

◆ **The Array Transformation group**— Indicates the current system of reference and allows you to set incremental or total amounts for each transform. You click the left arrows if you want to enter incremental amounts; click the right arrows if you want to enter the total amounts. The Re-Orient parameter causes clones to follow the direction of a rotation when it is checked. When the Uniform parameter is checked, Y and Z scaling are disabled and the X scale value is applied to all axes (**Figure 5.53**).

Figure 5.53 The Array Transformation group allows you to choose the transformations you will use in the array and set their parameters.

ADVANCED TRANSFORMS

A grid array is a two-dimensional array of objects arranged in rows and columns on a plane. A lattice array adds the dimension of height.

To create a grid array:

1. Select an object.

2. From the main toolbar, choose a reference coordinate system and a transform center ⊞.

3. Choose the Array tool ✴.

4. In the Type of Object group, choose a clone type.

5. In the Array Dimensions group, choose 2D.

6. In the 1D Count field, enter the number of clones you want in each row.

7. In the 2D Count field, enter the number of clones you want in each column.

8. In the Array Transformation group, enter incremental or total amounts for each transform you want to perform on the clones. For a simple grid without rotation or scaling, just enter a Move value for X in order to space apart the columns (**Figure 5.54**).

9. In the Y input field of the 2D Incremental Row Offsets, enter the amount of space you want between each row (**Figure 5.55**).

10. Click OK to create the array.

    The grid array appears (**Figure 5.56**).

To create a lattice array:

1. Follow the steps for creating a grid array.

2. In the Array Dimensions dialog box, choose 3D.

3. In the Count field, enter the number of clones for the vertical dimension. Then enter the offset amount in the Z field.

4. Click OK to create the array (**Figure 5.57**).

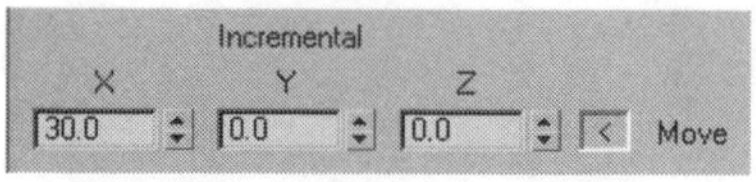

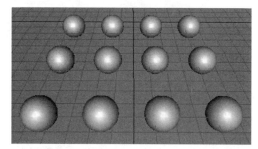

Figure 5.54 This setting will move the columns of the grid apart 40 units.

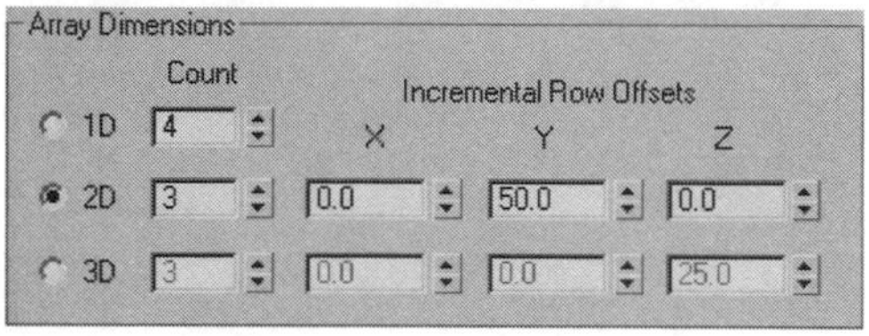

Figure 5.55 Entering a Y offset amount moves the rows apart. The values for a 3D array are grayed out.

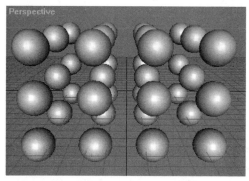

Figure 5.56 The resulting grid array.

Figure 5.57 You create a lattice array by entering 3D parameter values.

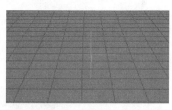

Figure 5.58 Create a Point helper object to serve as the center of rotation.

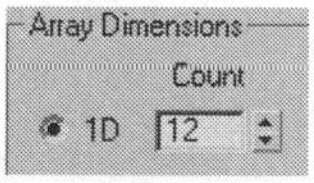

Figure 5.59 Setting the 1D Count to create a 12-object array.

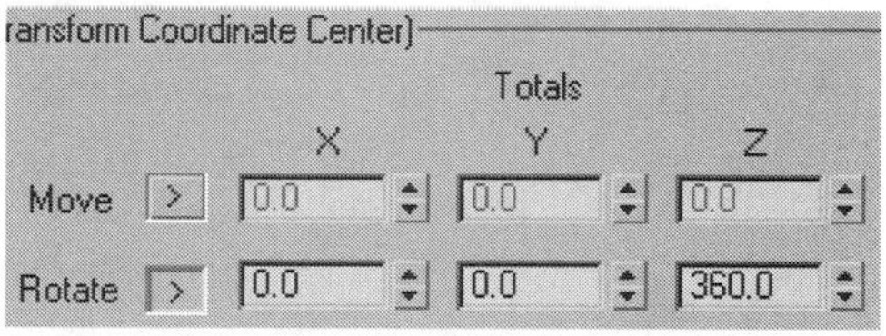

Figure 5.60 A total amount of 360 creates a circular array.

Figure 5.61 The resulting circular array. Notice that the teapots all follow the direction of rotation.

A circular array is a one-dimensional array of clones arranged in a circle.

To create a circular array:

1. In the Create panel, open the Helpers sub-panel .

2. In the Object Type rollout, click Point.

3. In any viewport, click the spot that you want to be the center of the array.
   A Point helper object appears (**Figure 5.58**).

4. Create or position the first object in the array . The distance between this object and the Point object will define the radius of the array.

5. From the transform center drop-down, choose Use Transform Coordinate Center .

6. From the reference coordinate system drop-down menu, choose Pick. Then click the Point object.

7. From the main toolbar, choose the Array tool .

8. In the Array dialog box, choose a clone type in the Type of Object group.

9. In the Array Dimensions group, choose 1D. Then enter the Count value for the number of objects you want to have in the array (**Figure 5.59**).

10. In the Array Transformation group, click the right arrow next to the word Rotate. Then enter Z = 360 degrees (**Figure 5.60**).

11. Enter any other transformations you want to add, if needed. Then click OK to create the array (**Figure 5.61**).

To create a spiral array:

1. Follow steps 1 through 10 for creating a circular array. (If you just completed step 11 and created a circular array, see the tip below.)

2. Adjust the number of objects in the array by changing the 1D Count parameter (**Figure 5.62**).

3. Multiply the Z rotation amount by the number of turns you want in the spiral. Then change the Z rotation amount to this value (**Figure 5.63**).

4. Enter a Z Move value to set the height increment or total height of the array (**Figure 5.64**).

5. Click OK.

   A spiral array appears, beginning with the original object (**Figure 5.65**).

✔ Tip

■ To adjust an array that you just created, click the Undo button or press Ctrl + Z. Then click the Array button. Your last settings are preserved, so you can quickly adjust them and create a new array.

The Snapshot tool creates multiple clones by taking "multiple exposures" of an animated object over time. Clones do not inherit the animation of the original object. (For more about animation, see Chapter 6, Basic Animation.)

Creating snapshot arrays of objects that are not animated creates multiple clones that are located in the same position as the original object.

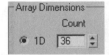

Figure 5.62 Adjust the 1D Count parameter to change the number of objects in the array.

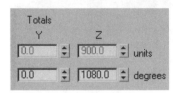

Figure 5.63 A total rotation of 1080° will cause the array to spiral three times.

Figure 5.64 This sets the height increment to 25 units.

Figure 5.65 The resulting spiral array, as seen in an ActiveShade View.

ADVANCED TRANSFORMS

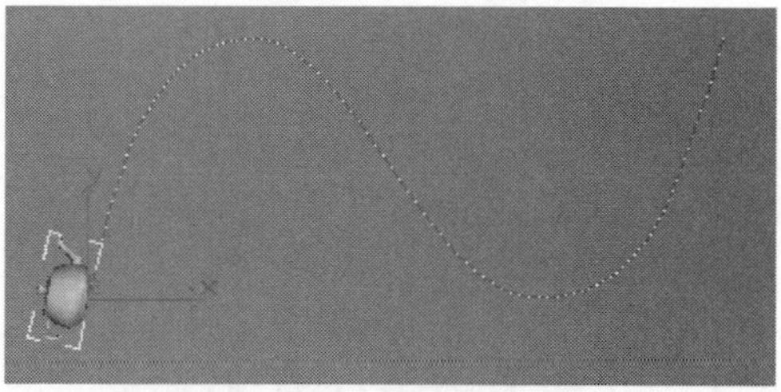

Figure 5.66 You see what an object's animation path looks like when you turn on its trajectory.

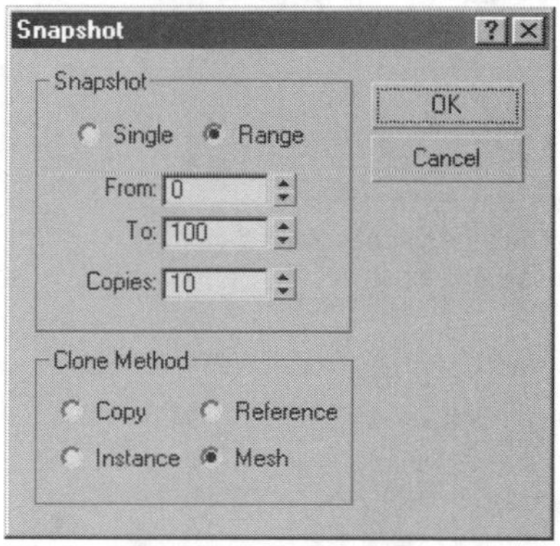

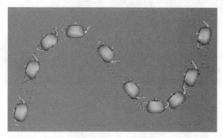

Figure 5.67 The Snapshot dialog box allows you to choose the number and type of clones you will create in a snapshot array.

Figure 5.68 The clones in the snapshot array follow the object's trajectory. The spacing of the clones depends on the speed of the object.

In addition to the usual clone options of copy, instance and reference, you also have the option of creating mesh clones. Mesh clones are mesh object copies made from an original object that may or may not be a mesh object. For example, you can create mesh clones from splines, compound objects, or particle systems.

To create a snapshot array:

1. Select an animated object.

2. Right-click on the object and choose Properties from the quad menu.

3. In the Object Properties dialog box, turn on Trajectory.

   The trajectory of the object appears (**Figure 5.66**).

4. Choose Snapshot 📷 from the Array fly-out in the Main Toolbar.

5. In the Snapshot dialog box, set the Snapshot to Range and enter the number of copies you want to create (**Figure 5.67**).

6. In the Clone Method group, select a clone type or accept the default (Mesh).

7. Click OK.

   A snapshot array appears along the trajectory of the original object (**Figure 5.68**).

✔ Tip

■ Snapshot arrays do not count the original object as part of the array. Instead, it creates a copy of the object in the exact same location. Compare this to the Array tool, which includes the original object as part of the final array.

The Spacing tool creates an array by distributing clones along a path, not unlike a Snapshot array (**Figure 5.69**). The main difference is that the Spacing tool has more parameters for arranging clones and does not use movement to determine spacing. The Spacing tool also does not offer the mesh clone type.

The main parameters of the Spacing tool are:

◆ **Count**—Sets the number of clones.

◆ **Spacing**—Sets the distance between clones.

◆ **Start Offset**—Determines how far away from the starting point the first clone will appear.

◆ **End Offset**—Determines how far away from the end point the last clone will appear.

As you check and uncheck parameters, the drop-down list below updates to reflect the current combination. You can also lock the offset values. If you choose a setting from the drop-down list, it will automatically check or lock your parameters (**Figure 5.70**).

In the Context group, you specify how you want to measure distance between the clones: from center to center or edge to edge. By default, clones in the array will "follow" the path, meaning they align to the direction of the path. But if you uncheck Follow in the Context menu, they will orient in the same direction as the original object (**Figure 5.71**).

When you use the Spacing tool to distribute clones along an existing spline path, the first vertex of a spline is always used to set the start point for spacing. (To learn how to change the first vertex of a spline, see Chapter 8, Editing Meshes.)

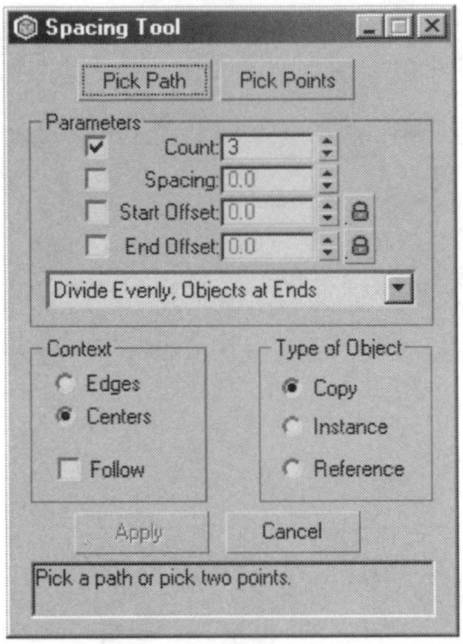

Figure 5.69 The Spacing tool creates an array of clones along a path.

Figure 5.70 The current selection of the Parameters drop-down list updates to reflect parameter combinations, and provides shortcuts to these combinations.

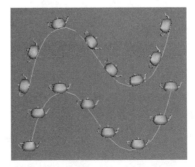

Figure 5.71 Clones follow the path by default, but you can also orient them in the same direction.

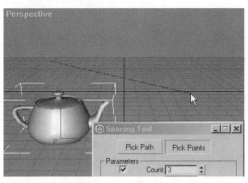

Figure 5.72 Clicking points in a viewport to define a path.

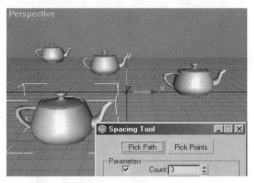

Figure 5.73 Three clones appear by default.

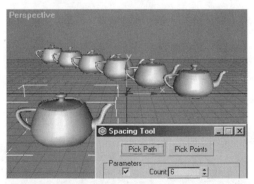

Figure 5.74 Setting the number of clones in the Count field automatically updates the number of clones in the array.

To space objects along a path:

1. Select an object.

2. In the main toolbar, choose the Spacing tool ▦ from the Array flyout.

   The Spacing Tool dialog box appears.

3. In the Type of Object area, select a clone type.

4. In the Context area, choose a spacing option.

5. Click Pick Path and then click a spline to use as a path.

   or

   Click Pick Points. Then click two different locations in a viewport to define a path (**Figure 5.72**).

   Three clones appear along the path from the start to end (**Figure 5.73**).

6. In the Count field, set the number of clones that you want in the array (**Figure 5.74**).

   As you change the Count, the number of clones updates in the viewports, and the Spacing parameter updates interactively.

7. If you want, you can choose a distribution option from the drop-down list.

   or

   Enter start and end offset values manually. The distribution of clones updates to match.

8. When you are satisfied with the array, click Apply and close the dialog box.

✔ Tip

■ The Spacing tool does not count the original object as part of the array.

The Align tool uses transforms to align the position, orientation, or scale of one or more objects to another object.

To align objects:

1. Select the object you want to align. This becomes the current object (**Figure 5.75**).

2. Choose the Align tool 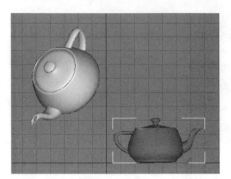 from the main toolbar.

3. Click the object you want to align to. This becomes the target object.

   The Align Selection dialog box appears (**Figure 5.76**).

4. Accept the default alignment reference point—the center of each object—or choose another option for each object.

   Minimum and Maximum refer to opposite edges of the object's bounding box.

5. Check the position, orientation, and scale of each axis in the target object to which you want to align the current object.

   As you check each axis, the current object aligns with that axis of the target object (**Figure 5.77**).

6. Click Apply to apply the alignment and reset the parameters.

7. Click OK when the alignment is complete.

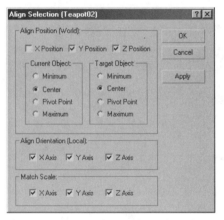

Figure 5.75 Select the object you want to align.

Figure 5.76 Aligning the position, orientation, and scale of the teapots.

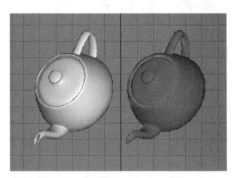

Figure 5.77 The teapots are align in all ways except the X position.

ADVANCED TRANSFORMS

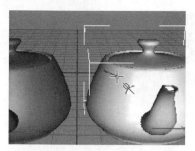

Figure 5.78 When you click on the first object, a blue surface normal appears.

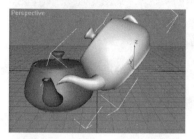

Figure 5.79 The surface normal of the first object aligns to the surface normal of the second object.

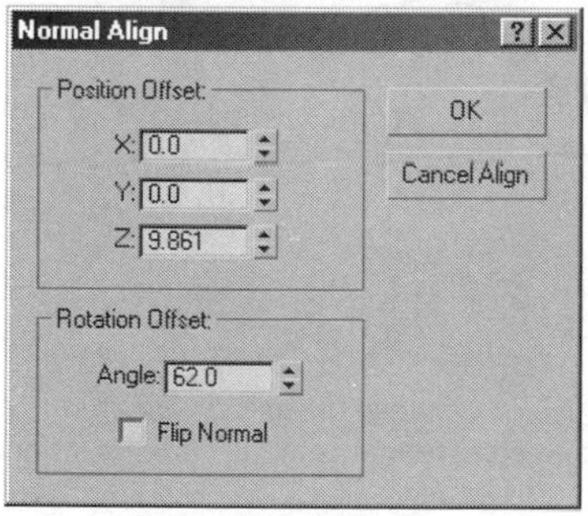

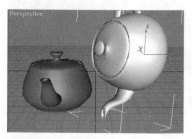

Figure 5.80 In the Normal Align dialog box you set position and rotation offsets for the normal aligned objects.

Normals are perpendicular vectors that stick out from the center of every face in a mesh. When you align the normal of one face to the normal of another, they align so that the faces just touch.

To align objects to normals:

1. Select an object.

2. Choose the Normal Align tool ⬚ from the Align flyout.

3. Click the surface of the first object with the normal align cursor.

   A blue surface-normal symbol appears (**Figure 5.78**).

4. Click the surface of the second object.

   The Normal Align dialog box appears. The surface normal of the first object aligns to the surface of the second object (**Figure 5.79**).

5. In the Normal Align dialog box, enter a Position Offset value if you want to reposition the aligned object. If you want to rotate the aligned object around the surface normal, enter a Rotation Offset value. Check Flip Normal if you want to flip the object upside down (**Figure 5.80**).

6. Click OK to complete the alignment (**Figure 5.81**).

✔ Tips

- Use the Place Highlight tool ⬚ in the Array flyout to align a selected light to the surface normal of an object: simply click the surface of the object.

- Use the Align Camera tool ⬚ in the Array flyout to align a selected camera to the surface normal of an object: simply click the surface of the object.

Figure 5.81 After offsetting and rotating an object along its surface normal.

The Align to View tool in the Align flyout aligns an object to the screen coordinates of the active view using the object's pivot point center and local axes for reference.

To align an object to a view:

1. Select an object.

2. Choose the Align to View tool  from the Align flyout.

   The Align to View dialog box appears (**Figure 5.82**).

   The object aligns the currently selected axis in the Align to View dialog box to the active view (**Figure 5.83**).

3. Change the axis of alignment, if necessary, in the View Align dialog box (**Figure 5.84**).

4. To flip an object 180° in the axis of alignment, check Flip in the dialog box (**Figure 5.85**).

5. Click OK.

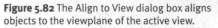

Figure 5.82 The Align to View dialog box aligns objects to the viewplane of the active view.

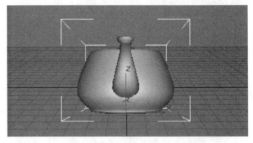

Figure 5.83 The object aligns to the currently selected axis.

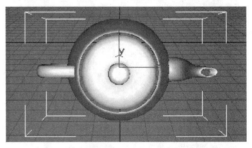

Figure 5.84 When you change the axis of alignment, the object immediately reorients in the direction of the axis.

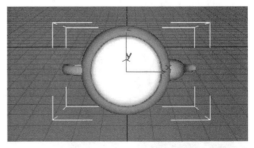

Figure 5.85 Check Flip to reverse the alignment 180°.

MODIFYING OBJECTS

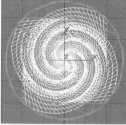

Figure 6.1 Top: A box that has been tapered and twisted. Bottom: A wireframe view of the box from the Top viewport.

Modifiers change the structure and appearance of objects. With the dozens of modifiers that ship with 3ds max 4, you can bend, twist, taper, ripple, wave, lathe, and extrude objects (**Figure 6.1**). Objects can be squeezed, sliced, stretched, or smoothed. You can even turn them inside out.

Like transforms, multiple modifiers can be applied in succession to obtain cumulative results. As you apply a succession of modifiers, they are tracked in an ordered list that stays with the object they modify. This list, or history, of modifiers is called the *modifier stack* (**Figure 6.2**).

Every time you apply a modifier, the object data is modified and passed up the modifier stack. Because the modifiers in the stack are completely accessible, you can adjust their parameters as often as you like. You can also turn off, rearrange, or remove modifiers from the stack. This flexibility gives the modifier stack its power for modeling, mapping, and animating objects.

Figure 6.2 The modifier stack shows that a Taper and a Twist modifier were applied to a box in that order.

Using Modifiers

Modifier commands are found in the Modify command panel (**Figure 6.3**) or the Modifier tab panel (**Figure 6.4**). To display the tab panels, right-click on the background of the main toolbar and choose Tab Panels from the menu.

Features of the Modify command panel include:

Object Name and Color—input fields for changing the name and color of objects.

Modifier List—a drop-down menu of all the modifiers that can be applied to the current selection.

The Stack Display—an area that lists all the modifiers in the stack of the current selection. A lightbulb icon 💡 next to each modifier indicates the active status of the modifier. Clicking the icon turns the modifier off or on.

Stack Tools—button-driven commands that control the modifier stack. They include:

- ◆ **Pin Stack**—Locks the modifier stack to the currently selected object. If another object is selected, the stack for the pinned object continues to be displayed.

- ◆ **Show End Result**—Turns the modifiers in the stack above it off or on. Previews the way the object will look when the entire stack has been evaluated.

- ◆ **Make Unique**—Converts instanced modifiers into copies.

- ◆ **Remove Modifier from the Stack**— Deletes the current modifier from the stack. Also unbinds space warps.

- ◆ **Configure Modifier Sets**—Allows you to create and display sets of modifier buttons (**Figure 6.5**).

Figure 6.3 The Modifiers command panel includes Name and Color inputs, the Modifier List drop-down menu, the stack display, stack tools, and modifier rollouts.

Figure 6.4 The Modifiers Toolbar contains shortcuts for the most commonly used modifiers.

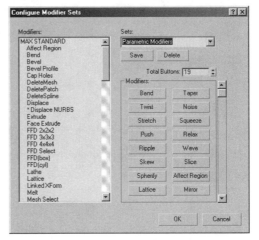

Figure 6.5 Modifier sets contain buttons for quick access to modifiers.

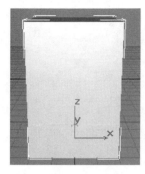

Figure 6.6 Select a box to modify.

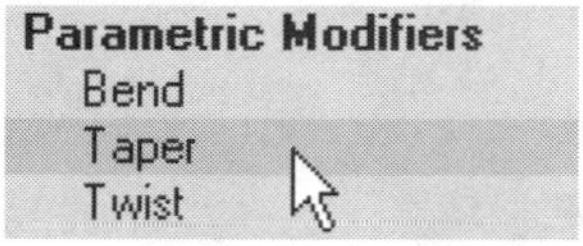

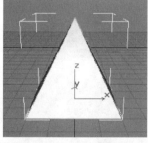

Figure 6.7 Choose a modifier from the Modifier List.

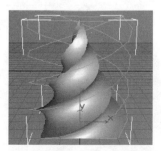

Figure 6.8 When you choose a modifier, it appears in the stack display at the top of the stack.

Figure 6.9 After adjusting the Taper modifier.

Figure 6.10 The result of applying a Twist to the tapered box.

To apply a modifier to an object:

1. Select an object (**Figure 6.6**).

2. Open the Modify panel 🎨.

3. Choose a modifier from the Modifier List drop-down menu (**Figure 6.7**).

or

Click a modifier button in a modifier set.

or

Click a modifier button in the Modifier tab panel.

or

Drag the name of a modifier from the Modifier List to the object.

The modifier is applied to the object. In the Modifier panel, the name of the modifier appears in the stack display, and the modifier parameters appear below (**Figure 6.8**).

4. Adjust the parameters of the modifier until the object looks the way you want it (**Figure 6.9**).

5. Apply as many modifiers as you want by repeating steps 3 and 4.

Every time you apply a modifier, it is added to the top of the modifier stack. When you adjust the parameters of each modifier, the object display updates in the viewports (**Figure 6.10**).

USING MODIFIERS

To remove a modifier from an object:

1. Select the modifier you want to remove by clicking its name in the stack display.

2. Click Remove Modifier from the Stack 🗑.

   The modifier is removed from the stack, and the modifier's effect upon the object ceases.

✔ Tips

- You can select multiple objects and apply modifiers to all of them at once.

- You undo the application and remove modifiers by clicking the Undo button ↶ or pressing Ctrl + Z.

The effect that modifiers have on an object depends upon the order in which they are evaluated. By clicking and dragging modifiers, you can rearrange modifiers in the stack so that they are evaluated in a different order.

To rearrange a modifier stack:

1. Select an object that has been modified (**Figure 6.11**).

2. Open the Modify panel 🖋.

3. In the stack display, click the modifier you want to move, and drag it to a new location in the stack (**Figure 6.12**).

   The modifier stack rearranges. The object in the viewport updates to reflect the new order of evaluation (**Figure 6.13**).

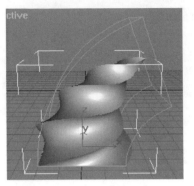

Figure 6.11 Selecting a box that has been modified.

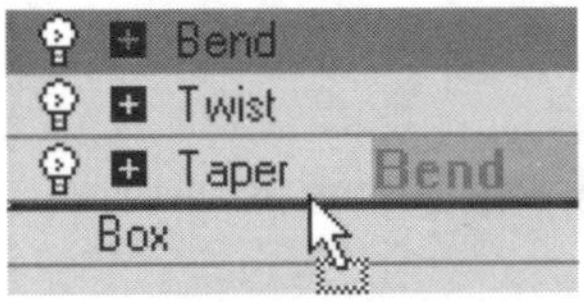

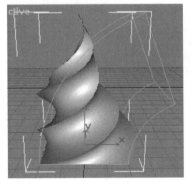

Figure 6.12 Dragging the Bend modifier from the top of the stack to the bottom.

Figure 6.13 The box changes shape, reflecting the different order of evaluation.

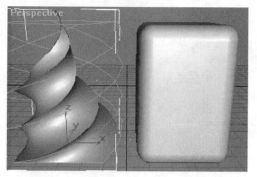

Figure 6.14 Selecting a box that has been modified.

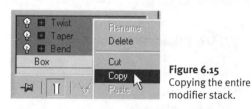

Figure 6.15 Copying the entire modifier stack.

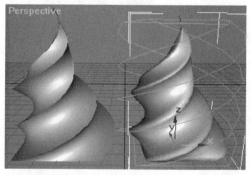

Figure 6.16 The result of pasting the modifiers onto the ChamferBox. Note that the ChamferBox has been set to a high face density.

Using the drag method, you can copy modifiers from a stack display of one object directly onto another object.

If you want to copy an entire modifier stack, it is easier to use the Copy and Paste commands.

To copy a modifier stack from one object to another:

1. Select a modified object (**Figure 6.14**).

2. Open the Modify panel ![icon].

3. In the stack display, click the modifier at the top of the stack. Then hold down the shift key and click the modifier at the bottom of the stack.
   The entire Modify stack is selected.

4. Holding down the Shift key, right-click on the selected modifiers, and choose Copy from the right-click menu (**Figure 6.15**).

5. Select the object that you want to paste the modifier stack onto.

6. In the stack display of that object, click just below the point where you want to insert the modifier. If the object does not have any modifiers in the stack, the name of the base creation object is selected.

7. Right-click the selection and choose Paste.
   The modifier is applied to the object (**Figure 6.16**).

✔ Tips

- Shift-dragging a modifier cuts it from the first object and pastes it onto the second.

- Ctrl-dragging instances a modifier before applying it to the second object, so that any changes you make to one modifier are replicated in the other.

- Use the Make Unique stack tool ![icon] to turn an instanced modifier into a copy.

- Pasting a modifier onto an incompatible object type has no effect on the object.

When you are satisfied with your modifications, you can choose to collapse the modifier stack.

Collapsing the modifier stack converts an object to an editable object and eliminates its modifier stack. Like taking a snapshot, collapsing the stack records the state of an object at a single moment in time. This stabilizes the object and saves memory because the program does not need to keep evaluating old parameters.

Because collapsing the stack eliminates creation parameters, make sure your object has enough segments, sides, and good basic proportions before you proceed.

To collapse the modifier stack:

1. Select a modified object.

2. Open the Modify panel.

3. In the stack display, right-click on any modifier.

   The right-click menu appears (**Figure 6.17**).

4. Click Collapse All.

   A warning appears to let you know that collapsing the stack removes all parameters (**Figure 6.18**).

5. Click Yes to collapse everything.

   or

   Click Hold/Yes if you want to save the scene in the hold buffer before collapsing the stack.

6. Click OK.

   All modifiers, their parameters, and the original creation parameters are collapsed. The object is converted to an editable object (**Figure 6.19**).

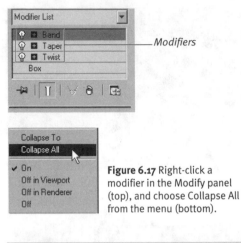

Figure 6.17 Right-click a modifier in the Modify panel (top), and choose Collapse All from the menu (bottom).

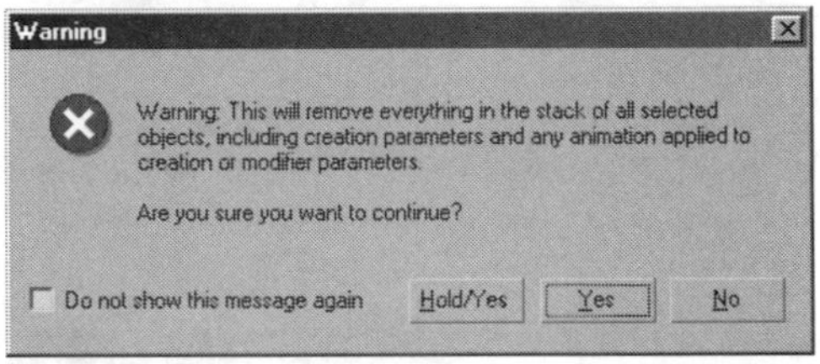

Figure 6.18 The Warning dialog box warns you of the consequences of collapsing the stack and gives you the option of holding the scene.

Figure 6.19 Collapsing the modifier stack freezes all the modifier parameters at their current state and replaces them with an editable object.

USING MODIFIERS

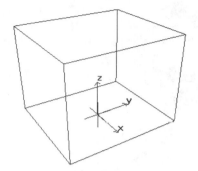

Figure 6.20 A modifier gizmo is a wireframe box that transfers the parameters of a modifier to an object. The center of the modifier lies within it.

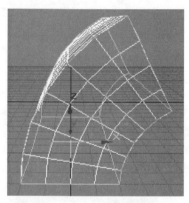

Figure 6.21 When you change the parameters of a modifier, you change the shape of its gizmo.

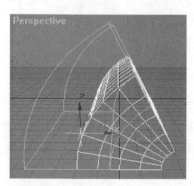

Figure 6.22 Transforming a gizmo changes its effect on an object.

Geometric Modifiers

Geometric modifiers use a wireframe box called a *modifier gizmo* to deform objects with respect to the axes of the gizmo and the modifier center (**Figure 6.20**). When you change the parameters of the modifier, the modifier gizmo changes shape. This in turn alters the shape of the object it modifies (**Figure 6.21**). (Modifier gizmos are not to be confused with transform gizmos, discussed in Chapter 5.)

Another way to affect the operation of a modifier is by selecting one of its components in the stack display and applying a transform. This can have a profound effect on the object it modifies (**Figure 6.22**).

Mesh objects deform by bending at their vertices, much like bones bending at joints. In order to deform objects smoothly, you usually need to increase the number of sub-objects that subdivide its surface so that the mesh can bend in smaller increments at each vertex. This is called increasing the density, or complexity, of a mesh.

Geometric modifiers are usually applied to geometry objects, but you can also apply them to shape splines and NURBS. In order to affect splines that are flat, you need to be sure to apply the modifier along the axes of the plane in which the spline is lying.

To facilitate your work, you start by learning how to display a modifier set that contains all the geometric modifiers and how to increase the complexity of a mesh primitive.

A Modifier set is a collection of buttons that apply modifiers to objects. 3ds max 4 ships with 11 modifier sets. You can choose to display any one of them, or configure your own modifier set.

Of the default sets, the Parametric modifier set is particularly useful for modifying mesh objects because it contains all the geometric modifiers.

To display the Parametric modifiers:

1. Open the Modify panel.

2. Click Configure Modifier Sets 🖼.

3. In the pop-up menu, choose Parametric Modifiers.

4. Click Configure Modifier Sets again. This time, choose Show Buttons.

   The Parametric modifier set buttons appear in the Modify panel. They are grayed out until you select an object (**Figure 6.23**).

Figure 6.23
The Parameters modifier set contains many geometric modifiers.

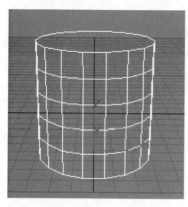

Figure 6.24 Select a box primitive.

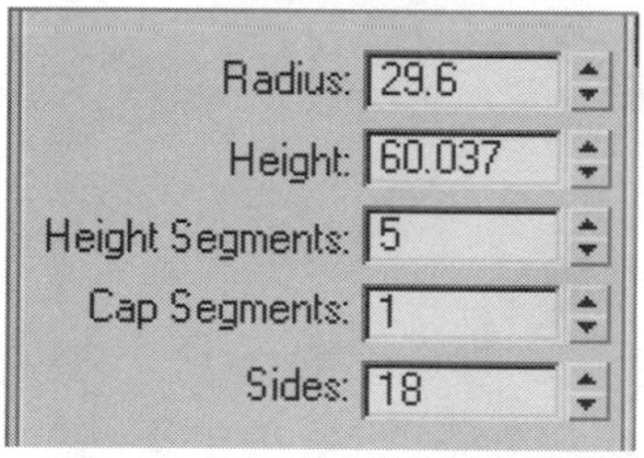

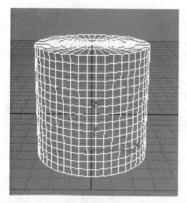

Figure 6.25 The creation parameters for a box. You increase the complexity of the box by increasing the number of length, width, and height segments.

![Figure 6.26 wireframe box illustration]

Figure 6.26 After increasing the complexity of the box.

If the object you want to deform is a mesh primitive, the simplest way to increase its density is by increasing its segments and/or sides parameters. However, if you convert a primitive to an editable mesh, you lose these parameters. In this case, the only ways you have of controlling mesh density is by hand-building faces using an edit modifier, or by applying a modifier that affects surface subdivision. For more information, see "Subdivision Modifiers" later in this chapter.

To increase the density of a mesh primitive:

1. Select a mesh primitive (**Figure 6.24**).

2. Open the Modify panel 🖊.

3. Select the name of the primitive from the bottom of the stack display.

   The creation parameters of the object appear in the Modify panel (**Figure 6.25**).

4. Increase the number of segments or sides to make your deformation smooth. If you are not sure how many divisions you will need, divide the surface evenly in all directions, or wait until you have applied your first geometric modifier and then return to this procedure.

   The mesh surface subdivides (**Figure 6.26**).

The Bend modifier bends an object uniformly throughout its geometry.

To bend an object:

1. Select an object (**Figure 6.27**).

2. 🖉 Open the Modify panel.

3. Click the Bend button.

   or

   Select Bend from the Modifier List
   (**Figure 6.28**)

   The Bend rollout appears (**Figure 6.29**).

4. Select a Bend axis.

   The Bend axis refers to the orientation of the modifier gizmo, which is not always the same as the orientation of the object.

5. Enter an Angle value in degrees, or drag the Angle spinner.

   The gizmo and the object bend together (**Figure 6.30**). If the object does not bend smoothly, increase the density of its mesh.

✔ Tips

- Changing the Direction parameter causes the object to bend perpendicular to the Bend axis.

- Check Limit Effect and enter a value to constrain the modifier to the upper or lower part of the object.

- If an object seems to lean or buckle or otherwise resists your attempts to deform it, try increasing the complexity of the mesh.

Figure 6.27 Select a box to bend.

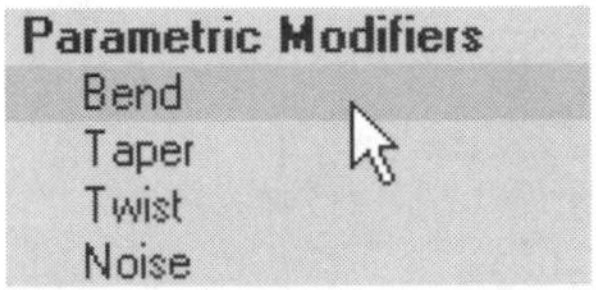

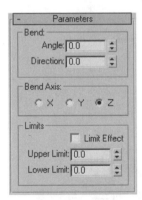

Figure 6.28 Select Bend from the modifier list.

Figure 6.29 The Bend rollout appears in the Modify panel.

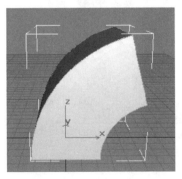

Figure 6.30 Bending the box in its Z axis. Notice that the gizmo and box bend together.

GEOMETRIC MODIFIERS

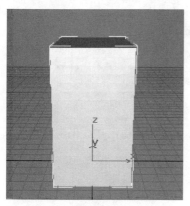

Figure 6.31 Select an object to twist.

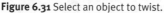

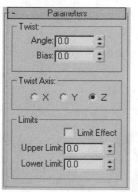

Figure 6.32 The Twist rollout appears in the Modify panel.

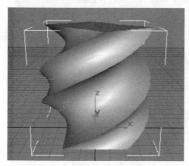

Figure 6.33 Twisting the box in its Z axis.

The Twist modifier causes an object to corkscrew along a central axis.

To twist an object:

1. Select an object (**Figure 6.31**).

2. Open the Modify panel 🖋.

3. Apply a Twist modifier.
   The Twist rollout appears (**Figure 6.32**).

4. Select a Twist axis for the gizmo.

5. Enter an Angle value in degrees, or drag the Angle spinner.

   The gizmo twists, and the object follows (**Figure 6.33**). If the object does not follow the gizmo smoothly, increase the density of its mesh along the axis that is being twisted.

✔ Tips

- Bias causes the object to twist more at one end of an axis than the other, like the Bias parameter of the Helix primitive.

- Check Limit Effect and enter a value to constrain the modifier to the upper or lower part of the object.

The Taper modifier tapers the sides of an object towards or away from a central axis.

To taper an object:

1. Select an object (**Figure 6.34**).

2. Apply a Taper modifier.

   The Taper rollout appears (**Figure 6.35**).

3. Select a primary axis.

   This sets the gizmo's central axis of tapering.

4. Select a Taper Axis for the Effect of the Taper gizmo.

   This determines which sides of the gizmo and object taper. Tapering is always symmetrical in the effect axis.

5. Enter an amount between -10 and 10, or drag the Amount spinner.

   The gizmo and the object taper together (**Figure 6.36**).

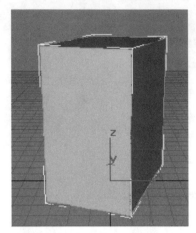

Figure 6.34 Select a box to taper.

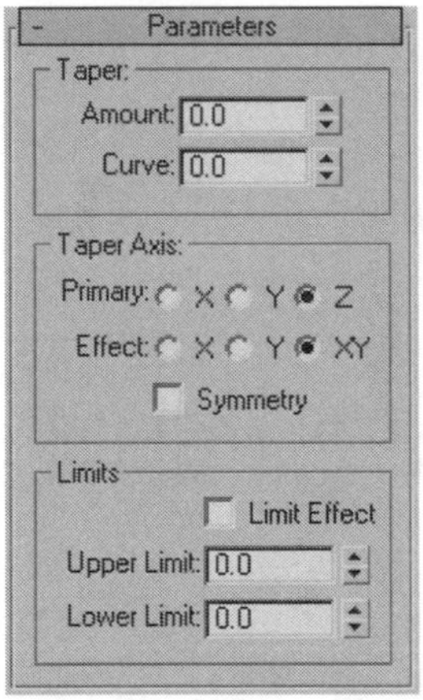

Figure 6.35 The Taper rollout appears in the Modify panel.

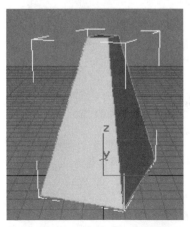

Figure 6.36 Tapering the box in its Z axis.

GEOMETRIC MODIFIERS

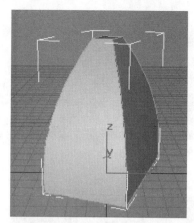

Figure 6.37 The result of adding a curve to the Taper modifier.

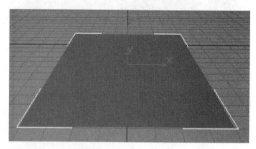

Figure 6.38 Select a plane object that has a lot of segments.

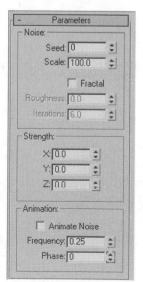

Figure 6.39 The Noise rollout appears in the Modify panel.

✔ Tips

- Enter a Curve value if you want to make the sides of the object curve as they taper (**Figure 6.37**).

- Check Symmetry if you want the taper to be symmetrical on both sides of the primary axis.

- Remember that you can animate nearly any parameter in 3ds max. For practice, animate each of these basic geometric modifiers by changing their parameters over time (see Chapter 7).

The random effect of Noise is very important because most surfaces in nature are irregular. On a small scale, Noise introduces surface texture to pristine, perfect surfaces, which makes them seem much more real. On a larger scale, Noise creates great surface contours for landscapes. Use it for rocks, hills, mountains, oceans, moons, asteroids, and alien planets.

To apply noise to a surface:

1. Select an object (**Figure 6.38**).

2. Apply a Noise modifier.
   The Noise rollout appears (**Figure 6.39**).

3. Set Scale to a number between 10 and 20 for starters.

continues on next page

GEOMETRIC MODIFIERS

155

4. Gradually increase the Strength parameters. For flat surfaces, you need only increase the one parameter that is perpendicular to the surface—usually the Z-axis.

The vertices of the mesh are increasingly displaced above and below the mesh surface in a random pattern (**Figure 6.40**). If the surface of the object becomes too choppy, go back to the bottom of the modifier stack and increase the density of the mesh.

5. For a rougher surface, check Fractal and increase the amount of roughness and the number of iterations (**Figure 6.41**).

✔ Tip

■ Checking Animate Noise automatically animates noise using the Frequency and Phase settings.

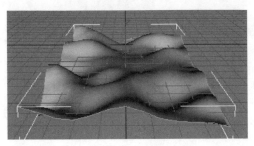

Figure 6.40 Noise randomly displacing the surface of the plane.

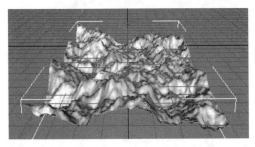

Figure 6.41 Fractal settings increase the roughness of the noise.

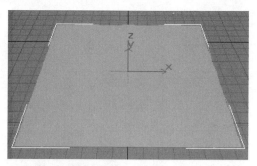

Figure 6.42 Select a plane object with a very dense mesh.

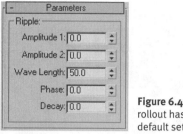

Figure 6.43 The Ripple rollout has effective default settings.

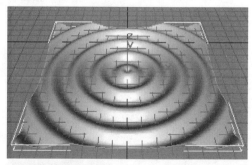

Figure 6.44 Rippling the Plane object with both amplitude settings.

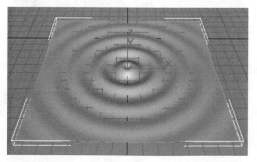

Figure 6.45 Decay causes the ripple effect to fall off from the center.

Ripple and Wave create wave patterns like ripples on water and shock waves in outer space. Because their parameters are exactly the same, only one modifier—Ripple—is shown here.

To ripple an object:

1. Select an object (**Figure 6.42**).

2. Apply a Ripple modifier .
    The Ripple rollout appears (**Figure 6.43**).

3. Adjust Amplitude 1 to affect rippling in one direction. Then adjust Amplitude 2 to affect the other direction (**Figure 6.44**).

4. Change the Wave Length as needed.

5. Use Decay if you want the ripple to fall off as it moves away from the modifier center (**Figure 6.45**).

✔ Tips

■ The Phase parameter helps you animate Ripple or Wave modifiers over time. You can also animate them by moving their centers or gizmos over time (see Chapter 7).

■ Two animation modifiers that deform geometry also work well for modeling objects:
    Melt collapses an object along an axis, giving it the appearance of melting.
    PathDeform deforms an object as it moves along a spline path of your choosing.

Normally, 3ds max evaluates transforms after modifiers, even though transforms may have been applied first. The XForm modifier is worthy of special mention because it gives you control over the order of evaluation by allowing you to place transforms anywhere in the modifier stack. Acting as a container, the XForm modifier can hold as many transforms as you like, or just one transform in each modifier. When you remove an XForm modifier, the transforms that it contains are removed as well.

No parameters come with the XForm modifier. The only inputs are the transforms you apply.

To use an XForm modifier:

1. Select an object (**Figure 6.46**).

2. Apply an XForm modifier.
   The XForm modifier has no parameters.

3. Move, rotate, and/or scale the object.
   The object is transformed, and the object transforms are placed in the modifier stack (**Figure 6.47**).

✔ Tips

- Moving the modifier center moves the center of rotation and scaling.

- A Linked XForm modifier causes an object to inherit the transforms of the object to which it is linked.

- The Transform quad menu allows you to quickly select transforms (**Figure 6.48**).

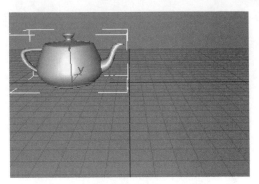

Figure 6.46 Select an object.

Figure 6.47 Moving the teapot on the XY plane. The transform will be stored in the XForm container in the modifier stack.

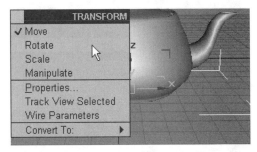

Figure 6.48 This context-sensitive menu allows you to change and constrain transforms.

Figure 6.49 The upper part of an FFD rollout.

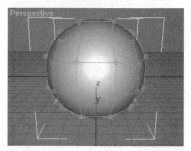

Figure 6.50 A free form deformation lattice of control points conforming to a sphere.

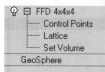

Figure 6.51 Selecting the control points sub-object in the stack display.

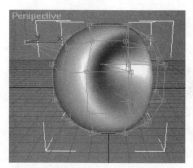

Figure 6.52 The result of moving a single control point back through a GeoSphere.

Free Form Deformation

Free form deformation (FFD) modifiers deform objects using a lattice of control points instead of a gizmo. The more control points in the lattice, the better you can articulate the deformation.

To freely deform an object:

1. Select a Mesh object.

2. Apply an FFD modifier.

   The FFD rollout for that modifier appears (**Figure 6.49**).

   A lattice of control points surrounds the object (**Figure 6.50**).

3. Click Conform to Shape.

4. In the stack display, access the sub-object components of the modifier by clicking the plus sign next to its name. Then select Control Points from the rollout (**Figure 6.51**).

5. Select and transform the control points of the lattice ⊕ ↻ ▯.

   Each control point deforms the part of the object that is closest to it (**Figure 6.52**).

✔ Tips

- Locking the control points makes them easier to transform and prevents them from being accidentally deselected. Remember to unlock them when you want to choose different control points.

- If you need to have finer control over your deformation, choose FFD Cyl or FFD Box, and click Set Number of Points to increase the number of points in the lattice.

Subdivision Modifiers

You control the surface complexity of a mesh primitive by adjusting its segments and sides parameters. Once a primitive has been converted to an editable object, however, these creation parameters disappear.

Tessellate increases the complexity of a mesh by subdividing edges and faces.

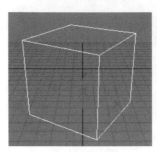

Figure 6.53 Select a box.

To tessellate a mesh:

1. Select a Mesh object (**Figure 6.53**).

2. Apply a Tessellate modifier.

    The Tessellate rollout appears (**Figure 6.54**).

    The complexity of the object increases automatically (**Figure 6.55**).

3. Try both the Edge and Face-Center options to see which one makes the object look better.

4. Increase the Iterations value to further increase the complexity of the mesh (**Figure 6.56**).

Figure 6.54 The Tessellate rollout offers two ways to increase mesh density.

✔ Tips

- Face-center divisions work better on objects with planar surfaces, such as boxes.

- To tessellate a limited surface area, select the area at a face level using Mesh Select before applying the Tessellate modifier.

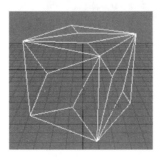

Figure 6.55 The box after one iteration of tessellation.

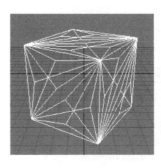

Figure 6.56 The tessellated box after a second iteration.

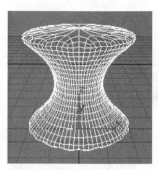

Figure 6.57 Select a mesh object to optimize.

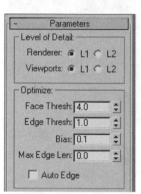

Figure 6.58 The Optimize rollout has different settings for viewport display and rendered output.

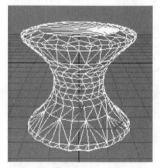

Figure 6.59 After optimizing the Mesh object.

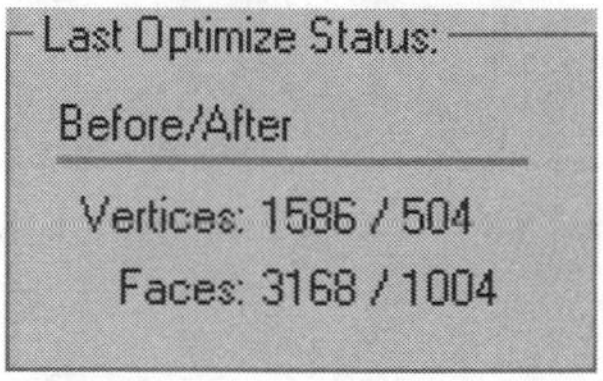

Last Optimize Status:

Before/After

Vertices: 1586 / 504

Faces: 3168 / 1004

Figure 6.60 This counter shows you the number of faces and vertices before and after the mesh is optimized.

The Optimize modifier intelligently reduces mesh density by eliminating coplanar faces, which are not needed for defining structural details and slow down your work.

To optimize a mesh:

1. Select an object (**Figure 6.57**).

2. Apply an Optimize modifier.
   The Optimize rollout appears (**Figure 6.58**).

3. Slowly increase the Face Threshold while keeping an eye on the viewports. Stop when curved surfaces begin to lose their smoothness.
   The number of faces decreases, reducing the complexity of the mesh (**Figure 6.59**).

✔ Tips

- Level of Detail has two settings: one for viewports and one for rendered output.

- To see how many vertices and faces have been eliminated, check the Before/After counter at the bottom of the rollout (**Figure 6.60**).

- For a complete description of Optimize parameters, see the online help files.

SUBDIVISION MODIFIERS

MeshSmooth works by adding an extra face for every vertex and edge in a mesh.

To MeshSmooth a mesh:

1. Select an object (**Figure 6.61**).

2. Apply a MeshSmooth modifier.

   The MeshSmooth rollout appears (**Figure 6.62**).

   The object is automatically smoothed using the default parameters (**Figure 6.63**).

3. Adjust the Subdivision Amount parameters.

   Slowly increase the Iterations value to increase the overall number of divisions in the mesh.

4. Reduce the Smoothness value to optimize the mesh.

✔ Tips

■ The MeshSmooth type is set to NURMS by default. NURMS stands for Non-Uniform Rational MeshSmooth, a humorous play on the term NURBS. For complete instructions on how to use the weighted control mesh and the other MeshSmooth types, see the online help files.

■ To avoid severely deforming objects with planar surfaces, make sure that the mesh has a reasonable number of divisions on each side before you apply MeshSmooth.

■ MeshSmooth can be used as a modeling tool because it rounds off corners and edges at the same time. Starting with rough, block forms, you can quickly create birds, fish, monsters, and spaceships. Try combining MeshSmooth with the Extrude modifier to convert splines to rounded forms.

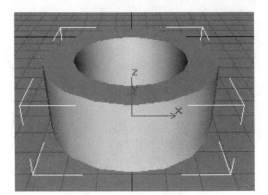

Figure 6.61 Select a tube.

Figure 6.62 The MeshSmooth rollout. As with Tessellate and Optimize, you increase the MeshSmooth effect by increasing the number of iterations.

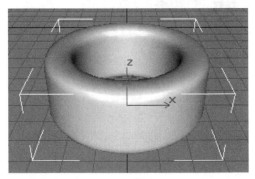

Figure 6.63 After MeshSmoothing the Tube. Note the rounded edges.

Figure 6.64 The more directly a surface normal points toward the light, the brighter its face is shaded by the program.

Figure 6.65 This Teapot object has two smoothing groups. One group has been smoothed; the other has not.

Modifiers That Affect Surface Rendering

Rendering is the process by which a 3D program draws an image of a 3D scene. There are a number of variables to take into account: the point of view; the system of projection; the position of objects; lighting; object properties such as color and visibility; the mode of display; and so on.

To speed up rendering, 3ds max shades only the outside surfaces of objects unless you set it to do otherwise. This means that each face is shaded only on one side—the side that the surface normal projects from. By comparing the angle of a normal to the source of light, the program determines how much intensity, or brightness, of light it should use to render each individual face (**Figure 6.64**).

In faceted shading modes, faces stand out distinctly on curved surfaces because each face is rendered with a different intensity. In smooth shading modes, faces blend together in a smooth gradient because the program averages the intensity values between normals. With the Smooth modifier, you can set smoothing for an entire object, or for discrete selections of faces (**Figure 6.65**).

The Normal modifier allows you to invert, or *flip* surface normals, so that the inside of a surface is shaded instead of the outside.

To flip the normals of an object:

1. Select an object (**Figure 6.66**)

2. Apply a Normal modifier.
   The Normal rollout appears (**Figure 6.67**).

3. Check Flip Normals.
   The surface normals of the faces are flipped. The opposite sides of the faces are rendered (**Figure 6.68**).

There are two ways you can flip normals of individual faces: by applying a Normal modifier to a selection of faces, or by clicking faces with Flip Normal mode enabled. The advantage of using Flip Normal mode is that you can see the results update in the viewport as you work.

To flip normals of individual faces:

1. Select an object.

2. Apply an Edit Mesh modifier or convert the object to an editable mesh.

3. Enable Face or Polygon level selection.

4. Open the Surface Properties rollout, and click Flip Normal Mode (**Figure 6.69**).

5. Click the faces that you want to flip.
   The faces flip interactively (**Figure 6.70**).

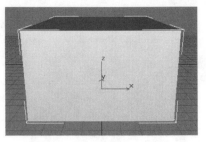

Figure 6.66 Select an object that you want to turn inside out.

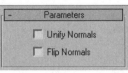

Figure 6.67 The Normal rollout has just two parameters.

Figure 6.68 After flipping the normals of the box

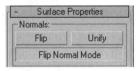

Figure 6.69 The Surface Properties rollout contains an option for flipping normals interactively.

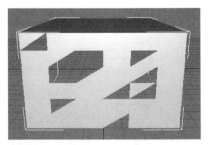

Figure 6.70 The result of flipping the normals of a selected faces in a box.

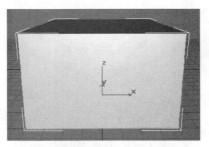

Figure 6.71 After unifying the normals of the box.

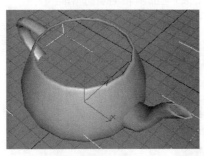

Figure 6.72 A lidless teapot makes a good practice object.

Figure 6.73 The STL-Check rollout gives you different options for checking the structure of a mesh.

Sometimes normals get flipped accidentally, such as when you import an object into 3ds max. You should suspect flipped normals whenever you see triangular holes in the surface of an object.

To unify normals:

1. Select an object that you suspect has flipped normals.

2. Apply a Normal modifier.

3. Check Unify Normals.

   The flipped normals are restored to their original orientation (**Figure 6.71**).

The STL-Check and Cap Holes modifiers find and fix actual holes in your mesh.

To fix holes in a mesh:

1. Select an object that has holes in it. For practice, try creating a lidless teapot by unchecking the lid element (**Figure 6.72**).

2. Apply an STL-Check modifier.
   The STL-Check rollout appears (**Figure 6.73**).

3. In the Errors group, check Open Edge. Then check Select Edges.

   continues on next page

4. Check the box next to Check.

The open edges become selected and turn red, indicating they are next to an open area (**Figure 6.74**).

5. Apply a Cap Holes modifier.

The holes are covered with new faces (**Figure 6.75**).

Note: the new faces may not be visible, but you can see the difference in the face count by viewing the object information in the Object Properties dialog box before and after applying the modifier.

✔ Tip

■ Use this combination of modifiers to fix holes in preparation for Boolean operations. (For information on Boolean operations, see Chapter 10, Compound Objects.)

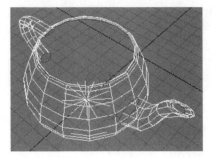

Figure 6.74 The STL-Check modifier selects open edges, which turn red. Here we see that the teapot has open edges around the lid, rim, spout, and handle.

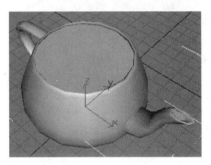

Figure 6.75 Applying a Cap Holes modifier automatically builds a cap on the openings of a teapot.

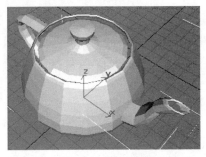

Figure 6.76 The Smoothing Groups rollout parameters allow you to smooth faces in numbered groups, or smooth an entire object.

You can smooth an object in its entirety, or you can smooth discrete selections of faces.

For mesh primitives, you control smoothing for the entire object by checking or unchecking the Smooth creation parameter. Editable objects do not give you this option, so you must apply a Smooth modifier instead.

To smooth an object:

1. Select a mesh object

2. Apply a Smooth modifier.

    The Smooth rollout appears (**Figure 6.76**). The object is unsmoothed (**Figure 6.77**).

3. Check Auto Smooth.

    The faces that meet at an angle that is less than the Threshold parameter are smoothed (**Figure 6.78**).

    continues on next page

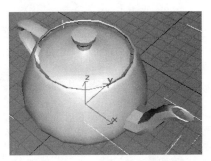

Figure 6.77 When you first apply a Smooth modifier it turns off smoothing for the object.

Figure 6.78 After checking Auto Smooth, every face that meets its neighbors at an angle greater than the smooth threshold is smoothed.

MODIFIERS THAT AFFECT SURFACE RENDERING

4. Increase the Threshold value until the most sharply angled faces are smoothed.

or

Uncheck Auto Smooth and click button number 1 in the Smoothing Groups area.

All the faces in the object are assigned to the same smoothing group. The entire object becomes smoothed (**Figure 6.79**).

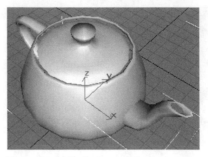

Figure 6.79 After increasing the smoothing threshold to 180°.

Creating Creases

Another use for the Smooth modifier is for creating creases. By assigning adjacent selections of faces to different smoothing groups, you can keep the program from smoothing the edges between them.

For the convenience of selecting and smoothing faces within the same modifier, apply an Edit Mesh modifier or convert the object to an editable mesh. Then enable face or polygon level selection and use the Surface Properties rollout to access smoothing commands (**Figure 6.80**).

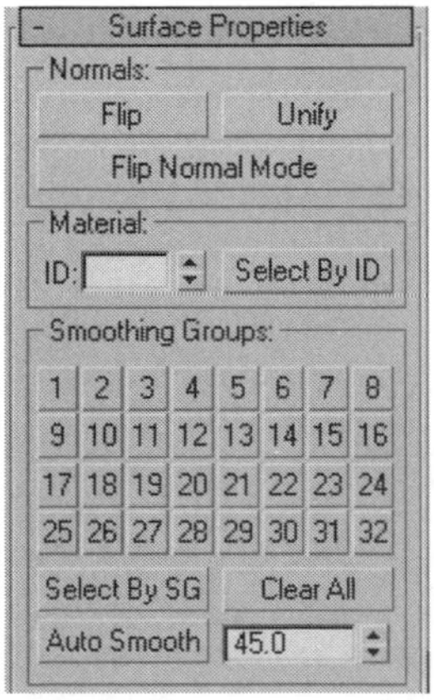

Figure 6.80 The Surface Properties rollout allows you to smooth selections of faces, as well as to select faces by smoothing group.

Figure 6.81 Select a star shape to extrude.

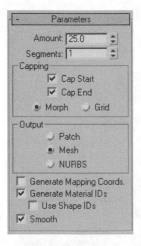

Figure 6.82
The Extrude rollout
has settings for the
amount of extrusion as
well as the number of
segments that will be
built on the sides.

Figure 6.83 The extruded star.

Generating Geometry

With modifiers you can create custom geometry objects by extruding, lathing, or beveling splines. The complexity of the output is determined by the number of vertex points on the original spline and the parameter settings in each modifier.

The Extrude modifier generates a mesh object by extruding a spline in a straight line along its Z axis.

To extrude a spline:

1. Select a spline object (**Figure 6.81**).

2. Apply an Extrude modifier.
   The Extrude rollout appears (**Figure 6.82**).

3. Enter an Amount value.
   The spline is extruded. If the spline is a closed shape, then a cap of faces is built in the enclosed area by default (**Figure 6.83**).

✔ Tips

- To increase the complexity of the output object, increase the Segments parameter.

- To create patches or NURBS objects, choose Patch or NURBS in the Output area.

- To extrude a spline along the path of another spline, see "Loft Objects" in Chapter 10 , Compound Objects.

GENERATING GEOMETRY

The Lathe modifier generates a mesh object by revolving a spline on an axis.

To lathe a spline:

1. Select a spline (**Figure 6.84**).

2. Apply a Lathe modifier.
   The Lathe rollout appears (**Figure 6.85**). The spline is lathed along its central Y axis (**Figure 6.86**).

3. Adjust the axis of revolution as needed.
   To use a different axis of revolution, click X or Z in the Direction group.

   To align the axis of revolution to the minimum, center, or maximum extents of the object, click Min or Max in the Align group (**Figure 6.87**).

   To make the axis of revolution able to be moved freely, click Lathe in the stack display and then click the Axis sub-object

Figure 6.84 Select a spline to lathe.

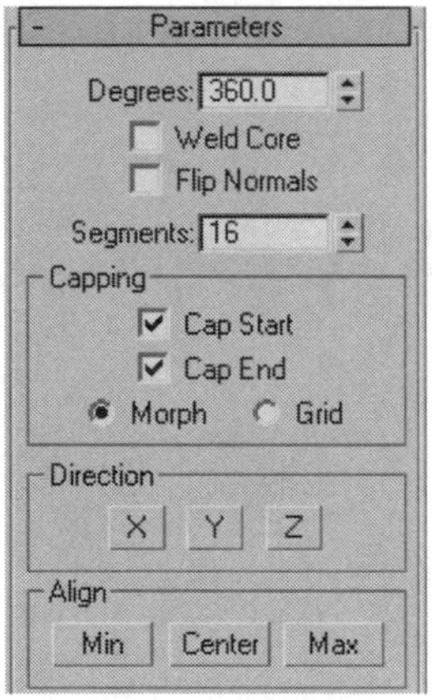

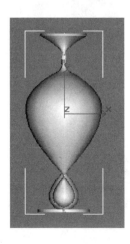

Figure 6.85 The Lathe rollout can be set for different object axes.

Figure 6.86 The lathed spline.

Figure 6.87 After clicking the Max button, the axis of rotation aligns to the right side of the shape.

✔ Tips

- To outline a shape spline, as in this example, see "To outline a spline" in Chapter 9.

- To lathe an object less than 360 degrees, decrease the Degrees parameter.

- Check Flip Normals if the object appears to be inside out.

- To increase the complexity of the lathed object, increase the Segments parameter.

- Enabling Weld Core causes coincident vertices along the axis of revolution to be welded together. Uncheck this box if you are creating morph targets so you can control the number of vertices that are generated. (See Chapter 10 for more information on morphing.)

The Bevel modifier extrudes a spline using different widths to bevel the edges.

To bevel text:

1. Select a Text Spline object (**Figure 6.88**).

2. Apply a Bevel modifier.

   The Bevel rollout appears (**Figure 6.89**). The text is capped.

3. In the Bevel Values rollout, enter a value for the Start Outline, or leave the value at 0.

   The starting width of the outline is set.

4. Set the Height and Outline values for Level 1.

   Height sets the initial extrusion amount, and Outline sets the bevel amount (**Figure 6.90**).

5. Set the Height and Outline values for Level 2 and, if needed, Level 3.

   Setting values for each level causes additional extrusion and beveling to be added to the text (**Figure 6.91**).

✔ Tips

- In the Parameters rollout, check Smooth Across Levels to smooth the edges of the levels.

- Bevel Profile is a related modifier that extrudes a spline using a second spline to define the outline of the beveled edge.

Figure 6.88 A text object can be extruded and beveled.

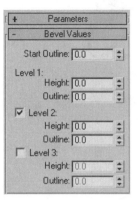

Figure 6.89 The lower half of the Bevel rollout.

Figure 6.90 After setting the initial extrusion and bevel amounts.

Figure 6.91 Rendered output of a two-level bevel.

ANIMATION

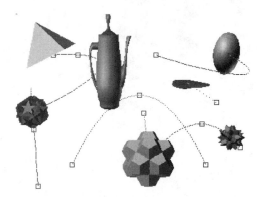

Figure 7.1 Animation brings a scene to life.

Animation introduces the concept of time. We recognize that time is passing by observing changes in our world: sunlight moving through the clouds, a beating heart, a ticking clock, bodies dancing to a beat, the steady rhythm of machines, rivers flowing to the sea, the turning cycles of the moon and stars. We also draw conclusions about the passage of time by comparing experience to memory: white hair, a wrinkled brow, an empty glass, an empty house. Time can make the world empty or full, high or low, light or dark, loud or soft, near or far, old or new.

According to Webster, the word animation is based on the Latin verb *animare*, which means, to give life to. This chapter tells you how to bring objects to life by changing their creation parameters and transforming them over time (**Figure 7.1**).

Applying traditional animation principles such as anticipation, squash and stretch, overlapping action, exaggeration, and follow-through can infuse your scenes with humor and bring them to life. An excellent reference to get you started is *The Illusion of Life: Disney Animation*, revised edition, by Frank Thomas and Ollie Johnston (Hyperion, 1995).

Keyframing

When you view a sequence of images in rapid succession, a physiological phenomenon called *persistence of vision* occurs, in which each image persists in your eyes and brain until the next image takes its place. This creates the illusion of continuous motion that we call animation.

In animation, images that you play back in sequence are called frames. The faster the frames play, the smoother the motion appears to be. Common playback rates are 15, 24, and 30 frames per second, or fps. That adds up to 900, 1440, or 1800 frames per minute of animation!

3D animation derives many of its terms and techniques from traditional animation methods, like the ones developed at Walt Disney Studios. In traditional cel animation, a head animator draws key poses, or *keyframes,* to show the high point of an action. Junior animators draw the frames in between, or *tweens,* that make the action appear to flow smoothly.

In 3D animation, you create keyframes by changing parameters or transforming objects over time. *Animation controllers* store these settings in *animation keys,* and act as your dream team of junior animators by instantly interpolating the values of all the tweens.

An *animation track* is a sequence of events that are governed by an animation controller. Animation tracks usually contain a series of animation keys, although some tracks contain graphic representations of their input, such as the ticks of a metronome or the waveform of a sound file.

In 3ds max 4, animation tools are found in the status bar, locks and controls area (**Figure 7.2**), the Motion panel (**Figure 7.3**), and the Track view (**Figure 7.4**). When tools appear in more than one area, preference is given to the area that is the most convenient to access and easy to use.

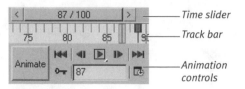

Figure 7.2 Animation tools in the status bar, locks and controls area.

Figure 7.3 You assign motion controllers and manipulate trajectories and keys in the Motion command panel.

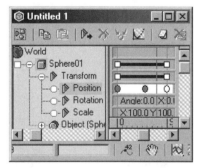

Figure 7.4 The Track view allows you to assign all animation controllers, and perform operations on both controllers and keys.

KEYFRAMING

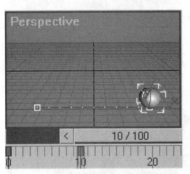

Figure 7.5 The readout on the time slider displays 0/100, indicating that you are at frame 0 of 100.

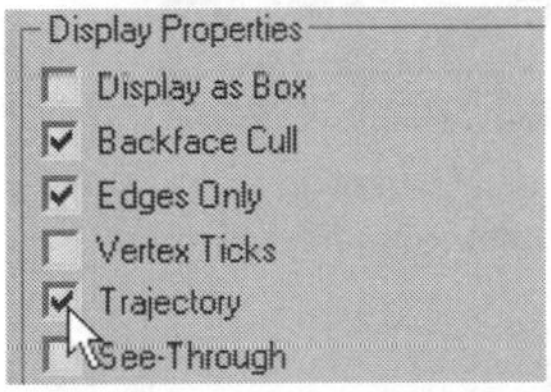

Figure 7.6 Turn on the trajectory in the Object Properties dialog box or the Display panel.

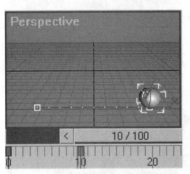

Figure 7.7 Making a change at frame 10 sets keys at frame 0 and frame 10. The trajectory shows the object's motion through space.

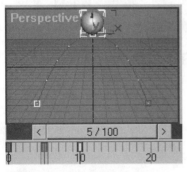

Figure 7.8 Setting a key at frame 5. Note that the trajectory curves to follow the object.

By default, time is measured as a sequence of frames. When you animate an object, 3ds max sets a *key* in the track bar at the current frame. This indicates that the frame is a keyframe, and provides a means of adjusting the animation.

To create a transform animation:

1. Drag the time slider all the way to the left (**Figure 7.5**).

2. Click the Animate button.

   The Animate button, time slider channel, and the active viewport boundary turn red.

3. Select an object.

4. Position, rotate, or scale the object to the state you would like it to be in at the beginning of the animation.

5. Turn on the object's trajectory display from the Object Properties dialog box or from the Display panel (**Figure 7.6**).

6. Drag the time slider to the right, so that the readout of the current frame number increases.

   The scene moves forward in time.

7. Transform the object in some way.

   A key is set in the track bar at frame 0 and at the current frame. If you moved the object, a red and white trajectory traces its path (**Figure 7.7**).

8. Drag the time slider back and forth to get a rough sense of the animation. This is called *scrubbing* the time slider.

9. Create additional keyframes as needed by moving the time slider and making more changes (**Figure 7.8**).

10. Click Play Animation.

    The animation plays back all frames in sequence from 0 to the final frame.

    If the object has a trajectory, it follows the trajectory from beginning to end.

11. Turn off the Animate button, or like the sorcerer's apprentice, you may get results you did not intend.

KEYFRAMING

175

You can animate virtually any parameter in 3ds max. You can set such scene parameters as background color, background animations, ambient light, and render-effect parameters.

For selected objects, you can set creation parameters and the parameters of any command that has been applied to them, including as modifiers, space warps, and material parameters.

To create a parametric animation:

1. Drag the time slider all the way to the left.

2. Click the Animate button .

   The Animate button, time slider channel, and boundary of the active viewport turn red.

3. Set the parameters of your scene or object to the state you would like it to be in at the beginning of the animation (**Figure 7.9**).

4. Drag the time slider to the right.

   The scene moves forward in time.

5. Change the parameters to the state you would like them to be in at this point in time (**Figure 7.10**).

   A key is set in the track bar at frame 0 and at the current frame.

6. Drag the time slider back and forth to get a rough sense of the animation.

7. Create additional keyframes as needed by moving the time slider and making more changes.

8. Click Play Animation .

   As the animation plays back, the parameters change over time (**Figure 7.11**).

9. Turn off the Animate button .

✔ Tip

■ Pressing the forward slash key (/) toggles animation playblack to start and stop.

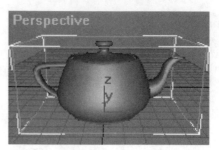

Figure 7.9 Setting the initial state of an object by applying a geometric modifier to it.

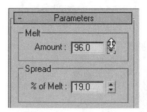

Figure 7.10 Changing parameters of a Melt modifier.

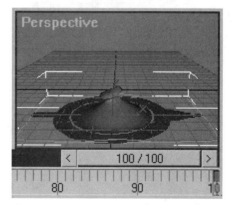

Figure 7.11 The object appears to melt into the grid when you play back the animation.

KEYFRAMING

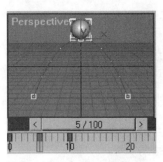

Figure 7.12 Selecting an object makes its animation keys appear.

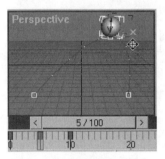

Figure 7.13 Adjusting a motion key adjusts the trajectory of an object.

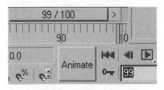

Figure 7.14 Entering a frame number moves the time slider to that frame.

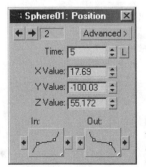

Figure 7.15 Opening the Key Info dialog box allows you to precisely adjust values.

You adjust keyframes by adjusting the animation values stored in their keys.

To adjust a keyframe:

1. Select an animated object.

   The animation keys of the object appear in the track bar (**Figure 7.12**).

2. Turn on the Animate button.

3. Click Key Mode toggle.

4. Click Next Key or the Previous Key until the time slider reaches the key you want to adjust.

5. Transform the object or change its parameter settings in the Modify panel.

   The values stored in the animation keys are adjusted. If the object has been animated to move through space, the trajectory of the object adjusts as well (**Figure 7.13**).

6. Click Play Animation.

   The animation plays back in the viewport, reflecting the adjustments you have made.

7. Repeat steps 4 through 6 until all the keyframes are set the way you want.

✔ Tips

- You can move the time slider to a specific frame by entering the frame number in the animation controls (**Figure 7.14**).

- Another way to adjust key values is by changing the XYZ Value parameters of the key info dialog box. To access this dialog box, right-click on the key and choose the object and key type from the list at the top of the pop-up menu (**Figure 7.15**)

KEYFRAMING

Working with Keys

Animation keys are the values of animated parameters or transforms at keyframes. By manipulating keys, you adjust the timing, duration, and repetition of your animation.

There are three ways you can work with keys: in the track bar, in the Motion panel, and in the Track View module. The easiest way to work with keys is in the track bar.

To select a key:

1. In the track bar, click the key that you want to select.

   The key and the track bar turn white (**Figure 7.16**).

2. To add to your selection, hold down the Ctrl key while clicking additional keys or dragging a selection region around them (**Figure 7.17**).

✔ Tips

■ To subtract a key from a selection, Alt + click on the key.

■ To see the range of your selection, right-click in the track bar and choose Configure > Show Selection Range (**Figure 7.18**). A black bar appears at the bottom of the track bar to indicate the range between the first and last key in your selection (**Figure 7.19**)

■ To filter keys in the track bar so that only parametric animation keys appear, right-click the track bar and choose Filter > Object from the pop-up menu.

■ To filter keys in the track bar so that only transform animation keys appear, right-click the track bar and choose Filter > All Transform Keys from the pop-up menu.

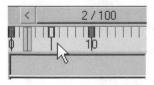

Figure 7.16 Selecting a key in the track bar.

Figure 7.17 Dragging a selection region around multiple keys.

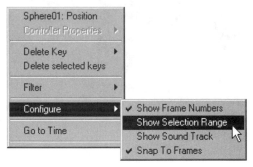

Figure 7.18 The Configure pop-up menu allows you to set different display options for the track bar.

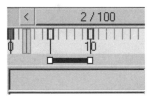

Figure 7.19 The selection range bar extends from the first key to the last key in your selection.

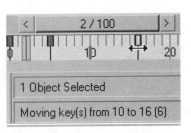

Figure 7.20 Dragging a key in the track bar.

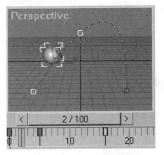

Figure 7.21 Moving a position key deforms the trajectory of an object.

Figure 7.22 Dragging a selection range bar moves the keys in the selection.

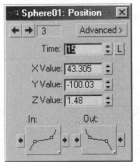

Figure 7.23 You can change the position of a key in time in the Key Info dialog box.

Moving keys in the track bar adjusts the timing of an animation. Moving keys closer together speeds up the animation. Moving keys farther apart makes the animation run slower.

To move a key:

1. Select a key by clicking it.

2. Drag the key to the left or right.

   As you drag the key, a small line marks the original location of the key until the mouse button is released. The prompt line displays the old frame number of the key, the new frame number, and the number of frames moved (**Figure 7.20**).

   If the object displays a trajectory, the trajectory will deform if you move a position key (**Figure 7.21**).

✔ Tips

- To move multiple keys, select the keys you want to move and drag any one of them. If the selection range bar is displayed, you can move your selection by dragging the range bar (**Figure 7.22**).

- Another way to move keys is by changing the Time parameter of the dialog box. To access this dialog box, right-click on the key and choosing the object and key type from the list at the top of the pop-up menu (**Figure 7.23**).

WORKING WITH KEYS

Cloning animation keys allows you to copy a portion of your animation and move it forward or backward in time.

If you clone an animation key and place it next to the original, the animation will pause between the clone key and the original key.

If you select and clone a group of keys, the animation of the entire group will be repeated.

To clone a key:

1. Select a key in the track bar.

2. Hold down the Shift key, and drag the key to a new location.

   A copy of the key is placed at the new location (**Figure 7.24**).

   If a trajectory is displayed, it will deform accordingly (**Figure 7.25**).

3. To clone multiple keys, make a multiple selection and then Shift-drag them.

✔ Tip

■ You can also clone keys by right-clicking the time slider to open the Create Key dialog box. There you select a key from one position (the source time) and copy it to another position (the destination time) (**Figure 7.26**).

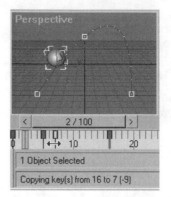

Figure 7.24 Dragging a clone (right) from an original key.

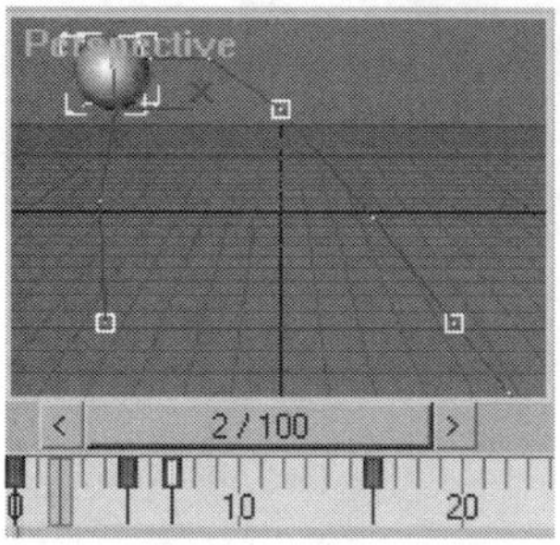

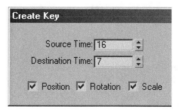

Figure 7.25 A trajectory deforms in response to cloning a key.

Figure 7.26 The Create Key dialog box allows you to clone keys to exact frame locations.

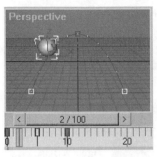

Figure 7.27 An object and its trajectory.

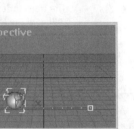

Figure 7.28 The trajectory after deleting the key.

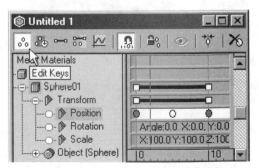

Figure 7.29 You can delete all the animation keys from an object using the track bar right-click menu.

Deleting keys removes animation data from objects.

To delete a key:

1. Select a key in the track bar (**Figure 7.27**).

2. Press the Delete key.
   The animation at that keyframe is removed from the object (**Figure 7.28**).

3. Deleting all keys removes all animation data from an object, so that the animation of the object ceases altogether.

To delete all keys:

1. Right-click on any key in the track bar.

2. Choose Delete Key > All from the right-click menu (**Figure 7.29**).
   All animation is removed from the object.

✔ Tip

■ You can also add, move, clone, and delete keys in the Edit window of the Track View 🔲 when it is set to Edit Keys mode (**Figure 7.30**).

Figure 7.30 The of the Track View Edit window.

You can adjust a trajectory in the viewports interactively by dragging its keys.

To adjust a trajectory:

1. Select an object that has a trajectory.

2. Open the Motion panel ⊚.

3. Click the Trajectories button.

   The Trajectories rollout appears (**Figure 7.31**).

   The trajectory of the object appears, if it was not already displayed (**Figure 7.32**).

4. Click the Sub-Object button to enable access to the object's keys.

5. Select and move ✛ a key in the trajectory.

   The trajectory deforms to follow the key (**Figure 7.33**).

6. Play the animation ▶ to see the results.

   The animation plays back in the viewports, following the new shape of the trajectory.

✔ Tip

■ You can select multiple keys, clone keys, and add and delete keys in a trajectory in much the same way you do in the track bar.

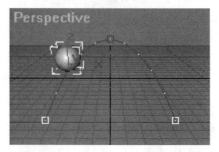

Figure 7.31
The Trajectories rollout of the Motion panel is where you adjust trajectories and their keys.

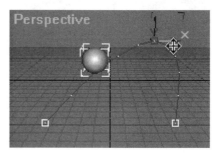

Figure 7.32 The trajectory before adjusting it.

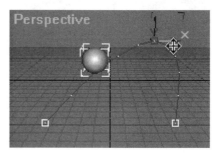

Figure 7.33 After adjusting keys in the trajectory.

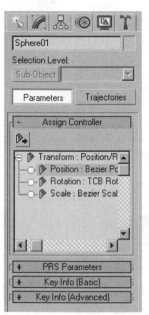

Figure 7.34
The Parameters
rollout of the Motion
panel contains four
tracks: the Position,
Rotation, and Scale
tracks, plus a general
Transform track.

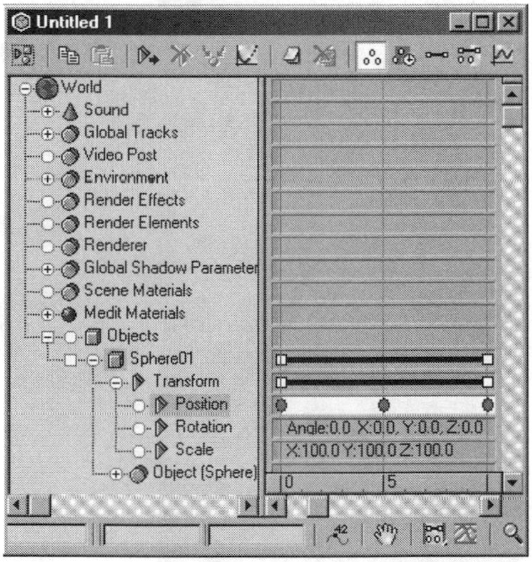

Figure 7.35 The Track View is a highly complex module
that includes tracks for every animatable parameter
and transform. When you select a track from the list
on the left, you can manipulate keys, time, ranges,
and function curves in the Edit window on the right.

Animation Controllers

Animation controllers store key values and
interpolate tween values using mathematical
functions.

You assign animation controllers to trans-
form animation tracks in the Motion panel
(**Figure 7.34**) or in the Track View module
(**Figure 7.35**).

In the Track View, you can also assign controllers to parametric animation tracks. In
addition, the Track View enables you to:

♦ add sound tracks

♦ create visibility tracks

♦ create animation cycles

♦ cut, copy, and paste controllers between
tracks

♦ edit keys

♦ edit time

♦ edit and position ranges

♦ edit function curves

♦ filter tracks

The following exercises use the Motion
panel by preference because of its relative
ease of use and because a book of this size
cannot do the Track View justice; that would
require another book. But to get you started,
the Track View is frequently referred to in
tips as an alternative method of working, and
presented in more detail when you need to
accomplish tasks that cannot be completed
in the Motion panel or the track bar, such as
editing function curves, adding sound tracks,
and creating animation cycles.

For more information on the Track View,
look up "Track View" in the 3ds max 4 User
Reference.

Five animation controllers stand out as being particularly useful for both parametric and transform animations:

Bézier—Interpolates tween values using an adjustable spline function that curves smoothly through key values by default. This is what causes trajectories to initially appear curved. The default controller for position and scale keys.

TCB—Interpolates tween values using a smooth function curve with tension, continuity and bias controls. The default controller for rotation keys.

Linear—Interpolates tween values using a linear function curve, so that change progresses steadily from one key to another. Use to create machine-like movements, or any other change that takes place at a constant pace.

Noise—Produces random values using fractal-based functions that use parameters instead of keys for input. Use to create random changes.

Audio—Converts the amplitude of sound waves from .avi and .wav files into scale values for X, Y, and Z. Use to make objects dance to music, or to lip-synch a character to the sound of its voice.

In the Track View, *function curves* display line graphs of the X, Y, and Z values generated by each animation controller. Like trajectories, function curves provide you with strong visual feed back about the nature of your animation (**Figure 7.36**).

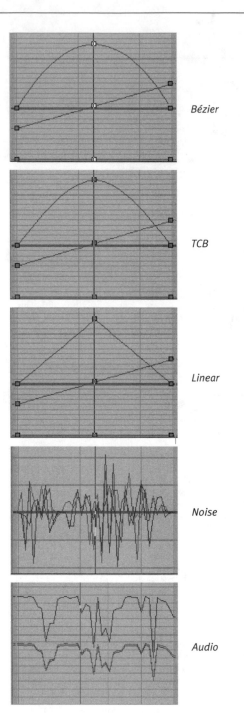

Bézier

TCB

Linear

Noise

Audio

Figure 7.36 The function curve of a bouncing ball for different controllers.

ANIMATION CONTROLLERS

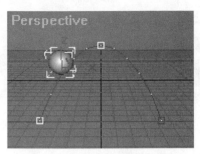

Figure 7.37 An object and its trajectory with a Bézier controller assigned.

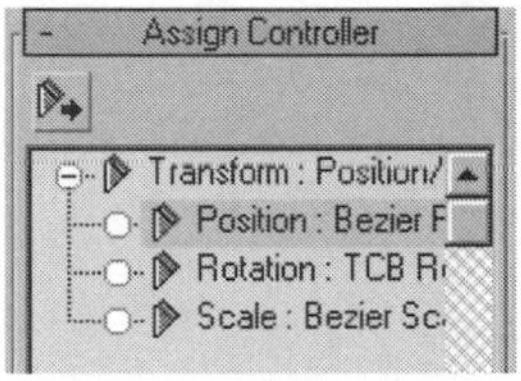

Figure 7.38 When you select an animation track, the Assign Controller button (top) becomes available.

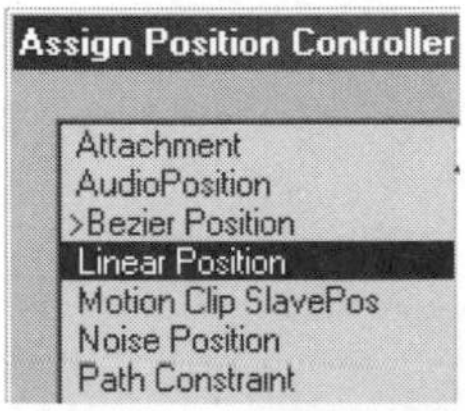

Figure 7.39 The Assign Controller dialog box presents all the controllers that can be applied to the selected track.

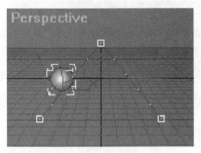

Figure 7.40 After assigning a Linear position controller to the object.

Every animation track has an animation controller assigned to it by default. In the Motion panel, you change controller assignments by selecting an animation track and choosing a new controller. Parameters vary from controller to controller. The Linear position controller (used in the example below) has no parameter settings.

To assign a controller:

1. Select an object (**Figure 7.37**).

2. Open the Motion panel 🖲.

3. In the Parameters rollout, open the Assign Controller rollout.

4. Select one of the four animation tracks. The Assign Controller button becomes available (**Figure 7.38**).

5. Click the Assign Controller button 🖲. The Assign Position Controller dialog box appears for that track (**Figure 7.39**).

6. Select a controller, and click OK. The controller is assigned to the track. The trajectory of the object updates to reflect the effect of the new controller (**Figure 7.40**).

7. Play the animation 🖲 to see the results.

✔ Tip

■ To assign a controller in the Track View, right-click on the word Objects in the list on the left and choose Expand All. Then select the track you want to reassign and click the Assign Controller button 🖲.

Bézier and TCB controllers allow you to adjust tween interpolation between each key. This affects the acceleration of objects.

Objects usually speed up or slow down gradually as they start, stop, or change direction. Abrupt acceleration or braking usually indicates extreme agitation, a collision, or mechanical motion.

To adjust a Bézier controller:

1. Apply a Bézier controller to a transform animation track.

2. In the Parameters rollout of the Motion panel 🔘, open the Key Info (Basic) rollout.

3. Use the arrows at the top left corner of the rollout to navigate to the key you want to adjust (**Figure 7.41**).

   The time slider advances to the next keyframe. At the same time, the object moves to the next key on the trajectory.

4. Click the In button and choose the Linear, Step, Slow, or Fast tangent type from the flyout (**Figure 7.42**).

   For position controllers, the trajectory of the object approaching the key changes shape (**Figure 7.43**).

5. Click the Out button, and choose the Linear, Step, Slow or Fast tangent type from the flyout.

   For position controllers, the trajectory of the object after the key changes shape (**Figure 7.44**).

6. Play ▶ the animation to see the results.

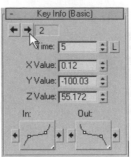

Figure 7.41 Advancing to the next key. The Key Info (Basic) rollout has inputs for time, XYZ values, and tangent types. The default tangent type is Smooth.

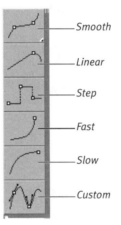

Figure 7.42 Tangent types.

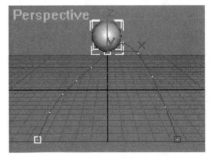

Figure 7.43 After assigning a Linear tangent type to the In parameter of the key.

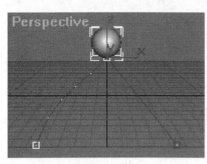

Figure 7.44 After assigning a Step tangent type to the Out parameter of the key.

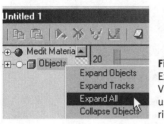

Figure 7.45 Expand the Track View hierarchy using the track right-click menu.

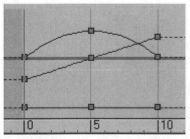

Figure 7.46 For the bouncing ball, the Y function slopes up and down, the X function increases steadily, and the Z function stays the same.

✔ Tips

■ You can also adjust controllers by right-clicking a key in the Track View or by right-clicking a key in the track bar and choosing the object and key from the top of the menu.

■ The tangent copy buttons ⬆⬇ next to the tangent typescopy tangent types to the next or previous tangent.

The Bézier Custom tangent type is the only tangent type that you can adjust using Bézier handles. You adjust Custom tangent types using function curves in the Track View Edit window.

To adjust a Custom tangent type:

1. Apply a Bézier controller to an animation track.

2. Set the tangent type of the key you want to adjust to Custom.

3. Open the Track View ▣.

4. In the Track View toolbar, click Function Curves ▥.

5. On the left side of the Track View, move the hierarchy list up by dragging on the white background area. Stop when the Objects track is near the top of the window.

6. Right-click Objects and choose Expand All (**Figure 7.45**).

7. Select the animation track you applied the Bézier controller to.

   The function curve for the animation track appears (**Figure 7.46**).

   In the function curve display, X values appear in red, Y in green, and Z in Blue.

continues on next page

8. At the bottom of the Track View, click Zoom Horizontal Extents ▨ to make the function curve fit in the Edit window. You can also choose Zoom Horizontal Extents Keys ▨ from the flyout to make the function curve fit from the first to last key.

9. Click Zoom Value Extents ▨ to make the function curve fit in the Edit window vertically.

10. In the Edit window, adjust the key by dragging it or dragging its Bézier handles.

    The function curve changes shape (**Figure 7.47**).

    If the object has a trajectory, the trajectory changes shape as well (**Figure 7.48**).

11. Play the animation ▣ to see the results.

With a TCB controller, you set acceleration in and out of keys using the Ease To and Ease From parameters. The Tension, Continuity, and Bias parameters affect the shape of the function curve and the shape of the object's trajectory, if it has one.

To adjust a TCB controller:

1. Apply a TCB controller to an animation track, such as the position track.

2. In the Parameters rollout of the Motion panel ⊙, open the Key Info rollout.

3. Use the arrows at the top left corner of the rollout to navigate to the key you want to adjust (**Figure 7.49**).

    The time slider advances to the next keyframe. At the same time, the object moves to the next key on the trajectory.

4. Adjust the Ease To and Ease From parameters to set the acceleration to and from keys. Use higher values to decrease acceleration, lower values to increase it (**Figure 7.50**).

5. Play the animation ▣ to see the results.

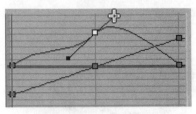

Figure 7.47 Dragging the Bézier handle of the second key.

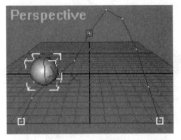

Figure 7.48 The trajectory deforms in response to the changes you made to the function curve of the position track.

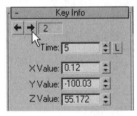

Figure 7.49 Click the arrow buttons to navigate to the key you want to adjust.

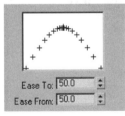

Figure 7.50 Increasing Ease To and Ease From to their maximum values causes the animation to slow down as it approaches the key and gradually speed up as it departs.

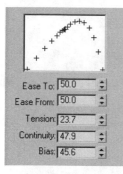

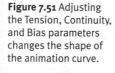

Figure 7.51 Adjusting the Tension, Continuity, and Bias parameters changes the shape of the animation curve.

Figure 7.52 The trajectory of a TCB position controller responds to the new key settings.

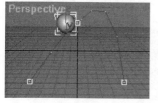

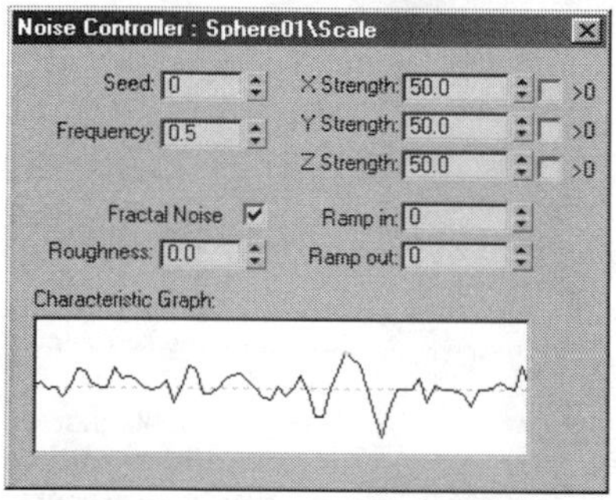

Figure 7.53 The Noise Controller dialog box allows you to make random changes to an animation track.

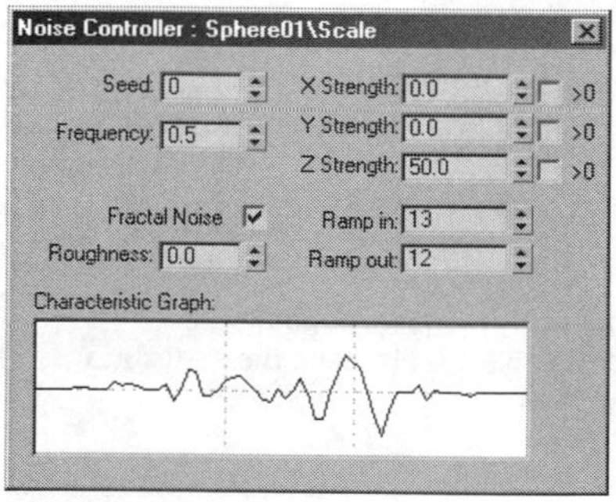

Figure 7.54 These settings will make the Noise gradually affect the Z direction and then taper off.

6. Adjust the Tension, Continuity, and Bias parameters to set the shape of the function curve:

   Adjust the Tension parameter to set the amount of curvature. Increased tension makes the function curve straighten out and slightly increases easing.

   Adjust the Continuity parameter to set the tangent value, similar to the action of a Bézier handle. Easing is unaffected.

   Adjust the Bias parameter to set the peak of the curve relative to the key. High bias moves the peak ahead of the key.

   The animation curve in the rollout changes shape (**Figure 7.51**). For position controllers, the trajectory of the object changes shape to match (**Figure 7.52**).

7. Play the animation ▶ to see the results.

You adjust the Noise controller by changing the seed value, frequency, roughness, strength, and ramping in and out parameters.

To adjust a Noise controller:

1. Apply a Noise controller to an animation track, such as the scale track.

   The Noise Controller dialog box appears (**Figure 7.53**).

2. Play the animation ▶ to see the results.

3. In the Noise Controller dialog box, adjust the shape of the noise graph by adjusting the seed value, frequency, roughness, strength, and ramping in and out parameters.

   To make the Noise smoother, uncheck Fractal Noise.

   To make the Noise affect a single direction, set two of the three X, Y, and Z Strength parameters to 0.

   To make the Noise ramp in and out slowly, increase the Ramp in and Ramp out values (**Figure 7.54**).

4. Play the animation ▶ to see the results.

You adjust an Audio controller by importing and manipulating a sound file, and by configuring the object's response to the amplitude (volume) of the sound wave.

To learn how to create a sound track, see the section entitled, "Adding Sound" later in this chapter.

To adjust an Audio controller:

1. Apply an Audio controller to an animation track.

   The Audio Controller dialog box appears (**Figure 7.55**).

2. In the Audio Controller dialog box, click Choose Sound.

3. In the Open Sound dialog box, navigate to a .wav or .avi file on your hard drive or network. Then click OK (**Figure 7.56**).

4. Set the base parameters, or use the default. This sets the state of the object at zero amplitude (when there is no sound).

   The default setting leaves the object unchanged during silence.

5. Set the target parameters of the object. This sets the state of the object at maximum amplitude (at peak volume) (**Figure 7.57**).

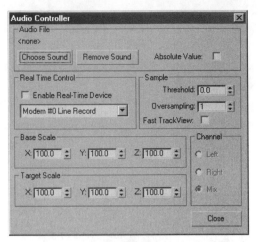

Figure 7.55 The Audio Controller dialog box allows you to control an animation track with an external sound file.

Figure 7.56 The Open Sound dialog box allows you to import a .wav file or an .avi file that has an audio stream from anywhere in your network.

Figure 7.57 Setting the target Z parameter to 500 makes the object scale along the Z axis by a maximum of 500%.

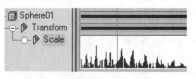

Figure 7.58 A sound wave in a scale track.

6. Close the Audio Controller dialog box.

   In the Track View, a sound wave appears in the animation track that you applied the audio controller to (**Figure 7.58**).

7. Play the animation ▶ to see the results.

✔ Tips

- To provoke a stronger response to the sound, check Absolute Value. This ensures that the target values are reached at maximum amplitude, rather than the *potential* maximum amplitude of the wave.

- To set a lower limit of response, increase the Threshold value.

- To smooth the sound wave, and the object's response to it, increase Oversampling.

Animation Constraints

Animation constraints are animation controllers that constrain transform animations with respect to one or more target objects. Two very useful constraints to know are the Path constraint and the LookAt constraint.

The Path constraint restricts an object to move along a path.

To assign a path constraint:

1. In the Parameters rollout of the Motion panel, assign a Path constraint to the position track of an object.

2. In the Path constraint rollout, click Add Path. Then pick an open or closed spline. The spline appears in the list of target paths (**Figure 7.59**).
   The object moves to the first vertex of the spline (**Figure 7.60**).

3. To make an object orient in the direction of the path, click Follow (**Figure 7.61**).

4. Play the animation [image]. The object follows the path from beginning to end (**Figure 7.62**).

✔ Tips

- If you are using a three-dimensional spline path and you want to make your object bank like a racecar through the curves, click Bank

- To change the beginning and end point of the animation, turn on the Animate button and adjust the % Along Path parameter.

- If you add multiple paths, the object will be constrained to an average distance between the paths. To make an object move closer or farther from the path, select the path and increase or decrease the Weight parameter.

- To make an animation deform like an eel as it follows a path, use a PathDeform modifier instead of a Path constraint.

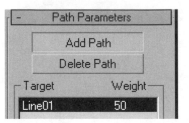

Figure 7.59 After adding Line01 as a path.

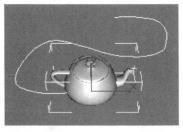

Figure 7.60 Adding a path causes the object to move to the first vertex of the spline. To reverse the order of vertices, see Chapter 8.

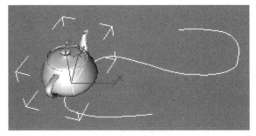

Figure 7.61 Check Follow to make the object orient along the length of the path.

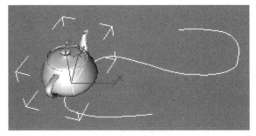

Figure 7.62 The object follows the path when you play the animation.

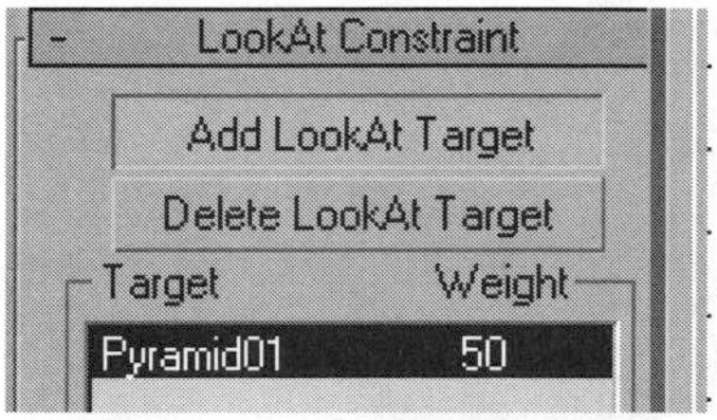

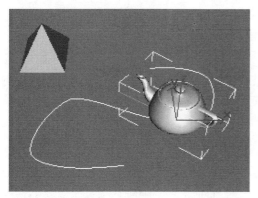

Figure 7.63 After picking Pyramido1 to be a LookAt target.

Figure 7.64 The teapot faces the pyramid no matter where it moves along the path.

The LookAt constraint causes an object to keep facing another object, no matter where the objects move in relation to each other. This can be used not only for geometry, but also for lights and cameras that follow objects through a scene.

To assign a LookAt constraint:

1. In the Parameters rollout of the Motion panel, assign a LookAt constraint to the rotation track of an object.

2. In the Path constraint rollout, click Add LookAt Target. Then pick a target object (**Figure 7.63**).

   The object rotates to face the target object.

3. Play the animation .

   The object faces the target, no matter where the objects are positioned in space relative to each other (**Figure 7.64**).

✔ Tip

■ To change the axis of orientation of the object, choose an axis in the Select LookAt Axis group.

Adding Sound

To import a sound file so that the sound plays back with the animation, you use the Track View.

To import a sound track:

1. Open the Track View ⊞.

2. Select the Sound track from the top of the scene hierarchy.

3. Right-click on Sound, and choose Properties (**Figure 7.65**).

4. In the Sound Options dialog box, click Choose Sound (**Figure 7.66**). Then choose a sound file.

   A waveform branch appears in the Track View hierarchy underneath the Sound track. Click the plus sign (+) next to the word Sound to see the waveform track (**Figure 7.67**).

5. Play the animation ▶ to hear the results.

✔ Tips

- By combining a sound track with audio controllers, you can make your scene objects dance to music.

- To see the sound wave in the track bar, right-click on the track bar, and choose Configure > Show Sound Track (**Figure 7.68**).

Figure 7.65 Choose Properties from the Sound right-click menu.

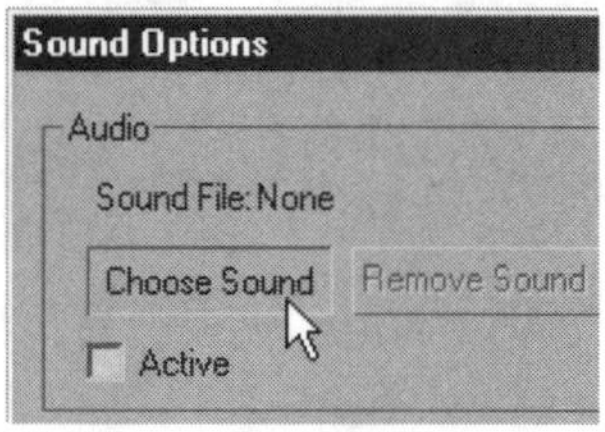

Figure 7.66 Choose a sound file in the Sound Options dialog box.

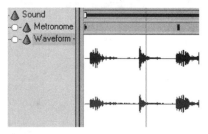

Figure 7.67 The Waveform track displaying a sound wave.

Figure 7.68 After turning on the sound track in the track bar.

ADDING SOUND

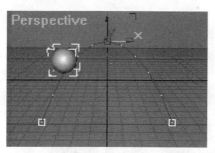

Figure 7.69 The object after animating a single cycle in the animation.

Figure 7.70 Expanding the Track View Hierarchy to see all tracks.

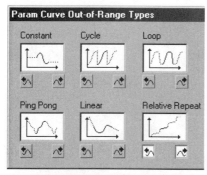

Figure 7.71 Choosing an animation pattern.

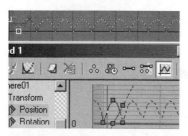

Figure 7.72 The function curve loops or cycles, depending on the pattern you chose.

Animation Cycles

If you want to create an animation that repeats cyclically outside of the range of its keys, you use Parameter Curves Out-of-Range Types. Patterns include:

◆ **Cycle**—Repeats the animation sequence.

◆ **Loop**—Repeats the animation sequence and smoothly interpolates between cycles.

◆ **Ping Pong**—Repeats the animation sequence backward and forward.

◆ **Relative Repeat**—Repeats the sequence and offsets repetitions to build on each other.

To cycle an animation:

1. Create a simple animation, such as a ball bouncing once over the course of 10 frames (**Figure 7.69**).

2. Click Open Track View 🖳 in the main toolbar.

3. On the left side of the Track View, move the hierarchy list up by dragging on the white background area. Stop when the Objects track is near the top of the window.

4. Right-click Objects, and choose Expand All from the pop-up menu (**Figure 7.70**).

5. Find the name of the object that you animated. Underneath it, you will find the object transforms. Click Position.
   The Position track is highlighted.

6. Click Function Curves 📈 in the toolbar at the top of the Track View module.
   The position function curve appears.

7. Click Parameter Curve Out-of-Range Types 📈 in the Track View toolbar.

8. Choose a pattern by clicking its graph (**Figure 7.71**). Then click OK.
   The pattern that you chose is reflected in the position function curve (**Figure 7.72**).

9. Play the animation 🖳 to see the results.

Linking Objects

To increase the possibilities of transform animation, you can create a one-way link between objects so that one object passes its transforms onto the other. The *child* object that inherits the transforms will then move, rotate, or scale in the same way as the *parent*.

By linking a series of objects together, you can create a branching tree structure called a linked hierarchy. This allows you to create sophisticated animation sequences involving multiple objects and complex motions.

Objects in linked hierarchies are referred to as if they are members of a family or parts of a tree:

◆ **Child**—An object that has been linked to another object.

◆ **Parent**—The object to which a child object is linked. Each child can have only one parent, but a parent object can have multiple children.

◆ **Grandparent**—The parent of a parent.

◆ **Ancestor**—The parent and all of a parent's parents.

◆ **Grandchild**—The child of a child.

◆ **Descendant**—The child and all of a child's children.

◆ **Root**—An object at the top of a hierarchy.

◆ **Scene**—The root of an object that is not linked to a parent.

◆ **Leaf**—An object at the end of a hierarchy.

◆ **Branch**—The path through a hierarchy from an ancestor to a leaf.

The Schematic View ⊞ is a module that allows you to view and modify linked hierarchies (**Figure 7.73**). It is accessed from the main toolbar and from the Graph Editors menu.

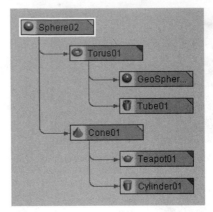

Figure 7.73 A linked hierarchy in the Schematic view displaying one grandparent, two parents, and four children.

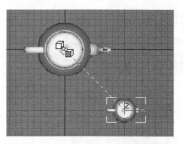

Figure 7.74 Release the mouse button when the link cursor turns white.

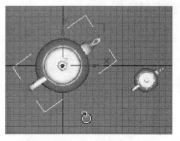

Figure 7.75 Moving the parent object causes the child to move with it.

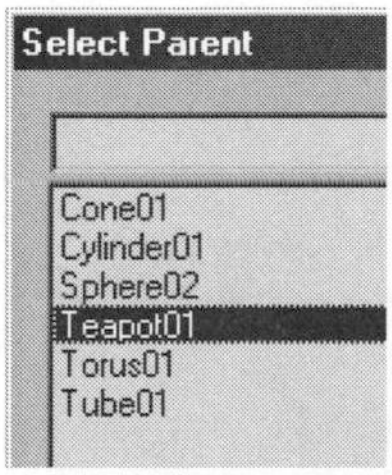

Select Parent

Cone01
Cylinder01
Sphere02
Teapot01
Torus01
Tube01

Figure 7.76 The Select Parent dialog allows you to pick a parent by name. The rest of the dialog box looks just like the Select Object dialog box, except the Select button says Link instead of Select.

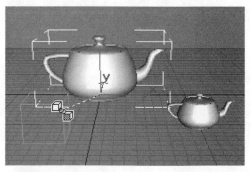

Figure 7.77 A dummy object can be used for an additional pivot point, or as a substitute for a more complex object.

The Select and Link tool links the pivot point of a child object to the pivot point of its parent. When linked, the child inherits the transforms of the parent. You cannot link a parent to its child.

To link an object:

1. Select an object.
   This will be the child object.

2. Choose Select and Link 🔗 from the main toolbar.

3. Drag the Link cursor from the selected object to a second object. When the upper box in the cursor turns white, release the mouse button (**Figure 7.74**).
   The second object (the parent) flashes, indicating that the objects are linked.

4. Test the link by transforming the parent object in some way.
   The child follows the parent (**Figure 7.75**).

5. Exit Select and Link mode by clicking the Select Object button 🔲.

✔ Tips

- To select a parent from a list, instead of by dragging, press the H key (**Figure 7.76**).

- If you need an additional pivot point for your animation, create a dummy object from the Helpers menu 🔲 to serve as a stand in. Dummy objects are non-rendering wireframe boxes that are often used for animating lights and cameras. They can also serve as proxies for more complex objects that you replace them with later (**Figure 7.77**).

The Unlink Selection tool halts the flow of transform data from parent to child.

To unlink an object:

1. Select a child object.

2. Choose Unlink Selection 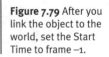 from the main toolbar.

3. Click the child object.
   The child object unlinks from its parent.

Using a Link constraint, you can make a child object switch links to different parent objects over time. This causes the child to inherit the transforms of each parent in sequence.

To animate link inheritance:

1. Select an object.

2. Open the Motion panel.

3. Open the Assign Controller rollout and highlight the Transform controller.

4. Click Assign Controller . Then choose the Link Constraint (**Figure 7.78**).

5. Move the time slider to frame 0.

6. In the Link Params rollout, click Link to World. Then change the Start Time to −1. This keeps the object from moving when you assign the first new link (**Figure 7.79**).

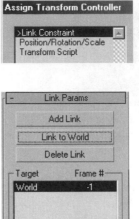

Figure 7.78 Assigning a Link constraint to the transform controller.

Figure 7.79 After you link the object to the world, set the Start Time to frame −1.

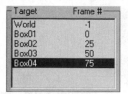

Figure 7.80 After linking the object to four boxes at frames 0, 25, 50, and 75.

Figure 7.81 The object is passed from one swinging box to another. Here at frame 45, Box02 is about to pass the sphere to Box03.

7. Move the time slider to frame 0.

8. Click Add Link. Then pick a target object to transfer link inheritance to.

9. Move the time slider to the point in the animation where you want to switch links.

10. Repeat steps 8 and 9 until you have added all the target objects you want (**Figure 7.80**).

11. Play the animation.

    As the animation plays back, the object changes links. The parent objects pass their transform animations to the child object (**Figure 7.81**).

✔ Tips

■ To adjust the timing of link transfers, move the time slider to the frame number in question. Then highlight a target object and drag the Start Time spinner.

■ To delete a link, highlight the link target in the target display and click Delete Link.

Configuring Time

Time is surprisingly flexible. It can move fast or slow, speed up or slow down, or appear to stand still. When you are immersed in work that you love, the hours fly by in the blink of an eye. At other times, when there is resistance, time crawls as slowly as the hands of a clock. In the mind of a child, a year lasts an eternity. But in the memory of an elder, years collapse into moments, like dewdrops suspended in a spider's web.

3ds max gives you the ability to manipulate time, and conduct the mysterious rites of relativity. With max, you can make frames run faster, or slow down to only a few frames per second. You can make an animation last longer or shorter, and you can even scale time up or down to change the speed of action and the timing of events.

The Time Configuration dialog box allows you to set time parameters such as length, playback rate and units of measurement. It also allows you to rescale time and control how time flows when you play back animations in the viewports. Access the Time Configuration dialog box in the status, locks and controls area by right-clicking on the animation controls or by clicking the Time Configuration button 🔲.

You set the length of an animation in terms of number of frames or units of time. Usually it is more convenient to work with frames.

To set the length of an animation:

1. Click Time Configuration 🔲.

   The Time Configuration dialog box appears (**Figure 7.82**).

2. In the Animation group, enter the length (**Figure 7.83**).

   The length of the animation changes. The distance between keys in the track bar shrinks or expands.

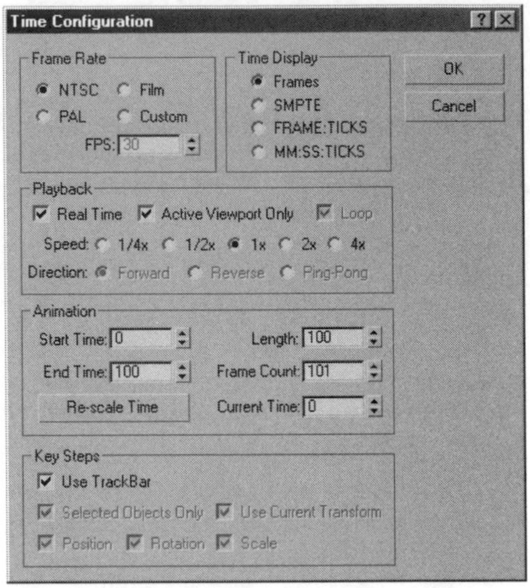

Figure 7.82 The Time Configuration dialog box allows you to set time parameters.

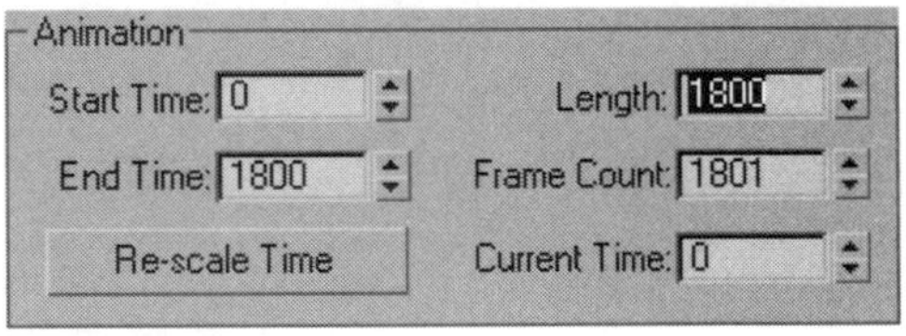

Figure 7.83 Setting the length of an animation to 1800 frames yields one minute of animation at 30 frames per second.

CONFIGURING TIME

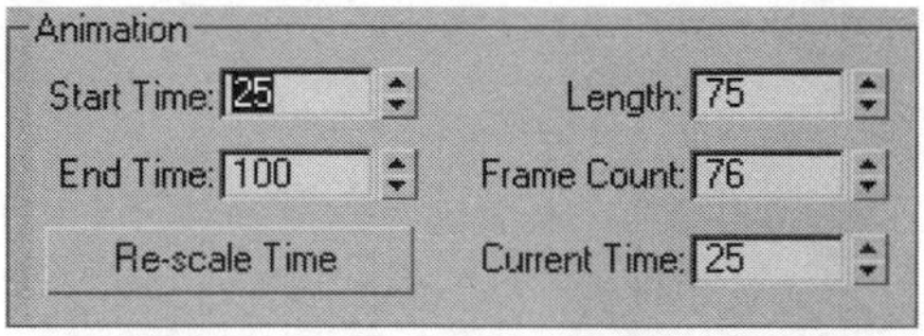

Animation

Start Time: 25   Length: 75

End Time: 100   Frame Count: 76

Re-scale Time   Current Time: 25

Figure 7.84 Entering a new start time sets the beginning point of the active time segment.

Animation

Start Time: 25   Length: 50

End Time: 75   Frame Count: 51

Re-scale Time   Current Time: 25

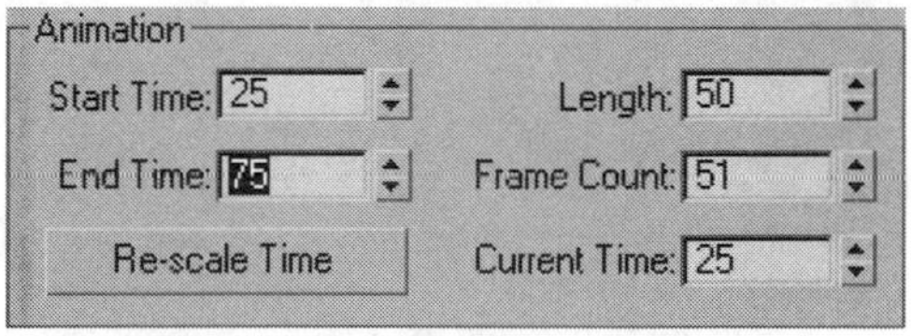

Figure 7.85 Entering a new end time sets the end point of the active time segment.

| < | 75 / 50 | > |

Figure 7.86 The time display on the time slider updates whenever you reconfigure time.

Technically, in 3ds max, you define the length of the active time segment, rather than the length of the animation itself. The active time segment is a period of time that is displayed on the time ruler and shown in the viewports. By default, the active time segment is set to the start and end point of the animation. Changing the start and end times of the active time segment shifts this window in time to wherever, or whenever, you need to work. The rest of the animation remains intact and out of view.

To specify an active time segment:

1. Open the Time Configuration dialog box ⬚.

2. In the Animation group, enter a Start Time value (**Figure 7.84**).

   The new start time becomes the first frame of the active time segment.

3. In the Animation group, enter an End Time value (**Figure 7.85**).

   The new end time becomes the last frame of the active time segment.

4. Click OK.

   The range of the active time segment changes. The change is reflected in the time slider, which shows a different start frame and length (**Figure 7.86**).

CONFIGURING TIME

Rescaling time moves animation keys in the active time segment farther apart or closer together. If time is scaled up, the timing of the animation slows down. If time is scaled down, the timing of the animation speeds up.

To rescale time:

1. Open or create an animated scene file.

2. Click Time Configuration 🖼 to display the Time Configuration dialog box.

3. In the Animation group, click the Re-scale Time button.

   The Re-scale Time dialog box appears (**Figure 7.87**).

4. Enter a new Length value.

   The active time segment scales up or down accordingly (**Figure 7.88**).

5. Click OK to close the Re-scale Time dialog box.

6. Click OK to close the Time Configuration dialog box.

7. Click Play Animation ▶.

   The animation plays back at a different speed.

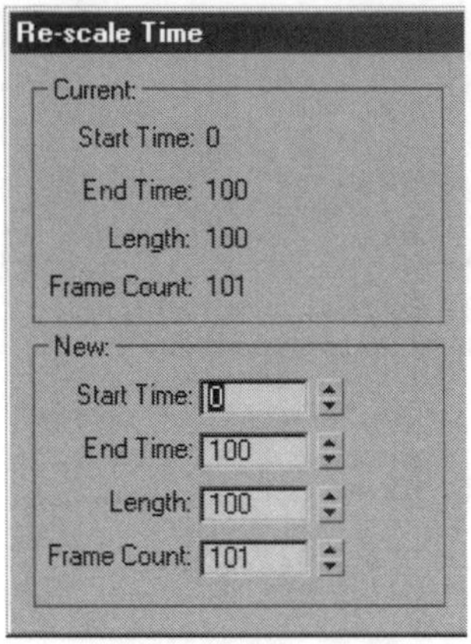

Figure 7.87 The Re-scale Time dialog box allows you to proportionally add and subtract tweens to make animation proceed slower or faster.

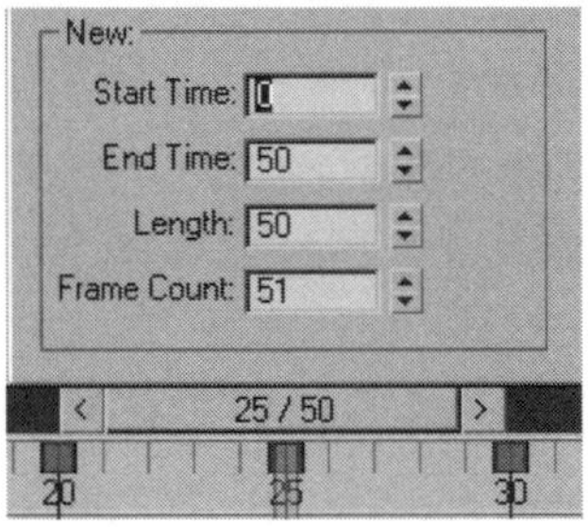

Figure 7.88 Changing the length in the Re-scale Time dialog box scales the active time segment.

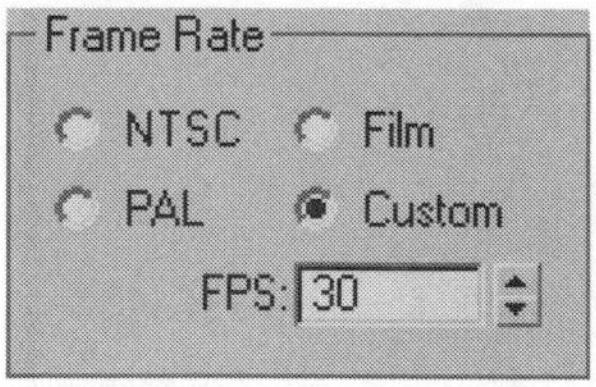

Figure 7.89 Choosing a frame rate.

The frame rate of an animation determines how fast new frames will appear when you play back an animation from a rendered output file. Higher frame rates produce smoother animations and yield larger files. Lower frame rates produce choppier animations and yield smaller files. You pick a frame rate based on the purpose of your animation. Standard frame rates include:

◆ **NTSC Video**—30 fps. Set by the National Television Standards Committee, NTSC is the standard used in the Americas and Japan.

◆ **PAL Video**—25 fps. PAL, or Phase Alternation Line, is the standard used for European television.

◆ **Film**—24 fps. This is the standard for making movies in the film industry.

For movies that you play back on a hard drive, the default, 30 fps, works very nicely. If you want to make your file smaller, try 15 fps, a rate that became popular for multimedia CD-ROMs. For Internet applications, you might try 12 or 8 fps to decrease download time over the Web.

See Chapter 13, Rendering, for a discussion of suitable file formats and compression codecs.

To set the frame rate of an animation:

1. Click Time Configuration 🔳.

   The Time Configuration dialog box appears.

2. In the Frame Rate group, choose a standard frame rate, or choose custom (**Figure 7.89**).

3. If you chose Custom, enter a frame rate in the FPS entry field. Some common rates for computer playback are 12, 15, and 30 fps.

4. Click OK.

   The length of the animation changes so that the playback time remains the same.

CONFIGURING TIME

A time code is a system of measuring and displaying time. 3ds max 4 offers four time code options:

- **Frames**—Measures time by frame number. This is the default.

- **SMPTE**—Measures time in minutes, seconds, and frames. SMPTE is the Society of Motion Picture Technical Engineers.

- **FRAME:TICKS**—Measures time in frames and ticks. A tick is 1/4800 of a second.

- **MM:SS:TICKS**—Measures time in minutes, seconds, and ticks.

To set the time code of an animation:

1. Click Time Configuration to display the Time Configuration dialog box.

2. In the Time Display group, click one of the four time code choices (**Figure 7.90**).

   The time code display updates in the Animation group, in the animation playback controls, and in the time slider (**Figure 7.91**).

3. Click OK.

The Time Configuration dialog box also allows you to control animation playback in the viewports, so that time appears to move faster, slower, or even backwards.

One of the most useful features allows you to play back an animation in all viewports at once.

To play back an animation in all viewports simultaneously:

1. Open or create an animated scene file.

2. Click Time Configuration.

   The Time Configuration dialog box appears.

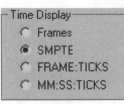

Figure 7.90 Choosing a time code.

Figure 7.91 The time code updates in the time slider and the animation playback controls.

CONFIGURING TIME

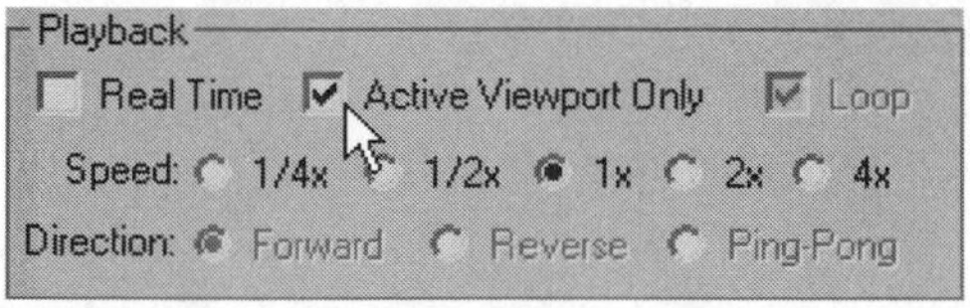

Figure 7.92 Unchecking Active Viewport Only enables animation playback in all viewports.

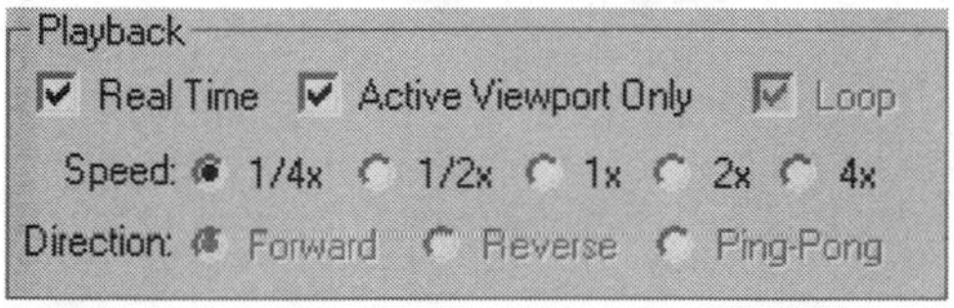

Figure 7.93 Changing animation playback speed for the viewports does not affect playback in the rendered output file.

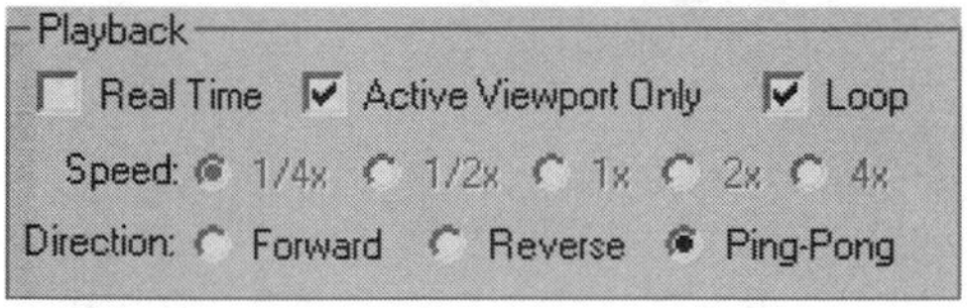

Figure 7.94 Choosing Ping-Pong causes playback to alternate directions in the viewports only.

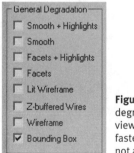

Figure 7.95 Adaptive degradation reduces viewport resolution for faster playback but does not affect rendered output.

3. In the Playback group, uncheck Active Viewport Only (**Figure 7.92**).

4. Close the dialog box.

5. Click Play Animation ▶.

The animation plays back in all of the viewports, unless a viewport is disabled.

✔ Tips

- To play back an animation in the viewports at quarter speed, half speed, double speed, or quadruple speed, check 1/4x, 1/2x, 1x, 2x, or 4x in the Playback group (**Figure 7.93**).

- To play back an animation in reverse, uncheck Real Time and select Reverse.

- To play back an animation in alternating forward and reverse, uncheck Real Time and select Ping-Pong (**Figure 7.94**).

- Adaptive degradation is a feature that reduces viewport display resolution in order to maintain animation playback speed. You will notice adaptive degradation kick in if you play back an animation with more polygons than your graphics card can handle in real time. If you prefer to play back your animation at full resolution and don't mind seeing your animation slow down, you can raise the level of degradation in the Adaptive Degradation panel of the Viewport Configuration dialog box (**Figure 7.95**), or you can activate Degradation Override 🔲 in the status bar, locks and controls area.

CONFIGURING TIME

EDITING MESHES

Figure 8.1 3D medical illustration requires highly detailed editing work.

Mesh editing is essential for character modeling, 3D medical illustration, or any other application that requires precision modeling (**Figure 8.1**). With this in mind, 3ds max 4 provides you with an abundant supply of tools for modeling mesh objects at the smallest level of detail.

Before you begin, it is important to evaluate the level of detail that you need. Will the work be visible when you play the animation? Will it be obscured by shadow? Lost in the distance? If so, you might want to concentrate on the larger issues of scene composition—materials, lighting, and timing—or on editing just those objects that appear prominently in the scene.

Selecting Mesh Sub-Objects

Sub-objects are a subset of an object's geometry. In order to manipulate mesh sub-objects, you must first select them. 3ds max 4 offers five levels of mesh sub-object selection (**Figure 8.2**):

◆ 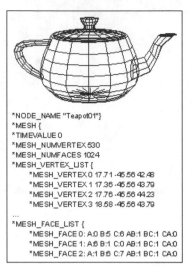 Vertex

◆ Edge

◆ Face

◆ Polygon

◆ Element

Vertices are point locations in space, defined by XYZ coordinates.

Edges are straight lines that have two endpoints. Each end point is a vertex.

Faces are triangular surfaces bounded by three vertices and three edges that connect the vertices.

Polygons are rectangular pairs of coplanar faces that share two vertices along a common edge.

Elements are discrete sets of contiguous faces that share vertices with all of their neighbors.

Methods of sub-object selection include:

◆ Clicking

◆ Region selection

◆ Choosing a named selection set

In addition, you can:

◆ Add to a sub-object selection by holding down the Ctrl key.

◆ Subtract from a selection by holding down the Alt key.

◆ Lock and unlock sub-object selections

◆ Invert sub-object selections

```
*NODE_NAME "Teapot01"}
*MESH {
*TIMEVALUE 0
*MESH_NUMVERTEX 530
*MESH_NUMFACES 1024
*MESH_VERTEX_LIST {
    *MESH_VERTEX 0 17.71 -45.56 42.48
    *MESH_VERTEX 1 17.36 -45.56 43.79
    *MESH_VERTEX 2 17.76 -45.56 44.23
    *MESH_VERTEX 3 18.58 -45.56 43.79
...
*MESH_FACE_LIST {
    *MESH_FACE 0: A:0 B:5 C:6 AB:1 BC:1 CA:0
    *MESH_FACE 1: A:6 B:1 C:0 AB:1 BC:1 CA:0
    *MESH_FACE 2: A:1 B:6 C:7 AB:1 BC:1 CA:0
```

Figure 8.2 An explicit description of the first few vertices and faces of the teapot. Note the coordinate locations of the vertices and their face grouping sequences.

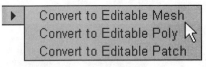

Figure 8.3 Converting an object to an editable mesh in the Transform quad menu.

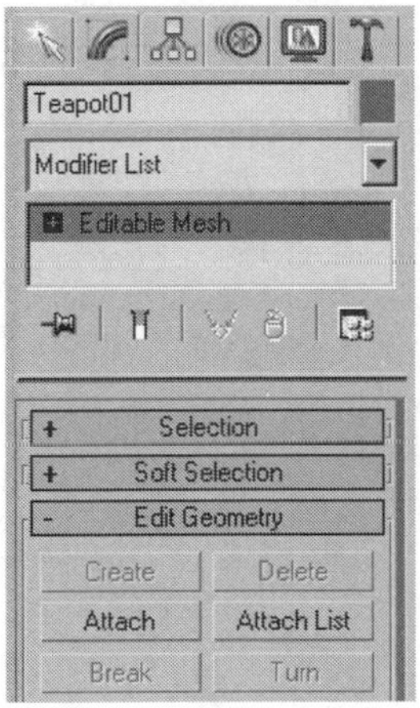

Figure 8.4 In the Modify panel, the editable mesh appears in the modifier stack display, replacing the original object type. Its parameters appear below.

Figure 8.5 Choose a Select or Edit modifier from the Modifier drop-down list.

Sub-object selection can only be performed when the Modify panel is open and a level of sub-object selection is chosen. When you are in a sub-object selection mode, object selection in the viewport is disabled.

To make a mesh object selectable at a sub-object level, you apply a mesh sub-object modifier, or you convert the object to an *editable mesh*.

Converting a mesh object to an editable mesh preserves the object in its current state by changing it from a mathematically defined parametric object to explicit descriptions of each of its sub-object components (**Figure 8.3**). Creation parameters and any modifiers that have been applied to the object are discarded.

To convert a mesh object to an editable mesh:

1. Select a mesh object.

2. Right-click on the object.

3. In the Transform quad menu, roll the cursor over Convert To. Then choose Convert to Editable Mesh from the pop-up menu (**Figure 8.4**).
    The object is converted to an editable mesh (**Figure 8.5**).

✔ Tip

■   You can also convert mesh objects by right-clicking on the name of the object in the modifier stack display and choosing Convert To: Editable Mesh.

The Mesh Select, Volume Select, and Edit Mesh modifiers allow you to select mesh sub-objects and preserve parameters at the same time.

To apply a mesh sub-object modifier:

1. Select an object.

2. Open the Modify panel 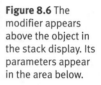.

3. Apply a Mesh Select, Volume Select, or Edit Mesh modifier (**Figure 8.6**).

   The mesh sub-object modifier is applied to the object (**Figure 8.7**). The select and edit parameters appear below.

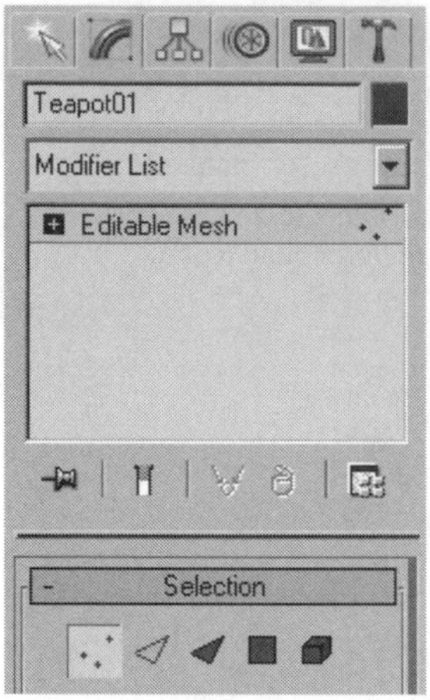

Figure 8.6 The modifier appears above the object in the stack display. Its parameters appear in the area below.

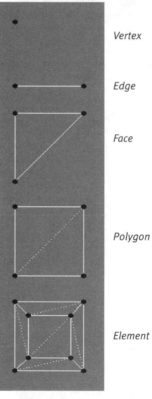

Figure 8.7 The five levels of sub-object selection.

Figure 8.8 You enable a level of sub-object selection by choosing a sub-object type.

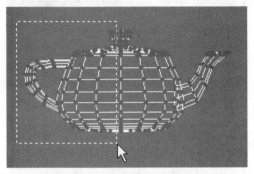

Figure 8.9 Selecting vertices with a selection region. Note that vertex ticks have become visible.

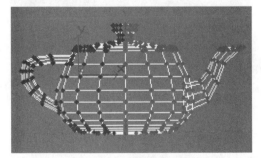

Figure 8.10 The selected vertices turn red.

Edit Mesh and editable meshes prepare objects for sub-object editing using conventional transforms or by using their built-in editing tools.

To select mesh sub-objects with Edit Mesh or within an editable mesh:

1. Select an editable mesh object, or an object that has an Edit Mesh modifier applied to it.

2. Open the Modify panel .

3. In the stack display, click the plus sign next to the Edit Spline modifier or the editable spline. Then choose a sub-object selection level from the drop-down list (**Figure 8.8**).

   The sub-object type becomes highlighted. Commands that can be applied at that level become available below.

4. Ctrl + click or drag a selection region around the sub-objects you want to select (**Figure 8.9**).

   The sub-objects turn red, indicating that they are selected (**Figure 8.10**).

✔ Tips

- Check Ignore Backfacing to prevent sub-objects on the far side of a mesh object from being selected.

- Check By Vertex to include adjacent edges and faces when you select vertices.

- To access sub-object selection mode from the keyboard, press Ctrl + B.

- To cycle through sub-object selection levels, press the Insert key.

SELECTING MESH SUB-OBJECTS

Select modifiers prepare objects for modification at the sub-object level. Their sole purpose is to pass sub-object selection data to the next modifier in the modifier stack.

Figure 8.11 Enabling face-level selection.

To select mesh sub-objects with Mesh Select:

1. Select an object that has a Mesh Select modifier applied to it.

2. Open the Modify panel .

3. Click the plus sign next to the Mesh Select modifier in the stack display. Then choose a sub-object selection level from the drop-down list (**Figure 8.11**).

   The sub-object type becomes highlighted. Commands that can be applied at that level become available below.

4. Ctrl + click or drag a selection region around the sub-objects you want to select (**Figure 8.12**).

   The sub-objects turn red, indicating that they are selected (**Figure 8.13**).

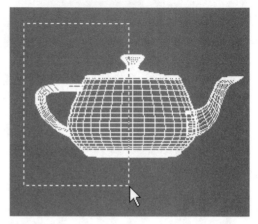

Figure 8.12 Dragging a selection region around faces in a teapot.

✔ Tips

■ Check Ignore Backfaces to prevent sub-objects on the far side of a mesh object from being selected.

■ Different sub-object selections can exist simultaneously at different levels of selection. With the Mesh Select modifier, you can import a selection from another sub-object level by clicking the buttons for that level in the Get from Other Levels group.

■ To verify the continuity of a mesh surface before performing a Boolean operation, enable edge selection and then click Select Open Edges.

■ You can also choose mesh sub-object selection levels from the Tools1 quad menu (**Figure 8.14**).

Figure 8.13 The selected faces turn red.

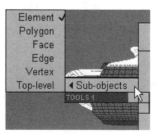

Figure 8.14 Choosing a sub-object selection level by right-clicking on a mesh object.

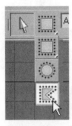

Figure 8.15 Use Fence Selection to select sub-objects within an irregular region.

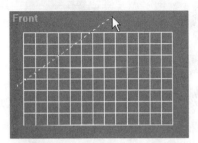

Figure 8.16 Drag to create the first side of the fence.

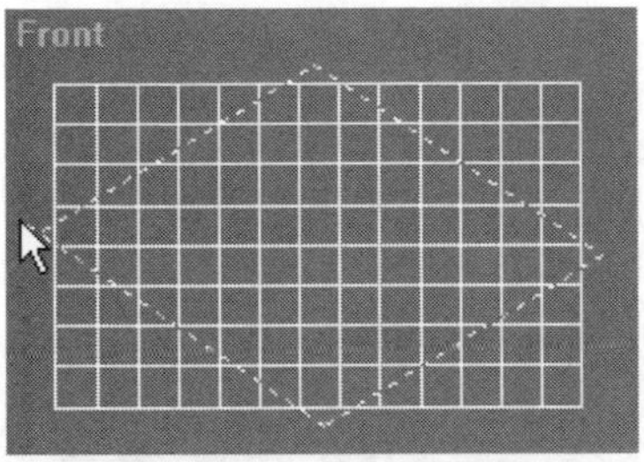

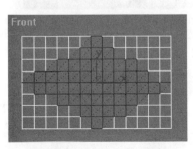

Figure 8.17 Move and click to create the rest of the fence.

Figure 8.18 Double-click to complete the fence. The sub-objects enclosed by the fence are selected.

Fence selection is a type of region selection that is especially well-suited to sub-object selection. By drawing a polygonal selection region, you can define a selection with great precision.

To make a sub-object selection with a fence:

1. Select an editable object, or an object that has a Select or Edit modifier applied to it.

2. Choose Fence Selection ⬚ from the Selection Region flyout (**Figure 8.15**).

3. Open the Modify panel ⬚.

4. Choose a level of sub-object selection by clicking an icon in the Selection rollout.

5. Place the cursor next to the sub-objects you want to select. Then drag to create the first side of the region (**Figure 8.16**).

6. Click to set the second point of the region.

7. Move and click the mouse to set more points, until the fence encloses all the sub-objects you want to select (**Figure 8.17**).

8. Double-click the mouse button.

   The sub-objects enclosed within the fence selection region turn red, indicating that they are selected (**Figure 8.18**).

SELECTING MESH SUB-OBJECTS

Circle selection is often used for editing radial objects, such as spheres, cylinders, and cones.

To make a sub-object selection with a circle:

1. Select an editable object, or an object that has a Select or Edit modifier applied to it, such as a cylinder.

2. Choose Circle Selection  from the Selection Region flyout (**Figure 8.19**).

Figure 8.19 Use Circle Selection for creating round or cylindrical selections.

3. Choose a level of sub-object selection by clicking an icon in the Selection rollout.

4. Place the cursor where you want the center of the selection to be. Then click and drag a circle until it encloses all the sub-objects you want to select (**Figure 8.20**).

5. Release the mouse button.

   The sub-objects enclosed within the circle turn red, indicating that they are selected (**Figure 8.21**).

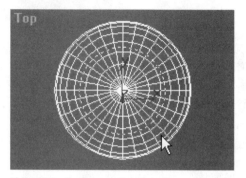

Figure 8.20 Dragging a circle from the center outward.

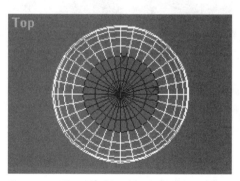

Figure 8.21 The sub-objects enclosed by the circle are selected.

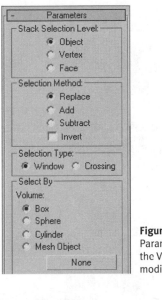

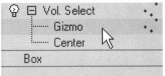

Figure 8.22 The Parameters rollout for the Volume Select modifier.

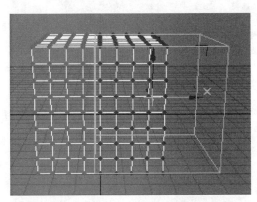

Figure 8.23 Click the plus sign next to a modifier to access the sub-objects of the modifier. The sub-objects of the Volume Select modifier are its Gizmo and Center.

Figure 8.24 The sub-objects enclosed by the volume are selected.

Use Volume Select on mesh objects to select vertices or faces within a three-dimensional area.

To make a sub-object selection with Volume Select:

1. Select a mesh object.

2. Open the Modify panel ![icon].

3. Choose Vol. Select from the Modifier drop-down list. The Volume Select modifier is applied to the object (**Figure 8.22**). A gold wireframe box called a gizmo appears at the extents of the object.

4. In the Stack Selection Level group, choose Object, Vertex, or Face.

5. Choose a selection method and a selection type, or use the defaults.

6. In the Select By group, choose a volume type.

   The gizmo changes to match the type of volume you choose. If you choose Mesh Object, click the None button. Then pick a mesh object to define the volume of selection.

7. In the modifier stack display, click the plus (+) sign next to Vol. Select. Then click Gizmo (**Figure 8.23**).

8. Position the Gizmo so that it encloses the vertices or faces you want to select. To position the gizmo, choose the Move tool and drag it, or drag the coordinate spinners in the status bar, locks and controls area.

   The sub-objects enclosed within the volume turn red, indicating that they are selected (**Figure 8.24**).

✔ Tips

- To fit, center, or reset the gizmo, click the Fit, Center, and Reset buttons in the Alignment group of the Parameters rollout.

- If you apply a Volume Select modifier to a spline object, it will convert the spline object to a mesh object.

Soft selection diminishes the effect of subsequently applied commands outside the bounds of the original selection.

To make a soft selection:

1. Make a vertex-level sub-object selection [icon] using any method (**Figure 8.25**).

2. Open the Soft Selection rollout.

3. Check Use Soft Selection. Then drag the Falloff spinner to adjust the degree of selection (**Figure 8.26**).

   The sub-objects in range of the soft selection change colors from red to orange to yellow to blue as you increase the falloff value. Red indicates the hottest selection where commands will be applied at full intensity; blue indicates the coolest selection where the effect of commands will diminish (**Figure 8.27**).

✔ Tips

- The Pinch and Bubble parameters affect the intensity of selection according the Soft Selection graph. For an example of how these parameters affect a sub-object transform, see "To move a vertex" in the next section.

- You can see falloff only at the vertex level, but with the select modifiers, you can get around this by using Get Vertex Selection to import the selection into another level. You can also soft-select sub-objects at the edge and face levels and import them to the vertex level to see the selection falloff.

Figure 8.25 A circle of vertices are selected on a sphere.

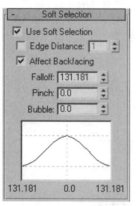

Figure 8.26 Check Use Soft Selection and drag the falloff spinner.

Figure 8.27 The colors of the vertices change from warm to cool to indicate the degree of selection.

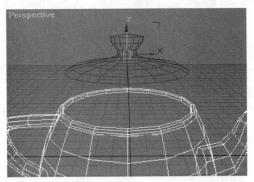

Figure 8.28 You can raise the lid of a teapot with a move transform after you select it at the element sub-object level.

Transforming Mesh Sub-Objects

You transform mesh sub-object to shape the details of your model. Since mesh structure is defined primarily by vertices, sub-object transforms are mostly applied at the vertex level.

Like sub-object selections, sub-object transforms are performed exclusively in the Modify panel. There are three ways to do this (**Figure 8.28**):

◆ Make a sub-object selection with a Mesh Select modifier and then apply an XForm modifier. When you apply your transforms, the XForm modifier will apply them to the sub-object selection. Use this option for animating sub-objects with transforms.

◆ Make a sub-object selection within an editable object and then transform the selection. Use this option for sculpting structural details.

◆ Make a sub-object selection with an edit modifier and then apply a transform. This option is used for modeling the details of objects when you want the operation to be reversible and you have plenty of RAM.

The Move tool is your primary tool for editing and animating vertices.

To move a vertex:

1. Select a vertex.

2. Optional: Apply a soft selection to the surrounding vertices.

3. If you used one of the select modifiers, apply an XForm modifier to the object.

4. Choose a reference coordinate system and an axis restriction. Note: You might find the Local Z axis to be a useful choice.

5. Optional: Lock the selection 🔒.

6. Move the selection ✥ (**Figure 8.29**).

   If you used a soft selection, the surface of the object will deform smoothly through the volume of the selection (**Figure 8.30**).

✔ Tips

- Changing the Pinch and Bubble parameters alters the distribution of soft selection intensity. This in turn changes how subsequent commands are interpreted (**Figure 8.31**).

- To transform a selection of vertices in the local axis of the object, rather than the local axis of each sub-object, make the selection and change the reference coordinate system to Pick. Then pick the object you are working on. This works around the problem of having multiple local axis tripods being active and obscuring your work.

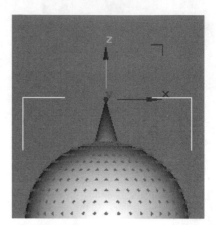

Figure 8.29 Selecting a vertex at the top of the sphere.

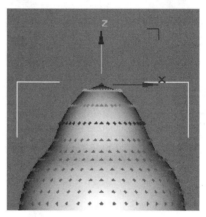

Figure 8.30 Applying a move transform to the sub-object selection.

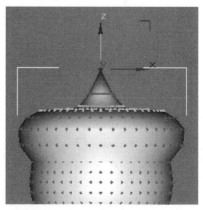

Figure 8.31 Pinch and Bubble after the distribution of soft selection.

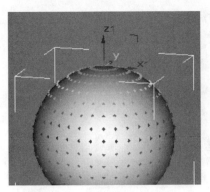

Figure 8.32 Selecting a vertex at the top of a sphere. A soft selection has been applied.

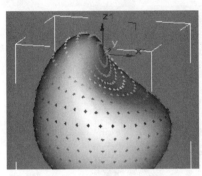

Figure 8.33 After rotating a single vertex, the object deforms.

Rotating a vertex rearranges the faces and edges that adjoin it, but does not deform the mesh surface unless you apply a soft selection.

To rotate a vertex:

1. Select a vertex (**Figure 8.32**).

2. Apply a soft selection to the surrounding vertices.

3. If you used one of the select modifiers, apply an XForm modifier to the object.

4. Choose a reference coordinate system and an axis restriction.

5. Optional: Lock the selection 🔒.

6. Rotate the selection ↻.

   The surface of the object deforms smoothly around the turning vertex (**Figure 8.33**).

Scaling vertices is a common way of making vertices move closer together or farther apart.

To scale vertices:

1. Select one or more vertices.

2. Optional: Apply a soft selection to the surrounding vertices.

3. If you used one of the select modifiers, apply an XForm modifier to the object.

4. Choose a reference coordinate system and an axis restriction, if you intend to use a non-uniform scale or squash.

5. Optional: Lock the selection 🔒.

6. Scale the selection ▣.

    The vertices move closer or farther apart (**Figure 8.34**).

    If you used a soft selection, you can make the sides of a mesh curve inward or outward (**Figure 8.35**).

✔ Tip

■ To change the density of vertices in a mesh surface, scale a single vertex using soft selection (**Figure 8.36**).

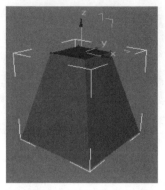

Figure 8.34 Scaling down vertices brings them closer together to achieve a taper effect.

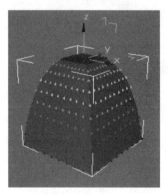

Figure 8.35 Scaling the top of a cube with soft selection and additional segmentation adds a curve to the taper action.

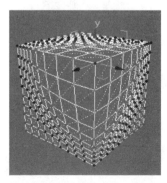

Figure 8.36 Scaling up the corner vertex that has been soft selected moves the surrounding vertices away from the corner.

TRANSFORMING MESH SUB-OBJECTS

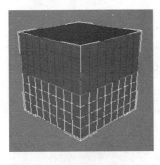

Figure 8.37 The Bend modifier gizmo surrounds the sub-object selection.

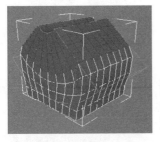

Figure 8.38 After applying the Bend modifier to the selected faces.

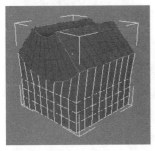

Figure 8.39 Soft selection radically alters how the mesh deforms.

Figure 8.40 Using soft selection controls the curvature of a Taper modifier.

Modifying Mesh Sub-Objects

Mesh sub-object selections are preserved in the modifier stack. When a mesh sub-object level is enabled, the sub-object selection saved at that level is passed up the modifier stack. If you change the level of selection, the selection made at that level will be passed along instead.

If you want to make a new sub-object selection at any level without losing the old selection, you simply apply another selection modifier and make a new selection.

To apply a modifier to a mesh sub-object selection:

1. Make a sub-object selection using Mesh Select or Volume Select.

2. Apply a modifier.

   The modifier is applied to the sub-object selection. If the modifier has a gizmo or lattice, the gizmo or lattice surrounds just the sub-object selection (**Figure 8.37**).

3. Adjust the parameters of the modifier.

   The modifier is applied to the sub-object selection (**Figure 8.38**).

   If you used soft selection, the effect of the modifier falls off gradually toward the unselected portion of the object (**Figure 8.39**).

✔ Tip

■ Using soft selection gives you a second option for controlling the curvature of a Taper modifier (**Figure 8.40**).

Editing Mesh Objects

To make a mesh object editable, you either apply an Edit Mesh modifier or convert the object to an editable mesh.

The advantage of using Edit modifiers is that they are flexible and non-destructive. With Edit modifiers, you apply a series of commands, save off clones, and then reverse the effect of the modifier by removing it from the stack. The disadvantage is that Edit modifiers add memory and computational overhead to your scene because they keep track of every command.

In comparison, editable meshes are more stable and have less overhead because they do not track commands in a modifier stack. For complex objects, this can significantly speed up editing operations (**Figure 8.41**). The disadvantage of editable meshes is that you cannot undo them after closing a file.

As a beginner, you may find Edit modifiers to be more forgiving. As you develop your skills and begin making more complex scenes, you will probably want to switch to editable meshes.

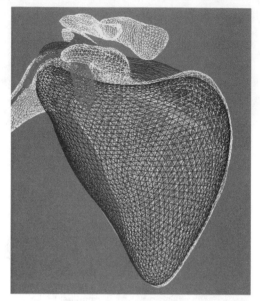

Figure 8.41 A high mesh density is often necessary for modeling details.

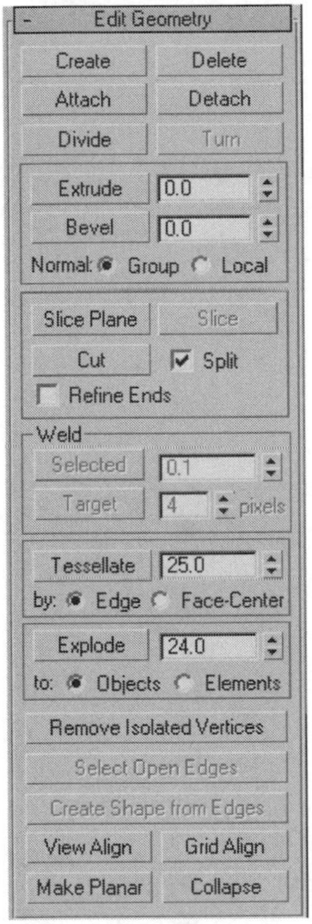

Figure 8.42
The Edit Geometry rollout for Edit Mesh and editable meshes. Only the commands for face level editing are enabled.

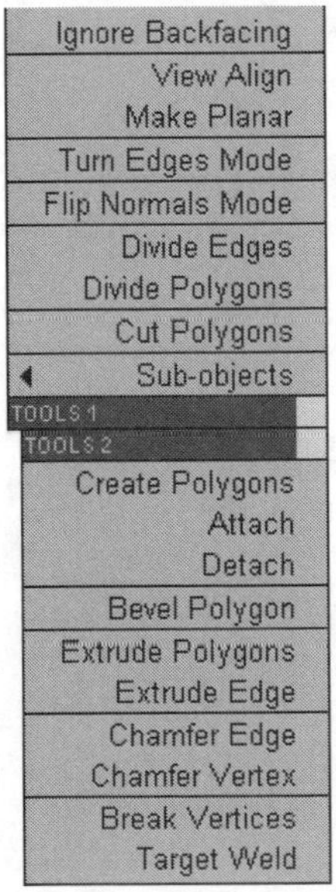

Figure 8.43 The right-click quad menus of an editable mesh contains two menus of mesh editing commands.

Mesh objects can be edited at the vertex, edge, face, polygon, element, and object levels. When you choose a selection level, the editing commands for that level become available in the Modify panel (**Figure 8.42**). You can also access these commands from the Tools1 and Tools2 quad menus when the Modify panel is open (**Figure 8.43**).

Object editing commands act upon the entire mesh. They are used primarily for attaching objects and controlling surface subdivision during displacement mapping (editable meshes only). The object level is the only level that allows you to attach multiple objects from a list.

The Attach, Delete, Remove Isolated Vertices, View Align, Grid Align, Make Planar, and Collapse commands can be used at every level. Other commands are specific to certain levels:

◆ Vertex-editing commands control the smallest details of mesh structure. Level-specific commands include Create, Detach, Break, Weld, Remove, and Vertex Colors.

◆ Edge-editing commands affect the interstices of a mesh. Level-specific commands include Divide, Turn, Extrude, Chamfer, Slice, Cut, Split, and Visibility.

◆ Face-editing commands change the rendering properties of a mesh, including shading, smoothing, visibility, and material assignments, as well as structure. Level-specific commands include Create, Detach, Divide, Extrude, Bevel, Slice, Cut, Split, Tessellate, Explode, Flip, Unify, Smooth, Material ID, and Vertex Colors.

◆ Polygon-editing affects coplanar pairs of faces. Polygon commands are the same as face-editing commands.

◆ Element-editing commands alter discrete collections of faces. Element commands are the same as face- and polygon-editing commands.

EDITING MESH OBJECTS

Table 8.1 shows the availability of editing commands at each level of sub-object selection:

Table 8.1

Mesh-Editing Commands and the Levels They Affect					
	VERTEX	EDGE	FACE	ELEMENT	OBJECT
Create	✓		✓	✓	✓
Delete	✓	✓	✓	✓	✓
Attach	✓	✓	✓	✓	✓
Detach	✓		✓	✓	✓
Break	✓				
Divide		✓	✓	✓	✓
Turn		✓			
Extrude		✓	✓	✓	✓
Chamfer	✓	✓			
Bevel			✓	✓	✓
Slice	✓	✓	✓	✓	✓
Cut		✓	✓	✓	✓
Split		✓	✓	✓	✓
Weld	✓				
Tessellate			✓	✓	✓
Explode			✓	✓	✓
Remove Isolated Vertices	✓	✓	✓	✓	✓
Select Open Edges Create Shape From Open Edges		✓			
View Align	✓	✓	✓	✓	✓
Grid Align	✓	✓	✓	✓	✓
Make Planar	✓	✓	✓	✓	✓
Collapse	✓	✓	✓	✓	✓
Flip			✓	✓	✓
Unify			✓	✓	✓
Smooth			✓	✓	✓
Material ID			✓	✓	✓
Vertex Colors	✓		✓	✓	✓
Visibility		✓			

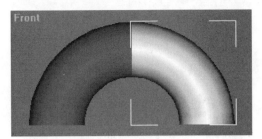

Figure 8.44 Select the mesh object that you want to attach other objects to.

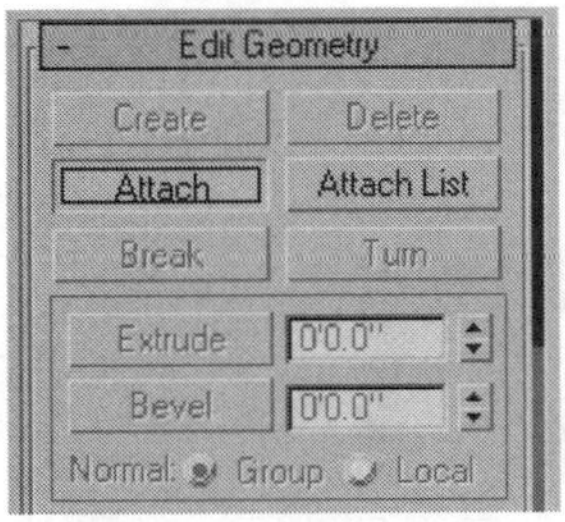

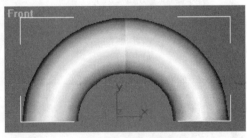

Figure 8.45 Click Attach before attaching objects.

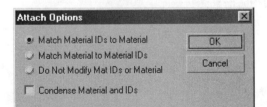

Figure 8.46 When you attach an object, it takes on the color of the object that it attaches to.

Figure 8.47 The Attach Options dialog box lets you choose how materials are combined.

The Attach command joins objects together and turns them into a single object with one name and one set of object properties. Each of the attached objects becomes a sub-object element.

Attach works at any level of sub-object editing, as well as at the object level.

To attach an object:

1. Select an object (**Figure 8.44**).

2. Open the Modify panel.

3. Convert the object to an editable mesh or apply an Edit Mesh modifier to it.

4. Enable a selection level or work at the object level (the default).

5. In the Edit Geometry rollout, click Attach (**Figure 8.45**).

6. Click the object you want to attach.

   The second object attaches to the first. It is now an element within that object.

   If the objects are different colors, the attached element will inherit the color of the object (**Figure 8.46**).

   If the attached element has a different material, you will be given a choice as to how to incorporate it into the material of the current object (**Figure 8.47**).

7. Click any other objects you want to attach.

8. Click the Attach button to turn off attach mode.

✔ Tips

■ Clicking Attach List brings up a list of attachable objects so that you select the object that you want to attach by name.

■ To smooth the seams between attached elements, use the Weld command (see the next task).

EDITING MESH OBJECTS

Welding eliminates vertices within a certain distance of each other so that adjacent elements are united as one.

To weld a mesh:

1. Select an object.

2. Open the Modify panel .

3. Convert the object to an editable mesh or apply an Edit Mesh modifier to it.

4. Enable Vertex level selection .

5. Select a set of adjacent vertices by dragging a selection region around them (**Figure 8.48**).

6. In the Weld group of the Edit Geometry rollout, click Selected (**Figure 8.49**).

   Vertices that are within the threshold value (located to the right of the Selected button) are welded together.

   The elements are joined together into one, and the seam in between them is smoothed (**Figure 8.50**).

7. If there are no vertices within the threshold distance, the Weld dialog box appears (**Figure 8.51**). To resolve this, increase the threshold value and click Selected again.

   or

   Select and scale the vertices so they draw tightly together. Then click Selected.

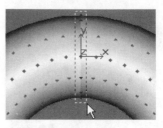

Figure 8.48 Selecting a group of vertices to weld.

Figure 8.49 Click Selected to weld the selection.

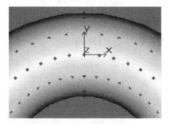

Figure 8.50 The smoothed seam.

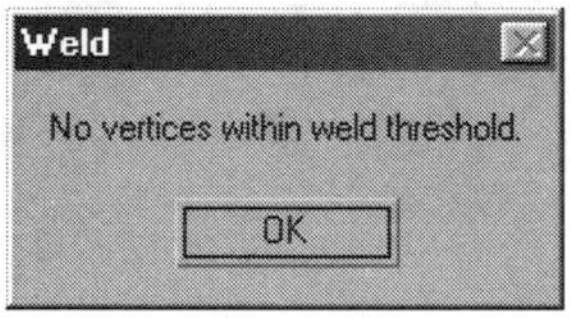

Weld

No vertices within weld threshold.

OK

Figure 8.51 The Weld dialog box appears if the vertices are too far apart to weld.

EDITING MESH OBJECTS

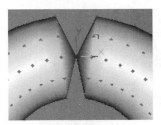

Figure 8.52 Collapse was used to weld all of a vertices on the seam into a single point.

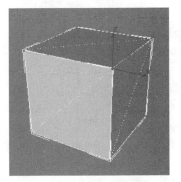

Figure 8.53 Selecting the corner of a box.

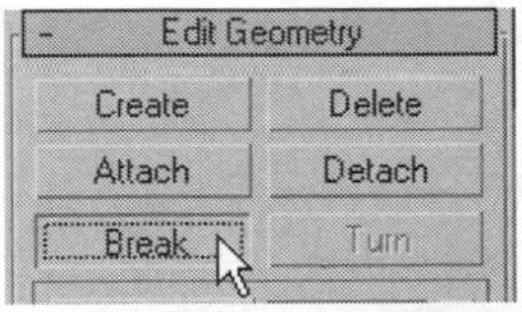

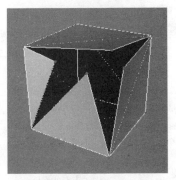
Edit Geometry

Create	Delete
Attach	Detach
Break	Turn

Figure 8.54 Click Break to clone the vertices.

Figure 8.55 After moving the faces apart by dragging their vertices. The dark interior is a result of unchecking the Backface Cull display property.

✔ Tips

- Remove Isolated Vertices deletes vertices that are not connected to faces with edges.

- View Align and Grid Align align selected vertices and faces to the plane of the view or the plane of the grid, respectively.

- Make Planar flattens the selection onto a plane whose normal is the average of all the normals of the faces attached to the vertices.

- Collapse is like a super-powerful weld command that merges selected vertices into one vertex at the center of the selection (**Figure 8.52**).

The Break command is the opposite of Weld; it clones vertices and assigns them to adjoining faces. This allows you to pull faces apart from a corner where they had originally been joined.

To break a vertex:

1. Select an object.

2. Open the Modify panel.

3. Convert the object to an editable mesh or apply an Edit Mesh modifier to it.

4. Enable Vertex level selection.

5. Select a vertex (**Figure 8.53**).

6. In the Edit Geometry rollout, click Break (**Figure 8.54**).

   The vertex is broken. You can now pull apart the adjoining faces (**Figure 8.55**).

✔ Tip

- To break off a selection into a separate element, use the Detach command.

Detach turns sub-object components into discrete elements, separate objects, or separate objects that are copies of the current selection.

To detach part of a mesh:

1. Select an object.

2. Open the Modify panel 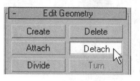.

3. Convert the object to an editable mesh or apply an Edit Mesh modifier to it.

4. Enable a selection level.

5. Select the sub-object components that you want to detach (**Figure 8.56**).

6. In the Edit Geometry rollout, click Detach (**Figure 8.57**).

   The Detach dialog box appears (**Figure 8.58**).

7. In the Detach dialog box, choose whether you want to detach the selection into an element, a separate object, or a clone. (Clone copies the current selection into a new object, and ensures that no geometry is removed from the original.)

8. Name the new object or clone in the Detach dialog box or accept the default.

   The selection is detached. You can now select and move it independently (**Figure 8.59**).

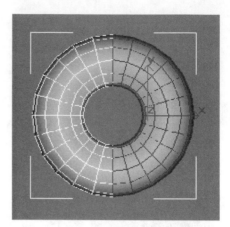

Figure 8.56 Selecting the right half of the torus.

Figure 8.57 Click Detach to create a new object or element.

Figure 8.58 Detaching a new object.

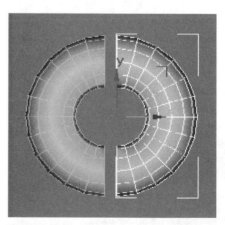

Figure 8.59 After exiting sub-object mode, you can select and move the new object.

EDITING MESH OBJECTS

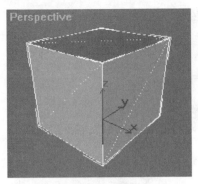

Figure 8.60 Select an edge.

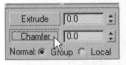

Figure 8.61 Click Chamfer to start the chamfer operation.

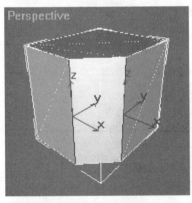

Figure 8.62 The chamfered edge.

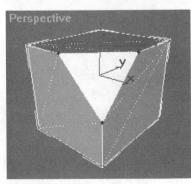

Figure 8.63 The chamfered vertex.

Chamfering creates an edge or corner that appears to have been filed down.

Chamfering an edge splits an edge in two. Two new faces are created between the new edges. Adjoining faces subdivide accordingly.

To chamfer an edge:

1. Select an object.

2. Open the Modify panel.

3. Convert the object to an editable mesh or apply an Edit Mesh modifier to it.

4. Enable Edge level selection.

5. Select an edge (**Figure 8.60**).

6. In the Edit Geometry rollout, click Chamfer (**Figure 8.61**).

7. Drag the Chamfer spinner, or enter a value in the Chamfer field.

   The edge splits, chamfering the edge (**Figure 8.62**).

Chamfering a vertex splits a vertex into multiple vertices that move away from its original location down every edge that connects to it. New edges and faces are created automatically.

To chamfer a vertex:

1. Select a mesh object.

2. Open the Modify panel.

3. Convert the object to an editable mesh or apply an Edit Mesh modifier to it.

4. Enable Vertex level selection.

5. Select a vertex.

6. Click Chamfer.

7. Drag the Chamfer spinner or enter a value in the Chamfer field.

8. The vertex splits, chamfering the corner (**Figure 8.63**).

Extruding is a quick way to build geometry. You can extrude edges, faces, polygons, or elements. Use Extrude to add details to an existing model or to build a low-polygon model from scratch.

To extrude a polygon:

1. Select an object.

2. Open the Modify panel [icon].

3. Convert the object to an editable mesh or apply an Edit Mesh modifier to it.

4. Enable Polygon level selection [icon].

5. Click a polygon to select it.

6. In the Edit Geometry rollout, click Extrude (**Figure 8.64**).

7. Drag the polygon.

   or

   Drag the Extrude spinner.

   or

   Enter an extrude value.

   The polygon extrudes from the surface of the mesh (**Figure 8.65**).

   The extrude amount is reset to zero. The polygon remains selected in case you want to extrude it again.

✔ Tips

- Extruding edges creates planar extrusions. Extruding faces creates triangular-shaped extrusions. Extruding elements creates a wall of extrusion between adjacent elements (**Figure 8.66**).

- Combining transforms with a polygon extrusion is a great way to create a low-poly model (**Figure 8.67**).

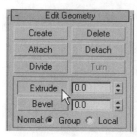

Figure 8.64 Click Extrude to create new faces.

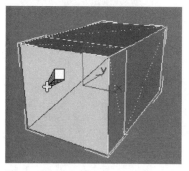

Figure 8.65 Extruding the front polygon of a box by dragging.

Figure 8.66 After extruding the handle, lid, and spout elements of a teapot.

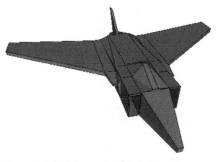

Figure 8.67 This low-poly jet fighter was created from a box using a series of Extrude commands.

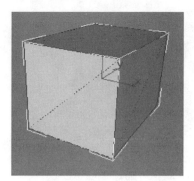

Figure 8.68 Selecting all the faces in a box to slice. Note that Edges Only is turned off.

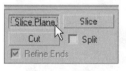

Figure 8.69 Use Slice Plane to subdivide an object along a plane.

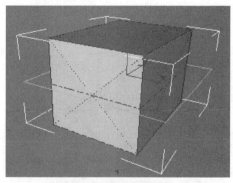

Figure 8.70 After clicking the Slice button, new edges appear along the plane of the Slice Plane.

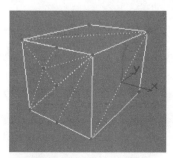

Figure 8.71 After dividing the edges on the front left polygon.

The Slice command divides a mesh in two. You access the Slice command from any level of sub-object selection.

To slice a mesh:

1. Select an object.

2. Open the Modify panel .

3. Convert the object to an editable mesh, or apply an Edit Mesh modifier to it.

4. Enable any sub-object selection level.

5. Select the sub-objects you would like to slice (**Figure 8.68**).

6. In the Edit Geometry rollout, click Slice Plane (**Figure 8.69**).

   The slice plane appears in the middle of the object. Like the Section object, it appears limited, but it actually extends infinitely into space.

7. Place the slice plane where you want it to slice the object.

8. Click Slice.

   All edges and faces intersected by the slice plane are subdivided (**Figure 8.70**).

✔ Tips

■ The Split option divides an object into two separate elements by creating duplicate vertices at every point of intersection.

■ Create Shape from Open Edges selects all the open edges in a mesh object and clones them into a new shape. Used with the Slice command, it sections an object.

■ The Divide command divides edges as you click on them individually (**Figure 8.71**).

■ The Cut command divides all edges on the visible surface that you drag across.

■ The Turn command rotates an edge and connects it to the other vertices of the two faces it divides.

The Delete command deletes sub-object selections at any level.

To delete part of a mesh:

1. Select an object.

2. Open the Modify panel.

3. Convert the object to an editable mesh, or apply an Edit Mesh modifier to it.

4. Enable the selection level of the components you want to delete.

5. Select the part of the mesh that you want to delete (**Figure 8.72**).

6. Click Delete or press the Delete key.

   If you are working at the Edge, Face, Polygon, or Element level, the Delete Face dialog box appears (**Figure 8.73**).

7. Click Yes.

   The selected part of the mesh is deleted (**Figure 8.74**).

✔ Tips

■ Isolated vertices are usually considered junk. They do not render, but they do add unnecessary confusion to your model. The only time you want to keep them is when you want to build new faces off of them.

■ If you have attached two objects that intersect one another, deleting the faces in the intersecting region will improve rendering performance.

■ Use the Create command to rebuild faces and vertices that have accidentally been deleted.

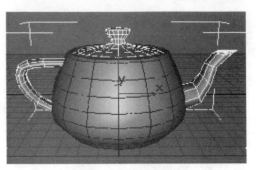

Figure 8.72 Selection the body of the teapot.

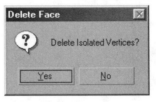

Figure 8.73 The Delete Face dialog box asks if you want to delete isolated vertices.

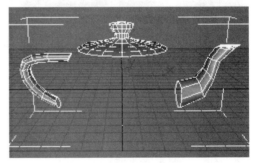

Figure 8.74 After deleting the body of the teapot.

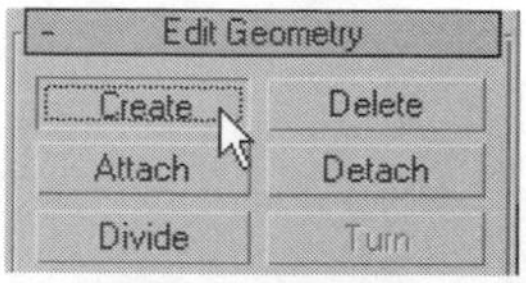

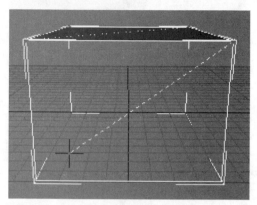

Figure 8.75 Click Create to start creating new geometry.

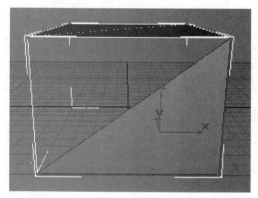

Figure 8.76 Click and drag from the first vertex counter-clockwise to the second vertex.

Figure 8.77 The new face appears on the front of the box.

The Create command gives you the ability to create new geometry from the ground up. With the Create command, you can create vertices, connect them with edges, and define faces and surfaces from scratch.

To create a face:

1. Select a mesh object that is missing some of its faces.

2. Open the Modify panel .

3. Convert the object to an editable mesh, or apply an Edit Mesh modifier to it.

4. Enable Face level selection .

5. In the Edit Geometry rollout, click Create (**Figure 8.75**).

    The vertex points of the object appear.

6. Click one of the vertices that you want to use to build the face.

7. Move the cursor to the next vertex, proceeding counterclockwise.

    A "rubber-band line" stretches from the first point to the second point (**Figure 8.76**).

8. Click the second vertex to set the second corner of the face.

9. Move the cursor to the final vertex, and click to anchor the last point of the face.

    The new face fills the hole in the mesh (**Figure 8.77**).

✔ Tips

- Click Auto Smooth in the Surface Properties rollout to smooth the face.

- Picking points in a clockwise order builds a face whose normal points away from you.

- If a face does not appear when you build it, click Unify in the Surface Properties rollout to flip the face.

EDITING MESH OBJECTS

EDITING SHAPES

Figure 9.1 Shapes were used to create the profiles of the apple, stem, seed, and core.

Shapes are primarily used as the source objects for 3D geometry, including flying logos for television, low-polygon models for 3D games, architectural and mechanical models, and morph targets for morph animation. They are also used as motion paths for animation and distribution paths for placing objects in a scene (**Figure 9.1**).

To fine-tune a shape, you apply transforms, modifiers, or edit commands to a sub-object selection. Transforms are mostly used for adjusting the curvature of a shape, although they can come in handy for arranging sub-objects within a shape. Modifiers are rarely applied at the sub-object level; more often they are applied at the object level after shapes have been edited.

Selecting Shape Sub-Objects

Shapes have three types of sub-objects that you can select (**Figure 9.2**):

◆ ⬛ **Vertex**

◆ ⬛ **Segment**

◆ ⬛ **Spline**

Vertices are point locations in space, defined by XYZ coordinates.

Segments are straight or curved line segments that connect two vertices.

Splines are a set of vertices and segments that connect them.

Methods of sub-object selection include:

◆ Clicking

◆ Region selection

◆ Choosing a named selection set

In addition, you can:

◆ Add to a sub-object selection by holding down the Ctrl key.

◆ Subtract from a selection by holding down the Alt key.

◆ Lock and unlock sub-object selections

◆ Invert sub-object selections

Sub-object selection can be performed only when the Modify panel is open and a level of sub-object selection is chosen. When you are in a sub-object selection mode, object selection in the viewport is disabled.

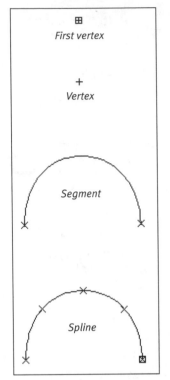

Figure 9.2 The sub-objects of a shape. The first vertex is a vertex with a square around it.

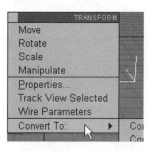

Figure 9.3 Right-click on the object and choose Convert To.

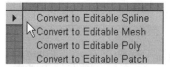

Figure 9.4 Converting an object to an editable spline.

Figure 9.5
In the Modify panel, the editable spline appears in the modifier stack display, replacing the original object type. Its parameters appear below.

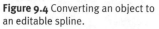

Figure 9.6 You can also convert objects in the modifier stack.

To make a shape object selectable at a sub-object level, you apply a shape sub-object modifier, or you convert the object to an *editable spline*.

(Note: editable splines are really editable shapes, rather than some generic spline type. The same goes for the Edit Spline modifier; it is really a shape modifier and cannot be applied to any other type of object.)

Converting a shape object to an editable spline preserves the object in its current state by changing it from a mathematically defined parametric object to explicit descriptions of each of its sub-object components (**Figure 9.3**). Creation parameters and any modifiers that have been applied to the object are discarded.

To convert a shape object to an editable spline:

1. Select a shape object.

2. Right-click on the object.

3. In the Transform quad menu, roll the cursor over Convert To. Then choose Convert to Editable spline from the pop-up menu (**Figure 9.4**).

   The object is converted to an editable spline (**Figure 9.5**).

✔ Tip

■ You can also convert shape objects by right-clicking on the name of the object in the modifier stack display and choosing Convert To: Editable Spline (**Figure 9.6**).

SELECTING SHAPE SUB-OBJECTS

The Spline Select and Edit Spline modifiers allow you to select shape sub-objects and preserve parameters at the same time.

Applying a Volume Select modifier converts a shape to a mesh object, so you cannot use it for editing shapes.

To apply a shape sub-object modifier:

1. Select an object.

2. Open the Modify panel ![icon].

3. Apply a Spline Select or Edit Spline modifier (**Figure 9.7**).

   The shape sub-object modifier is applied to the object (**Figure 9.8**). The select and edit parameters appear below.

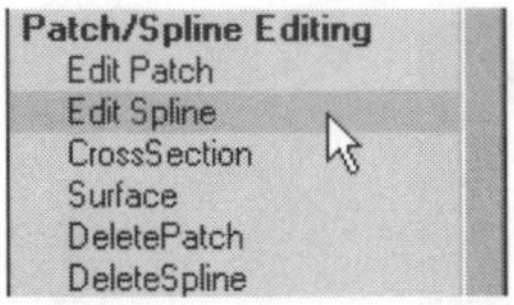

Edit Spline and editable splines prepare objects for sub-object editing with conventional transforms or with their built-in editing tools.

To select shape sub-objects with Edit Spline or within an editable spline:

1. Select a shape.

2. Open the Modify panel ![icon].

3. Convert the shape to an editable spline or apply an Edit Spline modifier to it.

4. In the modifier stack display, click the plus sign next to the Edit Spline modifier or the editable spline. Then choose a sub-object selection level from the drop-down list (**Figure 9.9**).

   The sub-object type becomes highlighted. Commands that can be applied at that level become available below.

5. Click or drag a selection region around the sub-objects you want to select (**Figure 9.10**).

   The sub-objects turn red, indicating that they are selected. If you select Bézier vertices, Bézier handles appear (**Figure 9.11**).

Figure 9.7 Choose a Select or Edit modifier from the Modifier drop-down list.

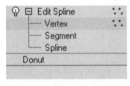

Figure 9.8 The modifier appears above the object in the stack display. Its parameters appear in the area below.

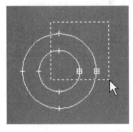

Figure 9.9 Choosing a sub-object selection level in the stack display.

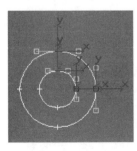

Figure 9.10 Dragging a selection region around some vertices in a donut.

Figure 9.11 The vertices turn red and sprout Bézier handles.

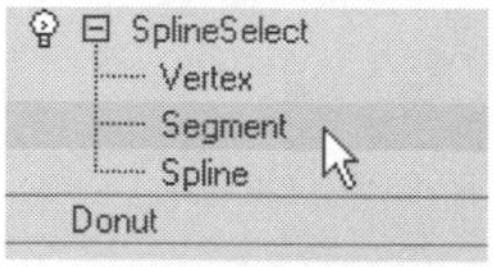

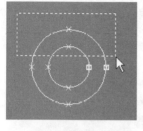

Figure 9.12 Enabling segment-level selection for a Spline Select modifier in the stack display.

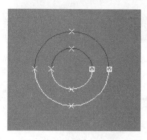

Figure 9.13 Dragging a selection region around segments in a donut.

Figure 9.14 The selected segments turn red.

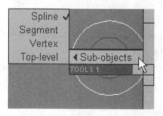

Figure 9.15 Choosing a sub-object selection level by right-clicking on a shape object.

✔ Tips

■ To access sub-object selection mode from the keyboard, press Ctrl + B.

■ To cycle through sub-object selection levels, press the Insert key.

To select shape sub-objects with Spline Select:

1. Select a shape.

2. Open the Modify panel 🖉.

3. Apply a Spline Select modifier to the shape.

4. In the stack display, click the plus sign next to the Spline Select modifier. Then choose a sub-object selection level from the drop-down list (**Figure 9.12**).

   The sub-object type becomes highlighted. Commands that can be applied at that level become available below.

5. Click or drag a selection region around the sub-objects you want to select (**Figure 9.13**).

   The sub-objects turn red, indicating that they are selected (**Figure 9.14**).

✔ Tips

■ Get Vertex Selection, Get Segment Selection, and Get Spline Selection create a selection based on adjacent sub-objects that are selected on other levels.

■ There is no Soft Selection option available for shapes.

■ You can also choose shape sub-object selection levels from the Tools1 quad menu (**Figure 9.15**).

You can soft select spline sub-objects with an Edit Spline modifier, or within an editable spline in order to control the affect of edit commands. Soft selection is not passed up the modifier stack and is not available with Spline Select.

To make a soft selection:

1. Make a vertex-level sub-object selection with an Edit Spline modifier, or within an editable spline (**Figure 9.16**).

2. Open the Soft Selection rollout.

3. Check Use Soft Selection. Then drag the Falloff spinner to adjust the degree of selection (**Figure 9.17**).

   The sub-objects in range of the soft selection change colors from red to orange to yellow to blue as you increase the falloff value. Red indicates the hottest selection where commands will be applied at full intensity; blue indicates the coolest selection where the effect of commands will diminish (**Figure 9.18**).

4. If you want to change the falloff pattern, apply Pinch and Bubble to the selection.

   To see an example of soft selection in action, see "To adjust the curvature of a shape" in the next section.

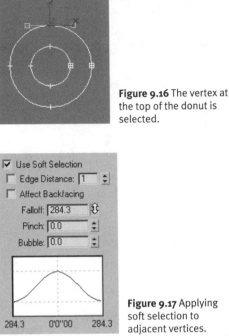

Figure 9.16 The vertex at the top of the donut is selected.

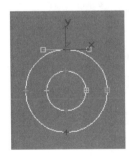

Figure 9.17 Applying soft selection to adjacent vertices.

Figure 9.18 The soft selected change color to indicate the intensity of selection.

SELECTING SHAPE SUB-OBJECTS

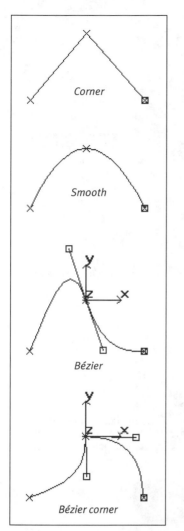

Figure 9.19 The four vertex types allow you to control the curvature of a spline.

Adjusting Curvature

The manipulation of shapes, and splines in general, is all about controlling curvature. Curvature controls are a property of vertices that control the curvature of neighboring segments. Because segments cannot bend more than 2° between steps, the number of steps in each segment governs the smoothness of its curve.

You adjust the curvature of segments by moving vertices, moving vertex controls, or converting to different vertex types:

Corner types produce straight line segments that protrude at any angle on either side of the vertex.

Smooth types produce gradually sloping curves and have no controls that you can adjust.

Bézier types have two control handles that can be dragged to affect each adjacent segment. The exception is endpoints, which have only one handle that can be dragged.

Bézier corner types have two control handles that can be dragged independently, or one if the vertex is an endpoint. Use this type to create sharp corners and curved segments.

For an illustration of each vertex type, see **Figure 9.19**.

Usually, the easiest way to adjust Bézier controls is by dragging them with the Move tool. You can also rotate and scale Bézier controls, but you can accomplish the same effect using the Move tool, and with better control. Rotating and scaling smooth and corner vertices has no effect.

Converting a vertex changes its type. This produces different options for curving segments or making them straight.

To convert a vertex:

1. Select the line.

2. Open the Modify panel .

3. Click on the point you want to convert. To convert multiple points at once, drag a selection region around them (**Figure 9.20**).

4. Right-click on a selected point.

5. In the Tools1 quad menu, choose a vertex type from corner, smooth, Bézier, or Bézier corner.

   To produce the most evenly rounded curves, choose smooth (**Figure 9.21**).

   The vertex points convert to the new type, and the segments adjacent to the vertex adjust accordingly (**Figure 9.22**).

✔ Tip

■ To produce smooth, adjustable curves, convert vertices to the smooth type before converting them a second time to Bézier (**Figure 9.23**).

Figure 9.20 Selecting all the vertices in a jagged line.

Figure 9.21 Choose a vertex type in the Tools 1 quad menu.

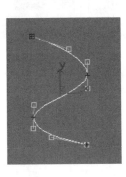

Figure 9.22 After converting the vertices to the smooth type.

Figure 9.23 Bézier handles will now allow you to adjust the curve.

ADJUSTING CURVATURE

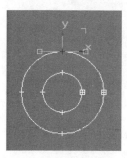

Figure 9.24 After selecting the vertex.

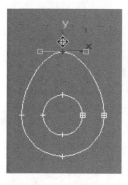

Figure 9.25 Moving the vertex affects the adjacent segments.

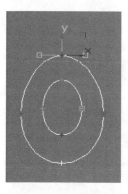

Figure 9.26 Soft selection spreads the effect of the deformation.

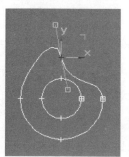

Figure 9.27 Dragging Bézier handles gives you precise control over curvature.

You adjust the curvature of a shape by adjusting vertices along its path.

To adjust the curvature of a shape:

1. Select a shape with the Move tool.

2. Open the Modify panel .

3. Enable Vertex level selection.

4. Select a vertex that is adjacent to the segments you want to adjust (**Figure 9.24**).

5. Optional: Soft select the vertex by increasing the selection falloff.

6. Move the vertex.

   The adjacent segments scale and bend as you move the vertex (**Figure 9.25**).

   If you applied soft selection to the adjacent vertices, they will deform as well (**Figure 9.26**).

7. To adjust curvature with more precision, convert the vertex to a Bézier or Bézier corner vertex. Then move the Bézier control handles toward, away from, or around the vertex.

   The curvature of the segments adjacent to the vertex adjust (**Figure 9.27**).

ADJUSTING CURVATURE

You smooth a curve at the shape level by increasing the number of steps between vertices. By checking Adaptive, you can increase the number of steps in such a way that they are distributed more liberally along tighter curves.

To smooth a shape:

1. Select a shape (**Figure 9.28**).

2. In the Modify panel, open the General rollout of the shape.

3. Increase the number of steps.

   or

   Check Adaptive (**Figure 9.29**).

   The shape becomes smoother (**Figure 9.30**).

✔ Tip

■ Checking Adaptive disables the Optimize and steps parameters, and introduces a lot of steps. If you are planning to extrude or lathe a shape, it is probably better not to use Adaptive because the resulting mesh will be more complex than needed. (Lofts have their own optimize and adaptive controls, so they are not affected by the complexity of the shapes that generate them.)

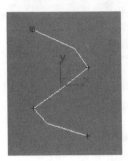

Figure 9.28 Selecting a line that has only one step between vertices.

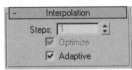

Figure 9.29 After checking Adaptive, the Steps and Optimize parameters become unavailable.

Figure 9.30 The line is smoothed as a result of adding more steps in between the vertices.

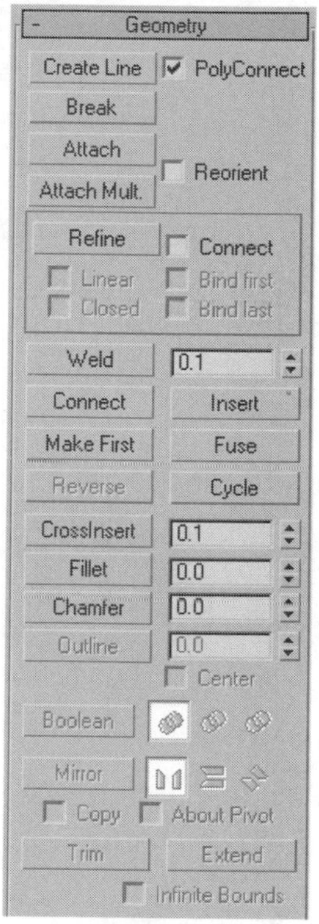

Figure 9.31 The Geometry rollout for Edit Spline and editable splines.

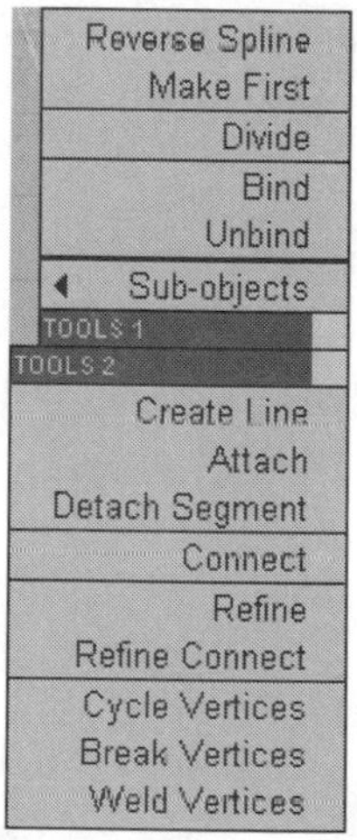

Figure 9.32 The right-click quad menus of an editable spline contains two menus of spline editing commands.

Editing Shapes

Shape objects can be edited at the vertex, segment, spline, and object levels. When you choose a selection level, the editing commands for that level become available in the Modify panel (**Figure 9.31**). You can also access these commands from the Tools1 and Tools2 quad menus (**Figure 9.32**).

Object editing commands act upon the entire shape. They attach shapes, create lines, and insert vertices. The object level is the only level that allows you to attach multiple objects from a list.

The Attach, Create Line, Insert, Hide, Unhide All, and Delete commands can be used at every sub-object level. In addition, the following commands are specific to certain levels:

◆ Vertex-specific commands are the most abundant. They include Break, Refine, Weld, Connect, Make First, Fuse, Cycle, Cross Insert, Fillet, Chamfer, Bind, and Unbind.

◆ Segment-specific commands are the fewest in number. They include Break, Refine, Divide, and Detach.

◆ Spline-specific commands are similar to element commands in that they affect discrete shapes within a spline. They include Reverse, Outline, Boolean, Mirror, Trim, Extend, Close, Detach, and Explode.

EDITING SHAPES

245

Table 9.1 shows the availability of editing commands at each level of sub-object selection:

Table 9.1

Spline Editing Commands and the Levels They Affect		
	VERTEX	**SEGMENT**	**SPLINE**
Create Line	●	●	●
Break	●	●	
Attach	●	●	●
Attach Mult.	●	●	●
Refine	●	●	
Weld	●		
Connect	●		
Insert	●	●	●
Make First	●		
Fuse	●		
Reverse			●
Cycle	●		
Cross Insert	●		
Fillet	●		
Chamfer	●		
Outline			●
Boolean			●
Mirror			●
Trim			●
Extend			●
Hide	●	●	●
Unhide All	●	●	●
Bind	●		
Unbind	●		
Delete	●	●	●
Close			●
Divide		●	
Detach		●	●
Explode			●

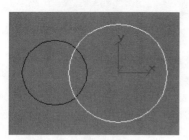

Figure 9.33 Select a shape object.

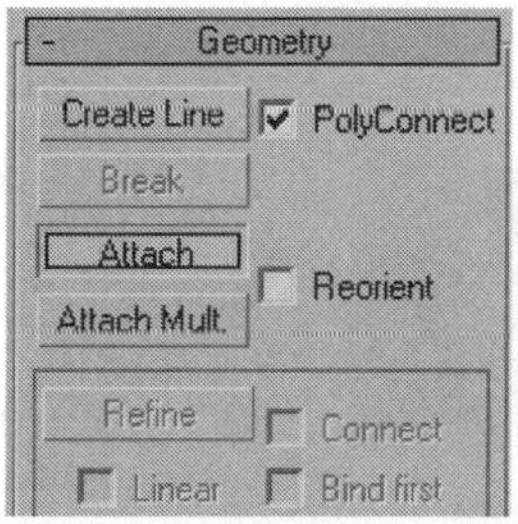

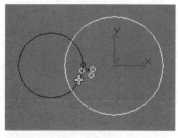

Figure 9.34 Click Attach in order to add another shape to the object.

Figure 9.35 Click a second shape to attach it to the first.

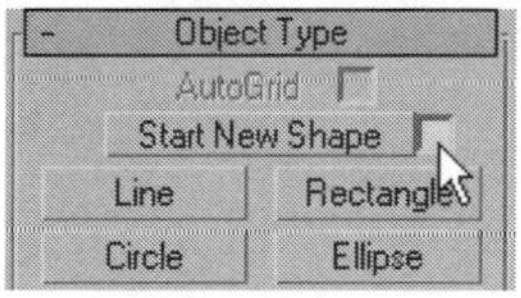

Figure 9.36 Unchecking Start New Shape allows you to attach shapes as you create them.

Attaching shapes creates a multi-shape object. You can use the Attach command at any level.

To attach a shape:

1. Select a shape (**Figure 9.33**).

2. Open the Modify panel 🖊.

3. Convert the shape to an editable spline or apply an Edit Spline modifier to it.

4. In the Geometry rollout, click Attach (**Figure 9.34**).

5. Click the shape you want to attach (**Figure 9.35**).

   The second shape is attached to the first.

6. Continue clicking shapes to attach them, or click Attach to end attach mode.

✔ Tips

- Clicking Attach Mult. brings up a list of attachable shape objects so that you can attach multiple shapes at one time.

- To attach shape shapes as you create them, uncheck the Start New Shape checkbox on the Shape creation menu (**Figure 9.36**).

Welding joins the end points of attached splines into a single vertex. You can use it for modeling, connecting motion paths, or cleaning up 2D drawings that are imported from CAD programs.

To weld vertices:

1. Select a shape.

2. Open the Modify panel [icon].

3. Convert the shape to an editable spline, or apply an Edit Spline modifier to it.

4. Enable Vertex level editing [icon].

5. [icon] Move one of the end points onto the other so that they coincide.

   When you release the mouse button, the Edit Spline dialog box appears (**Figure 9.37**).

6. Click Yes.

   The vertices weld and become one vertex (**Figure 9.38**).

✔ Tips

- You can also use the Weld command to set a weld threshold and weld selected vertices (**Figure 9.39**).

- A quick way to tell if coincident vertices in a spline are welded is to click Show Vertex Numbers in the Selection rollout and see if there is only one number at the vertex.

- The Fuse command brings vertices together without welding them.

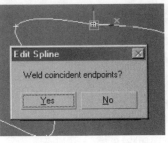

Figure 9.37 You can weld vertices by dragging one end point on top of another.

Figure 9.38 After welding the vertices into one.

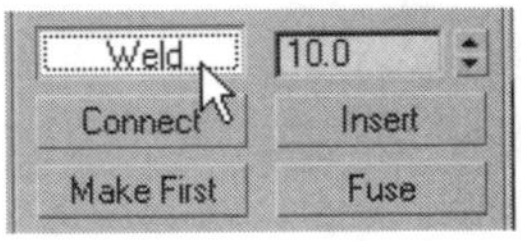

Figure 9.39 Use the Weld button to weld selected vertices within a set distance.

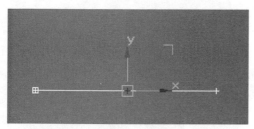

Figure 9.40 Select a vertex.

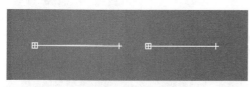

Figure 9.41 After you break a spline, you can separate the cloned vertices.

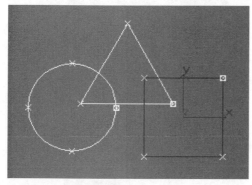

Figure 9.42 Select a spline.

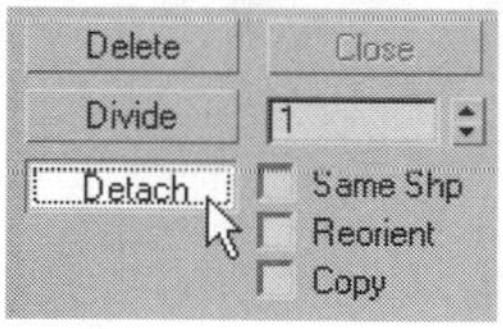

Figure 9.43 Click Detach to separate a sub-object selection.

The break command cuts a spline apart at a vertex point.

To break a spline:

1. Select a shape.

2. Open the Modify panel 🖉.

3. Convert the shape to an editable spline, or apply an Edit Spline modifier to it.

4. Enable Vertex level editing ∷.

5. Select a vertex where you want to break a spline (**Figure 9.40**).

6. In the Geometry rollout, click Break.

   The vertex is cloned and converted to a first vertex. You can now move the vertex apart from its clone (**Figure 9.41**)

The Detach command reverses the Attach command by detaching segments or splines into separate shapes.

To detach a spline:

1. Select a shape.

2. Open the Modify panel 🖉.

3. Convert the shape to an editable spline, or apply an Edit Spline modifier to it.

4. Enable Spline level editing ⌢.

5. Select the spline you want to detach (**Figure 9.42**).

6. In the Geometry rollout, click Detach (**Figure 9.43**).

7. Click OK to accept the default name for the detached shape.

   The spline is detached to a new shape.

✔ Tips

- You use the same procedure at the segment level to detach a segment.

- Explode is a fast way to detach segments or splines all at once. You can explode to detached shapes or to attached splines. Explode only works at the spline level.

Connect builds a straight line segment between two end points of a spline, regardless of the tangent values of the vertices that connect.

To connect two vertices:

1. Select a shape.

2. Open the Modify panel 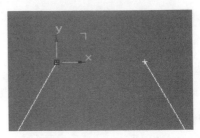.

3. Convert the shape to an editable spline, or apply an Edit Spline modifier to it.

4. Enable Vertex level editing .

5. Select an end vertex (**Figure 9.44**).

6. In the Geometry rollout, click Connect (**Figure 9.45**).

7. Drag the mouse cursor from the selected vertex to another end vertex (**Figure 9.46**).

   The vertices are connected by a segment (**Figure 9.47**).

Figure 9.44 Select an end vertex to connect.

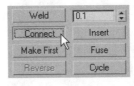

Figure 9.45 Click Connect.

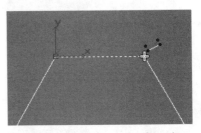

Figure 9.46 Drag a connection from the first end vertex to the next.

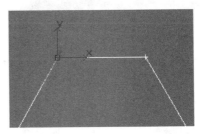

Figure 9.47 After connecting the two vertices, a straight segment is drawn between them.

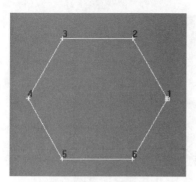

Figure 9.48 The first vertex of the NGon is on the right.

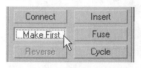

Figure 9.49 Use Make First to reorder the vertices.

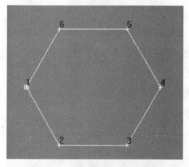

Figure 9.50 Now the first vertex of the NGon is on the left. The numbering still proceeds counterclockwise.

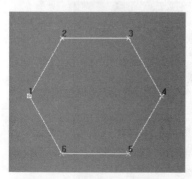

Figure 9.51 After using the Reverse command, the numbering proceeds clockwise.

Every shape has a first vertex at one end, or in the middle if it is a closed shape. The first vertex is important for determining the starting point of a motion path or the beginning point of a loft path.

The Make First feature allows you to choose which vertex of a shape is first.

To set a first vertex:

1. Select a shape.

2. Open the Modify panel 🖌.

3. Convert the object to an editable spline, or apply an Edit Spline modifier to it.

4. Enable Vertex level editing ⁙.

5. In the Selection rollout, click Check Show Vertex Numbers.

   Vertex numbers appear by each vertex, numbering the vertices in order from beginning to end. The first vertex has a square around it (**Figure 9.48**).

6. Select a vertex at the end of an open spline, or anywhere on a closed spline.

7. Click Make First in the Geometry rollout (**Figure 9.49**).

   The selected vertex becomes the first vertex. The vertex number changes to 1, and the square moves to enclose the vertex mark (**Figure 9.50**).

✔ Tips

- Clicking the Cycle button advances a vertex selection to the next vertex in a spline. If the shape contains more than one spline, the selection will cycle from one spline to the next and then back to the beginning.

- The Reverse command reverses the direction, or vertex order, of a single spline. The Reverse command is available only at the Spline selection level (**Figure 9.51**).

Chamfer splits a vertex into two vertices and spread them apart evenly. If the vertex is on the corner of a shape, the corner is filed down to a 45-degree angle.

To chamfer a vertex:

1. Select a shape that has a distinct corner (**Figure 9.52**).

2. Open the Modify panel ![icon].

3. Convert the shape to an editable spline, or apply an Edit Spline modifier to it.

4. Click Vertex ![icon].

5. Select a vertex.

6. In the Geometry rollout, click Chamfer (**Figure 9.53**). Then drag the Chamfer spinner or enter a value to set the chamfer distance.

   The vertex splits into two vertices, which spread apart along the length of the spline. If they are on a corner, they chamfer the corner (**Figure 9.54**).

✔ Tip

■ Fillet works the same way as the Chamfer command, except that it rounds a corner to an arc (**Figure 9.55**).

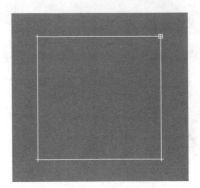

Figure 9.52 A rectangle is a good shape to use to learn about Chamfer and Fillet.

Figure 9.53 Use the Chamfer spinner to set the chamfer distance.

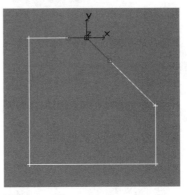

Figure 9.54 The rectangle corner after chamfering.

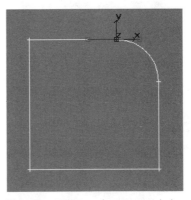

Figure 9.55 Fillet produces a rounded corner.

EDITING SHAPES

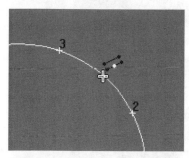

Figure 9.56 Use Refine to add new vertices to a spline.

Figure 9.57 The Refine cursor tells you that you can click to add a vertex.

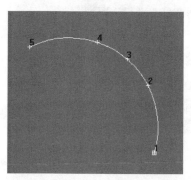

Figure 9.58 The new vertex stays in numeric sequence with the rest.

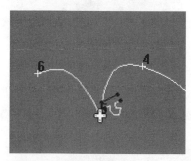

Figure 9.59 Use Insert to add a vertex and move it at the same time.

You refine a shape by adding vertices to it. This makes curved shapes bend more smoothly. If the refined shape is extruded, lathed, or lofted, the resulting shape object will have more faces.

To refine a shape:

1. Select a shape.

2. Open the Modify panel .

3. Convert the shape to an editable spline, or apply an Edit Spline modifier to it.

4. Enable Vertex level editing .

5. In the Geometry rollout, click Refine (**Figure 9.56**).

6. Place the cursor over a segment.

    The cursor changes to the Refine cursor (**Figure 9.57**).

7. Click the spline at the point where you would like to add the vertex.

    A new vertex appears, subdividing the segment you clicked on. If the vertex numbers are visible, they update accordingly (**Figure 9.58**).

✔ Tips

- You can add as many vertices as you wish so long as the Refine button is active.

- You cannot create a stand-alone vertex. Vertices must always be connected to at least one segment in a spline.

- The Insert command allows you to add vertices and move them at the same time (**Figure 9.59**).

- Cross Insert adds two vertices at the juncture of two intersecting splines. It does not connect, weld or fuse the vertices.

- Divide is a segment-level command that adds a vertex to the middle of a segment.

You delete shape sub-objects with the Delete command, or by pressing Delete on your keyboard.

To delete any part of a shape:

1. Select a shape object.

2. Open the Modify panel .

3. Convert the shape to an editable spline, or apply an Edit Spline modifier to it.

4. Enable the level that you want to edit 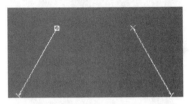.

5. Select the part of the spline that you want to delete (**Figure 9.60**).

6. Press the Delete key, or click the Delete button in the Geometry rollout.

   The selection is deleted (**Figure 9.61**).

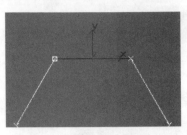

Figure 9.60 Select the portion of the object that you want to delete.

Figure 9.61 After deleting the segment.

Figure 9.62 Dragging the Outline spinner. A positive number offsets to the inside of the spline; a negative number offsets to the outside.

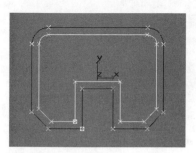

Figure 9.63 An outline has been added to the spline.

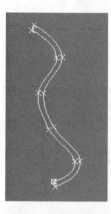

Figure 9.64 Because the profile was enhanced using Outline, the vase will have thickness when lathed.

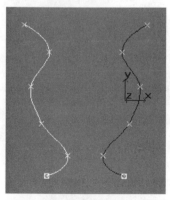

Figure 9.65 Use Mirror to flip or clone a spline.

The Outline command offsets a spline sub-object a specified distance from the original.

Outline is used in architectural modeling to add thickness to walls. You can also use it to add thickness to a lathed object.

To outline a spline:

1. Select a shape object that contains one or more splines.

2. Open the Modify panel ✐.

3. Convert the shape to an editable spline, or apply an Edit Spline modifier to it.

4. Enable Spline-level editing ∿.

5. Select the spline you want to outline.

6. Drag the Outline spinner or enter a value to specify the distance between the original spline and the outline (**Figure 9.62**).

   A new spline is created that outlines the spline you selected. This spline remains part of the shape (**Figure 9.63**).

✔ Tips

■ If you want to offset the spline and its outline an equal distance on either side of the original, activate the Center checkbox.

■ Outline the profile of a vase to add thickness to the vase when it is lathed (**Figure 9.64**).

■ The Mirror command flips splines vertically, horizontally, or both. It also gives you the option of cloning your spline (**Figure 9.65**).

Spline Boolean operations combine overlapping spline sub-objects and delete portions based on how they overlap. Each of the spline sub-objects that you operate on is referred to as an *operand*.

- ◆  **Union**—Deletes the overlapping portion of splines that intersect.

- ◆ **Subtraction**—Deletes the part of the first spline that overlaps the second, and the part of the second spline that does not overlap the first.

- ◆ **Intersection**—Deletes the non-overlapping portion of intersecting splines.

To perform a Boolean operation on a shape:

1. Select a compound shape object that has two or more overlapping splines.

2. Open the Modify panel.

3. Convert the shape to an editable spline, or apply an Edit Spline modifier to it.

4. Enable Spline level editing.

5. Select a spline sub-object to be the first operand (**Figure 9.66**).

6. In the Geometry rollout, click Boolean (**Figure 9.67**).

7. Click a Boolean button to choose a Boolean operation.

8. Click a spline sub-object to be the second operand (**Figure 9.68**).

   The Boolean operation is performed on the two operands (**Figure 9.69**).

9. Continue clicking operands until the shape is complete (**Figure 9.70**).

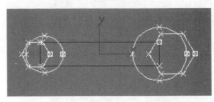

Figure 9.66 Select the rectangle to be the first operand. The other shape sub-objects are 2 circles and 2 NGons.

Figure 9.67 Click Boolean and choose an operation. Here, the Union operation is selected.

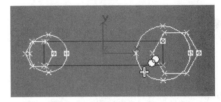

Figure 9.68 Clicking the second operand.

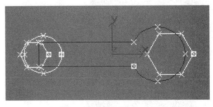

Figure 9.69 After performing a Boolean union on the first circle, the overlapping portions of the rectangle and circle disappear.

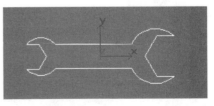

Figure 9.70 After the second circle is added and the NGons are subtracted, the final product is a wrench template, which can then be extruded.

EDITING SHAPES

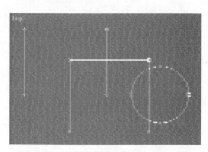

Figure 9.71 This is a single shape made up of two rectangles and a circle.

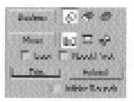

Figure 9.72 The Trim button turns yellow when it is active.

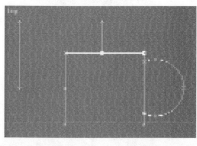

Figure 9.73 The lines inside the center spline are trimmed away.

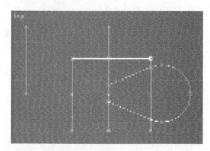

Figure 9.74 The lines are extended to the center spline.

Trim deletes the portion of a shape that extends beyond the area of intersecting spline sub-objects.

The Trim command has the same requirement as Boolean operations in that the splines you are working with must be part of the same shape.

To trim a shape:

1. Select a compound shape object that has at least two overlapping splines (**Figure 9.71**).

2. Open the Modify panel 🖉.

3. Convert the shape to an editable spline, or apply an Edit Spline modifier to it.

4. Enable Spline level editing ⌃.

5. Click the Trim button (**Figure 9.72**).

6. Select the lines that you want to remove (**Figure 9.73**).

   The lines are trimmed up to where they intersect the nearest spline.

✔ Tips

■ Click the Extend button and see what happens when you click the lines that you just trimmed (**Figure 9.74**).

■ Note that you do not have to select one of the splines to use Trim or Extend. You simply activate the button and start picking lines you want trimmed or extended.

EDITING SHAPES

257

COMPOUND OBJECTS

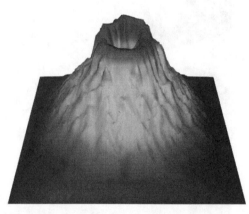

Figure 10.1 This terrain model of a volcano was created with actual contour line data.

Compound objects combine two or more objects into one. They greatly assist complex modeling operations and facilitate certain animation techniques, such as 3D morphing. 3ds max 4 ships with nine types of compound objects: Boolean, Connect, Scatter, ShapeMerge, Terrain, Conform, Loft, Morph, and Mesher.

Compound objects combine some of the best characteristics of modifiers and arrays. With compound objects, you can deform, cut, join, remove, and extrude surfaces. You can create ordered or random arrays of clones. You can also create surface terrain models from contour lines (**Figure 10.1**).

When you apply a compound object command to individual objects, the objects become operands of the compound object operation—meaning that they are operated upon. Compound object commands cannot be used to select the first object, so you must select an object before choosing a compound object command. Commands for creating compound objects are found in the drop-down menu of the Create/Geometry branch.

Creating Boolean Objects

Boolean algebra was invented by British mathematician George Boole for combining and manipulating sets of mathematical symbols. In 3D graphics, Boolean operations are applied to sets of mesh faces, or sets of spline segments. This chapter covers Boolean operations for mesh objects. For spline Booleans, see Chapter 9, Editing Shapes.

3D Boolean operations use additive and subtractive techniques, just like in traditional sculpture. In sculpture, you add to a form by applying mass, and subtract from a form by carving away mass. In Boolean operations, you add and subtract mass by combining objects.

Boolean operations always work on two objects. The first object that you select is called operand A. The second object is called operand B. The type of Boolean operation and the position of the objects determine the final result (**Figure 10.2**):

◆ **Union**—Combines both operands into one object and removes intersecting faces.

◆ **Subtraction (A-B)**—Subtracts the volume of operand B from the volume of operand A. Builds an interior surface on operand A by adding the enclosed faces of operand B to it. The rest of operand B's faces are deleted.

◆ **Subtraction (B-A)**—Subtracts the volume of operand A from the volume of operand B. This operation uses faces from operand B to cover the hole that would otherwise remain.

◆ **Intersection**—Deletes the nonintersecting volume of the two operands and uses the faces of the interpenetrating surfaces to build a new object.

◆ **Cut**—Cuts open the surface of operand A with the volume of operand B. No faces from operand B are added to operand A. Instead, faces are refined, split, or deleted in operand A along the intersection of its surface with operand B.

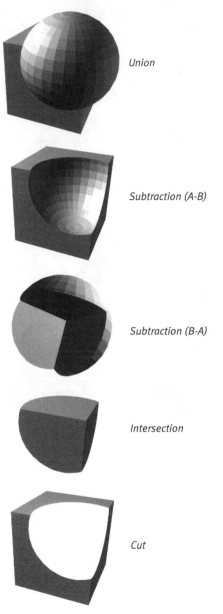

Union

Subtraction (A-B)

Subtraction (B-A)

Intersection

Cut

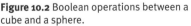

Figure 10.2 Boolean operations between a cube and a sphere.

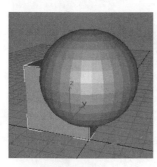

Figure 10.3 Select the first operand.

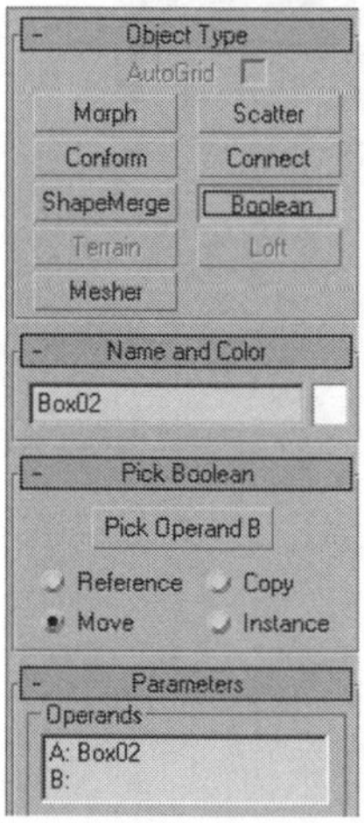

Figure 10.4 The Create panel shows the selected object assigned to operand A.

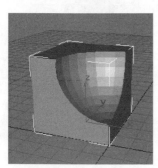

Figure 10.5 Subtraction (A-B) is the default Boolean operation.

Figure 10.6 The sphere has taken a bite out of the box.

Subtraction is the most commonly used Boolean operation.

To perform a Boolean subtraction:

1. Position ✛ ↻ two mesh objects so that they intersect.

2. Select the object you want to operate on (**Figure 10.3**).

3. In the Create panel 🎮, open the Geometry sub-panel and choose Compound Objects from the drop-down list. Then click Boolean in the Object Type rollout.

   The Boolean rollout appears. The selected object is already assigned to operand A (**Figure 10.4**).

4. In the Parameters rollout, choose Subtraction (A-B) (**Figure 10.5**).

5. Click Pick Operand B, and click the intersecting object.

   The volume of the second object is subtracted from the first (**Figure 10.6**).

6. To subtract the first object from the second, click Subtraction (B-A).

✔ Tip

■ Boolean operations sometimes fail to work properly, although they have improved significantly since the program was first released. However, it is still a good idea to hold your scene (using Edit > Hold) before performing a Boolean operation. That way, if the operation fails, you can retrieve the scene from the hold file using Edit > Fetch. For more information on how to make Boolean operations a success, see "Tips for Performing Successful Boolean Operations" later in this section.

The product of a Boolean intersection looks like the piece you drilled out in a subtraction. If the operands do not intersect, both disappear.

To perform a Boolean intersection:

1. Position ⊕ ↺ two mesh objects so that they intersect.

2. Select one of the objects (**Figure 10.7**).

3. Apply a Boolean command.

4. In the Parameters rollout, choose Intersection (**Figure 10.8**).

5. Click Pick Operand B, and the click the second object.

   The non-intersecting faces are removed, leaving the intersection of the two objects (**Figure 10.9**).

✔ Tip

■ To change Boolean operations interactively, so that you can compare the effect of each, click on the different operations in the Parameters rollout.

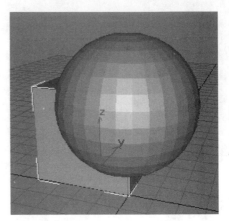

Figure 10.7 Select an operand. It doesn't matter which object you pick.

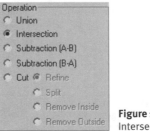

Figure 10.8 Choose the Intersection operation.

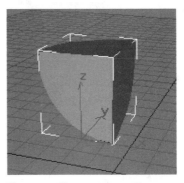

Figure 10.9 The non-intersecting faces are deleted.

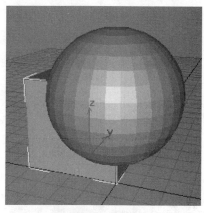

Figure 10.10 Position the two objects, and then select the one you want to cut.

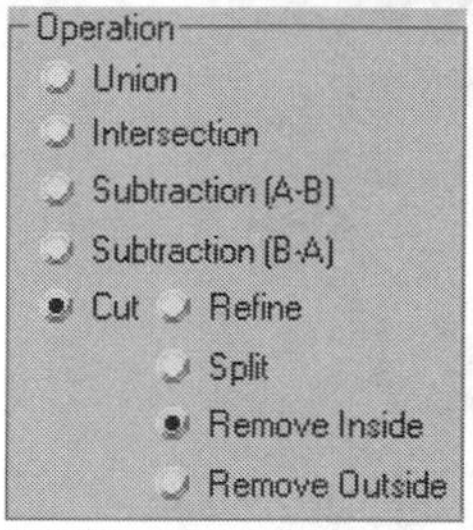

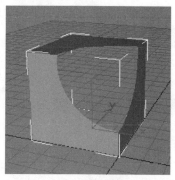

Figure 10.11 Choose the Cut > Remove Inside operation.

Figure 10.12 The sphere cuts a hole in the box without leaving any faces.

The Boolean cut operation has four variations:

◆ **Refine**—Adds new faces to operand A where it intersects the surface of operand B.

◆ **Split**—Adds two sets of new faces to operand A where it intersects the surface of operand B. Each of these sets of faces is used to define a separate element in the mesh so that the mesh can easily be split apart.

◆ **Remove Inside**—Deletes faces from operand A that are enclosed by the volume of operand B. This option works like Subtraction, except that it does not add faces to operand A.

◆ **Remove Outside**—Deletes faces from operand A that are not enclosed by the volume of operand B. This option works like Intersect, except that it does not add faces to operand A.

To perform a Boolean cut:

1. Create two intersecting objects.

2. Select the object you want to cut (**Figure 10.10**).

3. Apply a Boolean command.

4. In the Parameters rollout, choose Cut (**Figure 10.11**).

5. Click Pick Operand B, and then click the second object.

   The first object is cut by the second one (**Figure 10.12**).

Boolean operands can be animated after a Boolean operation has been performed. The results can be elegant and magical to watch and have a wide variety of applications.

To animate a Boolean:

1. Select a Boolean object. For this example, use an object that has been created by subtraction.

2. Open the Modify panel .

3. In the Display area, check Result + Hidden Ops (**Figure 10.13**).

   The hidden operand appears in wireframe (**Figure 10.14**).

4. In the modifier stack display, click the plus sign next to the word Boolean. Then click Operands (**Figure 10.15**).

5. Click the Animate button .

6. Drag the time slider to a new position.

7. Drag the wireframe operand all the way through the solid operand (**Figure 10.16**).

8. Turn off Show Hidden Operand.

9. Click Play Animation .

   The hole created by the hidden operand moves smoothly through the solid operand.

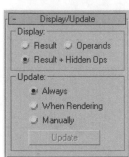

Figure 10.13 In the Modify panel, check Result + Hidden Ops.

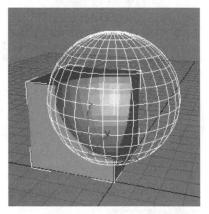

Figure 10.14 You can now see the wireframe sphere that was subtracted from the box.

Figure 10.15 Turning on Sub-Object lets you manipulate and animate Boolean operands.

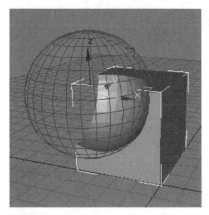

Figure 10.16 The space created by the subtracted operand seems to move through the solid operand.

CREATING BOOLEAN OBJECTS

Tips for Performing Successful Boolean Operations

Boolean objects can sometimes become unstable or fail, which may cause them to disappear or perform operations incorrectly. In this event, undo the operation and try these tips:

◆ Increase the number of faces on the simpler operand and try again. Boolean operations work best when the density of each mesh is roughly equal.

◆ Reposition the operands slightly.

◆ Collapse the operands' modifier stacks before using them.

◆ Make sure the operands are not too complex. Complexity can cause Boolean operations to take hours, and then fail. Decrease the number of segments or apply an Optimize modifier and collapse the stack before trying again.

◆ To escape from a Boolean operation, press the Esc key to end the operation.

◆ Good operands should have a closed, continuous surface that is not self-intersecting. Use the STL-Check modifier to check for open edges, double edges, double faces, internal faces, or unwelded vertices. (See "To fix holes in a mesh" in Chapter 6.)

◆ Another way to check a mesh object for holes is to apply a Mesh Select modifier and choose Edge level selection. Then click Select Open Edges. Edges that do not have a face on both sides will turn red.

◆ Teapots and Hedra are poor Boolean operands because of their internal self-intersecting faces. To overcome this obstacle, perform a Union operation between two clones.

◆ Avoid using operands that have long, skinny faces. To shorten faces in objects, try adding extra height segments to primitives and adding extra steps when you are lofting, extruding, or lathing objects.

◆ When performing a series of Boolean operations, deselect the object between operations.

◆ If you are performing multiple Boolean operations on a model, collapse the stack and convert the model to an editable mesh between operations. This changes the object to an explicitly defined model, rather than a parametrically defined one, which is far more stable.

◆ If the Boolean operation is so unstable that it disappears when you convert it, try exporting it as a .3ds object and then importing it back into your scene.

◆ Another way to stabilize a Boolean operation is to apply a Snapshot command using the Mesh setting. This produces an editable mesh that you can use instead.

◆ Applying an Optimize modifier with a low (0.1) face threshold can sometimes help.

◆ If you are not planning to animate the Boolean operation, try using the Collapse utility in the Utility panel instead. The Collapse command outputs an editable mesh. By holding down the Ctrl key, you can pick and operate with multiple operands in succession.

The Connect objects operation can connect two or more mesh objects by building bridges between holes in their surfaces. Use Connect objects to create architectural structures, furniture, handles, tools, and other manufactured objects. You can also use Connect objects to connect fingers to a hand or to connect appendages to a torso.

To create a Connect object:

1. Create 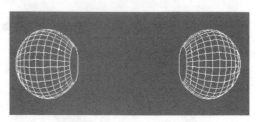 two mesh objects.

2. Make a hole in the surface of each object by deleting some sub-objects ⬜ or by performing a Boolean cut operation.

   For symmetrical output, create one object with a hole and then mirror/clone it.

3. Position the objects ⊕ ↻ so that the holes face each other within a 90-degree angle (**Figure 10.17**).

4. Select one of the objects.

5. Open the Create panel and choose Geometry > Compound Objects > Connect.

   The Connect rollout appears. The selected object is assigned as operand 0 (**Figure 10.18**).

6. Choose a clone type for your next operand, just as you would with a Boolean operand.

7. Click Pick Operand, and click the second mesh object.

   A mesh structure bridges the gap between holes in the operands (**Figure 10.19**).

8. Smooth the bridge in the middle and at either end by checking Bridge and Ends.

9. Increase the number of segments and adjust the tension to make the bridge bulge or shrink (**Figure 10.20**).

Figure 10.17 Positioning the objects so the holes face each other.

Figure 10.18 The selected object is assigned as operand 0.

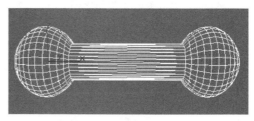

Figure 10.19 The result of connecting two spheres.

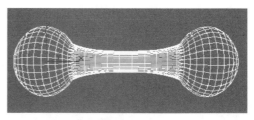

Figure 10.20 The result of adjusting the number of segments and tension setting.

CREATING BOOLEAN OBJECTS

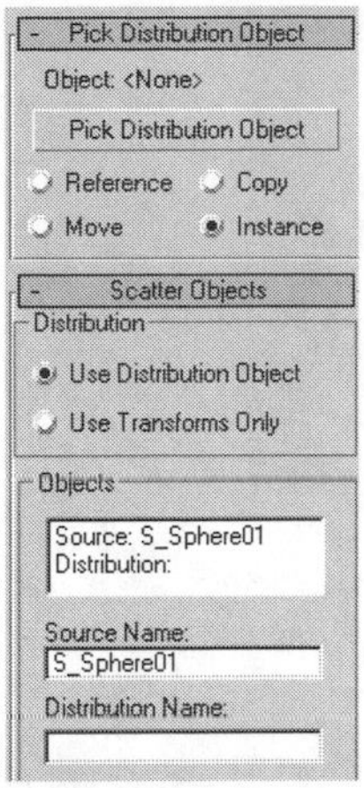

Figure 10.21 The Scatter panel shows the selected object assigned as the source.

Figure 10.22 The result of scattering teapots on a planar surface.

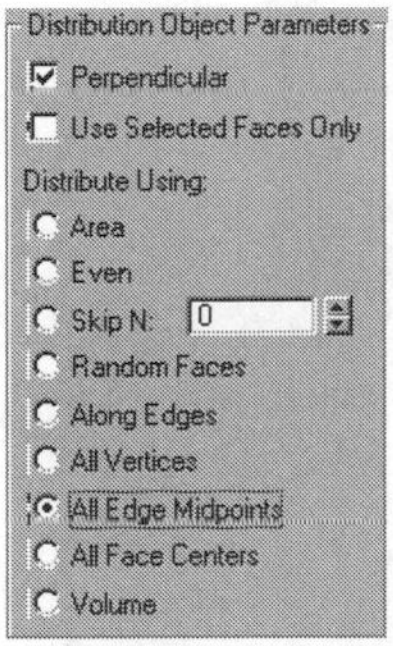

Figure 10.23 Setting All Edge Midpoints in the Scatter panel.

Figure 10.24 The result of scattering teapots on a planar surface using the All Edge Midpoints option.

The Scatter objects operation distributes clones of a source object over the surface or within the volume of a distribution object.

To create a Scatter object:

1. Select or create a mesh object to scatter.

2. Open the Create panel, and choose Geometry > Compound Objects > Scatter.

   The Scatter rollout appears. The selected object is assigned to be the source object (**Figure 10.21**).

3. Choose a clone type.

4. Click Pick Operand. Then click a mesh object to be the distribution object.

   The source object positions itself on the surface of the distribution object.

5. In the Source Object Parameters group, enter a value for the number of duplicates.

   Clones of the source object arrange themselves evenly over the surface of the distribution object (**Figure 10.22**).

6. Try each of the distribution methods by clicking the radio buttons in the Distribution Object Parameters group (**Figure 10.23**).

   All Vertices, All Edge Midpoints, and All Face Centers ignore the Duplicates value and create regular arrays (**Figure 10.24**).

✔ Tip

■ To create a random distribution of objects within a volume, use a mesh object that encloses volume as the distribution object and check Volume in the Distribution Object Parameters group.

You use the ShapeMerge command to embed shapes in a mesh surface or to cut shapes out of it. The faces, vertices, and edges created by embedded shapes are automatically selected at the sub-object level so that you can easily extrude, bevel, or assign materials to them.

To perform a ShapeMerge operation:

1. Position ⊕ ↻ a shape over the surface of a mesh object (**Figure 10.25**).

2. Select the mesh object.

3. Open the Create panel and choose Geometry > Compound Objects > ShapeMerge.

   The ShapeMerge rollout appears. The mesh object is assigned as the Mesh operand (**Figure 10.26**).

4. Choose a clone type and click Pick Shape. Then click the shape.

   The shape is embedded in the surface of the mesh (**Figure 10.27**).

5. Choose Cookie Cutter to cut the area enclosed by the shape out of the mesh surface. Check Invert to cut the surface away from the embedded shape area (**Figure 10.28**).

✔ Tip

■ To learn how to assign different colors to embedded shapes, see "To create a Multi/Sub-Object Material" in Chapter 13.

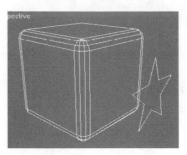

Figure 10.25 Getting a star shape ready to merge into a ChamferBox.

Figure 10.26 The ShapeMerge panel shows the ChamferBox assigned as the Mesh operand.

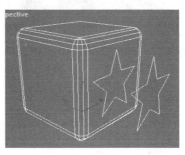

Figure 10.27 The star shape has been embedded into the ChamferBox surface.

Figure 10.28 Using Cookie Cutter to cut shapes out of a mesh.

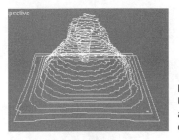

Figure 10.29 Using splines as the terrain contour lines.

Figure 10.30 The shape is assigned as Op 0 in the Terrain panel.

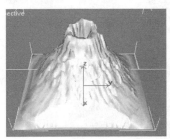

Figure 10.31 The Terrain compound object forms a volcano from the splines.

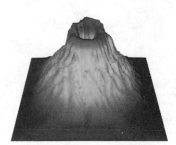

Figure 10.32 Using Color by Elevation to assign realistic shades to the volcano surface.

Terrains are 3D models that you make from contour line data. Terrains create landscapes for building sites, shadow studies, grading plans, and games. If you do not have any contour line models of landscapes, you can make one up using an array of closed splines, with each level being slightly smaller than the previous one.

To create a terrain:

1. Import a contour line data set, or create your own set of splines (**Figure 10.29**).

2. Make sure the splines are all attached as one object. If they are not, select a single spline and convert it to an editable spline. Then apply an Attach Multiple command and select the rest of the splines in the set.

3. Open the Create panel, and choose Geometry > Compound Objects > Terrain.

   The Terrain rollout appears (**Figure 10.30**). The contour lines are *skinned*—that is, a surface forms over them—and turned into a terrain (**Figure 10.31**). Note that complex contour lines may take a while to skin.

4. If any contour lines were skipped, click Pick Operand and click the contour line.

5. You can assign colors to each level of the terrain in the Color by Elevation rollout (**Figure 10.32**).

✔ Tip

■ To reduce the complexity of the mesh, open the Simplification rollout and choose Use $^1/_2$ of Lines or Use $^1/_4$ of Lines for vertical simplification or Use $^1/_2$ of Points or Use $^1/_4$ of Points for horizontal simplification.

Conform objects are compound objects created by "wrapping" the vertices of one object around the vertices of another. This causes the surface of the first object, called a *Wrapper object*, to conform to the surface of the second, the *Wrap-To object*. By placing the Wrapper object around the Wrap-To object, you can roughly duplicate the form of the Wrap-To object as if you were creating a very thin mold.

To create a Conform object:

1. Create ![icon] an object. This will be your Wrap-To object.

2. Create ![icon] a GeoSphere that is slightly larger than the Wrap-To object, and position it so it surrounds the first object. This will be your Wrapper object (**Figure 10.33**).

3. Open the Create panel and choose Geometry > Compound Objects > Conform.

    The Conform rollout appears. The selected outer object is assigned as the Wrapper object (**Figure 10.34**).

4. In the Vertex Projection Direction group, choose Along Vertex Normals (**Figure 10.35**).

5. In the Update group (near the bottom of the Parameters rollout), check Hide Wrap-To Object.

6. Click Pick Wrap-To Object, and choose a clone option.

7. In a wireframe view, click the inner object.

    The Wrapper object wraps around the Wrap-To object (**Figure 10.36**).

✔ Tip

- Use Conform objects to make text lie on the surface of a mesh object.

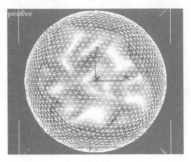

Figure 10.33 A GeoSphere encloses the Wrap-To object in preparation for creation of a Conform compound object.

Figure 10.34 The Conform panel shows the GeoSphere assigned as the Wrapper object.

Figure 10.35 Choosing Along Vertex Normals causes the wrapper vertices to move inward perpendicular to the object surface.

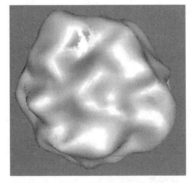

Figure 10.36 The GeoSphere is wrapped around the Wrap-To object and conforms to its surface.

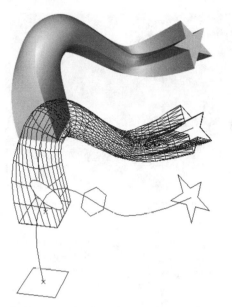

Figure 10.37 Using four shapes on a curved path to create an unusual lofted object.

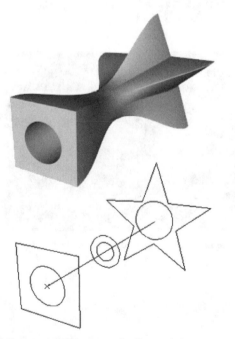

Figure 10.38 Using nested splines to loft an object with a hole through it.

Lofting Objects

Lofting is an incredibly versatile means of modeling and animating 3D forms. The term lofting comes from early methods of shipbuilding in which the hull of a ship was constructed from a series of cross-sections, or ribs, placed along its length. A structure called a loft supported the hull while the ribs were hoisted into place. The process of hoisting the ribs into the loft gave rise to the term lofting.

As in the shipbuilding days of yore, lofting creates a 3D object by placing cross-section shapes along a path. But instead of hoisting wooden ribs into a hull, lofting places shapes along a spline path. As each shape is added to the path, the loft builds a surface, or skin, to accommodate the different outlines of each (**Figure 10.37**).

A loft path can be angular or curved, open or closed, flat or three-dimensional, but it must be a single continuous spline. Shapes made up of more than one spline, such as a donut, cannot be used as a path. In contrast, shapes that you use as cross-sections of the loft can be made up of single or multiple splines. If splines are nested inside of each other, then each nested layer will be lofted together (**Figure 10.38**).

To loft an object, you start with either a path or a shape. If you start with a path and then get the cross-section shapes, the shapes will be arranged perpendicularly along the length of the path. If you start with a shape and then get a path, the path will be positioned along the local Z axis of the shape. For this reason, starting with the path and then getting the shapes is usually preferred because it is easier to predict where the loft will be built.

To loft an object with Get Shape:

1. Select a valid shape for a path (**Figure 10.39**).

2. Open the Create panel, and choose Geometry > Compound Objects > Loft.

   The Loft rollout appears. If the selected spline shape is not a valid path, the Get Shape button will be dimmed.

3. Click Get Shape, and choose a clone option. Accept the default option, Instance, if you plan to edit or animate the loft later (**Figure 10.40**).

4. Move the cursor over a shape.

   If the shape is valid, the cursor changes to a loft cursor (**Figure 10.41**). If the shape is invalid, the reason the shape is invalid is displayed in the prompt line.

5. Click the shape.

   The loft object appears. The shape, or a clone of it, is placed at the first vertex of the path and extruded along its length (**Figure 10.42**).

✔ Tips

- If you want to try lofting a different shape, click a new shape immediately after step 5. The new shape replaces the last shape you picked.

- Lofting a short line along a curved line creates a ribbon. Applying a two-sided material shades the ribbon on both sides.

- If you use shape objects that are made up of more than one spline, all shapes in the loft must contain the same number of splines, and the shapes must have the same nesting order, which is the number of splines that nest within.

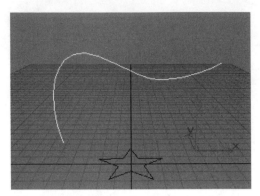

Figure 10.39 Selecting a spline line for the loft path.

Figure 10.40 The Loft panel provides Get Path and Get Shape functions.

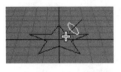

Figure 10.41 The mouse cursor is over a valid shape for lofting.

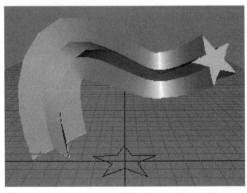

Figure 10.42 The shape is lofted along the entire path.

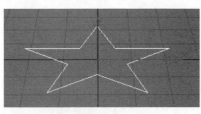

Figure 10.43 Selecting a valid shape for lofting.

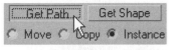

Figure 10.44 Activating the Get Path button using the Instance clone option.

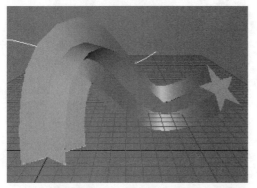

Figure 10.45 A loft generated using Get Path starts at the first shape.

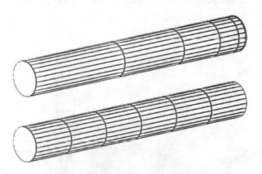

Figure 10.46 A loft path with uneven segment divisions uses Bézier end points (top); the problem is corrected by using Corner end points (bottom).

To loft an object with Get Path:

1. Select a valid cross-section shape (**Figure 10.43**).

2. Open the Create panel, and choose Geometry > Compound Objects > Loft.

   The Loft rollout appears. If the selected spline shape is not a valid shape, the Get Path button will be dimmed.

3. Click Get Path and choose a clone option (**Figure 10.44**).

4. Place the cursor over a shape you want to use as a path. Accept the default option, Instance, if you plan to edit or animate the loft later.

   If the shape is valid as a path, the cursor changes to a loft icon.

5. Click the shape.

   The loft appears, aligned to the local Z axis of the shape. The first vertex of the path is positioned at the pivot point of the shape (**Figure 10.45**).

✔ Tips

- If you want to try lofting a different path, click Get Path and click a new path. The new path replaces the last path you picked.

- To flip the orientation of the path, so that it follows the negative Z axis of the shape, hold down the Ctrl key when you click Get Path.

- Lines that are created by dragging Bézier end points generate uneven segment divisions, or steps, when used as paths (**Figure 10.46**). Converting the end points of the line to another vertex type and relofting the object corrects this problem.

You adjust the shapes, path, skin, and surface rendering of a loft in the Modify panel.

To add shapes to a loft:

1. Select a loft object.

2. Open the Modify panel 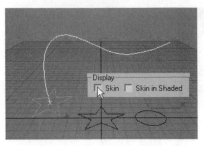.

Figure 10.47 Turning off the skin display so you can see the loft path and shapes.

3. In the Display group of the Skin Parameters rollout, uncheck Skin.

   The surface of the loft is hidden, making the path and shapes easier to see (**Figure 10.47**).

4. In the Path Parameters rollout, drag the Path spinner upward. Click Percentage or Distance to view the Path setting as a percentage along the path or as a distance in current units. Enable Snap if you want to snap to even intervals along the path.

   As you change the Path value, a yellow X moves along the path from the first shape to a new position, or level, on the path. This marks where the next shape will be added (**Figure 10.48**).

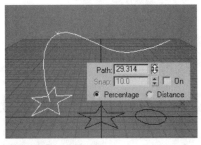

Figure 10.48 A small yellow X marks the point on the path where a new shape will be added.

5. Click Get Shape, and choose a clone option.

6. Click a shape.

   The shape, or a clone of it, is placed on the path at the current path level.

7. Repeat steps 4 through 6 until you have added all the shapes to the path that you want (**Figure 10.49**).

8. Turn Skin back on to see the results (**Figure 10.50**).

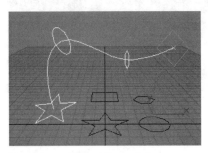

Figure 10.49 After adding a circle, an NGon, and a square to the path.

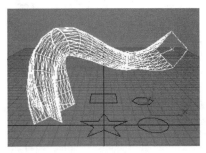

Figure 10.50 The skin of the loft object follows the contours of the shapes.

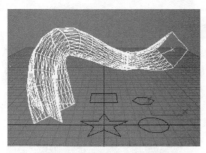

Figure 10.51 Selecting a loft object before replacing its shapes.

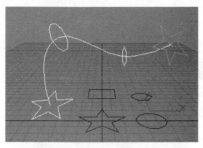

Figure 10.52 The star shape has replaced the original square at the end of the loft.

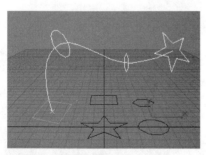

Figure 10.53 The square now replaces the star shape at the beginning of the path.

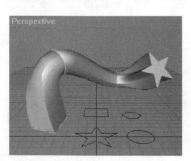

Figure 10.54 A shaded display of the finished loft.

To replace shapes:

1. Select a loft object (**Figure 10.51**).

2. Open the Modify panel.

3. Open the Skin Parameters rollout, and turn off the skin display.

   The surface of the loft is hidden.

4. Open the Path Parameters rollout, and navigate the path level to the shape you want to replace. Click one of the following:

   ◆ **Next Shape**—Moves up a level to the next shape in the path

   ◆ **Previous Shape**—Moves back a level to the previous shape in the path

   ◆ **Pick Shape**—Enables you to pick a shape by clicking it in the loft.

5. Click Get Shape, and click the shape you want to insert at that level.

   The new shape replaces the old shape in the loft (**Figure 10.52**).

6. Repeat steps 4 and 5 until you have replaced all the shapes you want to replace (**Figure 10.53**).

7. Turn Skin back on to see the results (**Figure 10.54**). To see how the loft looks in shaded mode, turn on Smooth + Highlights.

✔ Tip

■ You can also replace a path if you use Get Path to select the new path.

Adjusting skin complexity

Two factors govern the complexity of a loft:

◆ Shape steps are the number of segment divisions in the skin between each vertex of a cross-section shape. The number of shape steps determines the radial complexity of the loft.

◆ Path steps are the number of segment divisions in the skin between each cross-section shape on the path. The number of path steps determines the longitudinal complexity of the loft.

To adjust skin complexity:

1. Select a loft object, and set the viewport display to Wireframe (**Figure 10.55**).

2. Open the Modify panel .

3. Open the Skin Parameters rollout (**Figure 10.56**). By default, the Shape Steps and Path Steps are each set to 5.

4. Increase or decrease Shape Steps or Path Steps to increase or decrease the complexity of the loft (**Figure 10.57**).

✔ Tips

■ To optimize the number of path steps automatically, check Optimize Path. This checkbox is available only when Path Steps is selected in the Path Parameters rollout.

■ To automatically generate the best-looking skin, check Adaptive Path Steps. This checkbox is available only when Percentage or Distance is selected in the Path Parameters rollout.

■ Contour and Banking cause path steps to turn with the path in a flat plane and in 3D. Constant Cross-Section causes corners to be mitered correctly. These are all good options to leave checked (the default).

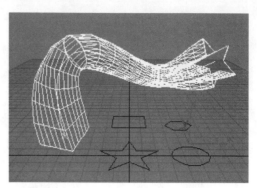

Figure 10.55 Set the viewport to Wireframe before adjusting skin complexity.

Figure 10.56 The Skin Parameters rollout lets you adjust skin complexity.

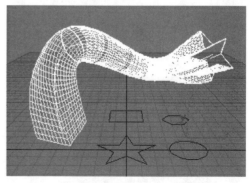

Figure 10.57 Increasing Shape Steps and Path Steps yields a better-looking, more complex loft object.

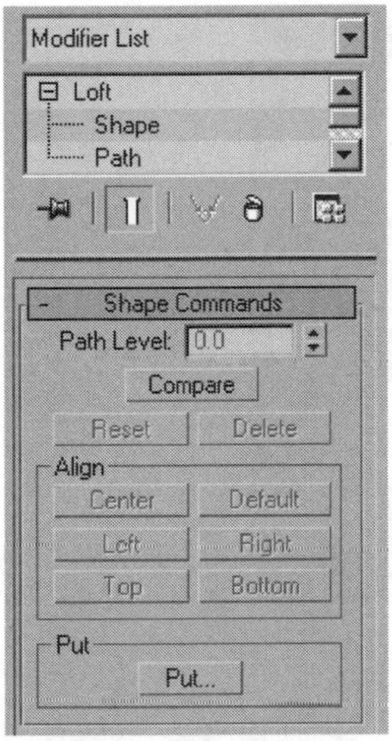

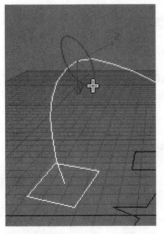

Figure 10.58 At the Shape sub-object selection level, you can manipulate the loft object's shapes interactively.

Figure 10.59 Selecting a loft shape in the viewport.

Editing Lofts

The sub-object components of a loft are the path of the loft and its cross-section shapes. You edit loft objects by editing shapes and paths at the sub-object level or by manipulating instances of the sub-object shapes used to create the loft.

Manipulating the original shapes is usually the easiest solution. Just select a shape, open the Modify panel, and edit, modify, or adjust the shape's creation parameters. Transforms are not passed on from original shape objects to instanced loft sub-objects unless you place them in an XForm modifier.

Loft sub-object editing commands are limited to aligning and cloning loft components, but once you are in sub-object mode, you can move, rotate, and scale cross-section shapes. You can also rotate paths along their Z axes. Because loft sub-object selections are not passed up the modifier stack, any modifiers that are applied at the sub-object level will have the unexpected result of modifying the entire loft.

The following exercises explain how to edit shapes at the sub-object level. You edit paths in much the same way, but you are limited to rotating and cloning them. Deleting a path deletes the entire loft object.

To select a loft shape:

1. Select a loft object, and turn off the skin display.

2. Open the Modify panel ![icon].

3. In the stack display, click the plus sign next to the word Loft. Then choose Shape from the sub-object level drop-down list (**Figure 10.58**).

4. Click a loft shape in a viewport.

   The shape is selected (**Figure 10.59**).

To remove a loft shape:

1. Select a loft shape.

2. Click the Delete button, or press the Delete key.

    The shape is removed from the loft object.

To transform a loft shape:

1. Select a loft shape.

2. Move ⊕, rotate ↻, or scale ◻ the shape.

    The shape is transformed in its local coordinate system. The skin updates to match the new position, orientation, or scale of the shape (**Figure 10.60**).

To clone a loft shape:

1. Select a loft shape.

2. Click Put in the Shapes Commands rollout.

    The Put To Scene dialog box appears (**Figure 10.61**).

3. Name the new shape, and then click OK.

    The copy or instance appears in the viewport at the origin of the home grid.

To align loft shapes to the path:

1. Select a loft.

2. Open the Modify panel 🖉.

3. Select ⬚ the Shape sub-object level.

    The Shape Commands rollout appears (**Figure 10.62**).

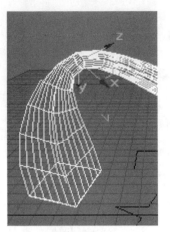

Figure 10.60 Reducing the diameter of the circle changes the diameter of that section of the loft.

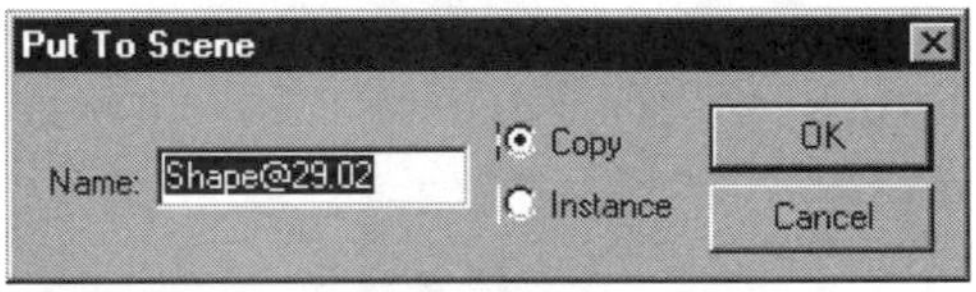

Figure 10.61 The Put To Scene dialog box lets you specify a name for the cloned shape.

Figure 10.62 The Shape Commands rollout provides access to the Compare functions.

ST. BASIL'S CATHEDRAL

Karl Raade, 2001

Image courtesy of Karl Raade
karl@lucaslearning.com

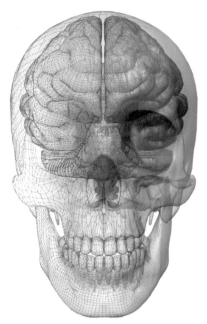

Brain and Skull
Darin Hakes, 1999

Image courtesy of Viewpoint Corporation
darin.hakes@viewpoint.com

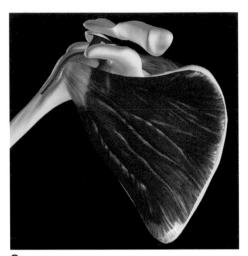

Shoulder
Michele Matossian, 1998

Image courtesy of UCSF School of Medicine, Department of Radiology
3d@lightweaver.com

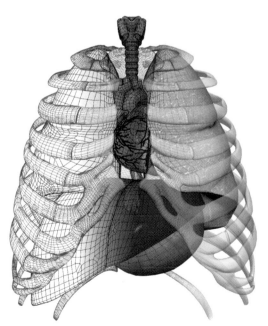

Internal Organs
Darin Hakes, 1999

Image courtesy of Viewpoint Corporation
darin.hakes@viewpoint.com

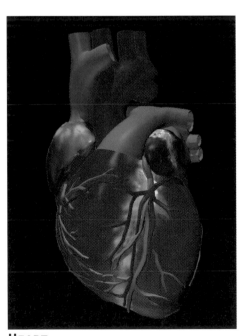

Heart
Sean Curtis, 1998

Image courtesy of Viewpoint Digital
sean.curtis@viewpoint.com

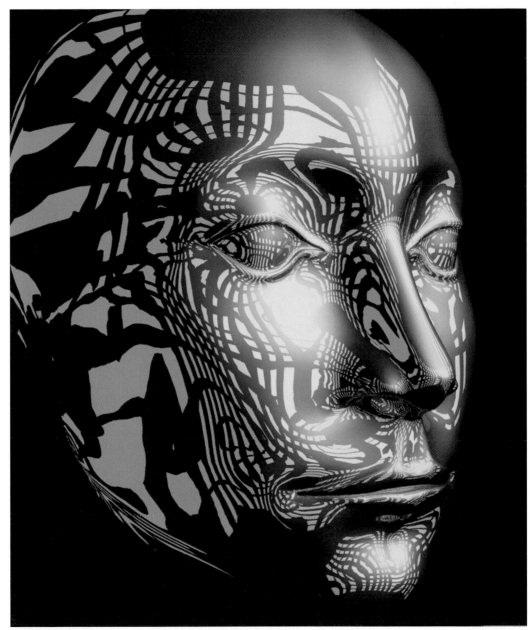

RayFlection
Bradford Stuart, 1999

Image courtesy of Autodesk, Inc.
brad.stuart@autodesk.com

MAY THE BLESSINGS BE
Clark Heist, 1998

Image courtesy of Clark Heist
clark.heist@autodesk.com

GOD IS GREAT. GOD IS GOOD.
Clark Heist, 1998

TAJ MAHAL Michele Matossian, 1997

CHRISTAMS TREE Grant Heath, 1998

OLD BUILDING Grant Heath, 2000

Image courtesy of Bob Prokopp *tippy@pacbell.net*

PRAIRIE Bob Prokopp, 1997

APPLES AND CHEESE Michele Matossian, 2001

From her upcoming tutorial CD-ROM on 3ds max 4. *www.lightweaver.com*

THE U.S.S. JOHN SHAFT Karl Raade, 1997

SCI-FI CHAIN REACTION Blur Studio, 1999

Images courtesy of Blur Studio

GEOGRAPHY
Grant Heath, 2000

Image courtesy of Viewpoint Corporation
grant.heath@viewpoint.com

TAHITIAN VACATION
Michele Matossian, 2001

From her upcoming tutorial CD-ROM on 3ds max 4

www.lightweaver.com

FOR THE CAUSE Blur Studio, 1999

HARLEY
Darin Hakes, 1999
Image courtesy of Viewpoint Corporation
darin.hakes@viewpoint.com

REPAIR SHOP
Darin Hakes, 2000
Image courtesy of Viewpoint Corporation
darin.hakes@viewpoint.com

GUNFIGHT FANTASY
Colby Acree, 2001
Image courtesy of Viewpoint Corporation.
colby.acree@viewpoint.com

CHAMELEON Jared Trulock, 1998

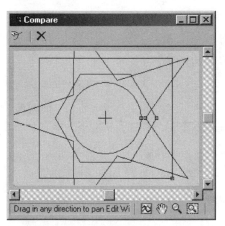

Figure 10.63 The Compare window shows you how shapes align to the path.

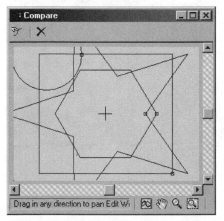

Figure 10.64 After changing the alignment of the circle.

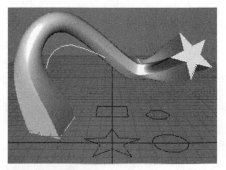

Figure 10.65 The loft moves above its path to follow the circle.

4. Click the Compare button.

The Compare window appears. A cross marks the position of the path as you look down its length.

Click Pick Shape 🐦 and click a shape to bring it into the Compare window.

Click Reset ✖ to clear the window.

The first vertex of each shape in the window is marked by a small square (**Figure 10.63**).

5. In the viewport, select the shape or shapes you want to align.

6. In the Shape Commands rollout, click the align buttons that best approximate the alignment you want. Click Default to return to the original alignment.

The selected shapes change alignment to the path. The new alignment is shown in the Compare window (**Figure 10.64**). The loft object updates in the viewports (**Figure 10.65**).

✔ Tips

- Lofting typically aligns the first vertex of each shape, but if the shapes vary widely in shape or complexity, these vertices may get out of alignment. The result is a loft that twists or stretches unpredictably. Use the Compare window to check and realign the first vertex of each shape.

- Fine-tune your shape alignment by moving or rotating shapes at the sub-object level.

You can animate lofts at the object level or at the sub-object level. At the object level, you animate a loft object as you would any other mesh object. At the sub-object level, you animate a loft strictly by animating instances or originals of the loft path and shapes. Applying transforms or modifiers directly to loft sub-objects does not generate any animation keys and has no effect on the loft object over time.

To animate a loft:

1. Select an original or instance of a loft shape or path (**Figure 10.66**).

2. Open the Modify panel 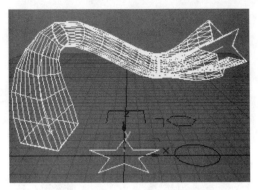.

3. Turn on the Animate button.

4. Drag the time slider to a new position.

5. Modify or transform the shape or path by changing its creation parameters or applying a modifier and changing the parameters of the modifier. An XForm modifier should be used for transforms (**Figure 10.67**).

6. Play back the animation.
   The loft changes over time.

Figure 10.66 To animate a loft, you can animate the shapes used to create the loft.

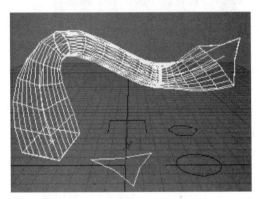

Figure 10.67 The loft animates as the star changes shape.

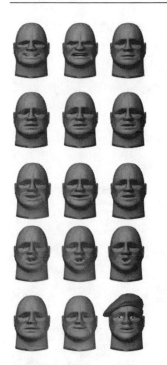

Figure 10.68 This figure from the 3ds max 4 tutorial (Commander_Lake_Tut_1.max) morphs from one expression to another.

Morphing Objects

3D morphing is a method of animation in which an object called a *seed* object changes shape to match a series of target objects. It is often used in character animation to change facial expressions and mouth position for lip-synching (**Figure 10.68**).

You can apply mesh morphing, patching, or NURBS to objects. The prerequisite for morphing mesh objects is that all target objects must have the same number of vertices as the seed object. This is because morphing moves the vertices of the seed object to corresponding vertices in the target objects. If the number of vertices is unequal, the morph animation will not work.

How do you model objects into different shapes with the same number of vertices? There are three main ways to do this:

◆ Modify clones of a geometry primitive.

◆ Create mesh objects from splines that have identical numbers of vertices using the Extrude, Lathe, or Loft command.

◆ If you want to morph existing mesh models that have unequal vertices, clone a high-density GeoSphere and make Conform objects of each seed or target object.

Once you have learned the basics of morphing, I recommend that you learn how to use the Morpher modifier for more sophisticated tasks. The advantage of the Morpher modifier is that it can be added repeatedly to the modifier stack, and it has over 100 channels for assigning morph targets. To go along with the Morpher modifier, the Morph material assigns materials to different channels of the Morpher modifier, allowing you to morph between materials. For instructions on applying Morpher modifiers and Morph materials, see the 3ds max 4 online help files.

To set the number of vertices on a spline:

1. Create  a spline object, such as a line.

2. Open the General rollout of the spline (**Figure 10.69**).

3. Uncheck Optimize and Adaptive.

4. Set the number of steps.

   The number of vertices is set.

To extrude or lathe seed and target objects:

1. Select a spline shape.

2. Use the Modeling Toolbar to apply an Extrude or Lathe modifier.

   The Extrude or Lathe rollout appears (**Figure 10.70**).

3. Set the number of segments.

4. If you use the Lathe modifier, make sure Weld Core is unchecked.

5. Set Capping to Morph.

   This arranges cap faces in a predictable pattern for morphing.

6. Repeat steps 1 through 5 using a spline with an equal number of vertices. Make sure that the Segments value is the same each time.

To loft seed and target objects:

1. Select a spline shape.

2. Loft the shape along a path.

3. In the Skin Parameters rollout, uncheck Optimize Shapes and Adaptive Path Steps, and set Capping to Morph (**Figure 10.71**).

4. Repeat steps 1 through 3 using loft shapes and paths with the same number of vertices.

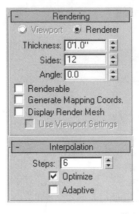

Figure 10.69 Use the General rollout to set a spline's vertex count.

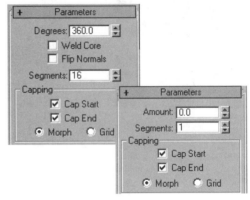

Figure 10.70 (left) Using Extrude to generate morph objects; (right) using Lathe to generate morph object

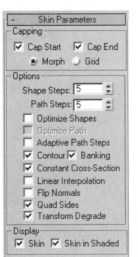

Figure 10.71 Use these Skin Parameters settings when creating morph objects.

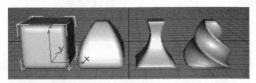

Figure 10.72 The ChamferBox is used as the seed object and thus appears first in the morph animation.

Figure 10.73 The Morph Targets list shows the ChamferBox as the first target.

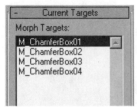

Figure 10.74 After all the morph targets have been picked, they appear in the list in the order that they'll appear in the morph animation.

Figure 10.75 The ChamferBox morphs into each shape in turn, ending up as the twisted box.

To create a morph animation:

1. Create ✎ a seed object and some target objects for morphing.

2. Select the seed object (**Figure 10.72**).

3. Open the Create panel, and choose Geometry > Compound Objects > Morph.

   The Morph rollout appears. In the Current Targets rollout, the seed object appears at the top of the Morph Targets list (**Figure 10.73**).

4. Click Pick Target, and choose a method for creating targets from your originals: Reference, Move, Copy, or Instance.

5. Click the morph target objects in the viewports.

   The target objects are added to the Morph Targets list (**Figure 10.74**).

6. Highlight the next target to which you want to morph the seed object.

7. Drag the time slider to the frame number or time where you want to set the first morph animation key. Note that it is not necessary to turn on the Animate button.

8. Click Create Morph Key.

   A key appears in the Track Bar at the current frame number or time.

9. To preview the animation, scrub the time slider back and forth. The seed object morphs to the target object automatically (**Figure 10.75**).

10. Repeat steps 6 through 9 until you are finished.

MORPHING OBJECTS

283

LIGHTS

Figure 11.1 Light conveys mystery and magic.

In nature, light flows like a luminous tide, revealing and concealing form. Light radiates, reflects, refracts, reacts, and softly diffuses into air. Light is warm or cool, high or low, near or far, bright or dim, harsh or soft. These qualities make a scene happy, sad, harsh, soft, romantic, dull, mundane or mysterious (**Figure 11.1**).

In the digital world, illumination is a calculated affair. Rendering algorithms, normal alignments, G-buffers, and Z-buffers determine the display of light and shadow. Where calculation fails, the eye of the artist must compensate.

The best lighting effects are achieved by artists who make themselves students of nature. Artists who study scene painting, drawing, photography, and cinematography develop sensitivity, awareness, and a practiced eye.

This chapter outlines the light sources available in 3ds max and how to control them.

Illuminating Scenes

In addition to making scenes more beautiful, working with light has practical applications. For instance, suppose you create a model of an office building for a prospective client. The client will want to see what it will look like under different lighting conditions. How will the building cast shadows? How will shadows be cast upon it? At what angle will light enter the windows at different times of the day and year?

The color and angle of a light place a scene in time and space. For morning or evening scenes, make the sun a warm color such as yellow, orange, or red. Then place the light source at a low angle (**Figure 11.2**). Cooler white lights placed at a high angle suggest the sun shining at midday. To make a mid-day scene more interesting, add clouds to the sky and project shadows from them (**Figure 11.3**). Fill lights above the ground should be blue or gray to match the sky. Fill lights below the ground should be green or brown to match the earth.

For night scenes, use a cool blue-white tint to suggest the light of the moon and stars (**Figure 11.4**). If there is fog, streetlights create warm, hazy cones of illumination. If there is a large or brightly colored object in the scene, match a nearby light to that color to create the effect of light radiating off of its surface.

Indoor lights also have color. Use warm, yellow colors for incandescent and halogen lights. Use a cold yellow-green color for fluorescent lighting. Be sure to create some fill lights to match the overall colors of the walls and carpets.

Figure 11.2 Morning in the mountains: angled light; long shadows.

Figure 11.3 Midday in the hills: cloud shadows add interest.

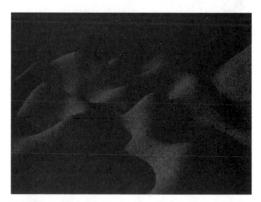

Figure 11.4 Moonlight in the desert: stars create the feeling of space.

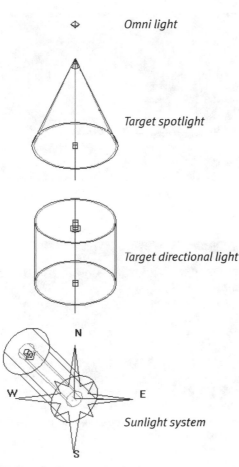

Omni light

Target spotlight

Target directional light

N

W

E

Sunlight system

S

Figure 11.5 The basic light types. Free spotlights and free directional lights look the same as their targeted counterparts, minus the target box.

Figure 11.6
The Light branch of the Create panel.

Creating Lights

As in nature, illumination in 3ds max is the product of a complex interaction of lights and objects. To participate, lights and objects must be placed so that there is a direct line of sight between them, and objects must be renderable.

The five types of lights and the sunlight system are designed to simulate light in the real world (**Figure 11.5**):

◆ **Omni lights**—Radiate light in all directions from a single source point. Can be moved through space without restriction.

◆ **Spotlights (target and free)**—Illuminate an area within a cone, similar to a stage light. Target spotlights point at a target that you aim. Free spotlights have no target, so they can be maneuvered more easily.

◆ **Directional lights (target and free)**—Like spot lights, directional lights use a cone of illumination, except that the cone sides are parallel. This is because directional lights have parallel rays, while spotlights spread light from a single source point.

◆ **Sunlight systems**—This is a hybrid light source that combines a free directional light with a Compass object. The compass helps you orient the light to a specific direction in the scene. The orbital distance, time, and location settings give the sun altitude and place it in the sky at a particular time and geographic location.

When you start up the program, 3ds max illuminates the scene with a diffuse light that has no fixed direction. As soon as you create a light, the default light is turned off and the new light illuminates the scene instead.

For all lights except sunlight systems, shadow casting is turned off by default. Ambient light, the diffuse background light of a scene that fills in shadow areas, is also turned off by default.

Lights are created in the Light branch of the Create panel (**Figure 11.6**).

Lighting a scene requires a bit of finesse. To make the process easier, you will start by creating a practice scene, and then add lights until the scene is fully illuminated. You will reuse this scene for studying more advanced light settings, as well as cameras, materials, and rendering.

To create the practice scene:

1. In the Perspective viewport, create some light gray objects and place them near the origin. Then place a white plane underneath (**Figure 11.7**)

   The neutral colors of the scene will make it easier to see the effects of light and color.

2. Right-click on the Perspective viewport label and change the Perspective view to an ActiveShade view.

   The ActiveShade view renders the scene at a higher resolution (**Figure 11.8**).

3. Zoom and pan the Front viewport so you will have plenty of room to place lights around the scene (**Figure 11.9**).

4. Choose File > Save, and name your scene PracticeScene.max.

5. Close the ActiveShade view by right-clicking in the viewport and choosing Close from the Tools1 quad menu.

6. Choose File > Save As to save a back up copy of your scene in case you accidentally save over the original. Name the back up copy PracticeScene00.max.

Figure 11.7 The practice scene consists of gray and white objects.

Figure 11.8 The ActiveShade view renders the scene at a higher resolution.

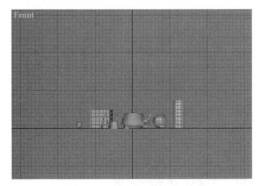

Figure 11.9 Give yourself plenty of room to work.

Figure 11.10 The image is scanned line by line in the virtual frame buffer.

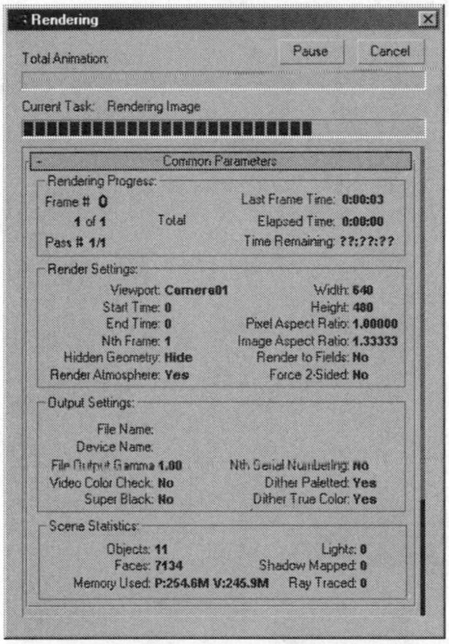

Figure 11.11 The Rendering dialog box keeps track of the progress of the rendering.

The scanline renderer provides high-resolution images for final output. Use this renderer to get the most accurate rendition of light and shadow.

To render a scene:

1. Open PracticeScene.max.

2. Right-click the view you want to render, unless you want to render the ActiveShade view. For ActiveShade views, left-click to activate. (Right-clicking in this viewport brings up the ActiveShade quad menus.)

3. Click Quick Render 🔘 in the main toolbar.

   The active viewport is rendered at high resolution in a separate window called a virtual frame buffer (**Figure 11.10**).

   The Rendering dialog box displays the progress of the rendering and other rendering information (**Figure 11.11**).

4. Review the image (**Figure 11.12**). Then close the virtual frame buffer.

✔ Tips

- To save an image, click the Save Bitmap icon 🖫 in the upper left-hand corner of the virtual frame buffer. You will be prompted to choose a file type and a name.

- The Render Type drop-down menu [View ▾] allows you to render a portion of the view. Change render types when you want to quickly review how selected objects or a selected region will render.

- Render Last 🔘 renders an image from the same view that was rendered previously, even if that view is no longer active. Use Render Last when you want to update lights in one viewport but render from another.

- Click the ActiveShade Floater button 🔘 on the extreme right of the main toolbar to render the current view as an Active-Shade view in a separate window.

Figure 11.12 The final high-resolution image can be saved to an image file.

Omni lights are the easiest to create and position.

To create an omni light:

1. Open PracticeScene.max.

2. Open the Lights branch  of the Create panel (**Figure 11.13**).

3. In the Object Type rollout, click Omni.

   The omni light parameters appear in the Create panel (**Figure 11.14**).

4. Click in the Front viewport.

   The light appears in the viewport, and the default lights are turned off (**Figure 11.15**).

   The ActiveShade view updates the illumination (**Figure 11.16**).

5. In the General Parameters rollout, decrease the Multiplier to about .5.

   The omni light dims.

6. In the Front viewport, move the omni light to the lower right-hand corner.

   The objects in the scene become lit from beneath. The plane does not block the light because its surface normals face away from the light.

7. In either the Top or Left viewport, move the omni light slightly in front of the scene.

   The light fills in the front of the objects.

Figure 11.13 You create lights in the Lights branch of the Create panel.

Figure 11.14 The omni rollout includes an intensity multiplier.

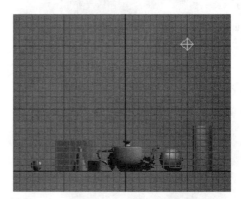

Figure 11.15 After creating the omni light in the Front viewport.

CREATING LIGHTS

Figure 11.16 The scene is now lit by the omni light.

Figure 11.17 After moving the omni light and turning down its intensity.

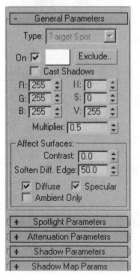

Figure 11.18
The spotlight rollout has the same basic parameters as the omni light.

8. Click in the ActiveShade viewport to activate it. Then click Quick Render (**Figure 11.17**).

9. Close the virtual frame buffer.

10. Save the scene as PracticeScene01.max.

    You can click the plus sign "+" next to the Save button in the Save File As dialog box to increment your file by +01.

Target lights have two components: a light source, and a target that the light points at. Having a target makes these lights easier to aim.

Target lights, both spot and direct, are created by clicking and dragging. The first click positions the source of the light. Dragging aims the light. Releasing the mouse button positions the target.

To create a target spotlight:

1. Open PracticeScene01.max.

2. Open the Lights branch of the Create panel.

3. In the Object Type rollout, choose Target Spot.

    The spotlight parameters appear in the Create panel (**Figure 11.18**).

continues on next page

4. In the Front viewport, click in the upper left-hand corner, and drag to the center of the scene. Release the mouse to place the target.

The target spotlight appears in the viewport (**Figure 11.19**).

The spotlight intensity is low because it uses the Multiplier that you set for the omni light, and because it is farther away from the objects (**Figure 11.20**).

5. In the General Parameters rollout, increase the intensity of the light by setting the Multiplier to 1.25. Then check Shadow Casting.

The scene brightens.

6. In the Top or Left viewport, move the spotlight slightly in front of the scene.

The light moves but the target stays put.

7. Click in the ActiveShade viewport to activate it. Then click Quick Render ⬛.

The spotlight illuminates the objects within its cone. The illuminated objects cast dark shadows. The effect of the fill light on the objects is not as noticeable (**Figure 11.21**).

8. Save the scene as PracticeScene02.max.

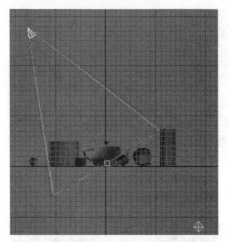

Figure 11.19 Placing the spotlight in the scene.

Figure 11.20 The spotlight is dim because it is farther away.

Figure 11.21 After turning up the intensity of the light.

CREATING LIGHTS

Figure 11.22
The directional light rollout has the same basic parameters as the omni light and the spotlight.

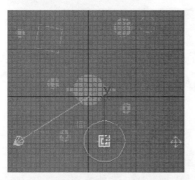

Figure 11.23 Place the free direct light directly over an object.

Figure 11.24 When you first set the direct light, it may be too bright.

Free lights are aimed without using a target. This makes them simpler to transform and animate.

Free spot and direct lights are created with a single click. The light is automatically aimed at the grid of the viewport in which you clicked (a.k.a. the construction grid).

To create a free directional light:

1. Open PracticeScene02.max.

2. Open the Lights 🔆 branch of the Create panel.

3. In the Object Type rollout, choose Free Direct.

   The directional light parameters appear in the Create panel (**Figure 11.22**).

4. In the Top viewport, click on top of an object that you would like to highlight.

   The free directional light appears in the viewport on top of the object (**Figure 11.23**).

5. In the Front or Left viewport, place the directional light above the object.

   The object is illuminated with a strong light (**Figure 11.24**).

6. In the General Parameters rollout, reduce the intensity of the light by setting the Multiplier to .4. Then check Shadow Casting.

7. Position the omni light under the plane and under the directional light to simulate light bouncing off the plane.

8. Click in the ActiveShade viewport to activate it. Then click Quick Render 🔘.

9. Save the scene as PracticeScene03.max.

CREATING LIGHTS

293

A sunlight system is a combination of a free directional light and a compass that sets the direction of the system. Shadows are turned on by default. Use sunlight when you want to know where shadows will fall over time.

To create a sunlight system:

1. Open PracticeScene.max.

2. Open the Systems ![icon] branch of the Create panel.

3. In the Object Type rollout, click Sunlight.

   The sunlight system rollout appears. The time is set to the time on your computer, and the location is set to San Francisco, CA (**Figure 11.25**).

4. In the Top viewport, click and drag to create the compass. Release to set the radius of the compass.

5. Move the cursor up or down to set the orbital distance of the sun from the Earth. Then click to create the light (**Figure 11.26**).

6. In the sunlight system rollout, set the time, date, and time zone for the light.

   This positions the sun in the sky. To position the sun geographically, click Get Location. This opens the Geographic Location dialog box, from which you choose a location by clicking on a map or picking from a list (**Figure 11.27**).

7. Open the Directional Parameters rollout in the Modify panel, and uncheck Overshoot. Then increase the Hotspot until the cone of illumination encompasses the entire scene, so that shadows will appear throughout.

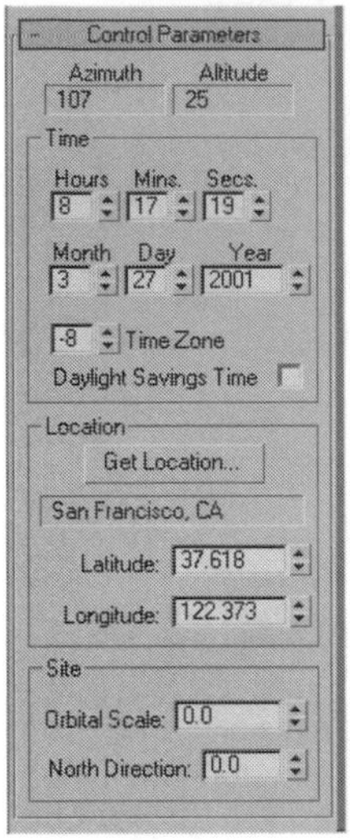

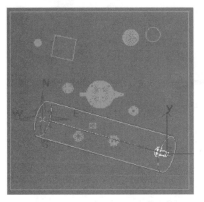

Figure 11.25 The sunlight system uses the time and date on your computer to position the light.

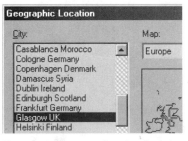

Figure 11.26 The compass sets the direction; the light illuminates the scene.

Figure 11.27 Get a new location from the list or click on a map of the world.

CREATING LIGHTS

Figure 11.28 Sunlight renders with sharp-edged shadows by default.

Figure 11.29 Default lights use frontal illumination.

8. Activate the ActiveShade viewport, and click Quick Render .

   Sunlight floods the scene. Shadows are crisp and precise (**Figure 11.28**).

✔ Tip

- After a sunlight system has been created, you change the system settings in the Motion panel. To change the direction of the system, rotate the compass in its local Z-axis.

When you start building a scene in 3ds max, the default lighting has no direction. No matter what viewport you look in, the light appears brightest on the sides of the objects that face you.

There is a second default lighting configuration that places two omni lights along a diagonal through the world origin, from the top-left-front to the below-right-back of the scene. This lighting is more realistic and interesting.

Once you have changed the default lighting to the second configuration, called 2 Lights, you can add the default lights to the scene. This allows you to select and adjust them, just as you would any other light.

To add default lights to a scene:

1. Open PracticeScene00.max.

2. Click Quick Render .

   The lighting appears to come from in front and above, no matter which viewport you render (**Figure 11.29**).

3. Open the Viewport Configuration dialog box from the viewport label right-click menu, or by right-clicking on any viewport control button.

continues on next page

CREATING LIGHTS

4. In the Rendering Method panel, check Default Lighting and choose 2 Lights (**Figure 11.30**). Then click OK.

The scene lighting changes direction (**Figure 11.31**).

5. Choose Views > Add Default Lights to Scene.

The Add Default Lights to Scene dialog box appears (**Figure 11.32**).

6. Check the default lights you want to add. Changing Distance Scaling dollies the lights toward or away from the origin.

7. Click OK, and save the scene.

The default lights are added to the scene and saved. The brighter light, named DefaultKeyLight, is positioned above and in the front of the origin. The dimmer light, named DefaultFillLight, is positioned below and to the right of the origin.

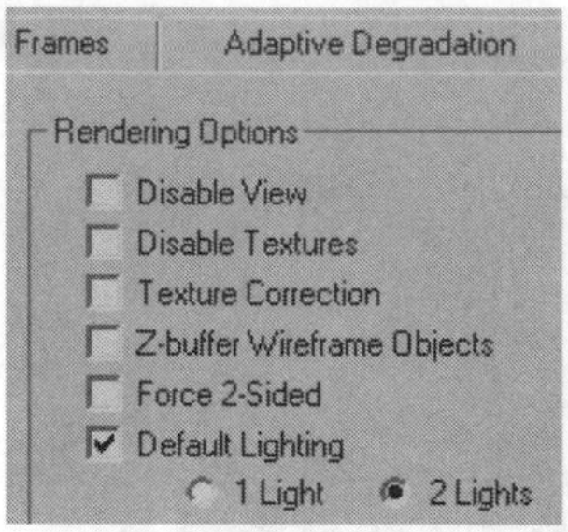

Figure 11.30 Changing the default lighting to two diagonally placed lights.

Figure 11.31 The ActiveShade view renders the two-light illumination.

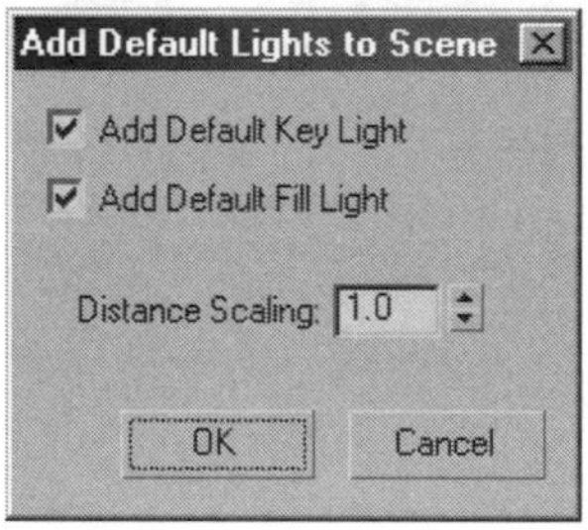

Figure 11.32 You can add one or both default lights, and scale them away from the origin.

Figure 11.33
The parameters of a spotlight are duplicated by the omni and directional lights.

Attenuation and Color

3ds max provides multiple controls for fine-tuning colors and gradations of light, and for determining the surfaces that light will affect. Common parameters for light rollouts include (**Figure 11.33**):

◆ **Type**—Sets the light type.

◆ **On**—Checking this box turns a light on. Uncheck to turn off a light. Default = On.

◆ **Cast Shadows**—Causes shadows to render. Uncheck to turn off shadows. Default = Off.

◆ **Color**—Sets the hue (chroma), saturation (purity), and value (intensity) of a light. Can be set by hue and whiteness, RGB, or HSV.

◆ **Include/Exclude**—Determines which objects are illuminated by the light.

◆ **Multiplier**—Controls the intensity, or brightness, of a light.

◆ **Contrast**—Sets the contrast between the ambient and diffuse areas of illumination.

◆ **Soften Diff. Edge**—Softens the edge between ambient and diffuse areas.

◆ **Diffuse**—Adds the light to diffuse (middle value) areas of illumination. Default = On.

◆ **Specular**—Adds the light to specular (high value) areas of illumination. Default = On.

◆ **Ambient Only**—Adds the light to the minimum level of scene illumination, regardless of the direction of the light. Default = Off.

◆ **Hot Spot and Falloff**—Sets the inner and outer boundaries of the cone of illumination.

◆ **Attenuation**—Fades a light over a limited distance at either end of its range.

continues on next page

ATTENUATION AND COLOR

297

◆ **Decay**—Diminishes the intensity of a light over its entire attenuation range.

◆ **Projector Map**—Projects an image or animation into a scene. Turns a light into a slide projector or movie projector.

Shadows have additional controls. These are explained in the section following this one under the heading, "Casting Shadows."

You can convert a light from one type to another in the Modify panel. When a light changes type, the illumination from the new light type replaces the illumination from the old type.

To convert a light:

1. Open PracticeScene03.max.

2. Select a light (**Figure 11.34**).

3. Open the Modify panel.

4. In the General Parameters rollout, choose a light type from the Type drop-down list.

   The new light type replaces the selected light, using the same settings (**Figure 11.35**).

   The name of the light remains unchanged. If the name of the light is Omni01 and you have just changed it to a target spotlight, this is probably a good time to rename it.

5. Activate the ActiveShade viewport, and render the scene.

   The new light type replaces the old and illuminates the scene (**Figure 11.36**).

✔ Tip

■ When you convert an omni light to any other type of light, it points toward the grid of the viewport is was created in.

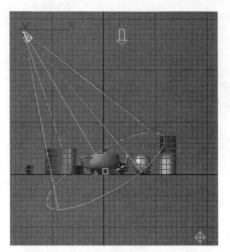

Figure 11.34 Select the light you want to convert.

Figure 11.35 Choosing a target light will add a target to the end of the light cone.

Figure 11.36 The directional light is narrower at the far end of its cone.

ATTENUATION AND COLOR

Figure 11.37 The practice scene before turning off the spotlight.

Figure 11.38 Uncheck the On box.

Figure 11.39 After turning off the spotlight, the scene is just illuminated by the omni light.

By default, lights illuminate all objects within range. Turning off a light ends their illumination.

To turn off a light:

1. Open PracticeScene02.max (**Figure 11.37**).

2. Select the spotlight.

3. Open the Modify panel.

4. Uncheck the On box in the General Parameters rollout (**Figure 11.38**). The light is turned off (**Figure 11.39**).

5. To turn the light back on, check the On box.

ATTENUATION AND COLOR

The Exclude command turns off the illumination of objects that are within range of a light. It can also turn off shadow casting.

To exclude objects from a light:

1. Open PracticeScene02.max.

2. Select the spotlight.

3. Open the Modify panel.

4. Click Exclude in the General Parameters rollout (**Figure 11.40**).

   The Exclude/Include dialog box appears.

5. Make sure Exclude and Both are selected in the upper-right corner.

6. Select the names of the objects or group of objects you do not want to be illuminated or to cast shadows.

7. Click the >> button.

   The names of the objects are moved to the Exclude list on the right (**Figure 11.41**).

8. Click OK.

9. Render the scene.

   The objects you have chosen to exclude neither receive illumination nor cast shadows when they render (**Figure 11.42**).

✔ Tip

■ Excluding just the spotlight illumination makes the objects look mysterious (**Figure 11.43**).

Figure 11.40 Click the Exclude button.

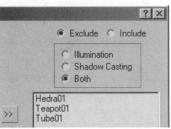

Figure 11.41 Turning off both illumination and shadow casting for the hedra, teapot, and tube.

Figure 11.42 The excluded objects are dark and float in the scene.

Figure 11.43 After excluding just the spotlight illumination.

ATTENUATION AND COLOR

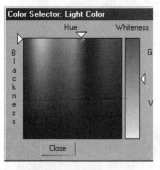

Color settings assign hue, value, and saturation to a light. The value of a color also affects its intensity. Brighter colors create brighter lights. Darker colors create dimmer lights.

Figure 11.44 Click the color swatch.

To set color:

1. Open PracticeScene02.max.

2. Select the spotlight.

3. In the General Parameters rollout, click the color swatch just to the left of the Exclude button (**Figure 11.44**).

4. Choose a color from the Color Selector dialog box. There are two basic methods:

   The most intuitive way to do this is to click in the Hue palette on the left and drag the Whiteness slider next to it (**Figure 11.45**).

   When precision is important, you can set numeric RGB or HSV values using the color sliders, input fields, or spinners on the right (**Figure 11.46**).

   As you change the color of the light, the lighting updates in the shaded viewports.

5. When you are satisfied with the result, close the Color Selector dialog box.

6. Render the scene to verify the results (**Figure 11.47**).

✔ Tip

- Light and color can be animated over time.

Figure 11.45 Picking a color using the palette and whiteness slider.

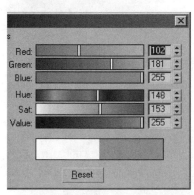

Figure 11.46 Picking the same color numerically.

Figure 11.47 Blue light gives the scene a more somber cast.

ATTENUATION AND COLOR

Global lighting commands shift the color of all the lights in a scene, including the default lights.

Initially, the color tint is set to white and the intensity multiplier is set to 1.0. Ambient light, which sets the minimum level of scene illumination, is set to black (no light).

Because ambient light brightens darker values, it reduces contrast across surfaces. Use this setting sparingly, so it does not wash out your scene.

To set global lighting:

1. Open PracticeScene03.max (**Figure 11.48**).

2. Choose Rendering > Environment.
   The Environment dialog box appears.

3. In the Global Lighting group, set the light's intensity by adjusting the Level (**Figure 11.49**).
   The scene brightens or dims (**Figure 11.50**).

4. Click the Tint color swatch.
   The Color Selector: Global Light Tint dialog box appears.

5. Choose a color from the Color Selector dialog box.
   The color of the illumination in the shaded viewports updates.

6. Click the Ambient color swatch.
   The Color Selector changes to the Color Selector: Ambient Light dialog box.

7. Drag the Whiteness slider to set the minimum level of illumination.
   Gradations of value become lighter throughout the scene.

8. When you are satisfied with the result, close the Color Selector: Ambient Light dialog box and the Environment dialog box.

9. Render the scene 🌀 to see the results (**Figure 11.51**).

Figure 11.48 Before affecting the global lighting of the scene.

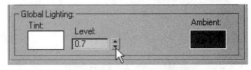

Figure 11.49 Reducing the global illumination.

Figure 11.50 All the lights are dimmed.

Figure 11.51 After decreasing the intensity of the global color and increasing the intensity of the ambient color.

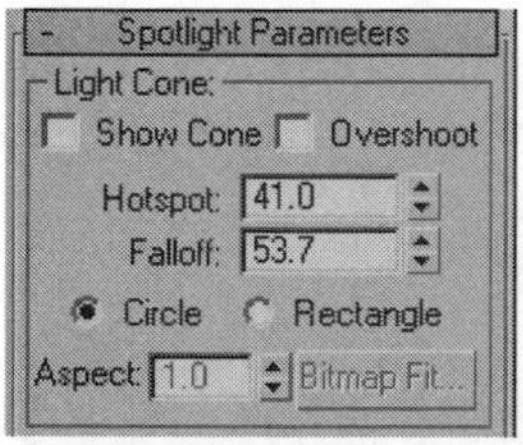

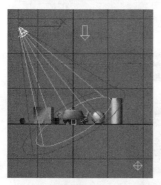

Figure 11.52 Adjust the hotspot and falloff in the spotlight parameters rollout.

Figure 11.53 The hotspot and falloff cones move apart.

Figure 11.54 The pool of light gains a softer edge.

Figure 11.55 The cone of the directional light narrows.

A light cone is actually made of two concentric cones: The inner core of illumination, or hotspot, and the outer edge of illumination, or falloff. Between the hotspot and falloff cones, the intensity of the light gradually decreases to zero.

To set the hotspot and falloff:

1. Open PracticeScene03.max.

2. Select the spotlight, and open the Modify panel.

3. In the Spotlight Parameters rollout, decrease the Hotspot value (**Figure 11.52**).

   The blue hotspot cone becomes narrower (**Figure 11.53**).

   In the ActiveShade viewport, the edge of the pool of light becomes softer (**Figure 11.54**).

4. Select the directional light.

5. Increase the intensity of the light to counteract the loss of illumination from the spotlight. You will probably need to triple it.

6. In the Directional Parameters rollout, decrease the Falloff amount so that both the Hotspot and Falloff cones become narrower.

7. Render the ActiveShade viewport.

   The pool of light from the directional light becomes smaller, but its edges remain sharp (**Figure 11.55**).

8. Save your scene as PracticeScene04.max.

✔ Tips

- Checking Overshoot causes the light to ignore the boundaries of the hotspot and falloff cones and spread throughout the scene. Shadows, however, will only be drawn within the cone of illumination.

- Click Rectangle to make the pool of light rectangular or square. The Aspect parameter sets the aspect ratio of the length and width of the rectangle. The Bitmap Fit button will match the aspect ratio to an external bitmap image, in case you want to project the image.

ATTENUATION AND COLOR

Projecting maps into a scene creates the illusion that there is more going on than meets the eye.

To project a map:

1. Open PracticeScene04.max.

2. Select the spotlight, and open the Modify panel.

3. In the Spotlight Parameters rollout, click the Projector Map button labeled None (**Figure 11.56**).

   The Material/Map Browser window appears.

4. Double-click Bitmap (**Figure 11.57**).

5. Choose a bitmap image using the Select Bitmap Image File dialog box. For this example, I chose the SCATR4.gif in the 3dsmax4/Maps/Lights folder.

   When you click Open, the bitmap image is projected by the spotlight onto the scene.

6. Adjust the intensity of the light. You will probably need to increase the Multiplier value from around 1.25 to about 1.5.

7. Render the scene to see the result (**Figure 11.58**).

✔ Tips

■ A black and white map that is designed to be used with a spotlight is called a *gobo map*.

■ Try some of the other maps in the Material/Map Browser such as Brick, Cellular, Checker, Dent, Gradient Ramp, Perlin Marble, and Smoke (**Figure 11.59**).

Figure 11.56 Click the Projector Map button.

Figure 11.57 Click Bitmap in the Material/Map Browser.

Figure 11.58 The SCATR4 map projects spots of light and shadow.

Figure 11.59 Projecting a checker map that has been tiled in the Material Editor.

ATTENUATION AND COLOR

Figure 11.60 Moving the spotlight produces strong side lighting all the way across the scene.

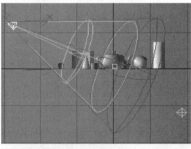

Figure 11.61
Check Use and Show for Far Attenuation.

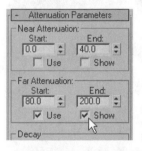

Figure 11.62 Setting the far attenuation range indicators.

Figure 11.63 After attenuating the light, the cylinder becomes darker.

Attenuation fades in a light near its source and fades out a light at the far end of its range.

To set attenuation:

1. Open PracticeScene02.max.

2. Select the spotlight.

3. In the Front viewport, move the spotlight to the lower left corner, so that it sits at about a 30° angle above the X-axis
   The scene is illuminated from the side (**Figure 11.60**).

4. Open the Modify panel, and open the Attenuation Parameters rollout.

5. In the Far Attenuation group, check Use and Show (**Figure 11.61**).
   The far attenuation ranges appear. In the ActiveShade view, the light from the spotlight will disappear if the objects are out of the light's current attenuation range.

6. Drag the Far Attenuation spinners so that the Start and End ranges just enclose the scene objects (**Figure 11.62**).

7. If necessary, increase the intensity multiplier in the General Parameters rollout.

8. Render the scene to see the final result (**Figure 11.63**).

✔ Tips

- Because light can continue shining forever, it is a good idea to use far attenuation so that the program won't waste time making unnecessary calculations.

- The Decay parameter increases the rate at which a beam of light diminishes as it moves away from its source.

ATTENUATION AND COLOR

Volume lighting is an atmospheric effect that is based on the real-world interaction between light and particulate matter such as fog, haze, dust, and smoke. It gives you the hazy glow of streetlights on a misty evening, the sweep of a lighthouse beacon on a foggy morning, or the rays of sunlight streaming through a window.

Volumetric lighting works with all types of light sources, although it is most commonly used with spotlights. Because volume lighting is a true 3D effect, you can render it only from viewports that use perspective projection.

To create a volume light:

1. Select a light that illuminates a scene.

2. Open the Modify menu.

3. Open the Atmospheres & Effects rollout. (Note: This rollout does not appear in the Create panel.)

4. Click the Add button (**Figure 11.64**).

5. Choose Volume Light from the Add Atmosphere or Effect dialog box (**Figure 11.65**). Then click OK.

6. Render the scene from a Perspective, Camera, or Light viewport.

   The light is rendered volumetrically (**Figure 11.66**).

✔ Tips

- Decreasing the size of the hotspot can make a volume light easier to control.

- By animating attenuation, you can make a volume light "touch down" and "beam up."

- Combining a projector map with volume lights can create extraordinary effects (**Figure 11.67**).

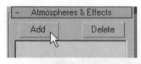

Figure 11.64 Click Add in the Atmospheres & Effects rollout.

Figure 11.65 Add Volume Light to the spotlight.

Figure 11.66 The volume light renders in three dimensions.

Figure 11.67 When added to a volume light, a Cellular map projects in three dimensions.

ATTENUATION AND COLOR

Figure 11.68 Shadow-map shadows have soft edges.

Figure 11.69 Ray-traced shadows have hard edges.

Figure 11.70 The Shadow Parameters rollout lets you adjust the appearance of shadows.

Casting Shadows

3ds max 4 provides two shadow types: shadow-map shadows and ray-traced shadows.

A shadow map is a bitmap that is projected from a light. It is created by the scanline renderer during a prerendering pass of the scene and applied during rendering. Shadow maps give shadows a soft edge, as if they are being diffused by the atmosphere (**Figure 11.68**).

Ray-traced shadows are more precise and sharp-edged than shadow-map shadows. They are calculated by tracing a ray from source to object. Use ray-traced shadows whenever you need to precisely locate shadows, such as in shadow studies for architectural siting (**Figure 11.69**).

The settings in the Shadow Parameters rollout affect both shadow-map and ray-traced shadows (**Figure 11.70**). You can add color and maps to shadows, and control their density (darkness). In addition, you can make shadows mix with light colors, giving them a more natural appearance.

Shadow maps create soft-edged shadows. They are the default for all types of lights except sunlight systems. Ray-traced shadows render more slowly, but they make excellent shadow studies because their edges are so crisp.

Using the Object Shadows drop-down menu, you can assign shadow maps or ray-traced shadows for any type of light.

To set the shadow type:

1. Open a scene that is illuminated and shadowed by lights (**Figure 11.71**).

2. Select the light that is casting shadows.

3. Open the Modify menu.

4. Open the Shadow Parameters rollout.

5. In the Object Shadows drop-down menu, choose a new shadow type (**Figure 11.72**).

6. Render the scene (**Figure 11.73**).

✔ Tip

■ Ray-traced shadows render more slowly when you use them with omni lights. If possible, use ray-traced shadows with spotlights or directional lights instead.

Shadow maps sometimes appear blurry, faint, or detach from the objects that cast them. Shadow-map parameters help you fix these problems:

◆ **Bias**—Offsets shadows from the object that casts them. Lower values move shadows closer to the object. Higher values move shadows away from the object.

◆ **Size**—Controls the accuracy of a shadow by setting the size of the bitmap that generates the shadow. If shadows appear fuzzy, then the size is too low. Higher values produce cleaner edges but take longer to render.

Figure 11.71 The practice scene is rendered with shadow map shadows.

Figure 11.72 Choose ray-traced shadows from the drop-down list.

Figure 11.73 After rendering the scene with ray-traced shadows.

Figure 11.74 The shadow appears blurry and indistinct.

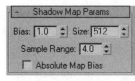

Figure 11.75 The Shadow Map Params rollout provides the means to correct shadow maps.

Figure 11.76 Increasing the map size and sample range focuses the shadow.

Figure 11.77 Adjusting the map bias brings the shadow bank into alignment.

◆ **Sample Range**—Controls the sharpness of shadows by averaging different-sized areas of the shadow map. If a shadow smudges, streaks, or creates moiré patterns, the Sample Range setting is probably too high. A Sample Range setting that is too low creates jagged shadows. Recommended values are between 2 and 5. You can also offset a high value by increasing the size of a shadow map or the amount of its bias.

◆ **Absolute Map Bias**—Determines how the map bias is computed in relation to the rest of the scene. If you render an animation and notice that the shadows flicker when you replay it, try checking this option to end the flicker.

Every time you adjust a shadow map, render the scene to check the result.

To adjust a shadow map:

1. Open a scene that has a problematic shadow map (**Figure 11.74**).

2. Select the light that casts the shadows, and open the Modify menu.

3. Open the Shadow Map Params rollout (**Figure 11.75**).

4. Adjust the Size and/or the Sample Range to increase the resolution of the shadow (**Figure 11.76**).

5. Adjust the Bias to move the shadow up to the object that casts it (**Figure 11.77**).

Ray-traced shadows always produce hard-edged shadows that rarely need correcting. They have two settings:

◆ **Bias**—Offsets shadows from the object that casts them. Lower values move shadows closer to the object. Higher values move shadows away from the object.

◆ **Max Quadtree Depth**—Controls the rendering speed of ray-traced shadows by setting the maximum size of the data structure that generates them. Lower values take longer to render but use less RAM. Higher values render faster but use more RAM.

To speed up rendering of ray-traced shadows:

1. Select a light that casts ray-traced shadows (**Figure 11.78**).

2. Open the Modify menu.

3. Open the Ray Traced Shadow Params menu.

4. Increase the Max Quadtree depth (**Figure 11.79**).

5. Render the scene.

   The scene renders faster.

Figure 11.78 This backlit scene has ray-traced shadows that are slow to render.

Figure 11.79 Increase the Max Quadtree Depth if you have plenty of RAM.

Figure 11.80 The object casts a black shadow.

Figure 11.81 Click the color swatch.

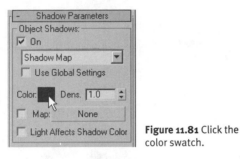

Figure 11.82 Choosing a light blue color.

Figure 11.83 The object now casts a light blue shadow.

You can set shadow color independently of the color of the light. Use this feature to introduce reflected color from nearby objects or from secondary light sources such as the sky.

To set shadow color:

1. Select a light that casts shadows in a scene (**Figure 11.80**).

2. Open the Modify menu.

3. Open the Shadow Parameters rollout.

4. Click the Color swatch (**Figure 11.81**)

5. Choose a color in the Color Selector: Shadow Color dialog box (**Figure 11.82**).

6. Render the scene.

   The shadow changes color (**Figure 11.83**).

The density parameter sets the value, or darkness, of the shadows without affecting their hue and saturation. Use this feature to fill in shadows or to make them more transparent.

To set shadow density:

1. Open a scene that has cast shadows (**Figure 11.84**).

2. Select a light that is casting shadows and open the Modify menu.

3. Open the Shadow Parameters rollout.

4. Set the Density value of the shadow (**Figure 11.85**).

5. Render the scene.

   The shadow becomes darker or lighter (**Figure 11.86**).

✔ Tips

■ To mix the color of the light with the shadow color, check Light Affects Shadow Color in the Shadow Parameters rollout.

■ To project a map into a shadow, check Map and click the None button.

Figure 11.84 The object casts a shadow of Density = 1.0.

Figure 11.85 Increasing the density of the shadow.

Figure 11.86 The shadow fills in.

CASTING SHADOWS

Figure 11.87 In this scene, the teapot overshadows the pyramid.

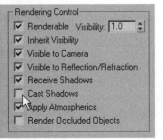

Figure 11.88 Turning off Cast Shadows for the teapot.

Figure 11.89 After turning off the teapot shadow.

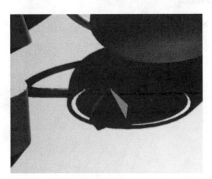

Figure 11.90 After turning off Receive Shadows for the pyramid.

A light can project shadows from the objects it illuminates or exclude those objects from casting shadows. But shadow casting is an arrangement between two parties: both the light and the object have to be set to cast shadows before shadows will be rendered.

Obviously, then, shadow casting is turned on for objects by default, since you have been able to turn them on and off by changing light settings. By the same token, shadow casting for objects applies to all lights, since renderable objects always cast shadows when you illuminate them.

If you turn off the shadow-casting property of an object, it will not cast shadows for any light.

To turn off shadow casting for an object:

1. Open a scene that is illuminated by a light (**Figure 11.87**).

2. Select an object that is casting a shadow.

3. Right-click on the object, and choose Properties from the Transform quad menu.

4. In the Object Properties dialog box, uncheck Cast Shadows (**Figure 11.88**).

5. Click OK.

6. Render the scene to see the results (**Figure 11.89**).

✔ Tip

- To prevent any shadows from falling across an object, uncheck Receive Shadows in its Object Properties dialog box (**Figure 11.90**).

Navigating Lights

When you activate a light view, the viewport window controls change to a new set of navigation buttons called the light viewport controls (**Figure 11.91**). By navigating lights with the light viewport controls, you can fine-tune their placement and animate them over time.

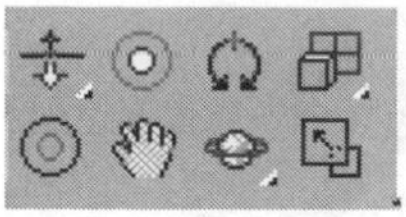

The names of light viewport controls are based on traditional terms for making movies. For a complete description of the light viewport controls, see **Table 11.1**.

Figure 11.91 The Light window controls navigate light viewports.

Table 11.1

Light Viewport Controls		
ICON	**NAME**	**DESCRIPTION**
	Dolly Light	Moves light along its local Z axis, or line of sight.
	Dolly Light + Target	Moves light and target along light's Z axis.
	Dolly Target	Moves target along light's Z axis.
	Light Hotspot	Changes the size of the hotspot.
	Roll Light	Rotates light around its Z axis.
	Zoom Extents All	Centers objects in all non-fixed viewports.
	Zoom Extents All Selected	Centers selected objects in all non-fixed viewports.
	Light Falloff	Changes the size of the falloff.
	Truck Light	Moves light and target parallel to the view plane.
	Orbit Light	Rotates light around its target.
	Pan Light	Rotates light. Target rotates around light.
	Min/Max Toggle	Toggles between viewport layout and full display.

Note: Free lights use virtual targets for the dolly, truck, pan, and orbit commands.

Figure 11.92 The Select Light dialog box prompts you to choose a light.

Figure 11.93 The light viewport shows how the scene looks from the standpoint of the light.

You can look at a scene from the point of view of a spotlight or a directional light.

To change a view to a light view:

1. Open a scene that has a spotlight or directional light in it.

2. Activate the viewport you want to change.

3. Type $ (Shift + 4).

   The Select Light dialog box appears (**Figure 11.92**).

4. Select a light, and click OK.

   The view in the viewport changes to the Light view (**Figure 11.93**).

To dolly a light:

1. Change a view to a Light view (**Figure 11.94**).

2. Click the Dolly Light button ⊕ in the Light viewport controls.

3. Drag the dolly cursor up or down in the Light viewport.

   The light moves in or out along its local Z-axis, or "line of shine" (**Figure 11.95**).

   The pool of illumination shrinks or expands (**Figure 11.96**).

✔ Tips

- To dolly a target, choose Dolly Target ⊕ from the Dolly Light flyout.

- To dolly a light and its target together, choose Dolly Light + Target ⊕ from the same flyout.

Figure 11.94 Open the spotlight viewport.

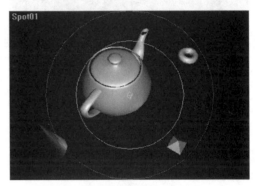

Figure 11.95 The scene enlarges in the viewport after you dolly the light closer to its target.

Figure 11.96 The pool of illumination shrinks as a result.

NAVIGATING LIGHTS

Figure 11.97 The scene before you truck the light.

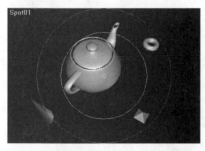

Figure 11.98 The view from the light shows the pool of illumination from above. .

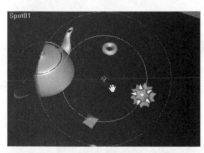

Figure 11.99 Use the panning hand to truck the light.

Figure 11.100 Compare the result to the light viewport.

The truck command moves a light and its target across a scene parallel to the plane of the light viewport.

To truck a light:

1. Open a scene with a light in it (**Figure 11.97**).

2. Change a view to a Light view (**Figure 11.98**).

3. Click the Truck Light button 🤚.

4. Drag the panning hand across the Light viewport.

   The light viewport moves across the scene (**Figure 11.99**).

   The cone of illumination moves as well (**Figure 11.100**).

NAVIGATING LIGHTS

Roll rotates a light along its line of sight. This affects the scene only if the light casts a rectangular cone or uses a projector map.

To roll a light:

1. Open a scene that is lit by a rectangular cone of illumination (**Figure 11.101**).

2. Change a view to a Light view (**Figure 11.102**).

3. Click Roll Light ⟳.

4. Drag the roll cursor across the Light viewport.

   The light rotates around its depth axis (**Figure 11.103**).

   The pool of illumination, and any maps that are being projected, roll with the light (**Figure 11.104**).

Figure 11.101 Using a rectangular cone of illumination, the light projects a Brick map onto the scene.

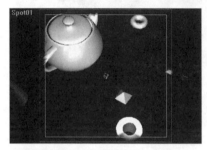

Figure 11.102 Before rolling the light.

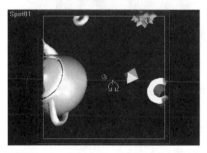

Figure 11.103 After rolling the light about 50°.

Figure 11.104 The map rolls with the projector.

Figure 11.105 This scene is mainly lit from above and to the left.

Figure 11.106 The view from the spotlight that provides most of the illumination.

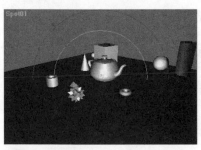

Figure 11.107 Orbiting the light around its target.

Figure 11.108 The scene is now illuminated from above and to the right.

Orbit Light a spot or directional light around its target. If the light is a free light, it uses a virtual target located at the end of the light cone.

To orbit a light:

1. Open a scene (**Figure 11.105**).

2. Change a viewport to a Light view (**Figure 11.106**)

3. Click the Orbit Light button 🔘 in the Light viewport controls.

4. Drag the cursor in the Light viewport.

   The light rotates around its target (**Figure 11.107**).

   The light orbits around the scene (**Figure 11.108**)

✔ Tip

- To align a light to a surface normal, select the light and choose Place Highlight 🔘 from the Align flyout. Then click the object. The light aligns to the normal and creates a highlight on the surface. It remains at the same distance from the object as it was before. For more information on controlling highlights, see Chapter 13, "Creating Materials."

NAVIGATING LIGHTS

Pan rotates a target around a light. If the light is a free light, it uses a virtual target located at the end of the light cone.

To pan a light:

1. Open a scene that is lit by a spotlight or a directional light (**Figure 11.109**).

2. Change a view to a Light view (**Figure 11.110**).

3. Click the Pan Light button  in the Light viewport controls, located on the Orbit Light flyout.

4. Drag the cursor across the Light viewport.

   The Light view pans across the scene (**Figure 11.111**).

   The light sweeps across the scene (**Figure 11.112**)

Figure 11.109 The light initially falls on the left front corner of the scene.

Figure 11.110 The view from the light viewport shows the area of illumination.

Figure 11.111 Panning the light across the scene.

Figure 11.112 The light sweeps across the scene.

Animating Lights

Lights are animated by keyframing or linking, or by assigning animation controllers to them.

Any numerical parameter of a light can be keyframed, including intensity, color, contrast, hotspot, falloff, attenuation and shadow density. You can also keyframe the position and orientation of a light using the move and rotate transforms and the light window controls. However, parameters that use check boxes cannot be keyframed.

Linking a light to a moving object ensures that the light will illuminate the object, or objects nearby—think running lights or headlights on a car. If the light is linked to a camera, the light will shine wherever the camera is pointed.

The Look At controller turns a light into a searchlight that always points at a target object. Moving the target over time is an easy way to animate the light. (Use a non-rendering pointer object if you do not want the target to be seen.) 3ds max automatically assigns the Look At controller to spotlights and directional lights, so all you need to do is tell the light where to look.

To make lights follow an object:

1. Open PracticeScene04.max and close the ActiveShade view. (Note: the scene may shift a little when you close the view.)

2. Link the omni light to the object above it (**Figure 11.113**).

3. Turn off the spotlight. Then increase the Multiplier of the directional light to 1.5 (**Figure 11.114**).

4. In the Modify panel, convert the directional light to a Target Direct type.

5. Open the Motion panel.

6. In the Look At Parameters rollout, click the Pick Target button (**Figure 11.115**). Then click the highlighted object.

7. Move the object.
   The lights follow the object (**Figure 11.116**).

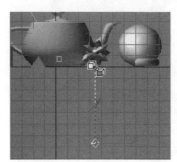

Figure 11.113 Linking the omni light to the hedra.

Figure 11.114 The hedra is lit from above and below.

Figure 11.115 Pick the hedra to be the Look At target.

Figure 11.116 When you move the hedra, the omni light and the target light follow it.

ANIMATING LIGHTS

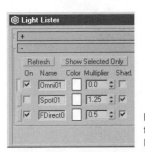

Figure 11.117 Adjust the light settings in the Light Lister utility.

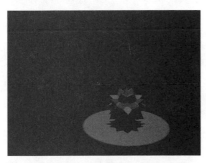

Figure 11.118 Start with a dim illumination.

Figure 11.119 As the overhead light brightens to full intensity, the fill light brightens with it.

Figure 11.120 Beam me up, Scotty!

By animating the intensity multiplier, you can make lights dim and brighten over time.

To animate light intensity:

1. Open PracticeScene04.max.

2. Close the ActiveShade view. Then pan the Perspective viewport so that the hedra is more central to the composition.

3. Choose Tools > Light Lister.

4. In the Light Lister dialog box, turn off the spotlight and set the omni Multiplier to 0 (**Figure 11.117**).
   The scene dims (**Figure 11.118**).

5. Turn on the Animate button and drag the time slider to frame 50.

6. In the Light Lister, set the directional light multiplier to 1.5. Then set the omni light multiplier to .5 (**Figure 11.119**).

7. Drag the time slider to frame 100.

8. Set the intensity of both the directional light and the omni light to 0.

9. Play back the animation.
   The lights brighten and dim to darkness.

✔ Tips

- To animate a light turning on and off, change the tangent type of the Multiplier keys to Step, or assign an On/Off controller to the Multiplier track.

- By cloning the directional light and adding volume and a projector map, you can create a transporter that beams up your objects (**Figure 11.120**).

CAMERAS

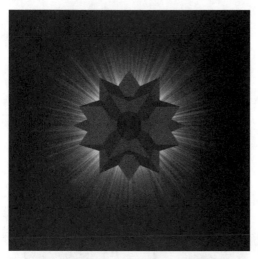

Figure 12.1 Looking up at the hedra in Figure 11.1.

In the previous chapters, you learned how to model and animate objects. With cameras, you determine how the audience views the scene.

Cameras make you the director of your own movie. To tell your story, you compose shots to show the part of the scene where the action takes place. As you become more experienced, you begin setting up shots from more informative, beautiful, mysterious, unusual, helpful, or surprising points of view (**Figure 12.1**).

This chapter discusses the different types of cameras, how to adjust them, and how to place them. You will also learn how to animate cameras by keyframing and using motion paths.

Viewing Scenes

Camera placement determines the composition of your final image. It tells the viewer what is important and places the viewer in the scene. By positioning a camera properly, you can transform a scene from mediocre to memorable.

If you want to make viewers feel as if they are participating in a scene, place the camera at eye level. For example, if you are designing an architectural walk-through, the eye-level camera creates the feeling that the viewer is actually taking a tour of the building (**Figure 12.2**).

To create a feeling of insignificance, place the camera close to the ground, so that it is level with an ant's point of view. This gives the viewer the impression that everything is huge and overwhelming by making objects loom steeply overhead (**Figure 12.3**).

Maybe you are re-creating a car accident scene and you want to show what led up to the accident. You might position a camera so it gives viewers the idea that they are in a helicopter that is keeping pace with the vehicle. Placing a camera high above a scene creates an omnipotent point of view, like that of a narrator (or lawyer) telling a story (**Figure 12.4**). Adding a second camera at eye level places your witness on the scene (**Figure 12.5**).

Close up shots give the impression of intimacy, like watching a character in a soap opera. Long shots create an impersonal feeling, like gazing across the vast sweep of the Western frontier. If you are working from an existing image, matching the shot may be the first step you take in creating a digital matte painting.

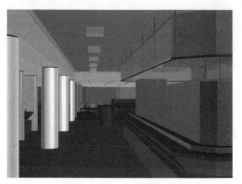

Figure 12.2 Proper camera placement makes viewers feel as if they are a part of the scene.

Figure 12.3 Use a low viewpoint to emphasize the insignificance of the viewer relative to the scene.

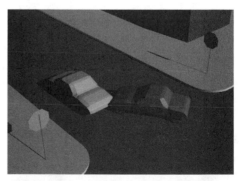

Figure 12.4 Place the camera overhead, aiming downward, for a storytelling viewpoint.

Figure 12.5 Using two vantage points often helps describe an incident better.

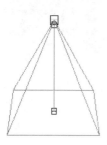

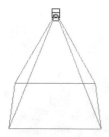

Figure 12.6 The camera cone is a pyramid whose tip is the camera. The target camera (top) displays a target at the focal length of the camera.

Figure 12.7 You can create two types of cameras in 3ds max: target cameras and free cameras

Creating Cameras

A camera is a nonrendering object that displays a view of a scene. The location and direction of the view is determined by the position and orientation of the camera.

Just as illumination can be considered an effect of a light, displaying a view can be considered an effect of a camera. To delimit a view, cameras use a field of view cone similar to the cone of illumination used by lights, except that the cone is actually pyramidal in shape. The angle of the cone ranges in arc from 0° to 175° across its width. The default field of view setting is 45°.

Like lights, cameras are either targeted or free (**Figure 12.6**):

◆ **Target Cameras**—Composed of two components: a camera and a target. Each component can move independently, but the camera always points at the target. This feature makes target cameras easy to aim.

◆ **Free Cameras**—Single-object cameras that use a virtual target. Free cameras move and rotate easily, which makes them better for animating complex camera movements.

Like other objects in 3ds max, you create cameras in the Create panel (**Figure 12.7**).

Target cameras are easy to aim. You create and aim a target camera by clicking and dragging.

To create a target camera:

1. Open a scene.

2. Open the Cameras branch of the Create panel.

3. Click Target Camera.

4. In the Top viewport, position the cursor where you want to place the camera. Use 3D snap to align the camera precisely.

5. Click to create the camera, and drag to aim it. Release the mouse button to set the target (**Figure 12.8**).

6. Activate a viewport, and type C to change the viewport to a Camera viewport.

   The viewport displays the view from the camera (**Figure 12.9**).

7. Adjust the position of the camera by moving and/or rotating it.

8. Aim the camera by moving its target.

   To select a target quickly, right-click on the camera, and choose Select Target from the Tools1 quad menu.

✔ Tips

- You can also change views to a Camera view using the viewport right-click menu.

- To match a camera to the Perspective view, activate the Perspective viewport and type Ctrl + C (**Figure 12.10**).

- To fine-tune the position of the camera, see "Navigating Cameras" later in this chapter.

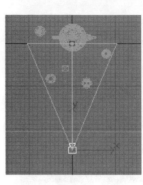

Figure 12.8 To aim the target camera horizontally in your scene, create it in the Top viewport.

Figure 12.9 The initial view from the target camera.

Figure 12.10 After matching the camera to the Perspective view. Note: The plane is mapped with a Checker map. See Chapter 14 for information on mapping objects.

CREATING CAMERAS

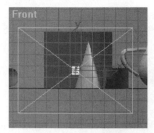

Figure 12.11 To point the free camera into your scene, create it in the Front viewport.

Figure 12.12 The initial view from the free camera.

Figure 12.13 The Select Camera dialog box lets you choose which camera to use.

Free cameras are easy to move. You create a free camera with a single click.

To create a free camera:

1. Open a scene.
2. Open the Cameras branch of the Create panel.
3. Click Free Camera.
4. Click the location where you want to place the camera.

   The camera appears in the viewport, facing the active grid (**Figure 12.11**).
5. Activate a viewport and type C to see the view from the camera (**Figure 12.12**)
6. Move or rotate the camera to position and aim it.

   or

   Match the camera to the Perspective viewport as explained in the tip for creating a target camera.

✔ **Tip**

■ If the scene includes multiple cameras, and none are selected, typing C opens the Select Camera dialog box so you can choose which camera to use (**Figure 12.13**).

CREATING CAMERAS

The Align Camera command aligns a camera to the surface normal of an object.

To align a camera to an object:

1. Select a camera.

2. Choose Align Camera  from the Align flyout in the main toolbar.

3. Place the cursor on the surface of an object.

4. Click and hold down the mouse button.

   A blue normal appears to indicate the direction of alignment (**Figure 12.14**).

Figure 12.14 Click and drag the movie-camera cursor to find a surface normal for aligning the camera. Then release the mouse button.

5. Drag the cursor until the normal points in the direction that you want to align the camera. Then release the mouse button.

   The camera aligns to the surface normal of the face that you clicked (**Figure 12.15**).

✔ Tips

- You can select a camera or its target from the camera viewport label right-click menu.

- To undo a camera movement, click Ctrl + Z.

Figure 12.15 The camera points at the teapot in line with the surface normal you selected.

You can also use an AutoGrid to align a free camera to the surface of an object while you are creating it (**Figure 12.16**).

AutoGrid is not available for target cameras, but you can convert a free camera to a target camera after the camera has been created.

To convert a camera:

1. Select a camera.

2. Open the Modify panel.

3. Select a new camera type in the Type drop-down list of the Parameters rollout (**Figure 12.17**).

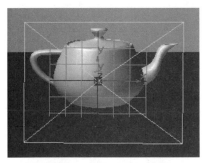

Figure 12.16 Use AutoGrid to align a free camera to an object upon creation.

Figure 12.17 Use the Type drop-down list to change the camera type.

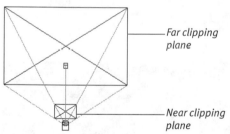

Figure 12.18 The parameters rollout is the same for target and free cameras.

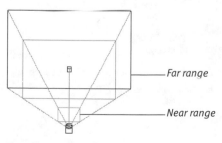

Far clipping plane

Near clipping plane

Figure 12.19 The clipping planes indicate which part of the scene the camera can see.

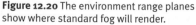

Far range

Near range

Figure 12.20 The environment range planes show where standard fog will render.

Adjusting Cameras

Target and free cameras have the same adjustments. The principle settings are lens size, clipping planes, environment ranges, depth of field, and motion blurring (**Figure 12.18**).

In 3ds max, the focal length of a camera can be adjusted by changing the size of its lens—just like with a real camera. When you change lenses, the focal length increases or decreases, and the field of view (FOV) widens or narrows.

The depth to which you can see in space is limited by two clipping planes: one near the camera, and one farther away along its line of sight. Objects not enclosed by these planes are not visible from the camera (**Figure 12.19**).

When you add an effect called standard fog to your scene, the fog is limited to a near and far range from the camera. This range is called the Environment range, and it allows you to define the region in which fog can obscure the scene (**Figure 12.20**).

Depth of field and motion blurring imitate the effects of real cameras by blurring objects that are outside of a certain radius. The radius can be defined by the target distance, or by a focal depth that you set especially for this effect.

ADJUSTING CAMERAS

You set the focal length of a camera by adjusting the size of its lens. Lenses range in size from 9.857mm to 100,000mm. For convenience, you can pick from a set of nine stock lenses ranging from 15mm to 200mm. Changing the size of the lens inversely affects the FOV setting.

To set the focal length:

1. Select a camera.

2. Type C to activate the view from that camera (**Figure 12.21**).

3. Open the Modify panel.

   The camera Parameters rollout appears.

4. Drag the Lens spinner (**Figure 12.22**).

   As the focal length increases, the field of view decreases. Objects in the Camera view appear closer, and the perspective flattens (**Figure 12.23**).

   Decreasing the focal length increases the field of view and deepens perspective.

✔ Tips

■ Select one of the stock lenses. The 15mm lens provides a wide-angle, fish-eye effect. At the other extreme, the 200mm lens zooms in tightly and flattens perspective.

■ Check Orthogonal Projection to make the Camera viewport flatten the scene as in a User view using orthogonal projection.

Figure 12.21 Setting the scene for experimenting with focal length.

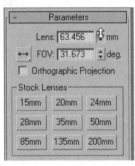

Figure 12.22 Increasing the lens size.

Figure 12.23 The camera zooms into the scene for a close-up shot.

Figure 12.24 Before changing the field of view.

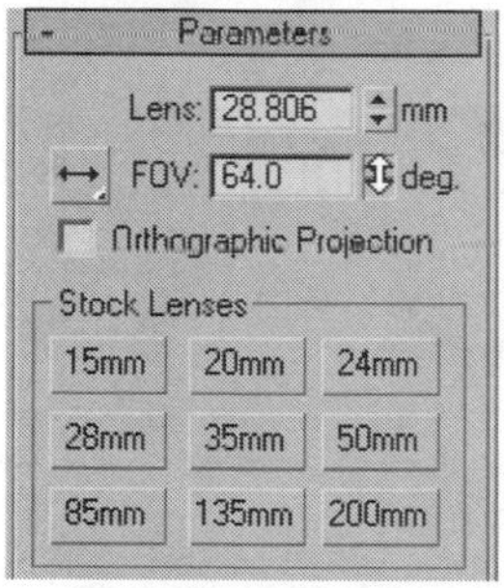

Figure 12.25 Increasing the field of view.

Figure 12.26 The camera zooms out, revealing more of the scene.

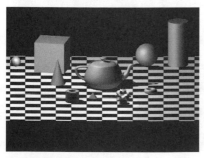

Figure 12.27 After checking Orthographic Projection the camera view looks like a User view.

The field of view sets the breadth of the camera view in degrees of arc. Views can range from 0° to 175° across. The field of view setting is inversely proportional to the focal length.

To adjust the field of view:

1. Select a camera.

2. Type C to activate the view from that camera (**Figure 12.24**).

3. Open the Modify panel to access the camera parameters.

4. Drag the FOV spinner (**Figure 12.25**).

   As the field of view increases, the focal length decreases. Objects in the Camera view appear further away, and the perspective flattens (**Figure 12.26**).

   Decreasing the field of view deepens perspective and makes objects appear closer.

✔ Tips

- The FOV Direction flyout ↔ changes the way the program measures the field of view.

- Check Show Cone to display the FOV cone even when the camera is not selected.

- To match a camera view to a background image, check Horizon. Then align the horizon line of the camera to the horizon line of the background image.

- You can also adjust the field of view using the Field-of-View button in the Camera viewport controls.

- By animating the field of view you can simulate the action of a zoom lens.

- Check Orthographic Projection to change the camera view to an axonometric view (**Figure 12.27**).

ADJUSTING CAMERAS

333

Clipping planes define the region of visibility within a camera's view cone along its *depth axis*, or line of sight. Objects positioned outside of this region are invisible to the camera. If a clipping plane intersects an object, the object is cut away.

To adjust clipping planes:

1. Select a camera.

2. Open the Modify panel.

3. In the Clipping Planes group, check Clip Manually (**Figure 12.28**).

   The clipping parameters become available in the rollout. The far clipping plane appears in the cone of the camera as a red rectangle with red diagonal lines. The near clipping plane is not visible yet because it is set to 0.

4. Type C to activate the camera view.

5. Adjust the near and far clipping planes dragging their spinners.

   As you drag their spinners, the clipping planes move toward or away from the camera (**Figure 12.29**). In the camera viewport, the front and/or back of the scene disappears (**Figure 12.30**).

✔ Tip

■ You can animate clipping planes to animate a cut-away view.

Figure 12.28 Turn on Clip Manually to set a specific clipping range.

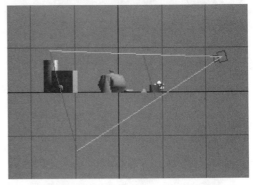

Figure 12.29 The clipping planes of this camera will be cutting off the front and back of the scene.

Figure 12.30 The rendered scene is missing some geometry in the front and the back.

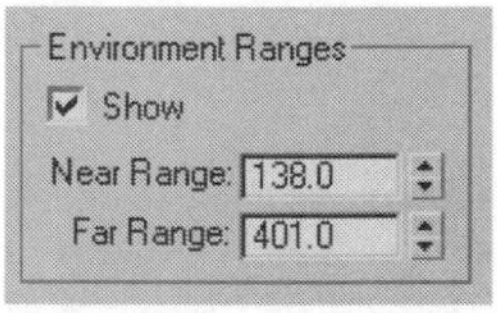

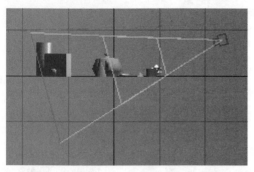

Figure 12.31 Turn on Show in the Environment Ranges group to display the environment range planes.

Figure 12.32 The environment ranges enclose the scene. The middle line indicates the target distance.

Figure 12.33 Fog renders just in between the environment range planes.

Standard fog is an atmospheric effect that fades objects as they move away from a camera. The Environment Range settings determine the near distance at which fog begins fading objects and the far distance at which it finally obscures them.

To set the environment range:

1. Open a scene with a camera in it.

2. Apply a standard fog effect to the scene. (This is explained in Chapter 14, Rendering Effects. Briefly: Choose Rendering > Environment. In the Atmosphere rollout, click Add. Then choose Fog, and click OK.)

3. Select a camera.

4. Open the Modify panel.

5. In the Environment Ranges group, check Show (**Figure 12.31**).

   The far range plane appears in the camera's view cone. The near range plane is set to zero by default, so it does not appear yet.

6. Drag the Near Range spinner to set the beginning of the fog.

   The light brown rectangle of the near range plane moves along the camera's line of sight.

7. Drag the Far Range spinner to set the point of full obscuration (**Figure 12.32**).

   The brown rectangle of the far range plane moves along the camera's line of sight.

8. Change to the Camera view by typing C.

9. Render the scene to view the effect.

   The fog is rendered between the Near Range and the Far Range distances (**Figure 12.33**).

ADJUSTING CAMERAS

Depth of field is a multi-pass rendering effect that blurs the foreground and background of a scene based on a focal point that you specify.

To apply depth-of-field blurring:

1. Select a camera that views a scene.

2. Activate the camera view.

3. Open the Modify panel.

4. In the Multi-Pass Effect group of the camera Parameters rollout, check Enable (**Figure 12.34**).

Figure 12.34 Enable multi-pass rendering for the depth-of-field effect.

5. Click Preview.

   The camera view wiggles for a few moments; then stops. The view is rendered with a small amount of depth-of-field blur both in front and beyond the target distance.

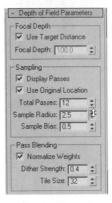

6. Increase the Sample Radius slightly (**Figure 12.35**). Then click Preview.

   The camera view shakes again. The depth-of-field blurring increases (**Figure 12.36**).

Figure 12.35 Increase the sample radius to increase the amount of blur.

7. Adjust the Sample Radius and preview the image until the blurring is sufficient.

8. Click Quick Render to see the result.

   The virtual frame buffer updates 12 times. Each time, the image gets brighter. When the rendering is complete, the image is blurred both in front and beyond the focal point (**Figure 12.37**).

Figure 12.36 Preview the image in the camera viewport.

✔ Tips

- To increase the offset amount of the blurred images, increase the Sample Bias amount.

- To adjust the depth of the focal point, adjust the target distance, or uncheck Use Target Distance and enter a Focal Depth amount.

- To make the rendered image appear grainier, uncheck Normalize Weights or increase the Dither Strength.

- For a complete description of Depth of Field parameters, look up multi-pass parameters in the Help files User Reference.

Figure 12.37 The image renders using multiple passes that are averaged together to create the blur effect.

ADJUSTING CAMERAS

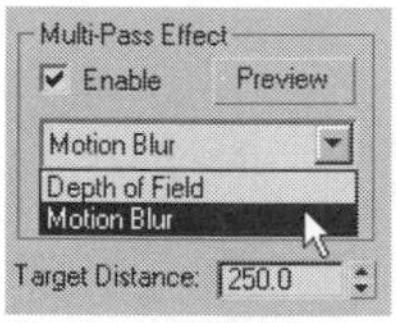

Figure 12.38 Enable multi-pass rendering for the motion blur effect.

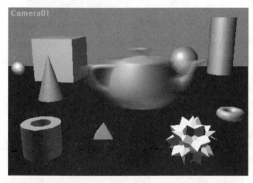

Figure 12.39 Increase the Duration and the Bias amounts.

Figure 12.40 Preview the image in the camera viewport.

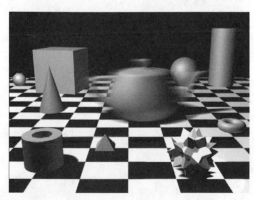

Figure 12.41 After multiple passes, the scene is rendered with motion blur.

Motion blur is a multi-pass rendering effect that creates a blurred trail behind a moving object.

To apply motion blur:

1. Select a camera that views a scene. The scene should contain an object that is animated to move across the camera view.

2. Activate the camera view.

3. Move the time slider so that the moving object is visible in the camera viewport.

4. Open the Modify panel.

5. In the Multi-Pass Effect group, check Enable. Then choose Motion Blur from the Multi-Pass Effect drop-down menu (**Figure 12.38**).

6. Click Preview.
   The object moves for the period of one frame. The view is rendered with a small amount of motion blur both in front and beyond the target distance.

7. Increase the Duration (frames) parameter to increase the amount of blur.

8. Adjust the Bias amount to weight the blur towards the two preceding frames or the two succeeding frames (**Figure 12.39**).

9. Click Preview to preview the image in the Camera viewport (**Figure 12.40**).

10. Adjust your settings. Then do a Quick Render to see the result (**Figure 12.41**).

✔ Tips

■ Clicking Preview has no effect it the camera view is not activated.

■ For a complete description of Depth of Field parameters, look up multi-pass parameters in the Help files User Reference.

Navigating Cameras

When you activate a camera view, the viewport window controls change to a new set of navigation buttons called the Camera viewport controls (**Figure 12.42**). By navigating cameras with the Camera viewport controls, you can fine-tune their placement and animate them over time.

The names of Camera viewport controls are based on traditional terms for making movies. For a complete description of the Camera viewport controls, see **Table 12.1**.

Figure 12.42 The Camera viewport controls navigate cameras.

Table 12.1

Camera Viewport Controls

Icon	Name	Description
	Dolly Camera	Moves camera along its local Z-axis, or line of sight.
	Dolly Camera + Target	Moves camera and target along camera's Z-axis.
	Dolly Target	Moves target along camera's Z-axis.
	Perspective	Dollies camera and changes its field of view.
	Roll Camera	Rotates camera around its Z-axis.
	Zoom Extents All	Centers objects in all non-fixed viewports.
	Zoom Extents All Selected	Centers selected objects in all non-fixed viewports.
	Field-of-View	Changes the angle of the camera lens.
	Truck Camera	Moves camera and target parallel to the view plane.
	Orbit Camera	Rotates camera around its target.
	Pan Camera	Rotates camera. Target rotates around camera.
	Min/Max Toggle	Toggles between viewport layout and full display.

Note: Free cameras use virtual targets for the dolly, truck, pan, and orbit commands.

The Dolly command moves a camera toward or away from a scene by moving the camera along its line of sight.

Figure 12.43 The scene before dollying the camera.

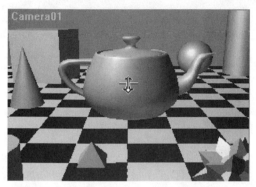

Figure 12.44 Dollying the camera into the scene.

Figure 12.45 After dollying in, the camera is closer, but the target remains in the same place.

To dolly a camera:

1. Select a camera.

2. Type C to change the active viewport to a Camera view (**Figure 12.43**).

3. Click the Dolly Camera button ⬚.

4. Drag the dolly cursor up or down in the Camera viewport (**Figure 12.44**).

   The camera moves along its Z (depth) axis, so that it moves closer toward, or farther away from, the objects it views. The objects grow or shrink in the view (**Figure 12.45**).

✔ Tips

- Dolly Camera has two additional flyout commands:

  Dolly Target ⬚ moves the target of the camera along its depth axis.

  Dolly Camera + Target ⬚ moves both the camera and its target along the camera's depth axis.

- You can animate the dolly command to gradually approach a point of interest, or back away and reveal the whole scene.

The truck command moves a camera and its target across a scene parallel to the plane of the Camera viewport.

To truck a camera:

1. Select a camera.

2. Type C to change the active viewport to a Camera viewport (**Figure 12.46**).

3. Click the Truck Camera button .

4. Drag the panning hand across the Camera viewport (**Figure 12.47**).

   The camera moves across the scene (**Figure 12.48**).

✔ Tip

■ Animate the Truck Camera command to simulate the view from a train or the side window of a car.

Figure 12.46 The scene before trucking the camera.

Figure 12.47 Trucking the camera across the scene moves both the camera and its target.

Figure 12.48 Afterwards, the camera looks at a different part of the scene.

NAVIGATING CAMERAS

Figure 12.49 The scene before rolling the camera.

Figure 12.50 Use Roll to bank, or tilt, the camera around its depth axis.

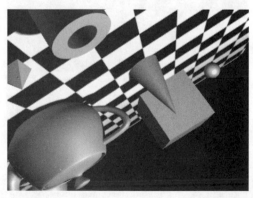

Figure 12.51 After rolling the camera, the scene looks tilted.

Roll rotates a camera along its line of sight, causing the scene to spin in the view.

To roll a camera:

1. Select a camera.

2. Type C to change the active viewport to a Camera viewport (**Figure 12.49**).

3. Click Roll Camera [icon].

4. Drag the roll cursor left or right in the Camera viewport (**Figure 12.50**).

   The camera rotates around its depth axis. The scene rolls in the view (**Figure 12.51**).

✔ Tip

■ Animate a camera roll to simulate a car rolling over. By combing a roll with a dolly command, you can simulate a plane diving into a spin.

Orbit rotates a camera around its target. If the camera is a free camera, it uses a virtual target located at the focal length of the camera.

To orbit a camera:

1. Select a camera.

2. Type C to change the active viewport to a Camera view (**Figure 12.52**).

3. Click the Orbit Camera button ⬚.

4. Drag the cursor across the Camera viewport (**Figure 12.53**).

   The camera rotates around its target. Objects in the scene appear to spin around the target (**Figure 12.54**).

✔ Tip

■ To create a simple fly-by animation, try orbiting a target camera around a point of interest over time.

Figure 12.52 Before orbiting the camera.

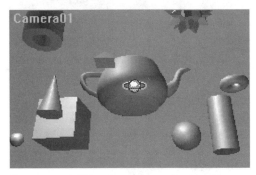

Figure 12.53 Orbiting the camera under the scene.

Figure 12.54 After orbiting the camera under the scene, the plane doesn't render because its normals face upwards.

Figure 12.55 Before panning the camera.

Figure 12.56 Panning pivots a camera and moves its target around it.

Figure 12.57 The camera faces a new direction.

Pan rotates a target around a camera. If the camera is a free camera, it uses a virtual target located at the focal length of the camera.

To pan a camera:

1. Select a camera.

2. Type C to change the active viewport to a Camera view (**Figure 12.55**).

3. Click the Pan Camera button, available from the Orbit Camera flyout.

4. Drag the cursor across the Camera viewport (**Figure 12.56**).

   The camera pivots, and the camera view sweeps across the scene (**Figure 12.57**).

✔ Tips

- Dragging the Pan cursor up or down in the Camera view tilts the camera, as if you were looking up and down a tall building.

- With the Pan command you can animate a camera as it slowly surveys a scene. Establishing the scene in this way gives the viewer a sense of reference.

- By panning rapidly around the scene over time, you can make it seems as if the viewer is in a car spinning out of control.

NAVIGATING CAMERAS

The Field-of-View command changes the size of the camera lens. As the field of view gets wider, the scene begins to distort like a fish eye lens. As the field of view gets narrower, the perspective flattens and the scene appears to have less depth.

To change the field of view:

1. Select a camera.

2. Type C to change the active viewport to a Camera view.

3. Render the view (**Figure 12.58**).

4. Click the Field-of-View button ▷.

5. Drag the cursor up or down in the Camera viewport (**Figure 12.59**).

    The field of view increases or decreases (**Figure 12.60**).

Figure 12.58 The scene before changing the field of view.

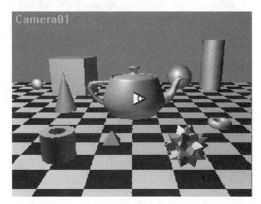

Figure 12.59 Dragging downward increases the field of view.

Figure 12.60 Afterwards, you can see more of the scene, but the camera remains in the same place.

NAVIGATING CAMERAS

Figure 12.61 The scene with normal perspective.

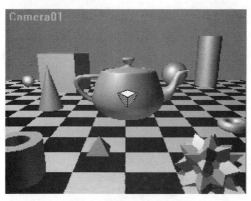

Figure 12.62 Increasing the perspective of the camera.

Figure 12.63 Exaggerated perspective adds a dramatic look to the scene.

The Perspective command dollies a camera and changes its field of view at the same time. This action preserves the essential composition of the scene while changing its perspective.

To change perspective:

1. Select a target camera.

2. Type C to change the active viewport to a Camera viewport.

3. Render the view (**Figure 12.61**).

4. Click the Perspective button.

5. Drag the cursor up or down in the Camera viewport.

   The view changes perspective and zooms a bit (**Figure 12.62**).

6. Render the scene (**Figure 12.63**).

✔ Tip

■ Holding down the Ctrl key while changing perspective accelerates the change.

Animating Cameras

Cameras have a wide range of controls that can be animated. You can animate Camera viewport controls, lens size, clipping planes and depth-of-field controls. You can also animate a camera by keyframing it or assigning it to a motion path.

To keyframe a camera:

1. Select a camera.

2. Type C to change the active viewport to a Camera view.

3. Aim the camera and adjust its settings for the opening shot (**Figure 12.64**).

4. Turn on the Animate button.

5. Move the time slider to the right.

6. Adjust the camera by navigating it with the camera viewport controls, by moving and rotating the camera and its target, or by adjusting its parameters (**Figure 12.65**).

7. Set additional keys by moving the time slider and adjusting the camera (**Figure 12.66**).

8. Play the animation ▶ to review the timing and smoothness of any camera motion. Most of the time, the camera will be moving too fast, and its motion will be jerky.

9. Adjust the speed of the camera by moving its keys further apart. To slow down the entire animation, re-scale time in the Time Configuration dialog box.

10. Continue to play back the animation and adjust it until you are satisfied.

✔ Tip

■ Linking a camera and its target to a dummy object and then moving the dummy can make a target camera easier to position.

Figure 12.64 The fog begins to roll in as the Environment ranges retract.

Figure 12.65 The Environment ranges enclose the teapot.

Figure 12.66 The fog encloses the last few objects as the Near and Far ranges approach the camera.

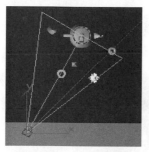

Figure 12.67 Pick an object to replace the camera target.

Figure 12.68 The camera keeps facing the teapot when it moves to the path.

Figure 12.69 The camera looks down at the teapot as it flies by.

Fly-by animations show the viewer how an object or area in a scene looks from different angles.

The default transform controller for a target camera is the LookAt controller. LookAt controllers limit rotation to the depth axis so that a camera will always look at its target.

When you combine a LookAt controller with a Path constraint, creating a fly-by animation becomes smooth and painless.

To create a fly-by animation:

1. Create a spline path for the camera, such as a line, an arc, a circle or an ellipse.
2. Position the shape above the objects.
3. Create a target camera.
4. In the Motion panel, open the LookAt Parameters rollout and click Pick Target (**Figure 12.67**). Then pick an object where you want the camera to look.

   The camera rotates to look at the target.
5. Open the Assign Controller rollout and assign a Path constraint to the position controller of the camera.
6. In the Path Parameters rollout, click Add Path, and then click your path.

   The camera moves to the first vertex of the path. It continues to look at the target (**Figure 12.68**).
7. Type C to activate the Camera viewport and turn on the camera's safe frame display.
8. Scrub the time slider.

   The camera flies by the target object (**Figure 12.69**).
9. In the Modify panel, adjust the field of view or other camera settings as needed.
10. Play back the animation to review the timing and composition. To change the beginning and end point of the animation, turn on the Animate button and adjust the Path constraint % Along Path parameter.

Walk-through animations are commonly used in architecture to show clients how the inside of a building will appear, but you can also use them to explore a landscape or any other type of scene.

To create a walk-through animation:

1. Create a line for the path of the camera that winds through your building or scene. Add enough steps to make the line smooth. For your first attempt, I suggest that you make the line parallel to the ground, and keep the curves as shallow as possible. Then position the line at eye-level.

2. Create a free camera.

3. In the Motion panel, assign a Path constraint to the position controller of the camera. Click Add Path and click the line.

    The camera moves to the first vertex of the line.

4. Check Follow, and choose an axis to make the camera look down the path. You may need to check Flip to make the camera look in the right direction (**Figure 12.70**).

    The camera looks down the animation path (**Figure 12.71**).

5. Type C to activate the Camera viewport. Then roll the camera until it is level.

6. Scrub the time slider to see what the camera sees as it moves down the path.

7. Rotate the camera to adjust its line of sight. Do not use navigation buttons; these reset the % Along Path parameter of the Path constraint to 100% at the current frame. (To fix this problem, turn on the Animate button and reset the last key to 100%.)

8. Adjust the height of the camera by moving the path up or down.

Figure 12.70 Check Follow, and choose an axis.

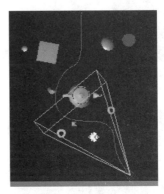

Figure 12.71 The camera looks down the path.

Figure 12.72 The camera walks the viewer through the scene.

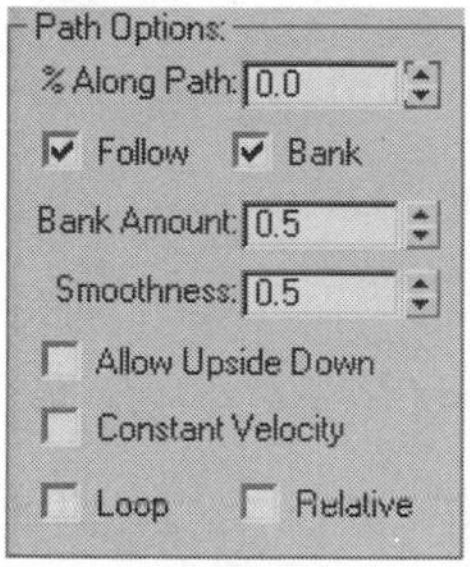

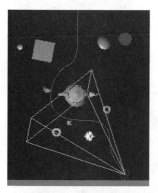

Path Options:
% Along Path: 0.0
☑ Follow   ☑ Bank
Bank Amount: 0.5
Smoothness: 0.5
☐ Allow Upside Down
☐ Constant Velocity
☐ Loop   ☐ Relative

Figure 12.73 Check Bank and set a Bank Amount.

Figure 12.74 Banking makes the camera roll along the path.

Figure 12.75 The scene appears to tilt as the camera banks through the turns.

9. Click Play Animation.

The camera walks the viewer through the scene (**Figure 12.72**).

10. Adjust the speed and timing of the animation by adjusting the animation keys.

To animate the view from a racecar, a swooping bird, or a fighter jet, you animate a free camera along a three-dimensional path and make the camera bank through the turns. Adding a LookAt constraint to the camera allows you to assign a separate target to the camera, such as a plane that is traveling by your side.

To create a fly-through animation:

1. Create a free camera, and assign it to a path, following the instructions for a walk-through animation.

2. In the Path Parameters rollout, check Bank (**Figure 12.73**).

The camera rolls around the path (**Figure 12.74**).

3. Activate the Camera view, and play back the animation.

The camera rolls as it passes through the turns (**Figure 12.75**).

To increase the amount that the camera rolls through turns, increase the Bank Amount.

4. Adjust the timing, motion, composition, and smoothness of the animation. Remember to turn on the Animate button when you need to set and adjust keys.

5. To make the camera move more smoothly, and ignore minor irregularities in the motion path, increase the Smoothness parameter. Decrease this value to less than 3 if you want more of a jerky camera motion.

6. Continue to adjust and play back the animation until you are completely satisfied.

ANIMATING CAMERAS

CREATING MATERIALS

Figure 13.1 All the objects in this scene use different materials.

Materials control how objects reflect and transmit light. They paint your scene with color, luminosity, transparency, and translucency, and they give objects their final finish: shiny or dull, glossy or matte, solid or wireframe, faceted or smooth (**Figure 13.1**).

Using the Material Editor, you can create and combine materials or add maps to different attributes. As your material evolves, the Material Editor builds a hierarchy of submaterials and maps called a *material tree*.

When you save your scene, material trees are stored in the .max file. You can also export them to custom libraries where they can be browsed and imported into other scenes.

Using the Material Editor

The Material Editor is divided into two main sections: the sample slot palette and button menus at the top (**Figure 13.2**) and the parameter rollouts underneath (**Figure 13.3**).

The sample slot palette is a high-resolution canvas for designing materials. Material controls along the edges of the palette allow you to browse, load, navigate, name, copy, save, and assign materials. The parameter rollouts contain settings for building and adjusting material trees.

Table 13.1

Material Controls	
	Sample Type
	Backlight
	Background
	Sample UV Tiling
	Video Color Check
	Save Preview
	Play Preview
	Make a Preview
	Select by Material
	Options
	Material Map Navigator
	Get Material
	Put Material to Scene
	Assign Material to Selection
	Reset Map/Material to Default Setting
	Make Material Copy
	Make Unique
	Put to Library
	Material Effects Channel
	Show Map in Viewport
	Show End Result (Active)
	Go to Parent
	Go Forward to Sibling

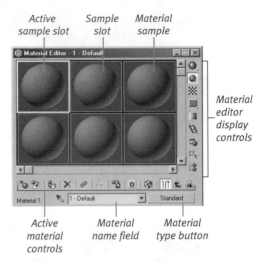

Active sample slot   Sample slot   Material sample

Material editor display controls

Active material controls   Material name field   Material type button

Figure 13.2 The sample slots and button menus.

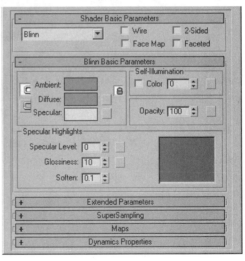

Figure 13.3 The material parameter rollouts contain settings for building and adjusting material trees. Rollouts vary according to material type.

USING THE MATERIAL EDITOR

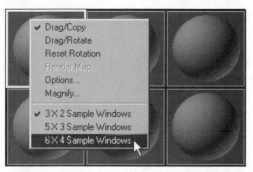

Figure 13.4 Choose 6 x 4 Sample Windows from the sample palette right-click menu.

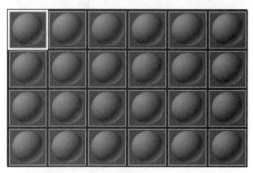

Figure 13.5 The palette refreshes, displaying 24 sample slots.

Figure 13.6 Rotating a sample cube by dragging in the sample slot.

Six sample slots appear in the palette by default, but there are actually 24 slots in all. You view the rest of the slots by scrolling the bar to the right and bottom, or by changing the display.

To navigate the sample palette:

1. Click Open Material Editor ⚃ in the main toolbar, or type M on your keyboard.

2. Drag the scroll bars below and next to the sample palette to view the other slots.

3. Click on a sample slot to activate it. Then right-click on the active sample slot.

   The sample slot right-click menu appears.

4. Choose 6 x 4 Sample Windows from the menu (**Figure 13.4**).

   The display refreshes to show 24 sample slots (**Figure 13.5**). Since all the sample slots are displayed, the scroll bars are disabled.

5. Right-click on the active sample slot and choose 5 x 3 Sample Windows.

   The display updates to 15 sample slots. The scroll bars are re-enabled.

✔ Tips

■ To magnify a sample slot, choose Magnify from the sample slot right-click menu, or double-click the slot. You increase the magnification of a sample slot by dragging a corner of its window.

■ Using the Sample Type flyout ⚃ ⚃ ⚃, you can change the sample object to see how a material will look on an object that more closely matches the shape of your model. You can also import a custom object. For instructions, see "Creating a Custom Sample Object" in the online help files.

■ The Drag/Rotate setting in the sample slot right-click menu allows you to rotate a sample object by dragging it (**Figure 13.6**).

The Material/Map Browser lets you browse for materials from material libraries, the Material Editor, and the current scene. You can also use the Browser to load materials and to select new material types.

To browse materials:

1. Open a scene that has some materials and maps in it, such as Earth.max.

2. Open the Material Editor.

3. Click Get Material 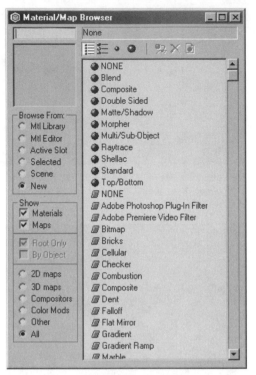.

   The Material/Map Browser appears.

   Materials appear next to blue spheres. Maps appear next to green parallelograms (**Figure 13.7**).

4. Uncheck Show Maps to hide the maps.

5. Choose a graphical display option by clicking an icon at the top of the Browser:

   View List + Icons

   View Small Icons

   View Large Icons (this one is slow)

6. Choose a source to browse from.

   As you choose each option, the materials that are available at that location appear in the Browser.

7. Scroll through the list and click on a material that interests you.

   A larger image of the material appears in the upper-left corner of the Browser window (**Figure 13.8**).

Figure 13.7 The Material/Map Browser displays all the available materials and maps.

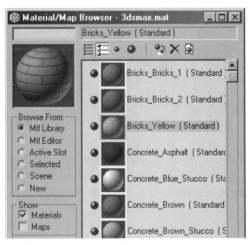

Figure 13.8 Click on a material to see a larger thumbnail image.

Using the Material Editor

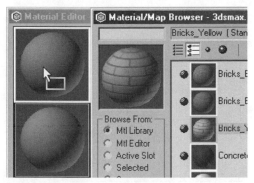

Figure 13.9 Drag a material from the list or from the large thumbnail.

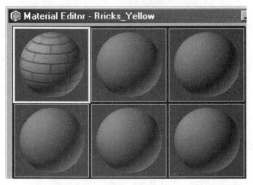

Figure 13.10 The material is copied into the sample slot.

In order to adjust materials, you must first load them into the Material Editor.

To load a material:

1. Open the Material Editor.

2. Click Get Material 🔘.

   The Material/Map Browser appears.

3. Browse through the material libraries until you find a material that you like.

4. Drag your selection from the Browser onto the sample slots in the Material Editor (**Figure 13.9**).

   The material is loaded into the Material Editor (**Figure 13.10**).

5. Close the Material/Map Browser.

✔ Tip

■ Double-clicking a material loads it into the active sample slot and closes the Material/Map Browser at the same time.

The Material/Map Navigator shows how a material is constructed and provides access to settings at every level of the material tree.

To navigate a material tree:

1. Load a material into a sample slot.

2. Click the Material/Map Navigator button 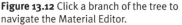.

   The Material/Map Navigator appears. It displays the material tree of the currently active sample slot in list format (**Figure 13.11**).

3. To browse through the material tree visually, choose a graphical display option by clicking an icon at the top of the browser.

4. Click a branch in the material tree (**Figure 13.12**).

   The Material Editor moves to the branch of the tree that you selected (**Figure 13.13**).

5. You can also navigate a material using the controls underneath the sample slots.

   Move to a deeper level by selecting from the drop-down list.

   Click Go to Parent 🔼 to move up a level.

   Click Go Forward to Sibling 🔽 to move across the material tree to a different branch at the same level of the tree.

✔ Tip

- A red icon indicates that Show Map in Viewport has been enabled for a given branch of a material tree.

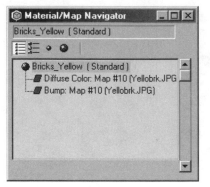

Figure 13.11 The Material/Map Navigator displays material and map trees.

Figure 13.12 Click a branch of the tree to navigate the Material Editor.

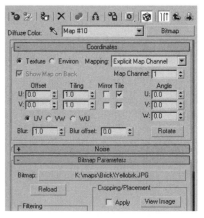

Figure 13.13 The Material Editor displays the branch of the tree that you selected.

USING THE MATERIAL EDITOR

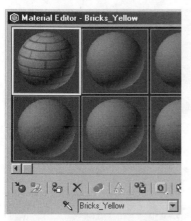

Figure 13.14 When you activate a sample slot, the name of its contents appears at the top of the Material Editor, and in the material name field.

Figure 13.15 Changing the name of the material.

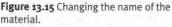

Figure 13.16 The new name appears in the Material/Map Navigator.

Names identify a material as being a unique entity that can be selected and manipulated.

To rename a material:

1. Activate a sample slot.

   The name of the material appears at the top of the Material Editor and in the material name field (**Figure 13.14**).

2. Highlight the name of the material in the material name field. Then enter a new name (**Figure 13.15**).

   The material is renamed.

3. Using the Material/Map Navigator, navigate to any branches of the tree that you would like to name.

4. Enter a new name in the name field.

   The branch of the material or map tree is renamed. The name appears in the Material/Map Navigator (**Figure 13.16**).

✔ Tip

■ As you build material trees, it helps to give each branch a descriptive name for easier reference.

You assign materials to objects by clicking or by dragging. In this way, you can quickly assign materials to all the objects in a scene.

When you assign a material to an object, the material becomes *hot*, meaning that the material is currently being used in the scene. Any changes that you make to a hot material instantly affect the object that it has been applied to.

To assign a material to an object by dragging:

1. Select a material in the Material Editor or the Material/Map Browser.

2. Drag the material onto an object.

   The material is applied to the object (**Figure 13.17**).

   If the material is loaded in the Material Editor, white triangles appear in the corners of the sample slot to indicate that the material is hot (**Figure 13.18**).

To assign a material to an object by clicking:

1. Select one or more objects.

2. Select a material in the Material Editor.

3. Click Assign Material to Selection .

   The material is applied to the object.

   Solid white triangles and a white border indicate that the material is hot, and the object that is using the material is currently selected (**Figure 13.19**).

✔ Tip

■ When you assign a mapped material to certain objects, you may be asked to supply mapping coordinates in order for the map to render correctly. See Chapter 14, Working with Maps, for more information.

Figure 13.17 Drag the material onto the object.

Figure 13.18 The material appears on the object. White corners appear on the sample slot to indicate that it is hot.

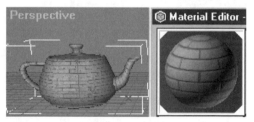

Figure 13.19 When the object you have assigned a material to is selected, the borders of the sample slot turn white.

Figure 13.20 Drag the sample slot to copy it onto one of its neighbors.

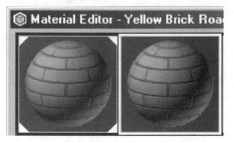

Figure 13.21 The copy is warm, and the original is hot.

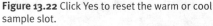

Figure 13.22 Click Yes to reset the warm or cool sample slot.

Figure 13.23 When you reset a hot material, you can choose whether to remove it from the objects it is assigned to.

Often the best way to create a new material is by copying a sample slot and adjusting its contents. The root and branches of the copied material have the same names and settings as the original.

If the original sample slot is hot, the copy is considered *warm* until you rename it, assign it to an object, or click the Put to Scene button.

To copy a sample slot:

◆ Drag a sample slot that contains the material or map you want to copy onto another sample slot (**Figure 13.20**).

The material is copied to the slot, replacing its previous contents (**Figure 13.21**).

Resetting clears the contents of a sample slot. Use the Reset command when you want to make more room in the sample palette, or remove materials and maps from the scene.

To reset a sample slot:

1. Select a sample slot.

2. Click Reset Map/Mtl to Default Setting ×.

 If the map or material is warm or cool (i.e., not used in the scene), the Material Editor dialog box appears (**Figure 13.22**).

 If the map or material is hot, the Reset Mtl/Map Params dialog box appears (**Figure 13.23**).

3. Click Yes in the Material Editor dialog box.

 or

 Choose an option in the Reset Mtl/Map Params dialog box, and click OK.

 The sample slot is cleared. If you chose Affect mtl/map in both the scene and the editor slot? then the map or material is removed from the scene as well.

✔ Tip

■ You can remove a material from selected objects using the UVW Remove utility located in the Utilities drop-down menu.

The Put to Scene command replaces a hot material with a warm copy of any material that has the same name.

The beauty of this arrangement is that you can make multiple copies of a material, make changes to the copies, and then substitute them for the original material by putting them to the scene. Using this method, you can freely experiment to find out which settings work best.

To put a material to a scene:

1. Activate a sample slot that contains a warm copy (**Figure 13.24**).

2. Click Put Material to Scene ⬚ .
   The Assigning Material dialog box appears.

3. In the Assigning Material dialog box, choose to replace the material (**Figure 13.25**).
   The warm copy becomes hot. The hot material becomes warm (**Figure 13.26**).
   All the objects that displayed the original material now display the hot copy.

4. If you want to edit a scene material that does not appear in the Material Editor, use the eyedropper to get it from the scene.

To pick a material from an object:

1. Activate an available sample slot.

2. Click the eyedropper icon ⬚ .

3. Click on an object (**Figure 13.27**).
   The material that is assigned to the object appears in the sample slot.

✔ Tip

■ To make a hot material cool, so that it is disconnected from the objects it is assigned to, click Make Material Copy ⬚ .

Figure 13.24 The warm copy on the right is activated.

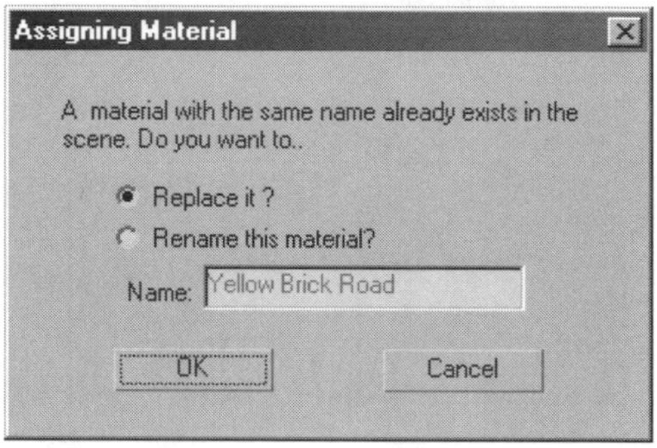

Figure 13.25 If you do not rename the material, it will replace other materials in the scene that have the same name.

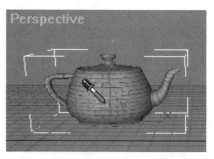

Figure 13.26 After you choose replace, the warm copy becomes hot and the hot original becomes warm.

Figure 13.27 Picking a material from an object.

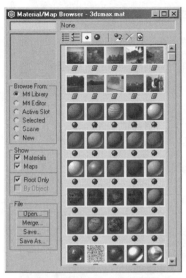

Figure 13.28 Viewing a material library. File commands appear at left.

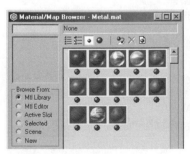

Figure 13.29 Material libraries are stored in the 3dsmax4\matlibs folder by default.

Using Material Libraries

3ds max 4 ships with 15 different libraries of materials and maps. They are categorized by content, such as Wood, Brick, Stones, Sky, Ground, Metal, Space, and Backgrounds. The default material library that appears when you first open the browser is called 3dsmax.mat. All material libraries have this .mat extension.

To open a material library:

1. Open the Material/Map Browser 🔳.

2. Click the Mtl Library radio button.

   The maps and materials in the current material library are displayed in the window on the right. On the left, the File group appears in the list of browsing commands (**Figure 13.28**).

3. In the File group, click Open.

   The Open Material Library dialog box appears. It displays the material libraries in the 3dsmax 4\matlibs folder (**Figure 13.29**).

4. Select a library and click Open.

   The material library opens (**Figure 13.30**).

✔ Tips

- The Merge command merges materials from a library that you select into the library that is currently loaded.

- Save lets you save the currently loaded material library, including any materials or maps you have added to it.

- Save As lets you save the materials and maps in the list into a new library.

Figure 13.30 After opening the Metal.mat material library.

USING MATERIAL LIBRARIES

A custom material library preserves your favorite materials and maps all in one place and keeps the master library from getting too large. I suggest that you create libraries by material category, such as Metallic or Architectural, or create separate libraries for different projects.

To create a library of scene materials:

1. Open a scene file in which materials have been assigned to objects.

   For practice, use one of the sample scene files that ship with the program.

2. Open the Material Editor.

3. Open the Material/Map Browser 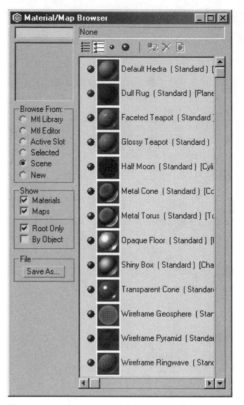.

4. Click the Scene radio button.

   A list of just the materials that are used in the scene appears (**Figure 13.31**).

5. Click the Save As button.

   The Save Material Library dialog appears (**Figure 13.32**).

6. Enter the name of the new library and click Save.

   Your new library contains all materials and maps used in the scene.

✔ Tips

■ You can also create a custom library by loading an existing library using the Delete from Library button to get rid of the materials you don't want, and then saving it with a different name.

■ Clicking Clear Material Library removes all materials from the currently loaded library. This does not affect the saved library file unless you click Save. Creating materials can take a lot of work. When you have a material that you like, you can put it in a custom material library.

Figure 13.31 Viewing materials used in the scene in figure 13.1.

Figure 13.32 Saving the scene materials to a library named Grayscale.mat.

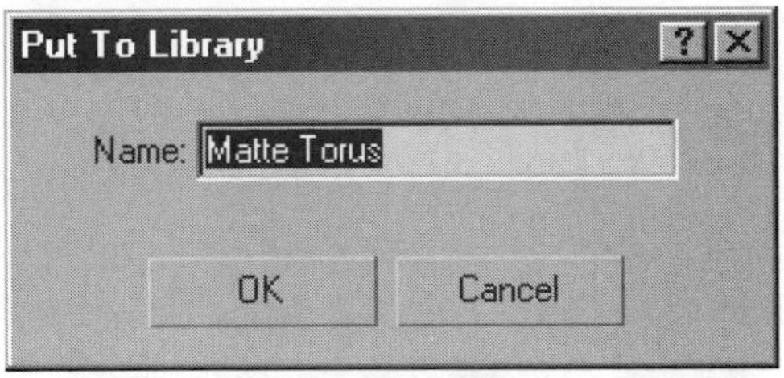

Name: Matte Torus

OK   Cancel

Figure 13.33 Adding a material to the current library.

To save a material to a library:

1. Activate the sample slot of the material or map you want to save.

2. Open the Material/Map Browser.

3. Load the library you want to save the material or map into.

4. Click Put to Library.

   Confirm the name of the material (**Figure 13.33**).

   The material or map is saved.

✔ Tip

■ If you want to delete a material from a library, select the material and click Delete from Library ✕ in the Material/Map Browser.

Creating Basic Materials

The default material in 3ds max 4 is the *Standard* material. But do not be misled by the name! Standard materials represent years of development that go back to the earliest DOS versions of 3ds max. Consequently, they have numerous controls and options for creating exquisitely beautiful and complex materials.

Standard materials start out with a solid, dull, and gray appearance. By setting basic parameters, you give them color, transparency, and brilliance (**Figure 13.34**).

A material color is actually made up of three colors that blend together (**Figure 13.35**):

Diffuse color is the primary color of the material. It predominates when a surface is directly lit.

Ambient color is the color of a material in the absence of direct light. It is strongly influenced by the ambient color of the environment.

Specular color is the color of specular highlights. It appears only in areas of strong illumination.

For the next few exercises, create a simple scene, such as a teapot, a plane, and a spotlight.

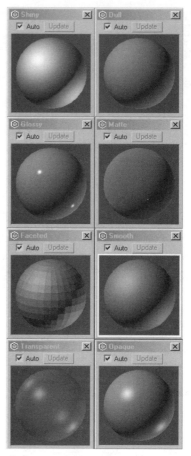

Figure 13.34 In each of these samples, just one setting has been altered.

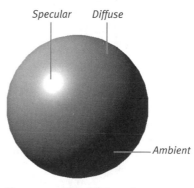

Figure 13.35 Materials have three basic colors that blend together.

Figure 13.36 A teapot is a good object for practicing on.

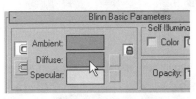

Figure 13.37 Click on the Diffuse color swatch.

Figure 13.38 After changing the material in the active sample slot to red.

Figure 13.39 The teapot turns red when you assign the material to it.

One usually begins by setting diffuse color, as this will be the predominant color of the material.

To assign a color to a material:

1. Open a practice scene (**Figure 13.36**).

2. Select a material in the sample palette by activating its sample slot.

3. Click the Diffuse color swatch in the Basic Parameters rollout (**Figure 13.37**). The Color Selector dialog box appears.

4. Select a color by setting the red, green, and blue amounts; by setting the hue, saturation, and value amounts; or by picking from the hue palette and value gradient.

    The Diffuse color swatch updates to display the color that you chose. Ambient color is locked to diffuse color by default, so the color is automatically copied from the Diffuse swatch to the Ambient swatch. The material sample object also changes hue (**Figure 13.38**).

5. Without closing the Color Selector, click the Specular color swatch and assign it a color.

6. Close the Color Selector dialog box.

7. Assign the material to an object.

8. Render the scene.

    The object takes on the color of the material (**Figure 13.39**).

✔ Tips

■ To unlock the ambient and diffuse colors, click the button to the left of the colors.

■ To copy a color, drag the color swatch that you want to copy onto another color swatch.

■ A quick way to create a specular color is to copy it from the diffuse color and then use the whiteness slider to make it lighter.

The Opacity parameter sets the opacity of a material from fully opaque to fully transparent.

To make a material transparent:

1. Select a material.

2. Click the Background button ▓.

   A multicolored test pattern appears in the background of the slot.

3. Drag the Opacity spinner downward (**Figure 13.40**).

   As you drag the spinner, the material becomes more transparent and the background becomes more visible through it (**Figure 13.41**).

4. Apply the material to an object.

5. Render the scene (**Figure 13.42**).

   The object is partially to fully transparent. If shadow casting is enabled, the shadows appear disproportionately dark and heavy.

5. To cast a shadow that adapts to the transparency of the object, change the shadow type of the key lights to ray-traced shadows (**Figure 13.43**).

✔ Tips

- You further control the darkness of shadows by adjusting the shadow density and shadow color of the light. You can also increase the self-illumination of the surface that the shadow is falling upon.

- If you want to limit the effects of a light to just transparent objects, clone the current light, and include only the objects that are casting or receiving transparent shadows.

- Transparent materials are easier to see if you make them shiny as well.

- To assign a bitmap to the background of a sample slot, click the Options ▓ button.

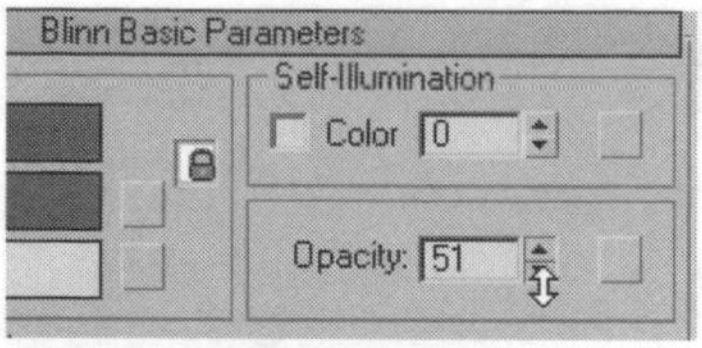

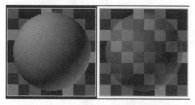

Figure 13.40 Reduce the Opacity value to make the material more transparent.

Figure 13.41 Turning on the background makes it easier to interpret the sample.

Figure 13.42 After assigning the transparent material to the teapot.

Figure 13.43 Raytraced shadows automatically adjust for transparency.

CREATING BASIC MATERIALS

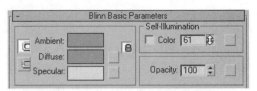

Figure 13.44 Increase the self-illumination of the material.

Figure 13.45 The dark values of the material brighten, reducing overall contrast.

Figure 13.46 After assigning the self-illuminated material to the teapot.

Self-illumination sets the minimum value of a material, regardless of the amount of light falling across its surface. Objects that are self-illuminated do not emit light or cast shadows.

To self-illuminate a material:

1. Select a material.

2. Increase the Self-Illumination amount (**Figure 13.44**).

   The material sample brightens (**Figure 13.45**).

3. Assign the material to an object.

4. Render the scene (**Figure 13.46**).

✔ Tips

- To self-illuminate an object with a color, check the Color box.

- Self-illumination brightens objects by reducing contrast. If your self-illuminated objects start appearing too washed out, reduce the amount of self-illumination.

- Self-illumination materials can be a great timesaver because they do not have the rendering overhead of lights. Try substituting self-illuminated objects for decorative lights, such as running lights on a ship or plane.

CREATING BASIC MATERIALS

Shininess is controlled by two settings: Specular Level and Glossiness.

Specular Level sets the intensity of the specular highlight. Higher values produce brighter highlights to make a surface appear shinier.

Glossiness controls the size of the specular highlight. Higher values produce a smaller highlight to simulate a high gloss surface.

To make a material shiny:

1. Select a material.

2. Increase the specularity of the material by increasing the Specular Level value (**Figure 13.47**).

   The highlights on the material sample brighten (**Figure 13.48**).

3. Assign the material to an object.

4. Render the scene.

   The object renders with a bright shine (**Figure 13.49**).

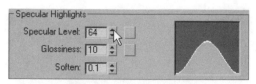

Figure 13.47 Increasing the specular highlights raises the specularity curve.

Figure 13.48 The shiny material has broad specular highlights.

Figure 13.49 After assigning the shiny material to the teapot.

Figure 13.50 Increasing the Glossiness value narrows the specularity curve.

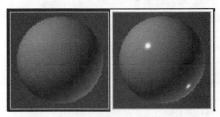

Figure 13.51 The glossy material has small, bright specular highlights.

Figure 13.52 After assigning the glossy material to the teapot.

To make a material glossy:

1. Select a material.

2. Increase the Specular Level. Then increase the Glossiness value (**Figure 13.50**).

   The highlights on the sample material become smaller, giving it the appearance of a highly polished surface (**Figure 13.51**).

3. Assign the material to an object.

4. Render the scene.

   The object renders with a glossy luster (**Figure 13.52**).

✔ Tips

■ You must set the Specular Level to a value greater than zero for the material to appear glossy.

■ To turn off the secondary lighting of a material sample, click Backlight 🔘.

The Shader Basic Parameter rollout offers four options for rendering surfaces: Wire, 2-Sided, Face Map, and Faceted.

The Wire option makes an object render in wireframe.

To make a wireframe material:

1. Select a material.

2. Open the Shader Basic Parameters rollout.

3. Check Wire (**Figure 13.53**).

   The material changes its display mode to wireframe (**Figure 13.54**).

4. Open the Extended Parameters rollout (**Figure 13.55**).

5. Select Pixels or Units to determine the measurement of the wireframe size. Pixels are pixels on your screen; units are scene units that are rendered in perspective.

6. Set the size of the wireframe.

   The wireframe becomes thicker or thinner as you change the size.

7. Assign the material to an object.

8. Render the scene.

   The object renders in wireframe. If shadow casting is turned on, the object casts wireframe shadows. All other parameters, such as color and shininess, remain the same (**Figure 13.56**).

✔ Tips

- You can animate the Size parameter to make an object fill in or wither away over time.

- Wireframe materials sometimes look better if you also make them 2-Sided.

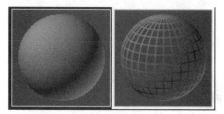

Figure 13.53 Check Wire in the Shader Basic Parameters rollout.

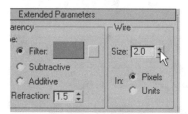

Figure 13.54 The material sample renders in wireframe.

Figure 13.55 Adjust the size of the wire and its units of measurement in the Extended Parameters rollout.

Figure 13.56 After assigning the wireframe material to the teapot.

Figure 13.57 Check Faceted in the Shader Basic Parameters rollout.

Figure 13.58 The material sample renders with facets.

Figure 13.59 After assigning the faceted material to the teapot.

Faceted shading renders coplanar faces with a single intensity value that is even across all faces.

Because intensity gradations are not calculated, faceted materials render faster than smooth ones.

To make a material faceted:

1. Select a material.

2. Open the Shader Basic Parameters rollout.

3. Check Faceted (**Figure 13.57**).

   The material changes its display mode to faceted (**Figure 13.58**).

4. Assign the material to an object.

5. Render the scene.

   The surface of the object renders with facets (**Figure 13.59**).

CREATING BASIC MATERIALS

The 2-Sided option makes a surface render on both the inside and outside. Because it shades both sides of each face, it takes longer to render.

To make a material two-sided:

1. Render an object that you can see the inside of, such as a teapot without a lid (**Figure 13.60**).

2. Select a material.

3. Open the Shader Basic Parameters rollout.

4. Check 2-Sided (**Figure 13.61**).

5. Assign the material to an object.

6. Render the scene.

   The surface of the object renders on both sides (**Figure 13.62**).

✔ Tip

■ Check Face Map to apply the entire material to each polygon on a surface. When used with mapped materials, this can create fascinating patterns depending on the structure of the mesh object you apply it to (**Figure 13.63**).

   Mapping coordinates do not need to be applied to the object because the face map uses the XYZ coordinates of each face.

Figure 13.60 Removing a lid from a teapot reveals that the inside is not rendered.

Figure 13.61 Check 2-Sided in the Shader Basic Parameters rollout.

Figure 13.62 The inside of the teapot renders after you assign it the 2-sided material.

Figure 13.63 After applying a Swirl mapped material to each coplanar pair of faces.

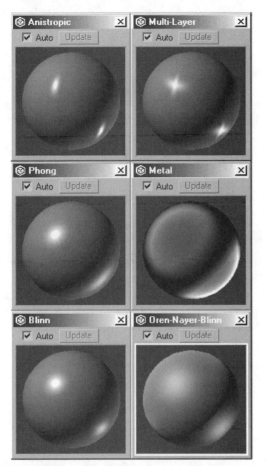

Figure 13.64 Different shader types produce different kinds of specular highlights.

Shaders determine how surfaces are rendered. The default Blinn shader type is a good all-purpose shader that will create most of the effects that you need. For more specialized purposes, such as glass and metal shading, try using one of the other shader types that give you more control, such as Anistropic, Multi-Layer, or Metal.

Shader types for Standard materials include (**Figure 13.64**):

◆ **Anistropic**—Calculates highlights from two different angles and renders them as ellipses. Good for creating hair, glass, or brushed metal.

◆ **Multi-Layer**—Similar to Anistropic, but with two highlights and two sets of highlight controls. Good for surfaces with more complex highlights.

◆ **Phong**—Calculates realistic highlights by averaging surface normals for every pixel. Good for creating strong, circular highlights.

◆ **Blinn**—A variation on Phong that uses softer highlights by default. Good for rendering bump, opacity, shininess, specular, and reflection maps.

◆ **Oren-Nayer-Blinn**—A variation on the Blinn shader that has additional controls for creating matte surfaces with dull, rough highlights.

◆ **Metal**—Creates sharply contrasting highlights with two peaks of specularity as found on metallic surfaces.

◆ **Strauss**—Creates sharply contrasting highlights like Metal, but with a single specular peak.

To change the highlights of a material:

1. Activate a sample slot.

2. Choose a shader type from the Shader Basic Parameters drop-down menu (**Figure 13.65**).

   The new shader is applied to the material.

Figure 13.65 Choosing a shader type from the drop-down list.

3. Adjust the color, opacity, and self-illumination of the shader.

4. Adjust the specular highlight parameters of the shader.

   Set the specular level and glossiness of the shader. (Strauss shaders have a single Glossiness parameter that also controls its specular level.)

   For Blinn, Oren-Nayer-Blinn, and Phong shaders, set the softness of the highlight.

   For Anistropic and Multi-Layer shaders, set the width and orientation of the highlights by adjusting the Anistropy and Orientation parameters.

   For the Strauss shader, use the Metalness parameter to adjust the contrast of the highlight.

5. Adjust the diffuse level and roughness of the Anistropic and Multi-Layer shadows.

6. Render the scene (**Figure 13.66**).

Figure 13.66 Multi-Layer shaders produce anistropic highlights that you can orient to different angles.

Blend

Composite

Shellac

Double Sided

Top/Bottom

Multi/Sub-Object

Figure 13.67 Compound material types combine materials in different ways. These materials combine a Checker mapped material with a Cellular mapped material.

Creating Compound Materials

Compound materials combine two or more materials in different ways. They are primarily for combining mapped materials, but you can use them for combining basic materials as well (**Figure 13.67**):

◆ **Blend**—Combines two materials by mixing them together. Similar to a Mix map. See "To create a Mix map" in Chapter 14.

◆ **Composite**—Adds, subtracts, or mixes up to 10 different materials based on their opacity and composite amount.

◆ **Double-Sided**—Combines two materials by assigning them to either the front or back faces of an object. Similar to 2-Sided materials, except that you use different materials on either side.

◆ **Morpher**—Shifts materials from one to another. Use them in conjunction with the Morph modifier.

◆ **Multi/Sub-Object**—Groups up to 1,000 materials into a single material. When you assign a multi/sub-object material to an object, it assigns the different materials to different faces based upon the material ID number of each face and material.

◆ **Shellac**—Combines two materials by assigning one to be a base material the second to be a shellac material. By adjusting the shellac color blend, you tint the base material with the shellac material.

◆ **Top/Bottom**—Combines two materials by assigning one to faces whose normals point upward and the other to faces whose normals point downward.

The Mix and Composite map types are very effective tools for blending and layering patterns. As a result, the Blend, Composite, and Shellac types are not employed as often as the others.

Double Sided materials assign two different materials to each side of an object. These materials are Standard materials by default, but you can replace them with any other type.

To create a Double Sided material:

1. Select a material sample.

2. Click the Type button, and select Double Sided from the list (**Figure 13.68**).
   The Replace Material dialog box appears

3. Choose to discard the current material or incorporate it into the Double Sided material. Then click OK.
   The Material Editor adds two sub-material branches to the material tree (**Figure 13.69**).
   The Double Sided material rollout appears at the top level, or root (**Figure 13.70**).

4. Name the Double Sided material. The name Double Sided is sufficient.

5. Click the Facing Material button.
   The Material Editor moves down one level to the Facing Material branch.

6. Create a material for the front faces. You can set parameters, choose a shader type, and add maps to the Material as you would to any other Standard material.

7. Click Go Forward to Sibling.
   The Material Editor moves to the Back Material branch.

8. Create a material for the back faces. Then click Go to Parent.

9. Assign the material to an object. Then render the scene (**Figure 13.71**).

✔ Tip

■ To blend the materials together as if you are seeing through a thin wall, set the translucency of the material as a percentage from 0 to 100.

Figure 13.68 The Material/Map Browser brings up a list of material types.

Figure 13.69 The Double Sided material contains two sub-material branches.

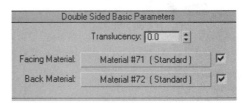
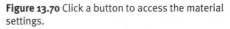

Figure 13.70 Click a button to access the material settings.

Figure 13.71 The Facing material is a shiny, black, transparent Standard material. The Back material is light gray and slightly self-illuminated.

CREATING COMPOUND MATERIALS

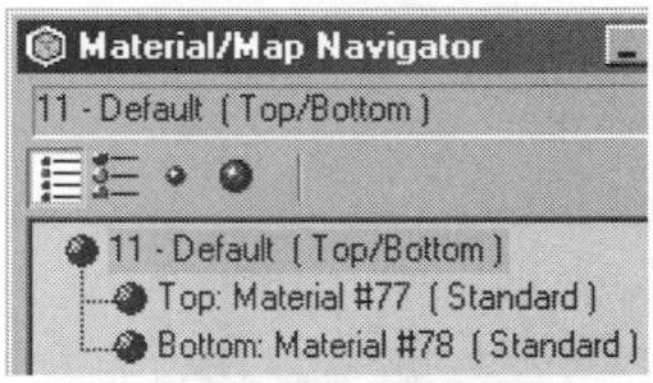

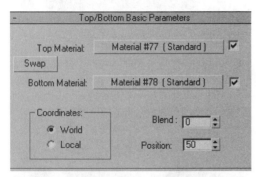

Figure 13.72 The Top/Bottom material contains two sub-material branches.

Figure 13.73 After designing your materials, choose a system of reference, a blending amount, and adjust their position.

Figure 13.74 The Top/Bottom material is positioned slightly over the middle of the teapot, and slightly blended together.

Top/Bottom materials assign two different materials to the top and bottom of an object.

To create a Top/Bottom material:

1. Select a material sample.

2. Click the Type button and select Top/Bottom from the list of materials.

   The Replace Material dialog box appears.

3. Choose to discard the current material or incorporate it into the Top/Bottom material. Then click OK.

   The Material Editor adds two sub-material branches to the material tree (**Figure 13.72**).

   The Top/Bottom material rollout appears at the top level, or root (**Figure 13.73**).

4. Name the Top/Bottom material. The name Top/Bottom is sufficient.

5. Click the Top Material button.

   The Material Editor moves down one level to the Top Material branch.

6. Create a material for the top faces. You can set parameters, choose a shader type, and add maps to the material as you would to any other Standard material.

7. Click Go Forward to Sibling .

   The Material Editor moves to the Bottom Material branch.

8. Create a material for the bottom faces. Then click Go to Parent .

9. To blend the materials together as if you are seeing through a thin wall, set the translucency of the material as a percentage from 0 to 10.

10. Choose a coordinate system. World coordinates align the position of the material to world space, even as you rotate the object.

11. Assign the material to an object. Then render the scene (**Figure 13.74**).

CREATING COMPOUND MATERIALS

Multi/Sub-Object materials allow you to assign different materials to different parts of an object by applying materials with a certain ID number to faces that are assigned matching ID numbers.

There are two ways to create Multi/Sub-Object materials: by assigning different materials to different faces and picking the material from the object, or by creating the material from scratch. Of these two methods, the first is simpler because it automatically assigns material ID numbers to faces as you assign materials to them.

To create a Multi/Sub-Object material:

1. Create three or four different materials (**Figure 13.75**).

2. Select some faces with an Edit Mesh modifier, or within an editable mesh.

3. Drag a material from a sample slot and drop it onto the selected faces.

4. Continue to select faces and apply materials to them. Then render the scene (**Figure 13.76**).

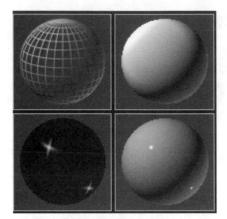

Figure 13.75 These four materials will be combined into one.

Figure 13.76 After assigning a different material to each element of the teapot.

Figure 13.77 The resulting Multi/Sub-Object material has four sub-materials.

5. Adjust the position of the materials by making new selections and dragging materials onto them.

6. Exit sub-object selection mode.

7. Activate an unused sample slot.

8. Click the eyedropper next to the material name field. Then click the object.

   The Multi/Sub-Object material is loaded into the sample slot. Its rollout appears below. Each sub-material that creates a branch in the material tree is assigned a different material ID number (**Figure 13.77**).

9. To change the material ID number of a material, enter a new number in the material ID entry field. The program will not allow you to enter duplicate material ID numbers.

✔ Tip

■ To display a Multi/Sub-Object material on another object, you must assign matching material ID numbers to its faces.

WORKING WITH MAPS

Figure 14.1 The Taj Mahal is mapped with scanned photographs.

Maps make your scene look real. By introducing texture and pattern, maps put grain in wood, rust on metal, streaks in paint, and frost on glass. They paint a blush on rosy cheeks and draw cracks on a concrete sidewalk. To set the stage, maps put stars in the sky, reflect the moon in the water, and place a scene in India or Spain (**Figure 14.1**).

3D artists routinely "dirty up" their models with maps to make them look real. To give a boat the appearance of age, you add texture maps of peeled paint, and make the edges look cracked and broken. A spaceship that has been through the stresses of hyperspace needs burns, dents, shockwave patterns, and faded insignia.

Scanners, digital cameras, and photo CDs are indispensable to the serious 3D artist for capturing these realistic details. To create custom maps, you should know at least one image-editing program, such as Adobe Photoshop or Corel Painter.

About Maps

A *map* is a pattern of color that is defined by a rectangular array of bits (as in a bitmap) or by a mathematical procedure (as in a procedural map).

You can add maps to lights, fog, backgrounds, materials, and other maps; however, you cannot assign a map directly to an object.

When you add a map to another map, it builds a hierarchy called a *map tree*. Map trees can either stand alone, or be part of a material tree. When you save your scene, map trees are stored in the .max file, but the maps that they reference remain external. Maps also remain external when you store map trees in material libraries.

About Mapping

Mapping is a mathematical function or procedure that projects maps onto objects, effects, and backgrounds. Different mapping functions serve different purposes (**Figure 14.2**):

Texture mapping transfers the pattern of a bitmap or procedural map onto the surface of a 3D object.

Procedural mapping uses the coordinates of a surface to generate patterns and variations in two or three dimensions.

Bump mapping creates the illusion of surface roughness by perturbing normals using the intensity values of a map.

Displacement mapping use the intensity values of a map to create "real" surface roughness by displacing faces.

Environment mapping surrounds objects with a map to quickly generate surface reflections. Environment background maps use *billboard mapping* to create a background that stays locked to the view.

Ray-tracing simulates the action of photons by tracing a ray of light as it bounces from one object to another to create highly accurate surface reflections.

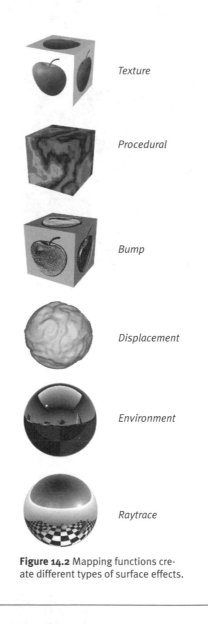

Texture

Procedural

Bump

Displacement

Environment

Raytrace

Figure 14.2 Mapping functions create different types of surface effects.

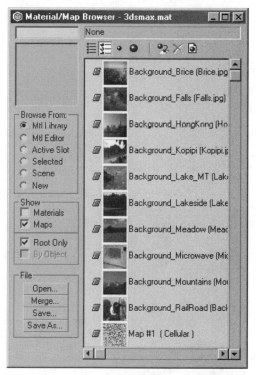

Figure 14.3 As you choose each option, the maps that are available at that location appear in the Browser.

Figure 14.4 A large thumbnail of the map appears in the upper-left corner of the Browser window.

Browsing Maps

The Material/Map Browser lets you browse and load maps from material libraries, the Material Editor, and the current scene. You can also use the Browser to load new map types.

To browse maps:

1. Open a scene that has some materials and maps in it, such as Earth.max.

2. Open the Material Editor.

3. Click Get Material 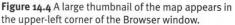.
   The Material/Map Browser appears.

4. Uncheck Show Materials so that just maps are displayed.

5. Choose a display option by clicking an icon at the top of the Browser.

6. Choose a source to browse from (**Figure 14.3**).

7. Scroll through the list and click on any map that interests you (**Figure 14.4**).

In order to create and adjust maps, you must first load them into the Material Editor.

To load a map:

1. Open the Material Editor.

2. Click Get Material .

    The Material/Map Browser appears.

3. Select a map from any source.

4. Drag your selection from the Browser onto a sample slot in the Material Editor (**Figure 14.5**).

    The map is loaded into the Material Editor (**Figure 14.6**).

5. Close the Material/Map Browser.

Figure 14.5 Drag the map onto a sample slot.

✔ Tips

■ Double-clicking a map in the list loads it into the active sample slot and closes the Material/Map Browser at the same time.

■ You can also load maps directly into materials. See "Adding Maps to Materials" later in this chapter.

Figure 14.6 The map appears as a thumbnail image that fills the sample slot from edge to edge.

■ You can browse and load bitmaps from your system or the Web using the Asset Browser utility. To access the browser, open the Utilities panel and click Asset Browser. Then choose Filter > All Images from the Asset Browser menu in order to automatically generate and display thumbnail images of all the bitmaps in the current folder (**Figure 14.7**). To load a bitmap, drag a thumbnail onto a sample slot.

Thumbnails of every image that you browse are stored in the 3dsmax4\abcache folder. To empty the cache or decrease its size, choose File > Preferences in the Asset Browser.

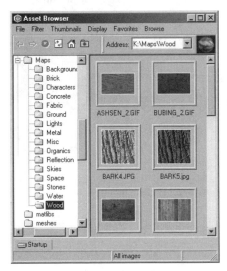

Figure 14.7 The Asset Browser allows you to browse and load bitmaps.

BROWSING MAPS

Figure 14.8 The Material/Map Navigator displays the components of a map tree.

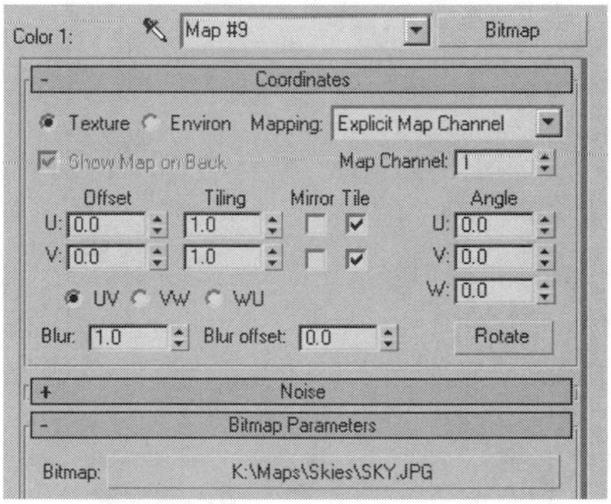

Figure 14.9 Select a branch in the map tree to view the parameter settings in it rollouts.

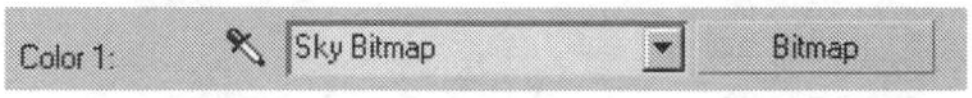

Color 1:   ✎   Sky Bitmap   ▼   Bitmap

Figure 14.10 Giving each branch a descriptive name helps you navigate map trees more easily.

The Material/Map Navigator shows how a map is constructed, and provides access to map settings at every level of its tree.

To navigate a map tree:

1. Load a map into a sample slot, or load a material that contains a map tree.

2. Click the Material/Map Navigator button ▣.

   The Material/Map Navigator appears. It displays the map tree of the currently active sample slot in list format (**Figure 14.8**).

3. To browse through the map tree visually, choose a graphical display option by clicking an icon at the top of the browser.

4. Click a branch in the map tree.

   The Material Editor moves to the branch of the tree that you selected (**Figure 14.9**).

5. You can also navigate a map using the controls underneath the sample slots.

   Move to a deeper level by selecting from the drop-down list.

   Click Go to Parent ▣ to move up a level.

   Click Go Forward to Sibling ▣ to move across the map tree to a different branch at the same level of the tree.

✔ Tips

■ Red icons indicate that Show Map in Viewport is enabled.

■ As you build a map tree, it helps to give each branch a descriptive name as you go along (**Figure 14.10**).

■ To save a map to the currently open material library, click Put to Library ▣.

Creating Maps

3ds max 4 ships with 35 different types of maps. Using the Material/Map Browser, you can browse map types by category (**Figure 14.11**):

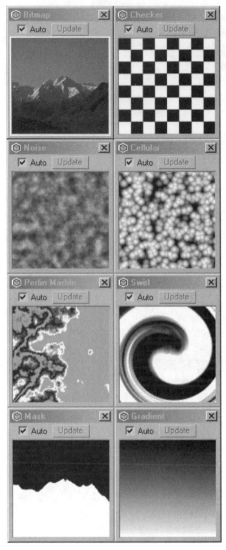

- ◆ **2D Maps**—Two-dimensional bitmaps, procedural maps, or filters used for texture mapping and special effects. Examples include the Bitmap, Bricks, and Checker map types.

- ◆ **3D Maps**—Solid texture procedural maps that can be added to surfaces and special effects. Examples include the Cellular, Dent, Noise, Perlin Marble, Planet, and Smoke map types.

- ◆ **Compositors**—Maps that combine multiple maps into a single map. Includes the Composite, Mask, Mix, and RGB Multiply map types.

- ◆ **Color Modifiers**—Maps that change the color output of a material or another map. Includes the Output, RGB Tint, and Vertex Color map types.

- ◆ **Other**—For creating surface reflections and refractions. Includes the Flat Mirror, Raytrace, Reflect/Refract, and Thin Wall Refraction types.

Figure 14.11 Maps come in a wide variety of patterns.

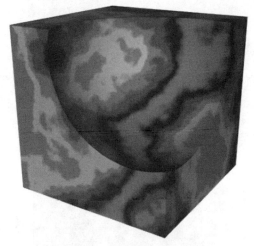

Figure 14.12 Subtracting part of a box reveals why 3D maps are called solid textures.

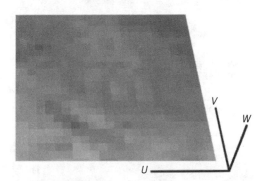

Figure 14.13 For UVW coordinates, the U axis corresponds to width, the V axis to height, and the W axis runs perpendicular to the UV plane.

Most maps contain map buttons that allow you to add other maps to them. You can also click the map type button to turn the currently active map into a sub-map that branches off a new map type.

Each map type has a rollout of parameters that is specific to that type, plus other standard rollouts such as the Noise and Output rollout. In addition, both 2D and 3D map types have Coordinates rollouts for adjusting the position, orientation, scale, and placement of maps on object surfaces.

2D maps and 3D maps are applied to objects in different ways. For a 3D map, the process is fairly simple: Take the XYZ coordinates from the surface of an object and plug them into a procedure. The procedure returns a series of RGB values and assigns them to the XYZ location that generated them, creating a pattern. When you cut away part of the object using a Boolean operation, you see that the pattern continues in three dimensions (**Figure 14.12**). This is why 3D procedural maps area also called *solid textures*.

Applying a 2D map to an object is not as straightforward because, like wrapping paper, it may not fit very neatly onto the 3D surface. To make this process a little easier, the coordinates of the surface and the coordinates of the map are converted to UV mapping coordinates, in which U and V correspond to the width and height of both the surface and the map. To enable rotation of maps on object surfaces, a third axis called the W axis is defined along a direction that is perpendicular to the UV plane (**Figure 14.13**).

Using UVW or XYZ coordinates, 2D and 3D maps are adjusted as follows (**Figure 14.14**):

◆ **Texture or Environment (2D maps)**— Sets the mapping function that will be applied.

◆ **Source (2D maps) or Mapping (3D maps)**—Determines the mapping coordinate system. Explicit Map Channel uses the coordinates of the current map channel.

◆ **Show Map on Back (2D maps)**— Enables a map to appear on the back of an object when planar mapping projection is in use.

◆ **Map Channel**—Determines which set of mapping coordinates will be used by the object.

◆ **Axes**—Sets the direction in which a map is offset, tiled, mirrored, or rotated.

◆ **Offset**—Sets the distance that a map is moved, or offset, from it original location.

◆ **Tiling**—Scales a map. Values greater than 1 or less than −1 shrink a map and cause it to repeat. Values between 1 and −1 enlarge a map.

◆ **Tile**—Enables tiling.

◆ **Mirror**—Flips 2D maps. If tiling is enabled, the map will repeat in a symmetrical pattern.

◆ **Angle**—Rotates a map around an axis.

◆ **Blur**—Blurs a map in world space depending on its distance from the viewplane. Helps prevent anti-aliasing.

◆ **Blur Offset**—Blurs a map in object space regardless of distance from the viewplane.

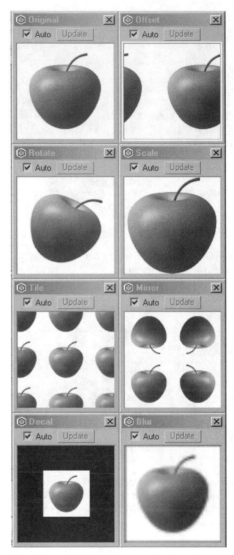

Figure 14.14 Adjusting the coordinates of a map changes its placement.

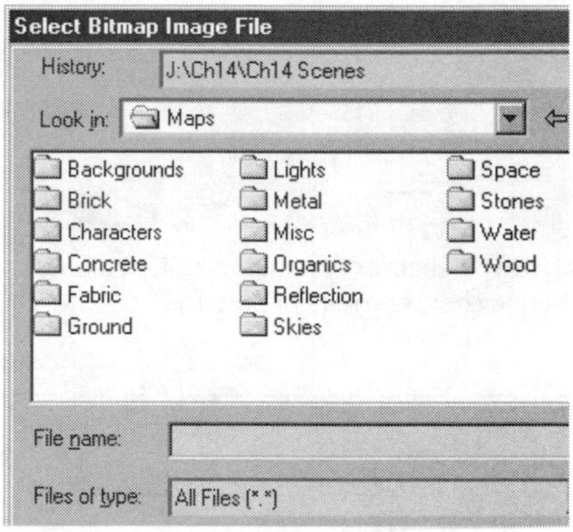

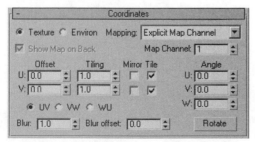

Figure 14.15 Select a bitmap from the 3dsmax4\Maps directory, a material library, or from an image file anywhere on your network.

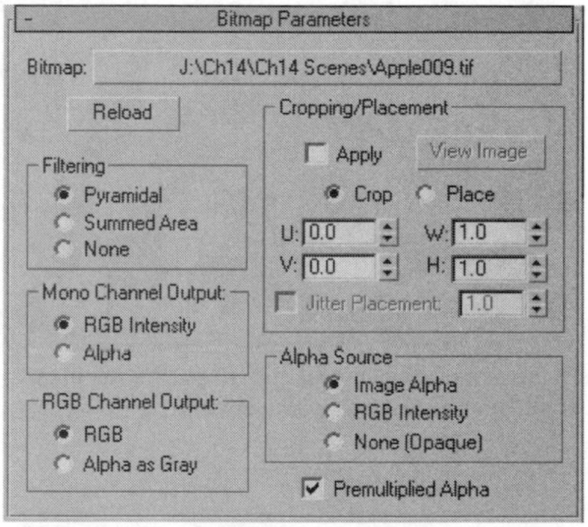

Figure 14.16 The Bitmap Parameters rollout controls how bitmap information is used.

Figure 14.17 You adjust the placement of a bitmap with the 2D Coordinates rollout.

Bitmaps are 2D maps that import color and alpha channel information from an external bitmap or movie file. In addition, they can reference Adobe Photoshop and Premiere filters.

To create a Bitmap:

1. Open the Material/Map Browser and click Show 2D Maps.

2. Drag a Bitmap onto an available sample slot.

3. In the Select Bitmap Image File dialog box, navigate to a map and open it (**Figure 14.15**).

   The map appears in the sample slot. Rollouts for the map appear below (**Figure 14.16**).

4. In the Bitmap Parameters rollout, click View Image. Drag the handles in the corners and along the sides of the image to crop it. Then close the window and check Apply.

5. In the Coordinates rollout, adjust the placement of the bitmap (**Figure 14.17**). See Figure 14.14 to view the results:

   ◆ To offset the map horizontally or vertically, adjust the U or V Offset amount.

   ◆ To rotate the map, adjust the W angle.

   ◆ To tile the map so that it repeats across the surface horizontally or vertically, increase the U or V tiling amounts.

   ◆ To mirror the map in either direction, check the U or V Mirror option.

   ◆ To create a decal, uncheck Tile and Mirror. To enlarge the width or height of the map, reduce the Tiling amount.

   ◆ Increase the Blur or Blur Offset amount to make the map appear softer.

✔ Tips

■ To reload a map after it has been updated, click Reload. This comes in handy when you are editing your maps in another program or rendering your own maps at the same time.

■ Choose the Summed Area option to help eliminate moiré patterns on tiled maps.

CREATING MAPS

389

Checker maps are 2D procedural maps that form a two-color checker pattern.

To create a Checker map:

1. Open the Material/Map Browser and click Show 2D Maps.

2. Drag a Checker map onto an available sample slot.

3. In the Checker Parameters rollout, select a color for each checker (**Figure 14.18**).

   or

   Click the map buttons next to the color swatches to replace the color with a map.

4. Adjust the Soften parameter if you want to blur the edges between checkers.

5. In the Coordinates rollout, adjust the placement of the map:

   ◆ Increase the U and V tiling coordinates to increase the number of checkers.

   ◆ Use the Offset and Rotate coordinates to move and rotate the checkers.

6. To disturb the checker pattern, open the Noise rollout and check On. Then adjust the Amount, Levels (or number of iterations), and Size of the noise (**Figure 14.19**).

   The edges of the tiled and rotated checker pattern wiggle and wave (**Figure 14.20**).

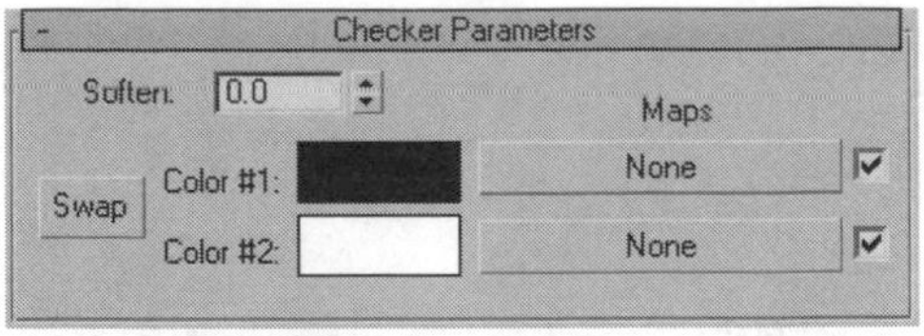

Figure 14.18 The Checker Parameters rollout allows you to choose checker colors or patterns.

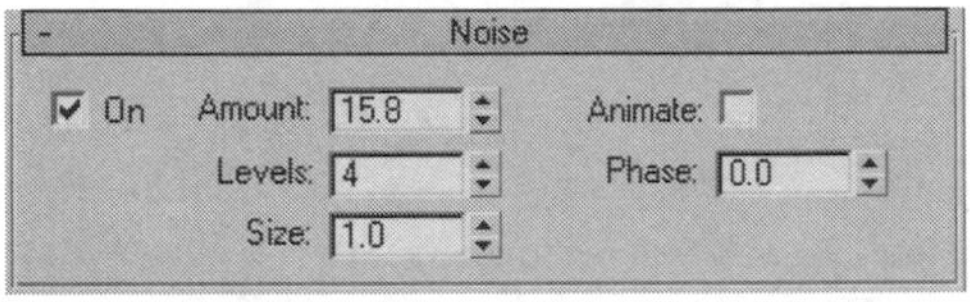

Figure 14.19 Use the Noise rollout to disturb the checker pattern.

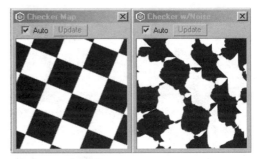

Figure 14.20 Left, tiling and rotating a checker map. Right, after adding noise to the map.

✔ Tips

- 2D maps all have Noise rollouts. Many other maps types have noise parameters built in.

- Bricks create patterns of brick and mortar based on traditional brick-laying patterns.

- Swirl maps create two-color swirls that can be twisted up, blurred, mapped, or sharply etched with smooth or rough edges.

- Gradient maps create a gradient of up to three colors. Each color can also be mapped.

- Gradient Ramp maps create an adjustable spectrum of colors using a wide variety of patterns and numerous controls.

A Noise map is a 3D map that creates random marks. Use Noise to roughen the colors of other materials and disturb the patterns of other maps.

To create a Noise map:

1. In the Material/Map Browser, click Show 3D Maps.

2. Drag a Noise map onto an available slot.

3. In the Noise Parameters rollout, set the size of the noise, and select a noise type (**Figure 14.21**).

   Fractal noise produces a more abundant grain. Turbulent is a type of fractal noise that creates a craggier look (**Figure 14.22**).

4. Select colors for the noise pattern or click the map buttons next to the color swatches to replace the color with a map.

5. To filter high- and low-intensity values, set the High and Low threshold levels. By setting these values close together, you can simulate a starry sky (**Figure 14.23**).

6. To increase the resolution of fractal or turbulent noise, increase the Level setting. This increases the number of iterations of the fractal function (Figure 14.23).

7. To change pattern of the noise, change the Phase setting. Animating this parameter changes the pattern of the noise over time.

8. Use Blur when you want to soften noise.

✔ Tips

- Falloff maps have advanced controls for creating three-dimensional gradients.

- Depending on the functions that are used to generate them, 3D maps create patterns or more randomly distributed marks.

  Dent, Smoke, Speckle, Splat, and Stucco maps create more random marks.

  Cellular, Marble, Perlin Marble, Planet, Water, and Wood maps create more distinct patterns.

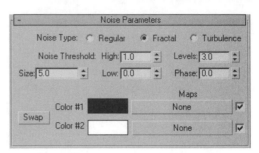

Figure 14.21 The Noise Parameters rollout allows you to set the size, type, color, and threshold parameters of the noise.

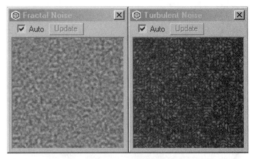

Figure 14.22 The Fractal and Turbulent options affect how the noise is shaded.

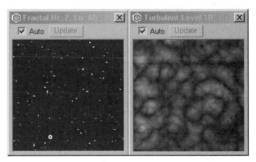

Figure 14.23 Use Noise maps to create starry skies and billowing smoke.

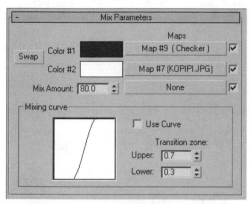

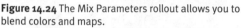

Figure 14.24 The Mix Parameters rollout allows you to blend colors and maps.

Figure 14.25 Mixing a Bitmap with a Checker map (left) and another Bitmap (right).

Figure 14.26 Placing a mask in the Mix Amount map button allows you to composite the island and the clouds without blending them.

A Mix map is a Compositor map that blends two maps together in varying proportions.

To create a Mix map:

1. In the Material/Map Browser, click Show Compositor Maps.

2. Drag a Mix map onto an available slot.

3. In the Mix Parameters rollout, select a color for each color swatch or build a compound map by adding a map to one or both map buttons (**Figure 14.24**).

4. Adjust the Mix Amount from 0 to 100% to blend the colors together (Figure 14.24).

   The maps mix together in the proportion that you designate (**Figure 14.25**).

5. To limit the upper and lower threshold of mixing, click Use Curve. Then adjust the transition zones of the mixing curve.

✔ Tips

■ By adding a black and white mask to the mix amount, you can filter out areas of each map (**Figure 14.26**).

■ The RGB Multiply map combines two maps and multiplies their color channels together. Use this to combine two bump maps together while retaining the strength of each. Or use it to tint the color of a map by adding it to one map button and changing the color of the swatch next to the other map button.

■ The Composite map allows you to composite up to 1000 maps in layers using alpha channels for masking.

■ The RGB Tint is a Color Mod map that adds a color tint to a material or map using separate channels for red, green, and blue.

■ The Vertex Color map enables the display of colors that have been applied to vertices. To learn more, look up the VertexPaint modifier and the Assign Vertex Colors utility.

An Output map allows you to adjust the hue, saturation, value, and alpha information of a map.

To adjust the output of a map:

1. Activate a map that you want to adjust.

   Bitmap, Cellular, Falloff, Gradient, Gradient Ramp, Mix, and Noise maps have Output rollouts built into them. To adjust the output of these map types, skip to step 5.

2. Click the Type button.

3. In the Material/Map Browser, click Show Color Mods. Then click Output.

4. In the Replace Map dialog box, choose Keep old map as sub-map (**Figure 14.27**).

5. In the Output Parameters rollout, click the map button and select a map type, or drag a map onto the button.

6. Check the options you want to apply (**Figure 14.28**):

   Invert reverses the colors of the map like the color negative of a photo (**Figure 14.29**).

   Clamp limits the intensity of a map when the RGB Level amount is increased.

   Alpha from RGB Intensity generates an alpha channel from the intensity of the red, green, and blue color channels of the map.

   Enable Color Map allows you to use the graph at the bottom of the rollout to adjust the intensity (value) range of a map.

7. Adjust the Output spinners.

   Output Amount controls the amount that the map will be added to a Composite map.

   RGB Offset lightens or darkens the map.

   RGB Level changes the saturation of the map.

   Bump Amount adjusts the bumpiness of a bump map independent of the Bump Amount parameter. This comes in handy when maps are mixed together in the Bump map.

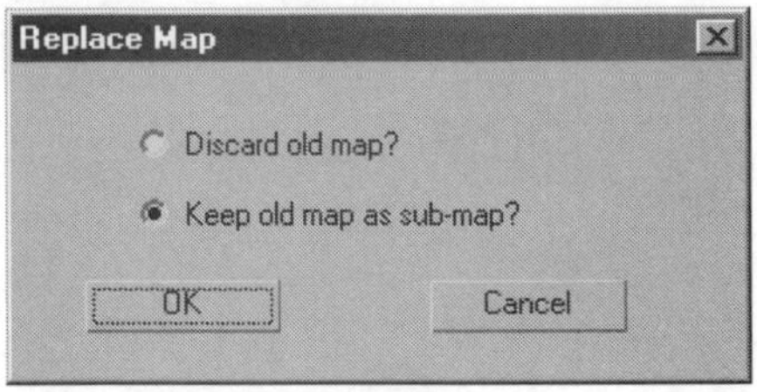

Figure 14.27 Choosing to keep a map as a sub-map adds another level to the material tree.

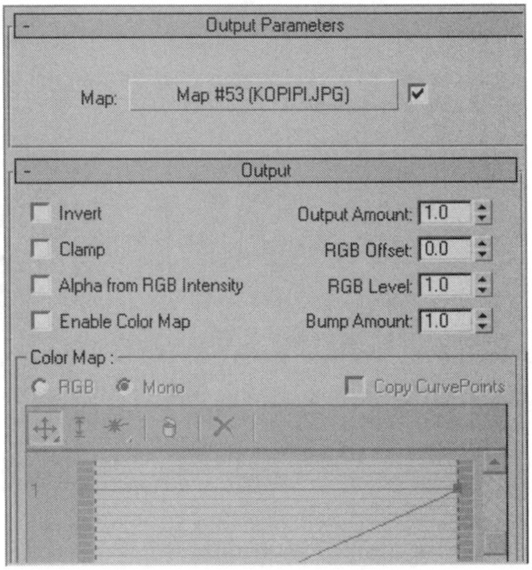

Figure 14.28 The Output rollout contains commands for altering the color properties of a map.

Figure 14.29 Checking the Invert option reverses map color information.

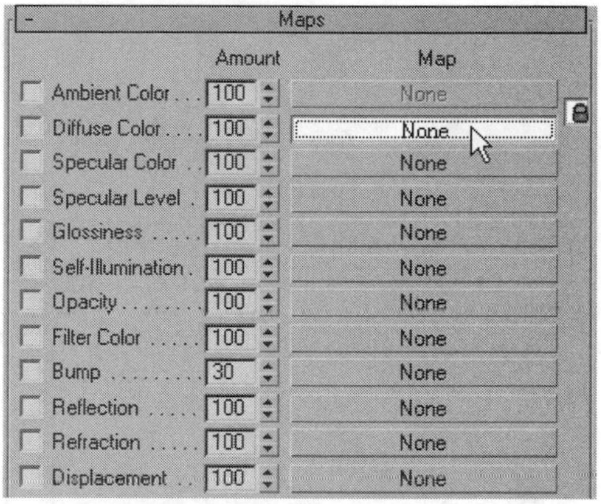

Figure 14.30 Click a map button to load a map into it.

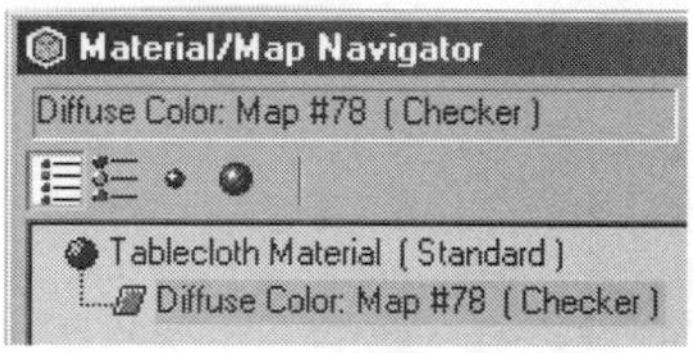

Figure 14.31 Adding a map to a map button builds a new map branch in the material tree.

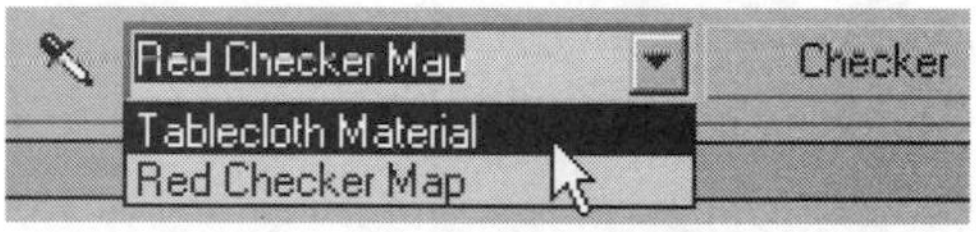

Figure 14.32 Use the material name field drop-down list to navigate back up the material tree.

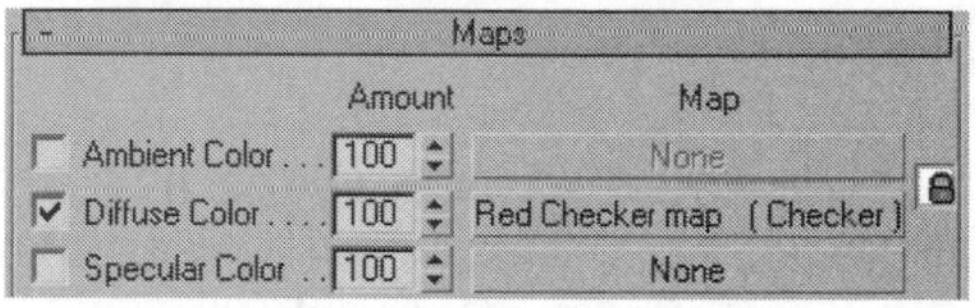

Figure 14.33 The name of the map appears on the map button.

Adding Maps to Materials

You cannot assign a map directly to an object. Instead, you add maps to materials and assign mapped materials to objects.

Materials can use the complete color information of a map, or just its intensity (light and dark) values. When you add a map to a material, the name of the map appears on a button in the Maps rollout. The amount of influence that the Map has on the material is set by the Amount spinner.

Because grayscale maps use about one third less RAM than color maps, use grayscale copies whenever you don't need color information. Viewing maps in grayscale also makes it easier to predict their effects.

There are two ways you can add a map to a material: by clicking or by dragging.

To add a map to a material by clicking:

1. Select a material sample by activating an available sample slot.

2. Open the Maps rollout.

3. Click a map button (**Figure 14.30**).
   The Material/Map Browser appears.

4. In the Material/Map Browser, double-click a map type.
   The map is added to the material tree (**Figure 14.31**). The Material Editor moves down the material tree to the map rollouts in the new map branch.

5. Name the map and adjust it as needed.

6. To move back up the material tree, click Go to Parent 🔼, or choose the name of the material from the material name field drop-down list (**Figure 14.32**).
   The Maps rollout reappears. The name of the map appears on the map button that you clicked earlier (**Figure 14.33**).

7. To turn off a map, uncheck the box next to the parameter in the Maps rollout.

The small gray buttons in the Basic Parameters rollout are duplicate map buttons that make it easier to add maps to the parameters.

To add a map to a material by dragging:

1. Select a material sample by activating an available sample slot.

2. Open the Maps rollout.

3. Drag a map from the sample palette or the Material/Map Browser and drop it onto a map button in the Maps rollout or the Basic Parameters rollout (**Figure 14.34**).

   An "M" appears on the map button to indicate that a map has been added it (**Figure 14.35**).

4. To adjust the parameters of the map, click the map button to navigate the Material Editor down to the map level.

✔ Tips

■ You can drag a map from one map button to another to copy, instance, or swap the map with another map (**Figure 14.36**). Instanced maps update whenever you change the parameters of any of the other instances.

■ When the map is turned off in the Maps rollout, the "M" on a small map button changes to a small "m" (**Figure 14.37**).

■ To clear a large or small map button, drag an empty map button over the map button you want to clear, or click the map button and choose NONE in the Material/Map Browser.

■ If you drag a map from the Asset Browser onto a material sample rather than onto a map sample or a material map button, it is automatically loaded into the diffuse map button of the material.

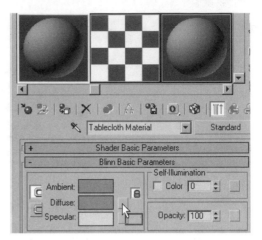

Figure 14.34 Dragging a Checker map onto the Diffuse map button.

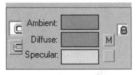

Figure 14.35 The "M" indicates that a map is loaded into the Diffuse color setting.

Figure 14.36 This dialog box allows you to copy, instance or swap a map.

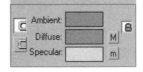

Figure 14.37 The small "m" indicates a map is inactive.

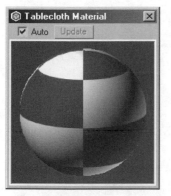

Figure 14.38 Adding a map to the Diffuse map button replaces the diffuse color of the material.

Figure 14.39 Click Show Map in Viewport to turn on viewport display of the map.

Figure 14.40 The diffuse map appears on the surface of the object.

Diffuse maps replace the overall diffuse color of a material with a map. Diffuse maps are often referred to as *texture maps*.

To add a diffuse (texture) map:

1. Select a material sample.

2. In the Basic Parameters rollout, click the small gray button next to the Diffuse color swatch. Then select a map in the Material/Map Browser.

   or

   Drag a map onto the button.

   The map replaces the diffuse color of the material (**Figure 14.38**).

3. Adjust the parameters of the map.

   The map updates on the material sample.

4. Click Go to Parent 🔼. In the Maps rollout, drag the Amount spinner to adjust the amount of influence that the map has over the diffuse color of the material.

5. Drag the panning hand downward on an empty part of the Maps rollout to access the Basic Parameters rollout.

   You can also use the thin scroll bar at right.

6. Adjust the basic parameters of the material.

   To increase the brightness of a map, increase the self-illumination of the material.

   To assign face-mapping coordinates to the map, click Face Map.

7. Assign the material to a mesh primitive, or to any other object that has mapping coordinates applied to it. (To learn how to apply mapping coordinates to objects, see the next section of this chapter.)

8. Click Show Map in Viewport 🔲. If the map looks askew, press Ctrl + T to correct the texture and update the display.

   The map appears on the surface of the object (**Figure 14.39**).

9. Render the scene (**Figure 14.40**).

Opacity mapping uses the intensity values of a map to calculate transparency. Lighter areas create more opaque surfaces. Darker areas create more transparent surfaces. Use this map type when you want to add edges to an object without increasing the complexity of its mesh.

To add an opacity map:

1. Select a material sample.

2. In the Basic Parameters rollout, click the small gray button next to the Opacity spinner. Then select a map in the Material/Map Browser.

   or

   Drag a map onto the button.

   Usually you choose a grayscale map that you have created specifically for this purpose. For practice, try using a checker map (**Figure 14.41**).

3. Adjust the basic parameters of the material. For instance, you might want to make the material two-sided by checking 2-Sided.

4. Assign the map to an object. Then click Show Map in Viewport .

   The opacity map appears as an opaque pattern on the surface of the object.

5. Click Go to Parent. Then click Show Map in Viewport at the root level.

   The object becomes transparent wherever the opacity map is dark (**Figure 14.42**).

6. Render the scene.

   If you checked 2-Sided, the inside surface of the object is visible through the transparent parts of the outside surface (**Figure 14.43**).

✔ Tips

- Ray-traced shadows cast shadows from the edges of an object's opacity map instead of from the edges of the object.

- You can use the alpha channel of a bitmap to generate an opacity map by setting Mono Channel Output to Alpha in the Bitmap Parameters rollout.

Figure 14.41 An opacity map adds a transparent pattern to a material.

Figure 14.42 You can get a good idea of how the object will render by viewing the opacity map in the viewport.

Figure 14.43 Checking 2-Sided makes the inside of the object visible through the transparent areas on the outside. To make the inside easier to read, Receive Shadows has been turned off in the Object Properties dialog box.

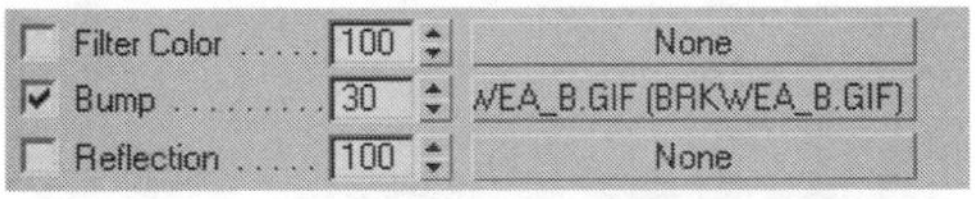

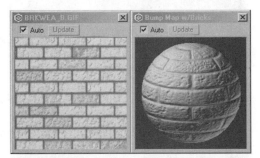

Figure 14.44 The bump map BRKWEA_B.GIF may be found in the 3dsmax4\Maps\Bricks folder.

Figure 14.45 Increasing the Bump amount increases the effect of the bump map.

Figure 14.46 The surface of the teapot appears bumpy. The silhouette of the object is unaffected.

A Bump map creates the illusion of displacement by altering how a surface is shaded. Artists often add bump maps to diffuse-mapped materials to make a texture-mapped surface look more convincing. For example, you could add a Noise map to make a surface look rougher, or a grayscale version of the texture map to make the bump pattern match the texture map.

You can also create your own bump maps by scanning textured surfaces into Photoshop or Painter or by rendering images from 3ds max.

To add a bump map:

1. Select a material sample.

2. Open the Maps rollout.

3. Add a map to the Bump map button (**Figure 14.44**).

4. Click Go to Parent 🔼.

5. Increase the Bump amount until the effect of the bump map is visible on the material sample (**Figure 14.45**).

6. Assign the material to an object.

   The map cannot be displayed in a viewport, even if you turn on Show Map in Viewport.

7. Render the scene (**Figure 14.46**).

   The surface of the object appears bumpy.

✔ Tips

- Reducing the Bump Amount to a negative number creates a inverted bump map in which light values indent and dark values are raised.

- A quick way to create a bump map is to drag an instance of the diffuse map onto the Bump map button.

- Noise and Dent are good choices for bump maps to make a surface look coarse or dirty.

- To make a map actually displace geometry, add it to the Displacement map button. Note that you will need to use a very dense mesh in order to obtain good results.

Applying Mapping Coordinates to Objects

Mapping coordinates match the pattern of a map to the surface of an object. When you assign a mapped material to an object, both the object and the map must have mapping coordinates assigned to them in order for the map to render properly.

Mesh primitives and compound objects are automatically assigned mapping coordinates when they are created. Other types of objects must have mapping coordinates assigned to them.

There are two ways to apply mapping coordinates to an object: by enabling the Generate Mapping Coordinates parameter of an object, or by applying a UVW Map modifier.

While generating mapping coordinates is very convenient, the UVW Map modifier offers several advantages. First, it allows you to apply mapping coordinates to objects that cannot generate them, such as editable meshes. Second, it allows you to adjust object mapping coordinates, which in turn adjust the placement of maps. Third, it allows you to change mapping channels in order to "tune in" different sets of material mapping coordinates. Finally, it allows you to choose a system of mapping projection using the gizmo of the UVW Map modifier, commonly known as a mapping gizmo.

The shape of a mapping gizmo determines the method of projection: planar, cylindrical, spherical, box, and so on (**Figure 14.47**). Map placement is further affected by the position, orientation, and scale of the gizmo.

For example, a planar gizmo projects a map in a single direction, like a slide projector (or a movie projector if the map is animated). If the surface is not parallel to the plane of the

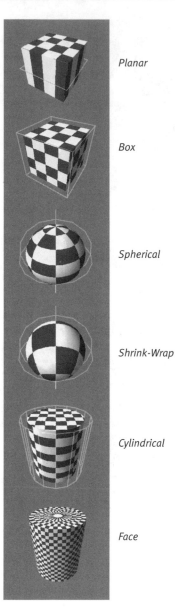

Planar

Box

Spherical

Shrink-Wrap

Cylindrical

Face

Figure 14.47 Map gizmos determine how a map is applied to an object. The Planar gizmo is the default type.

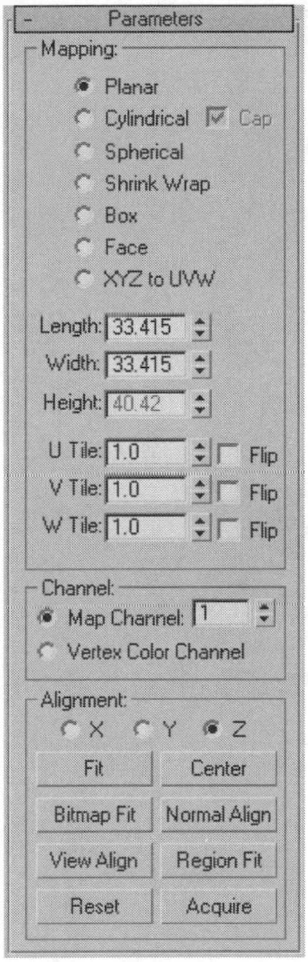

Figure 14.48 The UVW Map rollout adjusts the placement of a map on an object that it modifies. It does not adjust map placement for a material.

gizmo, the map stretches as the surface turns away from it.

If you want to avoid stretching the map, you choose a gizmo whose shape more closely resembles that of your object.

UVW Map modifiers have three groups of parameters for assigning mapping coordinates (**Figure 14.48**):

- **Mapping**—Determines the shape and proportions of the mapping gizmo. Sets parameters for tiling and flipping maps.

- **Channel**—Allows you to create up to 99 sets of mapping coordinates for an object. To display a channel, the UVW mapping coordinates of an object must be set to the same channel as the UVW coordinates of the map that is applied to it.

- **Alignment**—Matches the position, orientation, or scale of a gizmo to maps, objects, or the world.

Alignment commands include:

- **The X, Y, and Z buttons**—Aligns a mapping gizmo to the axes of the world coordinate system.

- **Fit**—Resizes a mapping gizmo to match to the size of the object at the extents of its bounding box. This may distort the proportions of a map.

- **Center**—Realigns a mapping gizmo to the selection center of an object.

- **Bitmap Fit**—Resizes a mapping gizmo in proportion to the size of a bitmap. This prevents distortion in bitmaps that are associated with the material being applied.

- **Normal Align**—Aligns a mapping gizmo to a face normal on the object by dragging the cursor over the surface of the object.

continues on next page

APPLYING MAPPING COORDINATES TO OBJECTS

- **View Align**—Aligns a mapping gizmo to the current view.

- **Region Fit**—Allows you to drag out the dimensions of a mapping gizmo.

- **Reset**—Returns a mapping gizmo to its default alignment.

- **Acquire**—Matches a gizmo to the mapping coordinates of another object.

In addition, you can affect the position, orientation, and scale of a gizmo by selecting it in the modifier stack and transforming it.

Generate Mapping Coordinates is a base parameter found in the creation rollouts of mesh primitives, shape primitives, editable splines, lathed objects, and extruded objects.

To generate object mapping coordinates:

1. Select an object.

2. Open the Modify panel and locate the Generate Mapping Coords. parameter.

   For mesh primitives, go to the bottom of the creation parameter rollout (**Figure 14.49**). The parameter is turned on by default.

   For lathed or extruded objects, go to the bottom of the Lathe or Extrude rollout.

   For spline objects, open the Rendering rollout.

3. Check the box.

   Mapping coordinates are applied to the object. If a mapped material is applied to the object, the map will now render correctly.

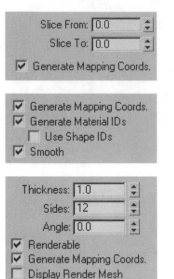

Figure 14.49 The Generate Mapping Coords. parameter for a primitive object (top), lathed object (middle), and a spline object (bottom).

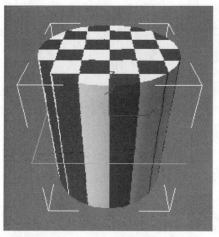

Figure 14.50 Planar mapping applies a map along an object's Z-axis. The map stretches along the sides of the object.

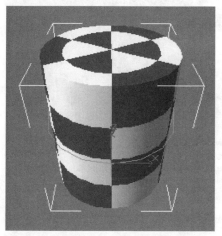

Figure 14.51 Spherical mapping wraps the map around the object and gathers it together at the poles of the sphere gizmo.

To apply mapping coordinates to an object:

1. Select an object.

2. Apply a UVW Map modifier.

   The modifier gizmo applies mapping coordinates to the object.

   Planar mapping coordinates are applied by default (**Figure 14.50**).

3. Select a gizmo type. Choose from Cylindrical, Spherical, Shrink Wrap, Box, Face, or XYZ to UVW (**Figure 14.51**).

4. To adjust the gizmo, use the Mapping and Alignment commands, or select the gizmo in the stack display and transform it.

✔ Tip

- Mapping coordinates are set to channel 1 by default. By changing channels in the UVW Map modifier, you can assign different mapping coordinates to each channel.

APPLYING MAPPING COORDINATES TO OBJECTS

Using Environment Maps

Environment maps add context to a scene and make it more interesting. Use them to add background images at rendering time and to create surface reflections on objects.

As scene backgrounds, environment maps provide additional visual information without your having to build everything that you see.

As surface reflections, environment maps give objects a finishing touch. Reflections are explained in the section following this one.

To create an environment map:

1. Load a map type into a sample slot.

   You can choose a simple 2D or 3D map, or build a compound map by mixing, masking, and mapping colors (**Figure 14.52**).

2. Adjust the parameters of the map type so that the image looks right toward you.

   To brighten the map, click the map type button and choose Output. Choose to keep the old map as a sub-map. Then increase the RGB output amount (**Figure 14.53**).

3. Adjust the coordinates of the map. Pay particular attention to size and placement.

   For 2D maps, be sure to change the coordinates of all maps and sub-maps from Texture to Environment. Screen mapping, which matches a map to the view-plane of a camera, is the default setting (**Figure 14.54**).

   Hint: Use Go to Forward to Sibling ![icon] to navigate to the branches of the map tree.

✔ Tip

- Use Screen mapping if you plan on using the environment map as a background image for your scene. Use Spherical Environment, Cylindrical Environment, and Shrink-Wrap Environment to control reflection maps.

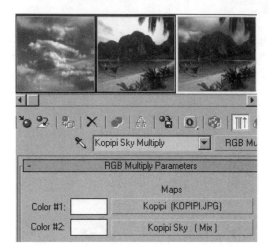

Figure 14.52 Any type of map can be turned into an environment map.

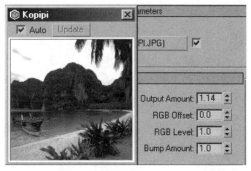

Figure 14.53 You often need to brighten a map before using it as an environment map.

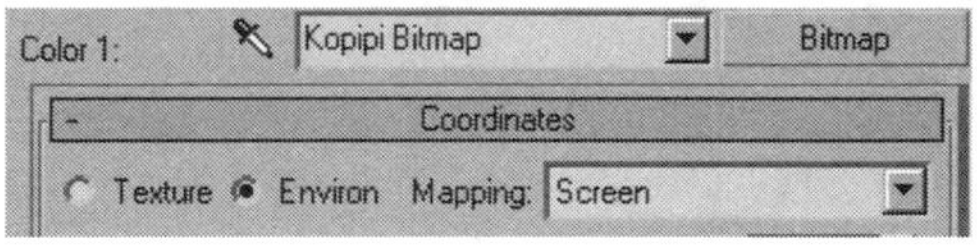

Figure 14.54 Choose the Environment option to turn a 2D map into an environment map.

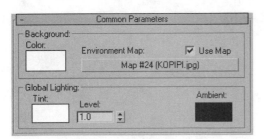

Figure 14.55 After loading a map onto the environment background map button.

Figure 14.56 Use the viewport background map and camera horizon to aid object placement.

Figure 14.57 The environment map renders in the background of the scene.

To add an environment map to the background:

1. Choose Rendering > Environment.

   The Environment dialog box appears. The Background Color parameters are at the top.

2. Drag an environment map onto the Environment Map button.

   or

   Click the map button and choose a map with the Material/Map Browser (**Figure 14.55**). (Loading a new map type automatically assigns environment coordinates to it.)

3. Press Alt + B. In the Viewport Background dialog box, check Use Environment Background and Display Background. Then click OK.

4. Arrange your objects using the viewport background and the camera horizon for reference (**Figure 14.56**).

5. Render the scene.

   The environment map appears behind the objects in the background (**Figure 14.57**).

6. To adjust the background, adjust the map in the Material Editor. If the map is not loaded into the Material Editor, drag an instance of the map onto a sample slot.

   continues on next page

✔ Tips

- To save rendering time, render the objects in the background of your scene to a high resolution image and then use the rendered image as an environment background map.

- Because environment background maps are locked to the viewplane, they do not change perspective when you move the camera. If you need to use a background that is located in space, position a plane behind your objects so that it is perpendicular to the line of sight of your camera. Then match the dimensions of the plane to the viewplane of the camera and assign it a mapped material that is not shiny and fully self-illuminated (**Figure 14.58**).

A Matte/Shadow material applies an environment screen map onto the surface of an object. This allows you to add shadows and reflections to the background image and create the illusion of objects moving behind parts of the background.

A Matte/Shadow material is a kind of a "cloaking device" that covers objects with the environment background. An object that is assigned a Matte/Shadow material is called a matte object.

When you render a matte object, it can cast shadows, receive shadows, or display reflections, even though it is invisible when you place it in front of an environment background.

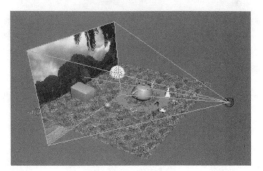

Figure 14.58 Create a background with a plane by matching it to the cone of a camera.

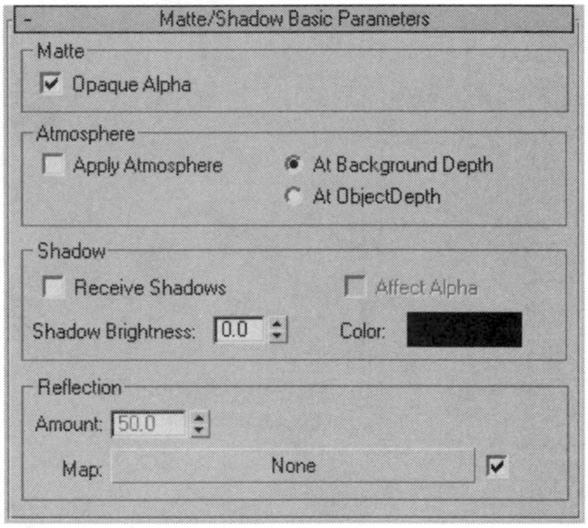

Figure 14.59 The Matte/Shadow material allows you to assign an environment background map to an object.

USING ENVIRONMENT MAPS

Figure 14.60 Hide the object behind a matte object.

Figure 14.61 When you render the scene, the object appears to be inside the background.

Figure 14.62 After checking Receive Shadows, the object appears to cast a shadow in the background.

By hiding part of an object behind a matte object, you can make the object appear as if it were located in the pictorial space of the background.

To place an object in a background:

1. Open a scene file that has an environment background image.

2. Select a material sample.

3. Click the Type button, and select Matte/Shadow from the list of materials. The Matte/Shadow rollout appears in the Material Editor (**Figure 14.59**).

4. Assign the material to an object. The object becomes a matte object. If you render the scene, the object disappears into the environment background.

5. Position one of the edges of the object so that it matches an object in the environment background image.

6. Place an object behind the matte object so that it emerges along the matched edge (**Figure 14.60**).

7. Render the scene (**Figure 14.61**).

8. To make a matte object receive shadows, check Receive Shadows in the Matte/Shadow Basic Parameters. You can also set the color and brightness of the shadow to match the environment map (**Figure 14.62**).

Reflection and Refraction

Everything that you see is an illusion of light. Earth and sun; sky and clouds; moon and stars; and every person, place, or thing is visible because of emitted or reflected light.

When light bounces off an object, it picks up some of the color of its surface. The more light bounces from object to object, the more color information it collects, and the more it spreads colors from one object to another.

Reflections are produced when the pattern of color information carried by rays of light bounce off a reflective surface into your eyes. You can think of a reflection as being the history of a beam of light told in the form of a visual image (**Figure 14.63**).

Figure 14.63 The Taj Mahal is reflected in a Flat Mirror map.

3D programs create reflections by simulating the interaction of light and objects in nature. To create reflections in 3ds max, you need to do three things:

- Assign a reflective material to an object.
- Surround the object with other objects, or an environment map.
- Illuminate the scene so that light reflects off the object and into the viewplane.

Your options for creating reflective materials include adding a Reflect/Refract map to a Standard material, adding a Flat Mirror map to a Standard material, or setting a Raytrace material to be reflective.

Reflection maps are locked to world coordinates so that they will appear constant as objects move through them. They only appear to move when the camera you are viewing them with moves. Because reflections are not tied to objects, objects do not need to be assigned mapping coordinates in order to display reflections.

Refraction causes light to bend when it passes through transparent objects. You can create refractions with a Reflect/Refract map or a

Figure 14.64 This chemistry visualization uses refraction mapping for the water and the glass.

Flat Mirror Parameters
Blur
☑ Apply Blur   Blur: 1.0
Render
○ First Frame Only
● Every Nth Frame: 1
☑ Use Environment Map
☐ Apply to Faces with ID: 1
Distortion
● None   ○ Use Bump Map   ○ Use Built-in Noise
Distortion Amount: 0.5
Noise
● Regular   Phase: 0.0
○ Fractal   Size: 10.0
○ Turbulence   Levels: 2.0
Note:
Unless "Apply Faces with ID" is checked, this material must be applied as a sub-material to a set of coplanar faces.

Figure 14.65 The rollout for a Flat Mirror map allows you to add an environment map to the reflection, and to disturb the reflection with built-in noise or with a bump map.

Figure 14.66 A Flat Mirror map makes a plane reflect the scene.

Figure 14.67 Adding noise to the map creates a ripple effect.

Raytrace map, but I find the refractions that are produced by Raytrace material to be more satisfactory and easier to control (**Figure 14.64**).

The best way to create reflections on a flat surface is with a Flat Mirror map.

To create a reflection on a flat surface:

1. Select a plane that has a few objects sitting on it.

2. Open the Material Editor.

3. Select one of the sample slots.

4. Click the Reset button to change the colors of the material to shades of gray.

5. Open the Maps rollout.

6. Click the Reflection Map button.
   The Material/Map Browser appears.

7. Select the Flat Mirror map type.
   The Flat Mirror Parameters rollout appears (**Figure 14.65**).

8. Click Assign Material Selection.

9. Render the scene.
   The planar surface reflects the scene (**Figure 14.66**).

10. To change which side of the object reflects, check Apply Faces with ID and change the ID number at right. This number corresponds to the Material ID number of the object's faces and can be reassigned at the face sub-object level of editing.

✔ Tips

- Flat Mirror maps work on only one of the flat sides of an object, usually the top side. To create reflections on more than one side, use a Multi/Sub-Object material and set each Flat Mirror map to a different material ID.

- An extruded shape also makes a good reflecting surface.

- Adding a little noise to a flat mirror map creates the appearance of ripples on water (**Figure 14.67**).

The fastest way to create reflections on a curved or irregular surface is with a Reflect/Refract map.

Reflect/Refract maps take snapshots of the scene from six directions and map them onto a surface using a cubic environment map.

To create a reflection on a curved surface:

1. Select a material that you want to add reflections to. For strong reflections, use a black glossy material with white specular highlights.

2. Open the Maps rollout.

3. Add a Reflect/Refract map to the Reflection map button.

4. In the Reflect/Refract Parameters rollout, make sure that the Source is set to Automatic and that Use Environment Background is checked (**Figure 14.68**).

5. Set the Blur or Blur Offset amount if you want the reflection to blur.

6. Apply the material to an object that has a curved or irregular surface.

7. Assign a background map to the environment of a scene.

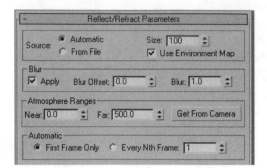

Figure 14.68 Use the Reflect/Refract map to create an automatic reflection.

Figure 14.69 Increasing the contrast of the material colors strengthens the reflection.

Figure 14.70 Reflections are usually secondary to the diffuse color of an object.

8. Activate a Perspective or Camera viewport. Then render the scene.

A reflection of the scene appears on the surface of the object. The reflection mixes with the base color of the material, but it does not mix with its specular highlights.

9. To give the reflection more contrast, so that it looks like a mirror, set the Ambient and Diffuse colors to black and the Specular color to white (**Figure 14.69**).

10. To mix the reflection with the diffuse color of the object, reduce the Reflect Amount in the Maps rollout (**Figure 14.70**).

✔ Tip

■ If an object intersects the object you are working with, it may not appear in the reflection. Correct this by moving the object.

REFLECTION AND REFRACTION

Raytrace maps eliminate seams by tracing a series of paths, or rays, from every pixel that you see on the viewplane into the scene. As the rays bounce from one object to another, they accumulate color and lighting information that they use to paint surface colors and reflections.

Because they require more calculation than cubic environment mapping, raytraced reflections take longer to render.

To create more accurate reflections on a curved surface:

1. Select a material and open the Maps rollout.

2. Add a Raytrace map to the Reflection map button.

3. In the Raytrace Parameters rollout, click the map button to assign an environment map to the background (**Figure 14.71**). Spherical coordinates are automatically assigned to the environment map.

4. Apply the material to an object.

5. Activate a Perspective or Camera viewport. Then render the scene.

   A reflection of the scene appears on the surface of the object. This time the reflection does not have any seams.

6. Adjust the brightness, contrast, and tint of the reflection by changing the colors of the material, the Reflect Amount, or by changing the output of the environment map. To antialias the reflection, click the Options button and check Global Antialiasing (**Figure 14.72**).

   Dim the reflection by reducing Reflect Amount.

✔ Tip

■ Adding a Reflect/Refract map or a Raytrace map to the Refract map button automatically produces a refraction instead of a reflection (**Figure 14.73**).

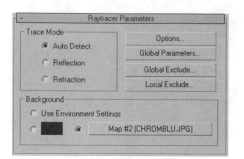

Figure 14.71 The Raytrace map rollout allows you to add an environment background map that encloses the surface of the reflecting object.

Figure 14.72 This highly polished reflection was created by adjusting the contrast of both the material and the map.

Figure 14.73 A refraction map inverts the scene that surrounds the refracting object.

REFLECTION AND REFRACTION

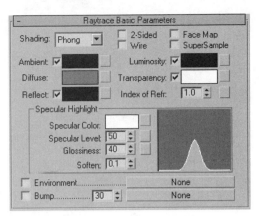

Figure 14.74 Setting Transparency to white is the same as making an object 100% transparent.

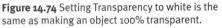

Figure 14.75 After adjusting the Raytrace Basic Parameters for a refracting crystal ball.

Figure 14.76 The crystal ball refracts the scene.

Raytrace materials map reflections using the same raytrace rendering engine as Raytrace maps. They have additional controls for creating refraction, transparency, translucency, and fog.

To create a refraction:

1. Click a sample slot.

2. Click the Type button and choose Raytrace from the Material/Map Browser.

3. In the Raytrace Basic Parameters rollout, set the Transparency color to white, or 100% transparent (**Figure 14.74**).

4. Set the Index of Refraction to a value between 1.5 and 2, depending on if your crystal is made of glass, quartz, or diamond. Higher values increase the curvature of the refracted image.

5. Set the Specular Level to 100 and the Glossiness to 90.

6. To make the crystal ball reflect as well as refract, uncheck Reflect and the increase the reflection amount by 5–15%. Higher amounts obscure the refracted image.

   If you are using an environment map, you may need to offset the U coordinates of the map to eliminate the map seam.

7. Click the Environment map button and select the map that you want to refract.

   You can also drag a copy of the scene's environment background map onto this button (**Figure 14.75**).

8. Assign the material to a sphere and render the scene (**Figure 14.76**).

✔ Tip

■ For more information on Raytrace materials and how to adjust them, see the help files.

RENDERING

Figure 15.1 The lens flare on the crystal ball was created with a render effect.

For thousands of years, artists have been drawing pictures. Starting with only a line, artists learned how to apply shading to form and color to light. After many centuries, they learned how to draw perspective: parallel perspective in the East, converging perspective in the West. Finally, in the twenty-first century, we are creating pictures out of our imaginations, using tools and media that could never have been foreseen. With 3ds max 4, artists can draw, paint, sculpt, and animate, and let the computer do the shading and perspective. For the first time, artists are working in a medium of light, moving bits of color and transparency and depth information through data channels and onto their screens. From the desktop to books, television, movies, and the Internet (not to mention new forms of multimedia production not even yet imagined), 3D graphics are here to stay.

This chapter shows you how to take the scenes you have created in your computer and send them out into the world. The basics of rendering still images are covered in Chapter 11, Lights. This chapter picks up where that explanation leaves off, and demonstrates how to set image output size, how to render images to different types of file formats, how to render animations, and how to create atmospheric and post-process effects (**Figure 15.1**).

Rendering Scenes

The Render Scene dialog box gives you all the tools you need to render still images and animations to image output files. But before you start rendering full-length animation files, I suggest that you do some testing to make sure that you get the results that you want.

The Render Types drop-down menu in the main toolbar allows you to select specific parts of your scene for test rendering (**Figure 15.2**).

Figure 15.2 The Render dialog box indicates rendering progress, displays Render settings, and gives you information about the contents of your scene.

- **View**—Renders the entire view.

- **Selected**—Renders just the objects that you select. If there is an image in the virtual frame buffer, the Selected type will render the selected objects on top of that image. Clicking Clear resets the virtual frame buffer.

- **Region**—Renders a rectangular region that you adjust. When you click the Render button, a dotted window with control handles appears in the viewport. Anything inside the window will be rendered at the last image resolution setting. When you are ready to render, click the OK button in the lower-right corner of the viewport.

- **Crop**—Renders a rectangular region and purges all other image data in the virtual frame buffer.

- **Blowup**—Renders a rectangular region and enlarges the area to fit the current image size.

- **Box Selected**—Renders only the volume specified by the current selection's bounding box, and lets you specify an image resolution for the objects being rendered.

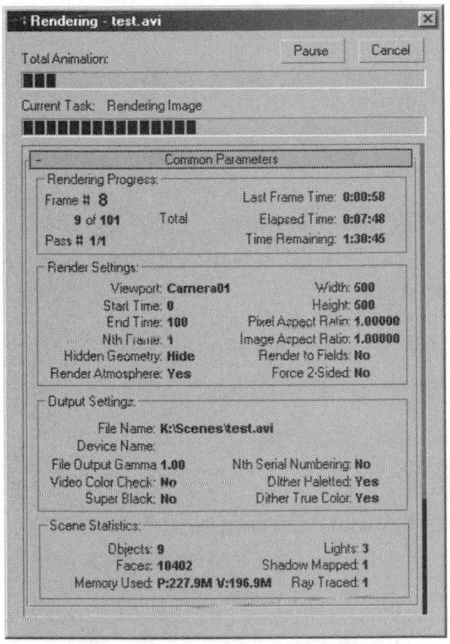

Figure 15.3 The Render Scene dialog box contains four rollouts. Options toggle the rendering of objects, maps, shadows, shading, and effects, and control color output for video.

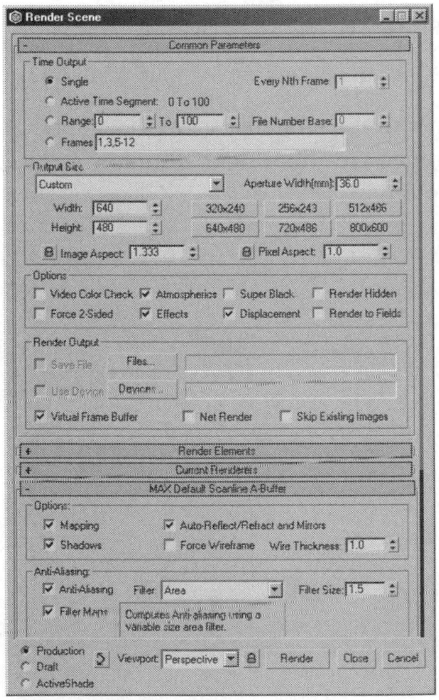

- ◆ **Region Selected**—Renders a region that is defined by the bounding box of a selection.

- ◆ **Crop Selected**—Renders a region that is defined by the bounding box of the current selection and crops out everything else.

As your scene renders, the Rendering dialog box appears. It indicates the progress of your rendering, frame by frame, and lets you know how long it took to render the last frame. Based on that time, it estimates how long it should take to render the rest of the animation (**Figure 15.3**).

The Rendering dialog box also displays settings used by the high-resolution scanline renderer to render your images for final output. You configure these settings in the Render Scene dialog box (**Figure 15.4**). To access the Render Scene dialog box, click Render Scene ⬚ on the main toolbar, or choose Rendering > Render. The keyboard shortcuts are Shift + R and F10.

Figure 15.4 The Render Type drop-down list gives you six ways to render a scene.

The Render Scene dialog box contains options that you can turn on and off to customize image output and save time during test rendering:

◆ **Video Color Check**—Verifies that pixels are within range of PAL or NTSC video thresholds.

◆ **Force 2-Sided**—Renders objects on both sides regardless of material assignment.

◆ **Atmospherics**—Renders atmospheric effects.

◆ **Effects**—Renders rendering effects.

◆ **Super Black**—Limits the darkness of pixels for video compositing.

◆ **Displacement**—Renders displacement maps.

◆ **Render Hidden**—Renders hidden objects.

◆ **Render to Fields**—Instead of using frames, renders to two fields of alternating lines for video output. Used for smoothing motion.

◆ **Save File**—Renders to an image file.

◆ **Virtual Frame Buffer**—Renders to the virtual frame buffer.

◆ **Net Render**—Renders multiple animations over a network, including the Internet.

◆ **Skip Existing Images**—Prevents saving over existing files that are part of a sequence.

◆ **Mapping**—Enables the rendering of maps.

◆ **Shadows**—Enables the rendering of shadows.

◆ **Auto-Reflect/Refract and Mirrors**—Enables the rendering of automatic Reflect/Refract maps.

◆ **Force Wireframe**—Makes objects render in wireframe regardless of material settings.

◆ **Wire Thickness**—Sets the thickness of the wire when Force Wireframe is enabled.

◆ **Anti-Aliasing**—Enables anti-aliasing.

◆ **Filter maps**—Enables pyramidal and summed area filtering of bitmaps.

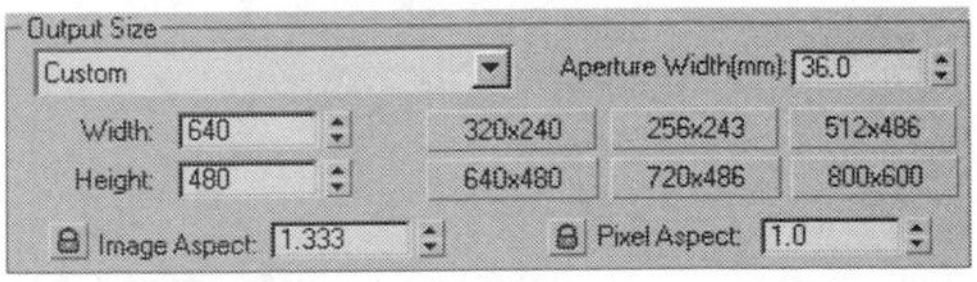

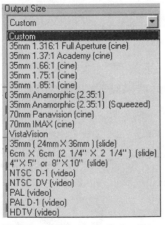

Figure 15.5 The Output Size group gives you presets, customization settings, and more.

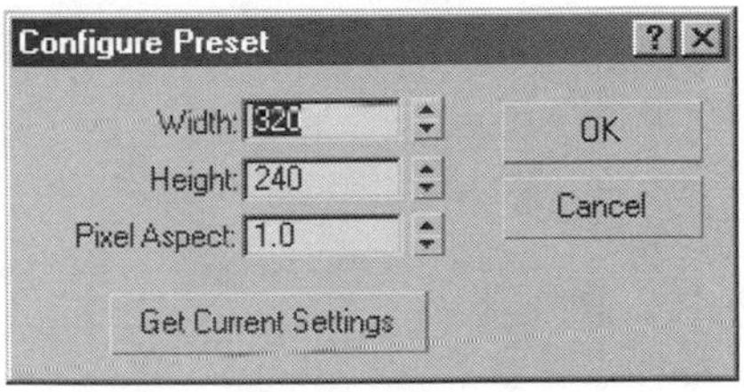

Figure 15.6 The Configure Preset dialog box lets you customize a preset output size.

Figure 15.7 If you're rendering for a standard cinematic or video resolution, such as IMAX, choose from the Output Size drop-down list.

The Output Size commands in the Render Scene dialog box determine the resolution of rendered images in pixel width and height. The default output size is 640 x 480 pixels.

To set the image output size:

1. Click Render Scene 🖼.

2. In the Output Size group, select an output size by clicking a preset resolution button or by entering values for width and height (**Figure 15.5**).

   The rendering size of the image is set.

✔ Tips

- Rendering defaults to a single image of the current frame. For testing, use a small image output size such as 320 x 240 pixels.

- Clicking the lock icon next to Image Aspect locks the image aspect ratio.

- Right-clicking a preset resolution button brings up the Configure Preset dialog box (**Figure 15.6**).

   The drop-down list in this group contains a variety of formats and presets for different applications (**Figure 15.7**).

You set the file type and destination of rendered output in the Render Output group. Still formats include: BMP, Kodak Cineon, EPS, JPEG, PNG, SGI, RLA, RPF, Targa, and TIF.

BMP is an uncompressed file format commonly found on Windows-based systems. It can be set to 8-bit (256 color) or 24-bit (True Color) output.

continues on next page

Targa and **TIF** are 32-bit uncompressed file formats that include alpha channel transparency information as well as RGB information. Used to create highly accurate files for video and print.

JPEG and **PNG** are commonly used on the Web for continuous-tone images. JPEG creates highly compressed 24-bit files with a minimum of loss. PNG files can be set to 8-bit, 24-bit, 32-bit, or 48-bit (281 trillion colors). Includes options for alpha channel transparency information and 8-bit or 16-bit grayscale output.

To select a name and file format:

1. Click Render Scene ⬚.

2. In the Render Output group, click Files. The Render Output File dialog box appears (**Figure 15.8**).

3. Choose a file format from the Save as Type drop-down list (**Figure 15.9**).

4. Enter a name for the image.

5. Click Save.

   Some file formats require extra configuration settings, so a configuration dialog box may appear (**Figure 15.10**).

   A check appears in the Save File checkbox of the Render Scene dialog box to let you know that the next rendering will be saved to a file (**Figure 15.11**).

✔ Tip

■ To create alpha channel image files at the same time that you render Targa files, check Alpha Split in the Targa Image Control dialog box. The alpha channel files will be named A_filename.tga, where filename is the name you assigned to the Targa file.

Figure 15.8 The Render Output File dialog box is similar to Save dialog boxes in other programs.

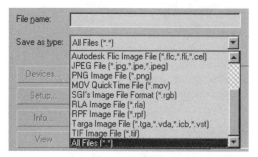

Figure 15.9 Choose your desired output file format from the Save as Type list

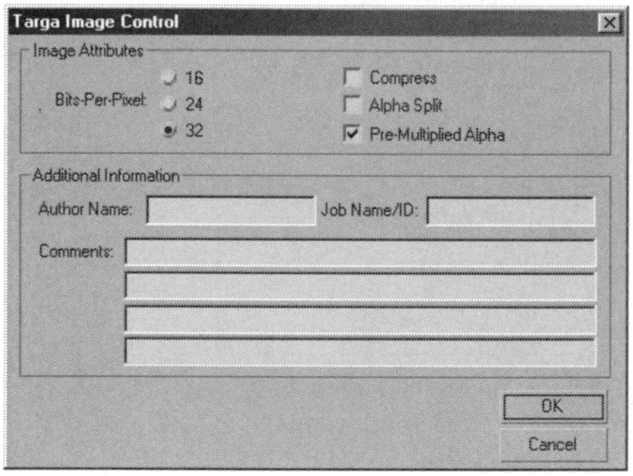

Figure 15.10 The Targa Image Control dialog box is an example of a configuration dialog box that gives you additional options specific to the output file format you choose.

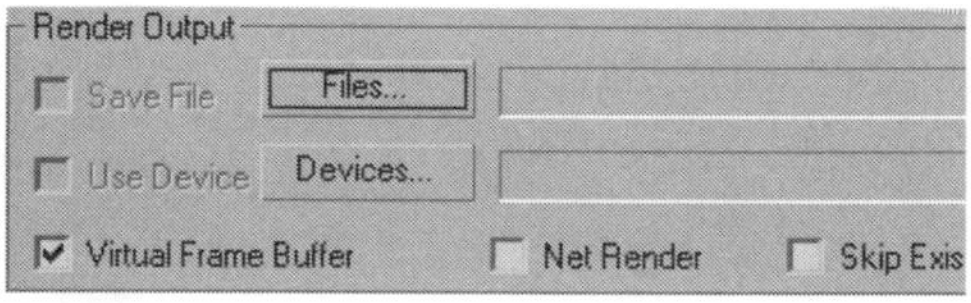

Figure 15.11 You can turn file saving on and off with the checkbox next to Save File.

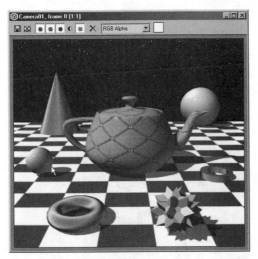

Figure 15.12 Save still image files by choosing Single in the Time Output group.

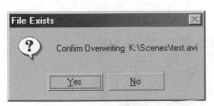

Figure 15.13 The virtual frame buffer window displays the rendered image.

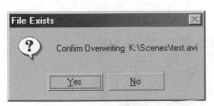

Figure 15.14 The File Exists dialog box asks for confirmation before overwriting a file.

In Chapter 11, you learned how to save a single image to a file using the virtual frame buffer. Using the Render Scene dialog box, you can save one or more images to file at the same time that they render in the virtual frame buffer.

To render a still image to a file:

1. Click Render Scene ⬚.

2. Choose an image size in the Output Size group.

3. Click the Files button, and then specify a name and still-image file format.

4. In the Time Output group, make sure that Single is selected (**Figure 15.12**).

5. Click Render.

   The current frame renders to the virtual frame buffer and to the file you selected (**Figure 15.13**).

✔ Tips

- To render a series of still frames that are sequentially numbered, choose a still-image file format and select Active Time Segment or Range in the Time Output group.

  If you select Range, specify the extent of the range by entering the numbers of the frames you want to render. Separate each frame with a comma or define sub-ranges using a hyphen between frame numbers.

- Sequentially numbered files can be used to create animated bitmaps in the Material Editor. See "IFL files" in the help files for more information about this option.

- Remember to uncheck Save File in the Render Scene dialog box if you do not want the program to save over your image file the next time that you render. Otherwise, the File Exists warning will appear to check if you want to overwrite the file (**Figure 15.14**).

RENDERING SCENES

The Time Output group sets the amount of time or the number of frames to render, using the time code chosen in the Time Configuration dialog box. (See Chapter 7, Animation, for a complete description of how to set time codes.) The default setting renders to a single frame.

You can render an entire active time segment or any range of frames that you specify. Take advantage of the Range and Preview options to test-render different parts of your animation.

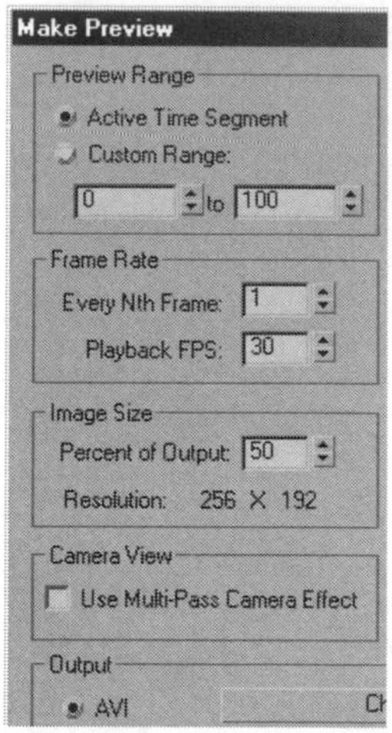

To render a preview animation:

1. Choose Rendering > Make Preview.

   The Make Preview dialog box appears (**Figure 15.15**).

2. Set the Preview Range, Frame Rate, and Image Size parameters, or accept the defaults.

3. Click Create. If necessary, choose a compression option.

   The preview window replaces the viewports. The preview renders in the center of the window (**Figure 15.16**).

4. When the preview has finished rendering, the Windows Media Player appears. It automatically plays back the preview (**Figure 15.17**).

✔ Tip

■ Previews are named _scene.avi and saved in the 3dsmax3/Preview folder by default. Use the Rendering > Rename Preview command if you want to save the preview to a new file that will not be saved over.

Figure 15.15 Use Make Preview to quickly produce a test rendering of your animation.

Figure 15.16 You can see the preview as it renders frame by frame in the preview window.

Figure 15.17 MAX uses the Windows Media Player to play back the preview.

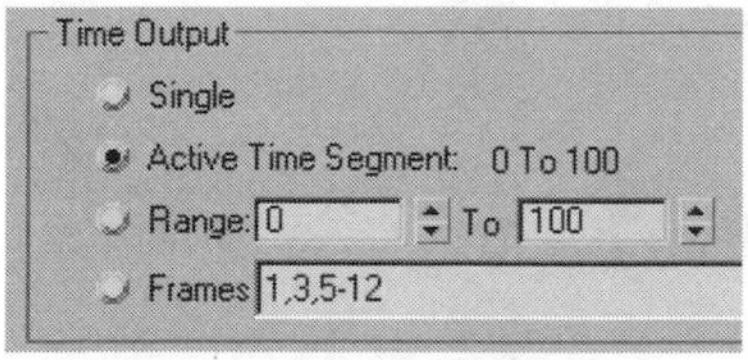

Figure 15.18 To render an animation, choose Active Time Segment or Range.

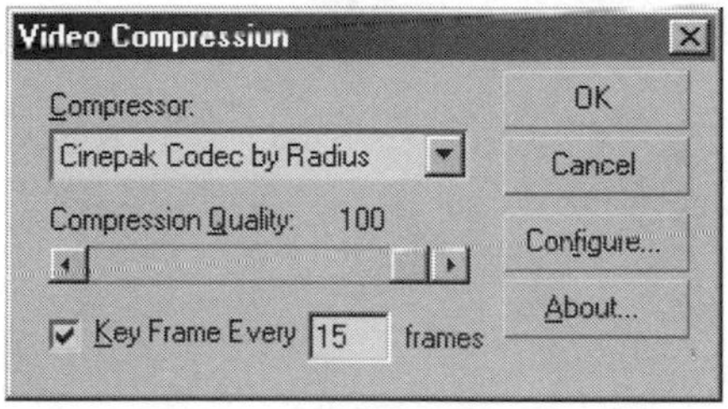

Figure 15.19 The Cinepak compression codec yields good results with AVI files.

Animation file formats include AVI, FLIC, and MOV.

AVI is the Windows movie format. This is the most common output for the Windows desktop.

MOV is the Apple QuickTime standard. Often used on the Web.

FLIC is an 8-bit file format developed by Autodesk for use with AutoCAD.

Different compression methods are available for each format, depending on your need for quality vs. file size. For basic experimentation, choose the AVI file format with Cinepak compression.

To render an animation:

1. Click Render Scene .

2. Choose an image output size.

3. In the Time Output group, select Active Time Segment or Range (**Figure 15.18**). If you choose Range, specify a range.

4. Choose a name and animation file format by clicking the Files button. When you click Save, the program prompts you to select a compression method or color palette (**Figure 15.19**).

5. Click Render.

   The active time segment or range renders to a movie file. To play back the movie, choose File > View File and navigate to the file you just saved.

   continues on next page

✔ Tips

■ Render uncompressed AVI files or a series of Targa images if you are going to process the file later in another application.

■ One of the best codecs, or compression methods, for MOV files is Sorensen Video.

■ For faster test rendering, increase the value of Every Nth Frame. Setting this parameter to 2 renders every other frame (**Figure 15.20**).

■ To eliminate banding, Choose Customize > Preferences > Rendering. Then uncheck True Color and Paletted output dithering.

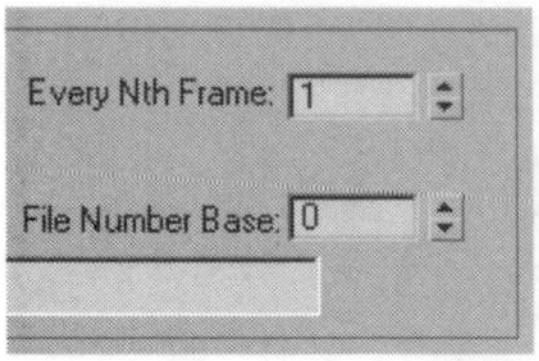

When the shutter of a real camera remains open for an extended period of time, any movement by the camera or the objects it views creates a blur.

Image motion blur simulates this effect by averaging images over multiple frames. In order for image motion blur to appear, either the object or the camera must be moving.

Image motion blur can also be applied as a rendering effect or a multi-pass camera effect.

To render image motion blur:

1. Select the objects you want to blur. Then right-click on the selection and choose Properties from the Transform quad menu.

2. In the Object Properties dialog box, check Enabled in the Motion Blur group. Then click the Image option (**Figure 15.21**).

3. Close the Object Properties dialog box and open the Render Scene dialog box.

Figure 15.20
For test rendering of animations at a higher quality than the preview, render every second or third frame.

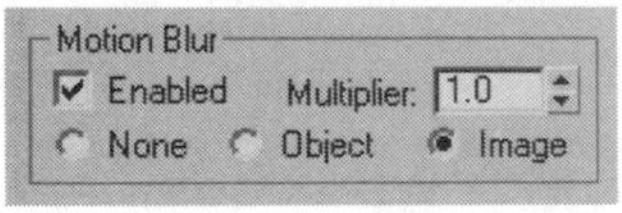

Figure 15.21 You must enable image motion blur in the Object Properties dialog box before motion blur will be applied.

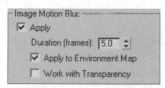

Figure 15.22 After setting image motion blur parameters in the Render Scene dialog box.

Figure 15.23 The moving teapot is blurred. The amount of blurring is proportional to the duration.

4. In the MAX Default Scanline A-Buffer rollout, adjust the Duration to set the number of frames that will be used to compute object motion blurring. Higher values increase the amount of blurring.

5. Check Apply to Environment Map to apply motion blur to reflections and refractions that use environment maps (**Figure 15.22**).

6. Render the scene.

   Moving objects that have image motion blur enabled are blurred along the path of their trajectories (**Figure 15.23**). If the camera is moving, everything in the scene that is not moving with the camera is blurred.

✔ Tip

■ For faster rendering, leave Work With Transparency unchecked unless you are having trouble blurring transparent objects, or the objects behind them.

Object motion blur smoothes the appearance of moving objects by rendering multiple transparent copies for every frame that is averaged. It does not take into account the movement of cameras. The purpose is to make animations play back smoother on the computer, rather than to make moving objects look blurry.

To render object motion blur:

1. Select the objects you want to blur. Then right-click on the selection and choose Properties from the Transform quad menu.

2. In the Object Properties dialog box, check Enabled in the Motion Blur group. Then click the Object option (**Figure 15.24**).

3. Close the Object Properties dialog box and open the Render Scene dialog box.

4. In the MAX Default Scanline A-Buffer rollout, adjust the Duration to set the number of frames that will be used to compute object motion blurring. Higher values increase the amount of blurring (**Figure 15.25**).

5. Adjust the number of Duration Subdivisions to set the number of transparent copies that will be rendered per frame. (Note: this value must always be greater than the sample level.) Then increase the number of Samples to set the amount of transparent dithering that occurs between copies. Higher values produce smoother results, but take longer to render.

6. For output to digital video, such as AVI files that you play back on your computer, turn off Color Dithering in the Rendering panel of the Preferences dialog box. This eliminates banding.

7. Render the scene.
   Moving objects that have object motion blur enabled are blurred along the path of their trajectories (**Figure 15.26**).

Figure 15.24 You must enable object motion blur in the Object Properties dialog box before motion blur will be applied.

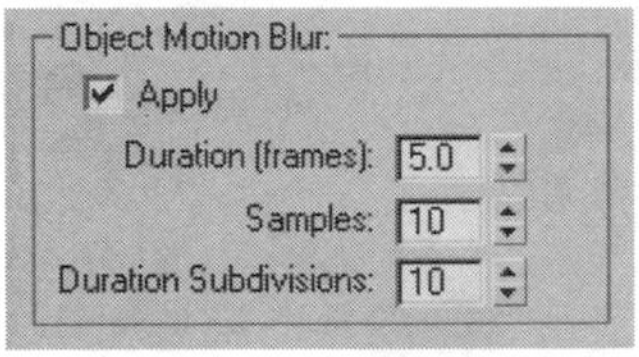

Figure 15.25 After setting object motion blur parameters in the Render Scene dialog box.

Figure 15.26 The moving teapot is blurred. The number of blurred copies is equal to the number of duration subdivisions.

✔ Tip

■ For smoother video output, render to fields. See "Fields" in the help files.

Figure 15.27 Volume light and volume fog add a little magic to an ordinary scene.

Rendering Effects

Rendering effects can be applied during the initial rendering pass or added post-process in successive passes and updates. Atmospheric rendering effects are always added during the first pass. Effects in the Rendering Effects dialog box are always added post-process (after the initial rendering pass).

Atmospheric Effects

Atmospheric effects are visual effects that create the illusion of fog, fire, smoke, and clouds. These effects appear when your render your scene.

Using the Environment dialog box, you can create the following effects (**Figure 15.27**):

◆ **Fog**—Adds smoke and fog effects to a scene. There are two kind of fog:

Standard fog fades objects toward the front or back of a view.

Layered fog fades objects toward the top or bottom of a view.

You can also make fog constant throughout a view.

◆ **Volume Fog**—Creates swirling smoke, fog, and cloud effects.

◆ **Volume Light**—Adds swirling smoke and fog to a light beam, creating the illusion of headlights on a foggy night or spotlights in a smoky theater.

◆ **Fire**—Creates smoke, fire, and explosion effects, including candles, campfires, fireballs, nebulae, and clouds. Fire is animated by default.

You define the extent of an atmospheric effect in different ways.

◆ Standard fog is defined by the environment ranges of the camera.

◆ Layered fog is defined by the horizon of the camera and a layered fog parameter setting.

◆ Volume light is defined by the cone of illumination of a light.

To limit the range of volume fog and fire effects, you create an object called an atmospheric gizmo and assign it to the effect. Atmospheric gizmos can be box-shaped, spherical, or cylindrical.

To create a gizmo:

1. Activate a Perspective viewport or a Camera viewport.

2. Open the Create panel and click the Helpers sub-panel.

3. From the drop-down menu, choose Atmospheric Apparatus (**Figure 15.28**).

4. Click a gizmo button.

   The parameters of the gizmo appear below (**Figure 15.29**).

5. Drag out the gizmo in a viewport.

   For SphereGizmos, check the Hemisphere parameter to make the gizmo a hemisphere (**Figure 15.30**).

6. Set the dimensions of the gizmo by adjusting its parameters.

7. Position the gizmo by moving or rotating it.

Figure 15.28
Choose Atmospheric Apparatus from the Helper sub-panel.

Figure 15.29
Choosing a SphereGizmo.

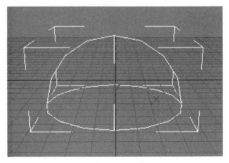

Figure 15.30 After checking Hemisphere, the SphereGizmo is cut in half.

RENDERING EFFECTS

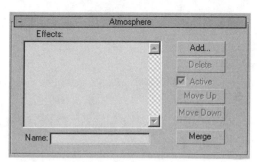

Figure 15.31 The Atmosphere rollout is part of the Environment dialog box.

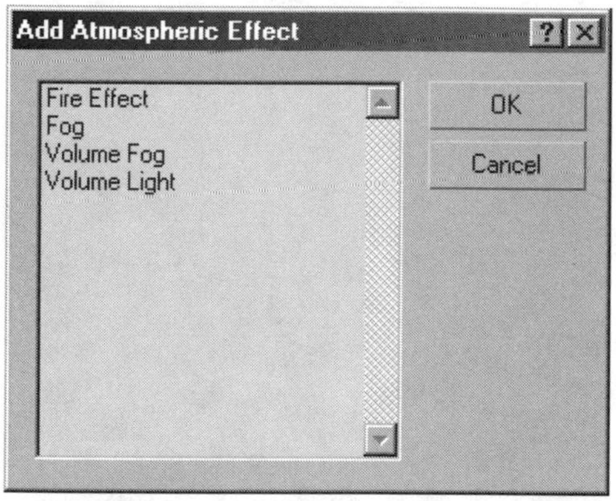

Figure 15.32 Choose an atmospheric effect from the Add Atmospheric Effect list.

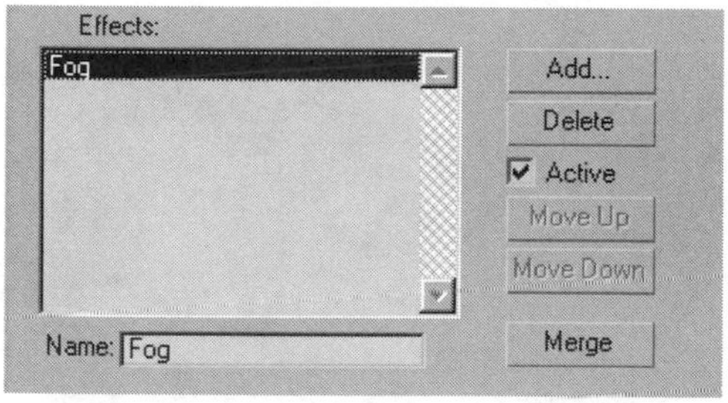

Figure 15.33 The Effects list lets you activate and deactivate individual effects.

To add an atmospheric effect:

1. Choose Rendering > Environment.

   The Environment dialog box appears (**Figure 15.31**).

2. Click the Add button.

   The Add Atmospheric Effect dialog box appears (**Figure 15.32**).

3. Double-click an effect.

   The atmospheric effect is added to the scene.

   The name of the effect appears in the Effects list (**Figure 15.33**). Active is checked by default. The Parameters rollout for the effect appears below.

4. If you have added a fire or volume fog effect, click Pick Gizmo. Then click a gizmo to define the boundaries of the effect.

✔ Tips

- To delete an effect, select the name of the effect from the Effects list and click the Delete button.

- To disable an effect temporarily, select the name of the effect from the Effects list and uncheck Active.

RENDERING EFFECTS

You can create two kinds of fog: standard fog, which fades the scene along your line of sight, and layered fog, which creates a vertical gradation between the earth and sky.

To create standard fog:

1. Select or create a targeted camera.

2. Set the Environment ranges of the camera to define the region that will be affected by the fog.

3. Activate the Camera viewport.

4. Open the Environment dialog box and add a Fog effect.

   The Fog Parameters rollout appears (**Figure 15.34**).

5. Choose Standard fog.

6. Render the scene to see the effect of the default settings (**Figure 15.35**).

7. Adjust the parameters of the fog.

   Choose Near or Far to fade a scene from the near range to far range or vice versa. Check Exponential to increase the rate at which the fog effect obscures the scene.

8. Render the scene to see the effects of each adjustment.

✔ Tips

- You can change the color of the fog by clicking the color swatch in the Fog Parameters rollout.

- Uncheck Fog Background if you don't want the fog to fade out the background (**Figure 15.36**).

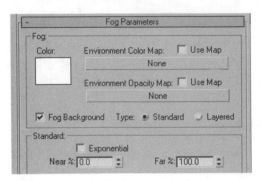

Figure 15.34 Use the Fog Parameters rollout to change the fog color, extents, and other parameters.

Figure 15.35 This scene uses the default settings for standard fog.

Figure 15.36 Turn off Fog Background for an unrealistic effect in which the scene objects are affected by fog, but the background is not.

RENDERING EFFECTS

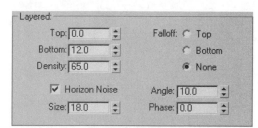

Figure 15.37 Layered fog parameters include Top, Bottom, and Horizon Noise to control the placement and edges of a layer of fog.

Figure 15.38 This layered fog uses the above settings to obscure the ground, but not the sky.

Figure 15.39 Adding an environment background map to fog creates unusual effects.

Layered fog always lies parallel to the world XY plane—that is, parallel to the top view. You limit the vertical extent of layered fog by setting parameters and moving the camera horizon.

Layered fog renders from perspective viewports, such as the Perspective or Camera viewports. It does not render from axonometric viewports.

To create layered fog:

1. Activate a Perspective or Camera viewport.

2. Open the Environment dialog box and add a Fog effect.

   The Fog Parameters rollout appears.

3. Choose Layered fog.

   The layered fog parameters become enabled (**Figure 15.37**).

4. Render the scene to see the effect of the default settings.

5. Set the Top of the fog to 0 and the Bottom to 10. Then set the Density to 65.

6. Check Horizon Noise and set the Size to 18 to add a rough edge to the fog. Then set the Angle to 10° below the camera horizon.

7. Render the scene (**Figure 15.38**).

✔ Tips

- Layered fog settings for the top and bottom of the fog can produce unpredictable results. The specific settings for fog in steps 5 and 6 above should help you get started.

- To make fog fall off at a faster rate, choose the Top or Bottom falloff options.

- Adding a map to the environment color map channel applies a texture map to fog. If you use the same texture map in the background, it can make objects appear to sink into the environment (**Figure 15.39**).

- Adding a map to the environment opacity map channel varies the opacity of the fog.

RENDERING EFFECTS

Volume fog uses noise to create an uneven distribution of fog.

To create volume fog:

1. Create an atmospheric gizmo and position it where you want to place the fog.

2. Open the Environment dialog box and add a Volume Fog effect.

   The Volume Fog Parameters rollout appears (**Figure 15.40**).

3. Click Pick Gizmo. Then click the gizmo.

4. Render the scene to see the effect of the default settings.

5. Adjust the opacity of the fog by increasing or decreasing the Density value.

   Check Exponential to increase the opacity of the fog more rapidly with distance.

6. Adjust the size and granularity of the blobs using the Size and Step Size spinners.

7. To decrease the brightness and contrast of the fog, increase the Uniformity value.

   To increase the brightness and contrast of the fog, choose Fractal or Turbulent noise.

   To reverse the areas of opacity and transparency, check Invert.

   To make the fog render in discrete patches, increase the low threshold amount and decrease the high threshold amount.

8. Render the scene (**Figure 15.41**).

✔ Tips

- The Phase and Wind parameters churn and blow fog over time. Use the Wind From The parameters to choose a wind direction. Use the Wind Strength to set the wind speed. If there is no wind, the fog will churn in place.

- You can assign volume fog to multiple gizmos, or assign each gizmo a separate effect (**Figure 15.42**).

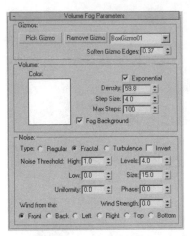

Figure 15.40 The Volume Fog Parameters rollout allows you to pick a gizmo, control opacity, and add noise to the fog effect.

Figure 15.41 Using the above settings, the volume fog creates patches of ground fog.

Figure 15.42 Two gizmos and two volume fog effects create steam coming out of a teapot.

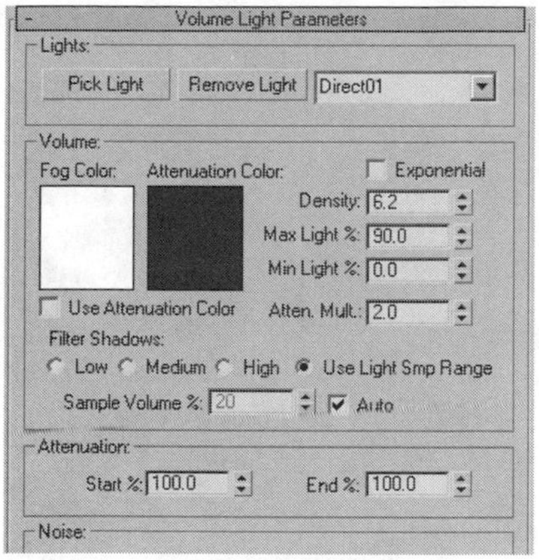

Figure 15.43 The Volume Light rollout contains settings that are similar to Volume Fog. It also allows you to control attenuation.

Figure 15.44 When combined with shadow maps, volume light creates 3D shadows.

Figure 15.45 Volume light created the rays of sunshine entering a hole in the ceiling.

In Chapter 11, you learned how to add volume to a light. Now you'll learn how to adjust the light as well.

To adjust a volume light:

1. Select a volume light and click the Setup button in the Atmospheres rollout.

   or

   Open the Environment dialog box and add a Volume Light effect. Then pick a light.

   The Volume Lights Parameters rollout appears (**Figure 15.43**).

2. Render the scene to see the effect of the default settings.

3. Adjust the color and density of the volume. Set the minimum and maximum intensity of the light, or use the defaults.

4. To attenuate the light so that it diminishes along its length, check Use Attenuation Color and select an attenuation color. Then adjust the attenuation multiplier and the attenuation start and end percentages.

5. To add noise to the light so that it looks like fog, check Noise On, and adjust the noise parameters. See "To create volume fog" for a description of how those parameters work.

6. Render the scene (**Figure 15.44**).

✔ Tips

- To create volumetric shadows, use shadow maps rather than ray-traced shadows.

- Use volume light to make a dramatic statement about space (**Figure 15.45**).

- Use volume light to put a glow around an omni light. Lens Effects (covered in the next section) provide a more convincing glow effect.

The fire effect creates flames, fireballs, explosions, and smoke that animate automatically. Fire renders only from perspective-type views.

To create a fire effect:

1. Create an atmospheric gizmo.

2. Open the Environment dialog box and add a Fire effect.

   The Fire Effect Parameters rollout appears (**Figure 15.46**).

3. Click Pick Gizmo and click the gizmo.

4. Render the scene to see the effect of the default settings.

5. Adjust the color and shape of the fire. Choose Tendril to make campfire flames, or Fireball to make rounder balls of fire. Increase the Stretch amount to make the flames straighter and taller. Increase the Regularity amount to make the flames more uniform.

6. Adjust the characteristics of the fire. Increase the Flame Size and Density amounts to make the flames larger and brighter. Increase the Flame Detail and Sample amounts to give the flames more distinct edges and higher resolution.

7. Render the scene (**Figure 15.47**).

✔ Tip

■ Using the Motion and Explosion parameters, you control how the fire burns, including the rate that it burns, whether or not it explodes, the timing of the explosion, whether or not the explosion produces smoke, and so forth.

   To see a complete description of the fire parameters, look up "Fire" in the help files.

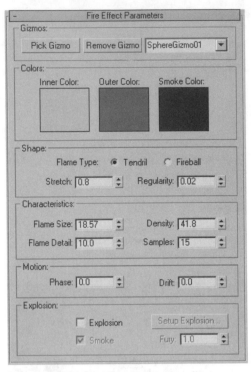

Figure 15.46 The Fire Effect Parameters rollout controls the appearance of flames, fireballs, explosions, and smoke.

Figure 15.47 Two separate fire effects were used to produce this burning bowl of oil.

Figure 15.48 Lens effects have been applied to this crystal ball to give it a sense of radiance.

Post-Process Effects

The Render Effects dialog box adds effects to your scene that are processed in the virtual frame buffer after an image has been rendered. Render effects include (**Figure 15.48**):

◆ **Blur**—Blurs an image uniformly, along one or two axes or from a center point. Includes advanced parameters for selecting what parts of an image will be blurred.

◆ **Depth of Field**—Blurs foreground and background along the line of sight while preserving focus with in a central region.

◆ **Motion Blur**—Blurs objects directionally to create the illusion that the objects are moving past the camera.

◆ **Film Grain**—Applies noise to a rendered image, like the grain on old film.

◆ **Brightness and Contrast**—Changes the brightness and/or contrast of a rendered image.

◆ **Color Balance**—Shifts the color balance of a rendered image using CMY/RGB sliders.

◆ **Lens Effects**—Simulates effects that are created by a camera lens and a bright light. Use this effect to create glows, starburst effects, streaking, and rainbows.

◆ **File Output**—Takes a snapshot of a scene and saves the image to a file or returns the image to the Effects stack for further processing.

Most effects give you the option of including or excluding background images from the effect.

Because the effects are evaluated in sequence, the Effects list is also called the Effects stack.

To add a rendering effect:

1. Choose Rendering > Effects.

   The Rendering Effects dialog box appears (**Figure 15.49**).

2. Click Add.

   The Add Effect dialog box appears (**Figure 15.50**).

3. Select the effect you want and click OK.

   The rendering effect is added to the scene.

   The name of the effect appears in the Effects stack (**Figure 15.51**). Active is checked by default. The Parameters roll-out for the effect appears below.

4. Click Update Scene.

   The scene renders in the Effects preview window. After a pause, the effect is applied.

5. Adjust the effect. Then click Update Effect.

   The effect updates in the preview window.

✔ Tips

- Some effects update more quickly than others. For fast-updating effects, try checking Interactive. This option updates effects automatically every time you change a setting.

- Effects are evaluated in order from the top to the bottom of the stack. To change the order of evaluation, highlight an effect and click Move Up or Move Down.

- To delete an effect, select its name from the Effects list and click the Delete button.

- To disable an effect temporarily, select the name of the effect and uncheck Active.

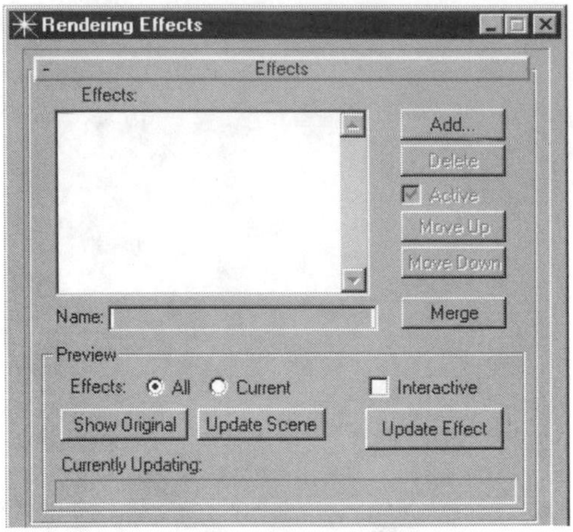

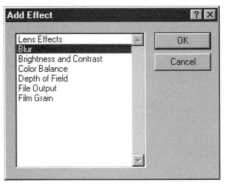

Figure 15.49 Use the Rendering Effects dialog box's Add button to create new effects.

Figure 15.50 Choosing an effect from the Add Effect dialog box.

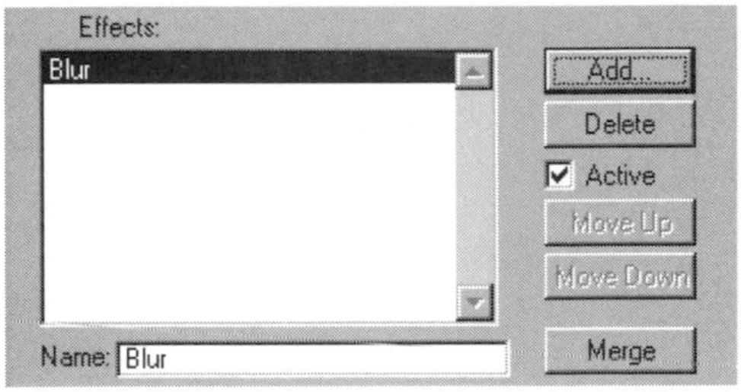

Figure 15.51 The effect is added to the Effects List.

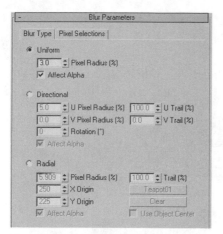

Figure 15.52 The Blur Parameters rollout allows you to choose from three different types of blurring.

Figure 15.53 After applying directional blur to the U direction with 100% trailing.

Figure 15.54 After applying radial blur with 100% trailing.

The Blur effect blurs an image after it has been rendered. You can blur an image evenly along the U and V axes, or around a central point.

To add blur:

1. Open the Rendering Effects dialog box and add a Blur effect.

   The blur effect is added to the Effects stack. The Blur parameters rollout appears below (**Figure 15.52**).

2. Click Update Scene.

   The scene renders from the active viewport. After a short pause, the blur effect is applied to the image. The blur effect is quite strong.

3. Reduce the Pixel Radius to decrease the amount of the blur. Then click Update Effect (**Figure 15.53**).

4. Choose the Directional option. Then adjust the U and V directional blurring to make the image blur along one or two axes.

5. Click Update Effect to see the result.

6. Choose the Radial option and update the scene. Then adjust the Pixel radius to control the amount of radial blur. Use the X Origin and Y Origin to locate the center of blurring, or click the button labeled "None" and then click an object to use as a focal point. Check Use Object Center to assign the pivot point of the object as the focal point of the effect.

7. Click Update Effect (**Figure 15.54**).

continues on next page

RENDERING EFFECTS

✔ Tips

- Trails add "direction" to your blur by weighting it more heavily toward one side or another.

- When checked, Affect Alpha blurs the edges of the alpha channel. To view this effect, click Display Alpha Channel ◐ in the virtual frame buffer.

- To blur an image more selectively, use the settings in the Pixel Selections tab panel. For information about these parameters, look up "Blur rendering effect" in the help files.

A depth of field effect blurs the foreground and background of a scene. The area that remains in focus is called the depth of field.

To add depth of field blurring:

1. Open the Render Effects dialog box and add a Depth of Field effect.

   The Depth of Field Parameters rollout appears (**Figure 15.55**).

2. Click Pick Node and click an object in the scene to be the focal point of the effect. (Hint: Type H to access the Pick Object dialog box.) Then click Update Effect.

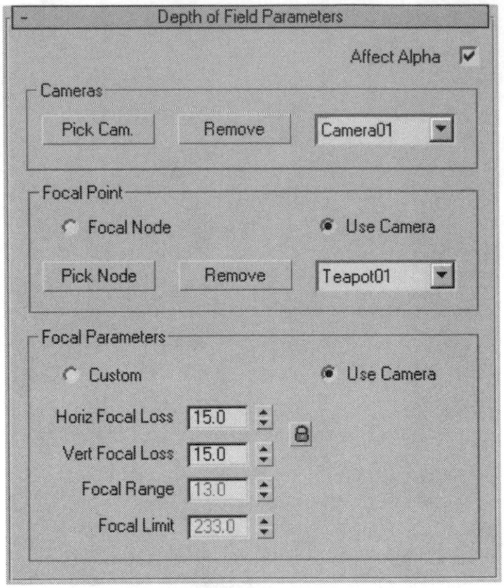

Figure 15.55 The Depth of Field Parameters rollout controls the placement of the depth of field and the amount of blurring outside the field.

Figure 15.56 Using the teapot for a focal node focuses the middle ground area around it.

Figure 15.57 Because the target of the camera is near the front of the scene, the middle and background of the scene are blurred.

3. In the Focal Parameters group, choose Custom. Adjust the strength of the blurring by modifying the horizontal and vertical focal loss settings.

To set the range of the depth of field in front of and behind the focal point, adjust the Focal Range. Objects outside of this range will be blurred.

To set the distance from the focal point at which blurring reaches its full amount, adjust the Focal Limit.

4. Click Update Effect.

The scene blurs outside of the depth of field (**Figure 15.56**).

5. To use a camera target as the focal node of the depth of field, click Pick Camera and select a camera in the scene. Then choose Use Camera in the Focal Parameters group and set the horizontal and vertical focal loss.

Note: Using a camera target to establish the depth of field disables the Focal Range and Focal Limit parameters and substitutes values based on the lens size of the camera.

6. Click Update Effect.

The scene blurs outside of the depth of field that is established by the camera target (**Figure 15.57**). To move the depth of field closer or farther away, use the Dolly Target command ⊕ in the Camera viewport.

The Motion Blur effect adds image motion blur to your scene. Image motion blur can also be applied from the Render Scene dialog box, and from the camera as a multi-pass camera effect.

To add image motion blur:

1. Select the objects you want to blur. Then right-click on the selection and choose Properties from the Transform quad menu.

2. In the Object Properties dialog box, check Enabled in the Motion Blur group. Then click the Image option (**Figure 15.58**).

3. Close the Object Properties dialog box and open the Render Effects dialog box. Then add a Motion Blur effect to the scene.

   The Motion Blur Parameters rollout appears (**Figure 15.59**).

4. Set the amount of motion blur that you want by increasing the Duration amount.

5. Click Update Effect.

   Objects that have image motion blur enabled and that are moving in relation to the camera during the current frame are blurred along the path of their trajectories (**Figure 15.60**).

✔ Tips

- For faster rendering, leave Work With Transparency unchecked unless you are having trouble blurring either transparent objects or the objects behind them.

- When you apply image motion blur from more than one place, the effects are added together, rather than replaced.

- A small amount of image motion blur is applied from the Render Scene dialog box by default. To turn off this effect, uncheck Image Motion Blur in the MAX Default Scanline A-Buffer rollout.

Figure 15.58 Enable image motion blur in the Object Properties dialog box.

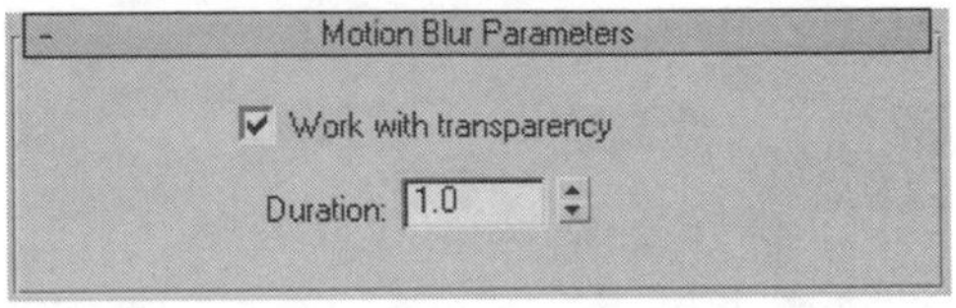

Figure 15.59 Adjust the amount of blurring by increasing the Duration amount.

Figure 15.60 Motion blur makes these objects jump for joy!

Figure 15.61 The Film Grain Parameters rollout sets the contrast of the grain and determines whether the grain will applied to the background.

Figure 15.62 A fine grain appears throughout the image.

Figure 15.63 After checking Ignore Background, the grain is not applied to the background image.

Film grain makes a rendered image look old and weathered, like the graininess you see on old movie films.

To add film grain:

1. Open the Render Effects dialog box and add a Film Grain effect.

   The Film Grain Parameters rollout appears (**Figure 15.61**).

2. Check Interactive.

   The scene renders in the Effects preview window. A small amount of grain is added.

3. Increase the Grain setting.

   The image becomes grainier (**Figure 15.62**).

✔ Tip

- If you do not want the background image to be affected by the grain, check Ignore Background (**Figure 15.63**).

The Brightness and Contrast effect changes the brightness and/or contrast of a rendered image.

To change brightness and contrast:

1. Open the Render Effects dialog box and add a Brightness and Contrast effect.

   The Brightness and Contrast Parameters rollout appears (**Figure 15.64**).

2. Check Interactive.

3. Set the brightness and contrast amount. Check Ignore Background to leave the background values intact (**Figure 15.65**).

4. Try reversing the brightness and contrast to see what happens (**Figure 15.66**).

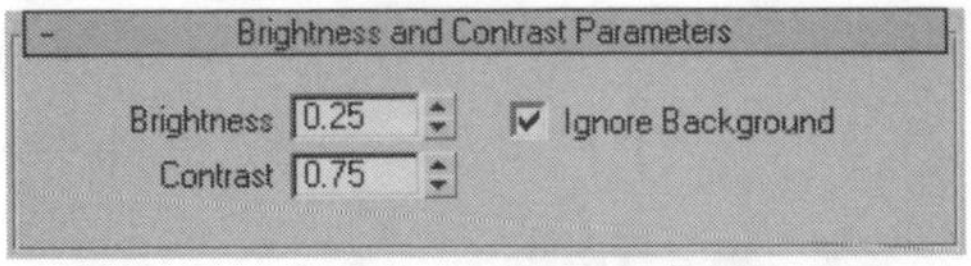

Figure 15.64 The Brightness and Contrast Parameters rollout sets the brightness and contrast of a rendered image.

Figure 15.65 After applying .75 brightness and .25 contrast and checking Ignore Background.

Figure 15.66 After applying .25 brightness and .75 contrast and checking Ignore Background.

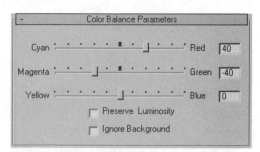

Figure 15.67 The Color Balance Parameters rollout allows you to adjust the amount of red, green, and blue in the image.

Figure 15.68 After shifting the color balance, the luminance values of the image are also affected.

Figure 15.69 Checking Preserve Luminosity and Ignore Background bring some semblance of balance back to the luminance values.

The Color Balance effect shifts the color balance of a rendered image using CMY/RGB sliders.

To shift the color balance:

1. Open the Render Effects dialog box and add a Color Balance effect.

   The Color Balance Parameters rollout appears (**Figure 15.67**).

2. Check Interactive.

3. Set the color balance by dragging the sliders (**Figure 15.68**).

✔ Tips

- Checking Preserve Luminosity preserves the range of values, but does not preserve their distribution across the range (**Figure 15.69**).

- The color channel buttons at the top of the Effects preview window allow you to view how much of each color is added.

The File Output effect saves the current state of an image as it is being processed in the Render Effects stack. Only effects that are listed above the File Output effect are applied to the output.

You can save alpha, luminance, or depth channel information to a separate file without affecting the assigned rendering output of your animation.

Alpha—Renders transparency information as a grayscale image. Environment background maps save to black.

Luminance—Renders the light to dark color information as a grayscale image.

Depth—Renders scene geometry that is within the clipping range of the camera, or in between two depth ranges that you specify, to a grayscale image. Objects that are closer to the camera appear lighter, while objects that are further away appear darker.

To render a channel:

1. Open the Render Effects dialog box and add a File Output effect.

   The File Output Parameters rollout appears.

2. Click Files. Then choose a location, name, and file format to render to.

3. Open the Channels drop-down menu and choose a channel (**Figure 15.70**).

4. Click Update Scene.

   The channel is rendered to the output file that you specified (**Figure 15.71**).

5. Change the channel selection and the output file name. Then click Update Scene (**Figure 15.72**).

✔ Tip

■ The Affect Source Bitmap takes the file that you output and feeds it back into the Effects stack so that further effects may be applied. The final result is saved to the output file that you specified for rendering the channel.

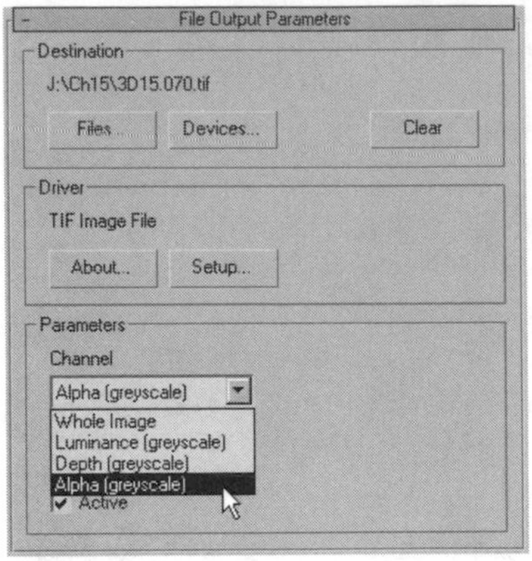

Figure 15.70 The File Output Parameters rollout allows you to save information from different channels to a grayscale output file.

Figure 15.71 The alpha channel information shows that the objects are solid and that the fog is semi-transparent.

Figure 15.72 The depth channel information displays objects as being darker the farther away they are from the camera.

RENDERING EFFECTS

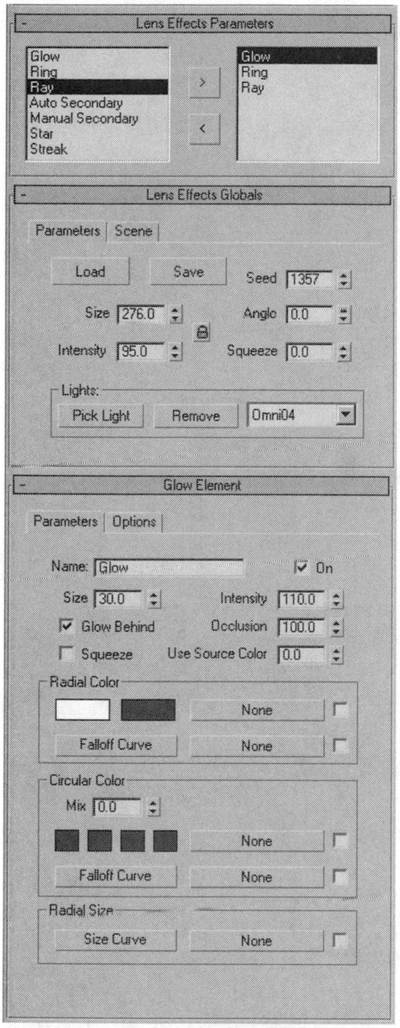

Figure 15.73 The Lens Effects Parameters rollout allows you to select from seven different effects.

Lens Effects simulate the effects that are created by a camera lens and a bright light. They include glows, starburst effects, streaking, and rainbows.

To add lens effects

1. Open the Render Effects dialog box and add a Lens Effect.

   The Lens Effects Parameters rollout appears.

2. Add the effects you want to apply by selecting them in the left window and clicking the right arrow button.

   The selected effects move to the right window (**Figure 15.73**).

   continues on next page

3. In the Lens Effects Globals rollout, click Pick Light and then select a light.

4. Click Update Effect to see the effect of the default settings.

5. Adjust the global size and intensity of the lens effects.

6. Adjust the size, color, and intensity of individual effects. To access the parameters of an effect, click the name of the effect in the right-hand window of the Lens Parameters rollout.

7. Click Update Effect (**Figure 15.74**).

✔ Tip

■ With judicious combination and careful adjustments, Lens effects can create mystical effects (**Figure 15.75**). To learn about the unique properties of each effect, look up "Lens effects" in the help files.

Figure 15.74 After applying the Glow, Ray, and Star effects to an omni light.

Figure 15.75 The Rainbow Cross is my vision of what the Logos might look like from outer space.

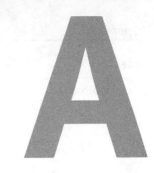

ICONS

3ds max 4 is replete with icons and buttons. To help you keep track, here is a list of all the icons I used in creating this book.

Table A.1

Main Toolbar			
	Undo		Restrict to XY
	Redo		Restrict to YZ
	Select and Link		Restrict to ZX
	Unlink Selection		Mirror
	Bind to Space Warp		Array
	Select Object		Snapshot
	Rectangular Selection Region		Spacing Tool
	Circular Selection Region		Align
	Fence Selection Region		Normal Align
	Selection Filter		Place Highlight
	Select by Name		Align Camera
	Select and Move		Align to View
	Select and Rotate		Named Selection Set
	Select and Uniform Scale		Open Track View
	Select and Non-Uniform Scale		New Schematic View
	Select and Squash		Material Editor
	Select and Manipulate		Render Scene
	Reference Coordinate System		Quick Render (Production)
	Use Pivot Point Center		Quick Render (Draft)
	Use Selection Center		Quick Render (Active Shade)
	Use Transform Coordinate Center		Render Type
	Restrict to X		Render Last
	Restrict to Y		Active Shade Floater
	Restrict to Z		

Table A.2

Command Panels	
	Create Panel
	Modify Panel
	Hierarchy Panel
	Motion Panel
	Display Panel

Table A.3

Create Panel	
	Utilities Panel
	Geometry
	Shapes
	Lights
	Cameras
	Helpers
	Space Warps
	Systems

Table A.4

Modify Panel	
	Pin Stack (Off)
	Pin Stack (On)
	Active/Inactive Modifier Toggle (Active)
	Active/Inactive Modifier Toggle (Inactive)
	Active/Inactive in Viewport (Active)
	Active/Inactive in Viewport (Inactive)
	Show End Result (Off)
	Show End Result (On)
	Make Unique
	Make Unique (Active)
	Remove Modifier From Stack
	Configure Button Sets

Table A.5

Status Bar, Locks and Controls	
	Selection Lock Toggle
	Absolute Mode Transform Type-In
	Offset Mode Transform Type-In
	Plug-In Keyboard Shortcut Toggle
	Crossing Selection
	Window Selection
	Degradation Override (Inactive)
	Degradation Override (Active)
	3D Snap
	2.5D Snap
	2D Snap
	Angle Snap
	Percent Snap
	Spinner Snap
	Animate
	Key Mode Toggle
	Go to Start
	Previous Frame
	Previous Key
	Play Animation
	Play Selected
	Stop Animation
	Next Frame
	Next Key
	Go to End
	Time Configuration

Table A.6

Viewport Controls	
🔍	Zoom
⊞	Zoom All
🔲	Zoom Extents
🔲	Zoom Extents Selected
⊞	Zoom Extents All
⊞	Zoom Extents All Selected
🔍	Region Zoom
▷	Field-of-View
✋	Pan
⟳	Arc Rotate
⟳	Arc Rotate Selected
⟳	Arc Rotate Sub-object
⧉	Min/Max Toggle

Table A.8

Light Viewport Controls	
⟟	Dolly Light
⟟	Dolly Light + Target
⟟	Dolly Target
◎	Light Hotspot
⟳	Roll Light
⊞	Zoom Extents All
⊞	Zoom Extents All Selected
◎	Light Falloff
✋	Truck Light
👁	Orbit Light
⟩	Pan Light
⧉	Min/Max Toggle

Table A.7

Camera Viewport Controls	
⟟	Dolly Camera
⟟	Dolly Camera + Target
⟟	Dolly Target
◈	Perspective
⟳	Roll Camera
⊞	Zoom Extents All
⊞	Zoom Extents All Selected
▷	Field-of-View
✋	Truck Camera
👁	Orbit
⟩	Pan Camera
⧉	Min/Max Toggle

Table A.9

Virtual Frame Buffer	
💾	Save Bitmap
🔳	Clone Virtual Frame Buffer
●	Display Red Channel
●	Display Green Channel
●	Display Blue Channel
◐	Display Alpha Channel
●	Monochrome
✕	Clear
RGB Alpha ▼	RGB Alpha
☐	Color Selector

Table A.10

Material Editor	
	Get Material
	Put Material to Scene
	Assign Material to Selection
	Reset Map/Material to Default Setting
	Make Material Copy
	Make Unique
	Put to Library
	Material Effects Channel
	Show Map in Viewport
	Show End Result (Inactive)
	Show End Result (Active)
	Go to Parent
	Go Forward to Sibling
	Pick Material from Object
	Material Map Navigator
	Select by Material
	Options
	Make a Preview
	Play Preview
	Save Preview
	Video Color Check
	Sample UV Tiling
	Sample UV Tiling
	Sample UV Tiling
	Sample UV Tiling
	Background
	Backlight
	Sample Type
	Sample Type
	Sample Type
	View List
	View List + Icons
	View Small Icons
	View Large Icons
	Update Scene Materials from Library
	Delete from Library

Table A.11

Schematic View	
	Clear Material Library
	Filters
	Hierarchy Mode
	Reference Mode

Table A.12

Sub-Object Levels	
	Vertex
	Edge
	Face
	Polygon
	Element
	Vertex
	Segment
	Spline
	Select Sub-Object

Table A.13

Track View and Motion Panel	
	Function Curves
	Parameter Out-of-Range Types
	Assign Controller
	Zoom Horizontal Extents
	Zoom Horizontal Extents Keys
	Zoom Value Extents

Table A.14

Spline Boolean Operations	
	Union
	Subtractions
	Intersection

ICONS

451

Table A.15

Lofting	
	Next Shape
	Previous Shape
	Pick Shape
	Pick Shape
	Reset

Table A.16

Lights and Cameras	
	Target Camera
	Free Camera
	Target Spotlight
	Free Spotlight
	Free Directional Light
	Target Directional Light
	Omni Light
	Sunlight System
	Light Include/Exclude Tool
	Light Lister Tool
	Field of View Direction

Table A.17

Tangent Types	
	Previous Key
	Next Key
	Copy to Previous Key
	Copy to Next Key
	Smooth
	Linear
	Step
	Slow
RGB Alpha	Fast
	Bézier

KEYBOARD SHORTCUTS

Keyboard shortcuts are a major time-saver and worth taking some time to master. To help you get started, I have listed them by function, and I include nearly every default shortcut found in the main user interface. I also note some useful shortcuts that you can assign yourself.

To see a complete alphabetical list of short-cuts, assign your own hotkeys, and save them to a file, choose Customize > Customize User Interface.

Table B.1

Scene File Operations	
Ctrl + Z	Undo Scene Change
Ctrl + A	Redo Scene Change
Ctrl + S	Save Scene
Ctrl + N	New Scene
Ctrl + O	Open Scene
Alt + Ctrl + H	Hold Scene
Alt + Ctrl + F	Fetch Scene
F1	Display Help Files

Table B.2

UI Display	
2, Y	Tab Panel Toggle
3	Command Panel Toggle
Alt + 6	Main Toolbar Toggle
Ctrl + X	Expert Mode Toggle

Table B.3

Viewport Display	
F	Front View
K	Back View
R	Right View
L	Left View
T	Top View
B	Bottom View
P	Perspective View
U	User View
C	Camera View
$	Light View
G	Grid Display Toggle
W	Minimize / Maximize View
D	Disable / Enable View
Shift + Z	Undo View Change
Shift + A	Redo View Change
Alt + B	Viewport Background Dialog Box
Alt + Shift + Ctrl + B	Update Viewport Background Image
1	Redraw All Views
Ctrl + T	Redraw Maps (Texture Correction)

Table B.4

Viewport Navigation	
Z	Zoom
assignable	Zoom All
Alt + Ctrl + Z	Zoom Extents
E	Zoom Extents Selected
Shift + Ctrl + Z	Zoom Extents All
assignable	Zoom Extents All Selected
Ctrl + W	Region Zoom
assignable	Field-of-View
Ctrl + P	Pan
V, Ctrl + R	Arc Rotate
W	Min/Max Toggle
[	Zoom in around cursor
]	Zoom out around cursor
Shift + Plus Sign*	Zoom in 2X
Shift + Minus Sign*	Zoom out 2X

* Plus Sign (+) and Minus Sign (-) on numeric keypad only

Table B.5

Object Selection and Display	
H	Select Object Dialog Box
Spacebar	Selection Lock Toggle
Page Up	Select Parent
Page Down	Select Child
Ctrl + F	Cycle Region Selection Method
Insert	Cycle Sub-Object Selection Level
F2	Shade Selected Faces Toggle
F3	Wireframe / Smooth Shaded Toggle
F4	Edged Faces Toggle
Shift + B	Box Mode Toggle
Shift + F	Show Safe Frames Toggle
Shift + C	Hide Cameras Toggle
Shift + L	Hide Lights Toggle
Shift + H	Hide Helpers Toggle
Shift + P	Hide Particles Toggle
Shift + O	Hide Geometry Toggle
Shift + W	Hide Space Warps Toggle
assignable	Hide Selected
assignable	Hide Unselected
assignable	Hide Frozen Objects
5	Unhide by Name
6	Freeze Selected

Table B.5 (continued)

Object Selection and Display	
7	Unfreeze All
Alt + X	See-Through Display Toggle
Q	Toggle Polygon Counter

Table B.7

Transforms	
X	Transform Gizmo Toggle
Page Up	Transform Gizmo Size Up
Page Down	Transform Gizmo Size Down
F5	Restrict to X
F6	Restrict to Y
F7	Restrict to Z
F8	Cycle Restrict to Plane
F12	Display Transform Type-In Dialog Box
Shift + I	Display Spacing Tool
Snape	2D, 2.5D and 3D Snap Toggle
A	Angle Snap Toggle
Shift + Ctrl + P	Percent Snap Toggle
Alt + A	Align
Alt + N	Normal Align
Ctrl + C	Match Camera To View
Ctrl + H	Place Highlight

Table B.8

Animation	
Home	Go To Start Frame
End	Go To End Frame
/	Play Back Animation
\	Sound Toggle

Table B.9

Rendering	
M	Display Material Editor
Ctrl + T	Texture Correction (Redraw Maps)
F9, Shift + E	Render Last
F10, Shift + R	Render Scene
Ctrl + I	Show Last Rendering

INDEX

INDEX

INDEX

INDEX

INDEX

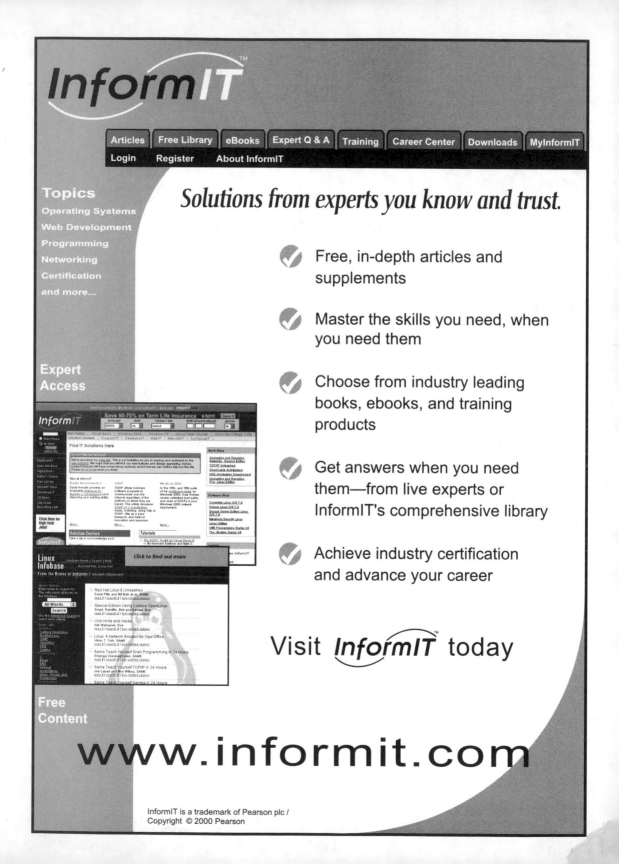